THE
Diſcovery of Witchcraft:

PROVING,

That the Compacts and Contracts of WITCHES
with *Devils* and all *Infernal Spirits* or *Familiars*, are but
Erroneous Novelties and Imaginary Conceptions.

Also diſcovering, How far their Power extendeth in Killing, Tormenting,
Conſuming, or Curing the bodies of Men, Women, Children, or Animals,
by Charms, Philtres, Periapts, Pentacles, Curſes, and Conjurations.

WHEREIN LIKEWISE

The Unchriſtian Practices and Inhumane Dealings of
Searchers and *Witch-tryers* upon *Aged, Melancholly*, and *Superſtitious*
people, in extorting Confeſſions by Terrors and Tortures,
and in deviſing falſe Marks and Symptoms, are notably Detected.

And the Knavery of *Juglers, Conjurers, Charmers, Soothſayers, Figure-Caſters,
Dreamers, Alchymiſts* and *Philterers*; with many other things
that have long lain hidden, fully Opened and Deciphered.

ALL WHICH

Are very neceſſary to be known for the undeceiving of *Judges, Juſtices*,
and *Jurors*, before they paſs Sentence upon Poor, Miſerable and Ignorant People;
who are frequenly Arraigned, Condemned, and Executed for *Witches* and *Wizzards*.

IN SIXTEEN BOOKS.

By REGINALD SCOT Eſquire.

Whereunto is added
An excellent Diſcourſe of the *Nature* and *Subſtance*
OF
DEVILS and SPIRITS,

Witchcraft
in Europe

Edited with an Introduction by
Alan C. Kors *and*
Edward Peters

University of Pennsylvania Press
Philadelphia

WITCHCRAFT

IN EUROPE

1100–1700

A Documentary History

The following selections are reprinted by permission. Caesarius
of Heisterbach from Heisterbach, *The Dialogue on Miracles,*
translated by H. Von E. Scott and C.C. Swinton Bland, copyright
1929 by Routledge & Kegan Paul Ltd.; Ralph of Coggeshall from
A.P. Evans and W.L. Wakefield, *Heresies of the High Middle
Ages: Selected Sources Annotated and Translated,* copyright ©
1969 by Columbia University Press; Thomas Aquinas, *Summa
Contra Gentiles* and *Summa Theologica,* copyright 1928 and 1912
by the Very Reverend Prior Provincial OP, Saint Dominics Priory,
London; documents 6 and 15 from Julio Caro Baroja, *The World
of the Witches,* English Translation copyright © 1964 by George
Weidenfeld and Nicholson, Ltd. (London); Jean Calvin
from *Calvin: Institutes of the Christian Religion,* Vol. XX, The
Library of Christian Classics, edited by John T. McNeill and
translated by Ford Lewis Battles. Published in the U.S.A. by The
Westminster Press. Copyright MCMLX, by W.L. Jenkins. Used
by permission; Reginald Scot from *The Discoverie of Witchcraft*
by Reginald Scot. Introduction by Hugh Ross Williamson. Copyright
© 1964 by Centaur Press, Ltd. Published in the United States of
America by the Southern Illinois University Press. Reprinted by
permission of Centaur Press, Ltd. and Southern Illinois University
Press; Montaigne from *The Complete Essays of Montaigne,*
translated by Donald M. Frame, with the permission of the
publishers, Stanford University Press. Copyright © 1948, 1957 and
1958 by the Board of Trustees of the Leland Stanford Junior
University; Spinoza from Benedict de Spinoza, *The Political
Works,* translated by A.G. Wernham 1958, used by permission of
the Clarendon Press, Oxford; Antonio Salazar de Frias from Charles
Williams, *Witchcraft,* copyright 1941 by Faber and Faber, Ltd.,
London.

Printed in the United States of America
ISBN: 0–8122–7645–0

Contents

Contents

Illustrations

Illustrations

The
Documents

INTRODUCTION:
The Problem of
European Witchcraft

Western minds, when confronted by the problem of witchcraft in primitive or non-Western cultures, assume most comfortably the attitudes and categories of formal or informal cultural anthropology. We know, and we find nothing unusual in this, that men, fearful and helpless before the awesome forces of the visible world, traditionally have sought to reach forces beyond that world to increase their meagre human powers and their abilities to control their own destinies. Men then assign to other men or acknowledge in them the extraordinary role of causing events not normally within the province of human determination. We see the beliefs, rites, and institutions of such "magic" as purposeful, whatever our views of their legitimacy and efficacy, and we speculate freely on the psychological, social, and explanatory functions which they serve. We understand, with varying degrees of satisfaction, why it is that the recognized holders of such magical powers—the witches, sorcerers, and shamans of other cultures—should be among the most feared and revered members of any society and why men's behavior toward them should take intensely particular and peculiar forms. Our orderings and explanations of magic may seem to us still inchoate or insufficient, but on the whole we preserve a sense of the final comprehensibility and clarity of such phenomena.

Confronted by the problem of witchcraft in Western culture, however, we feel ourselves faced with a much more complex problem. It seems to us far less comprehensible that *after* our alleged period of primitive experience in the West, after our "Dark Ages," during the centuries of dynamic intellectual experimentation, the Renaissance, the Reformation, and, more perplexing still, during that seventeenth century which we continue to consider "the Age of Reason" and "The Age of Scientific Revolution," Europeans engaged in a systematic and furious assault upon men and women believed to be witches manipulating the forces of the supernatural to effect evil in the world and bring Satan's kingdom to a complete and terrible fulfillment. The otherwise calm and analytic language of the social sciences suddenly appears inadequate to the task even of description alone, and the terms "craze," "mania," "superstition," and "aberration" record a recoil from our culture's past far more than they clarify and explain that past.

It is precisely those techniques of investigation and description so useful to the study of other cultures that we generally fail to apply to the study of our own: the suspension of absolute criteria of "truth" and "falsehood," of "sanity" and "insanity," and the impartial schematization of a people's worldview upon which so many aspects of its beliefs and behavior depend. If we are ever to understand or explain the phenomenon of European witchcraft, we must begin by appreciating Europe's sense of the ontology of the witches' world and the character of the participants involved. This collection of sources has been assembled to offer the English-speaking reader significant examples of the European view of that reality and those participants. During the period from 1100 to 1700 Europe's concern over the nature, activities, and numbers of witches became a major intellectual and juridical preoccupation of men from all walks of life and culminated in the widespread fears, trials, and executions that so arrest our attention. Our work will focus upon this period, from the development of a systematic theory of witchcraft to the end of the major persecutions and the formulation of criteria for scepticism and eventual disbelief.

European witch-beliefs antedate, of course, the period of pandemic fear and persecution. Historians, folklorists, and anthropologists, in fact, have long debated over the exact sources from which they were drawn. Celtic and Germanic folklore, biblical and patristic speculation on the nature of evil, Neoplatonism and the related philosophical spiritualism of late antiquity, and even the possible survival of "underground" ancient pre-Christian cults and covens have all been identified by one school or another as major contributors. From 1100 on, however, indistinct and often idiosyncratic strains of belief were systematized into a coherent and generally uniform system of theological and juridical dogma, the logical implications of which were the obligation of the Church and the secular courts actively to seek out and extirpate the witches and their defenders. In the pages of the texts under consideration here, one can witness the transformation of the wise-woman and occasional "sorcerer" of earlier days (who may often have been midwife, doctor, or adviser to a town or village) into the satanic witch of the period of persecutions. Two phenomena whose causal interaction with other social and intellectual conditions constitutes one of the great problems of European history become increasingly clear after 1100: the growing codification of witch beliefs centering on the universal malevolence and diabolism of the witches, and the growing awareness of the active and horrific dangers presented by the ever-increasing number of witches at large.

Before 1100, ecclesiastics and theologians were often sceptical of popular beliefs concerning witches and their magical powers. The Church, after all, had disarmed the last bastion of paganism by convincing men that belief in the Christian god protected everyone from the inept assaults of pagan demons. As the intellectual synthesis of witch beliefs progressed, however, it was precisely the ecclesiastics and theologians and other educated men who were to shape and channel popular opinion. As awareness of the theological and juridical ramifications of the reality of witchcraft spread, so did men's perception of the nature of the witches' activity; as the latter grew, so did the demand for theological and juristic clarification and response. From 1100 on, one can observe (and sometimes even date rather precisely) the appearance of certain common elements which both learned and popular opinion were to consider universally characteristic of witchcraft, and one can follow also the emerging realization that something new and dreadful in the history of Christendom had appeared. Many contemporary observers looked upon manifest witchcraft as quantitatively and qualitatively the single greatest threat to Christian European civilization. At the height of these fears, in the sixteenth and seventeenth centuries, men speculated on when and why the concerted and terrible assaults of the witches had begun. Some dated the crisis from the later fourteenth century, some from around 1500. Protestants later accused the Catholic clergy of fostering witchcraft through "popish blasphemies," and Catholics in turn proceeded to identify witchcraft first with traditional and recognized heresy and later with Protestantism itself. Almost all agreed, however, that intensive witchcraft was essentially a new danger and a particularly urgent one. This perception of the novelty and uniqueness of witchcraft by men of the fifteenth through the seventeenth centuries suggests the value of studying European witchcraft as a peculiarly time-bound phenomenon.

Few writers of the sixteenth and seventeenth centuries realized that the manifestations of witchcraft which they saw as growing rapidly around them had begun as early as 1100. They interpreted a substantial but inconsistent body of tales concerning witchcraft and magic, and earlier ecclesiastical scepticism as to their veracity, as evidence that before their own time witchcraft had not been the extensive threat it later became. Ecclesiastical injunctions against belief in magic and witchcraft increasingly were regarded as legitimately applicable only to the time of their utterance, before the magnitude of the witches' assault had reached its current awesome proportions. The development of theory concerning the witch prepared Europe for the identification of certain empirical phenomena as diabolical witchcraft. Once that identification was made, men were bound by their own world-view to the fact of persecution. In this sense, the problem of European witchcraft demands less the study of magic as pure folklore than the study of the intellectual, perceptual and legal processes by which "folklore" was transformed into systematic demonology, systematic persecution, and, as both contributing cause and resultant effect, to widespread, absolute, undeviating horror.

When the problem of witchcraft is seen in this light, the study of particular social, intellectual, and legal phenomena becomes essential. Before the twelfth century, Christian cosmology had not become the detailed common frame of reference—the literal blueprint of God's creation—which it was to be between 1100 and 1700.[1] Before the thirteenth century, there had existed no systematic and universal ontology as elaborate and thorough in its description of the interrelations among the elements of creation as was that of St. Thomas Aquinas and other scholastic philosophers.[2] Scholastic ontology gave to both demons and witches a logically consistent place within the Christian schema. Before the fourteenth century, there had existed no permanently established body of investigators and judges whose sole duty was to uncover and uproot theological error, including that of the witches, such as was at the disposal of the powers of the Inquisition.[3] Before the fifteenth century, there had been no widespread, literate, concentrated public subjected to widespread social strains and capable of mutually reinforcing that acute awareness of shared helplessness, danger, and constant terror which was an essential ingredient of any substantial witch scare or persecution.[4] Furthermore, and perhaps most important, once the witch had been irrefutably identified as the visible agent of evil upon the earth, then the social, political, and economic turmoils of the late medieval and early modern world, the agonizing disintegration of Christendom into warring religious camps, and the brutalizing and disheartening recurrence of plague and famine all served to heighten that sensibility to the forces of evil, to demonic powers, upon which the persecutions largely depended.[5]

At an intellectual and systematic theological level, the clarification of the ontological status and purposeful activities of Satan and his host of demons was essential to a changed perception of the witch, whose nature and fate were increasingly linked to those of the diabolical powers. The early Christians had inherited an eclectic unorganized theory of the power of evil in the world. Satan had appeared infrequently in the Old Testament, where he was depicted occasionally as a tempter of mankind but more usually as an obedient, accusing angel in particular service to God. In the Jewish apocrypha, however, more imbued as it was with the themes of eastern dualism, the Devil often was presented as the causal agent of all that is evil, a spirit in active rebellion against God. It is this latter concept that emerged as dominant in the New Testament—coupled, to be sure, with the unswerving promise of Christ's ultimate triumph over him. The book of *Revelation* referred to "that ancient serpent, who is called the Devil and Satan, the deceiver of the whole world," thus revealing Eve's tempter and Satan to be one and the same. In this role, Satan tempted both Judas and Christ. St. Paul logically warned the Christian congregations of the powers and wiles of this archfiend, and his *Epistle to the Ephesians* became the fundamental scriptural proof of diabolical character and intentions. By the fourth century, when St. Augustine was drawn to discuss the problem of the source and nature of evil by his dispute with the Manicheans, the notion of the Devil as the enemy of God and man was firmly enshrined in Christian belief. St. Augustine was to systematize this concept and place it in a meaningful context. By stressing to so great a degree the climactic effects of the fall from Eden and the continuing efforts of Satan to prey upon sinful human nature for the perdition of souls, he heightened the Christian awareness of the Devil's powers so that they seemed second only to those of God. When Thomas Aquinas turned to the codification of Christian theology in the thirteenth century, he thus found a clear source of dogma concerning Satan in the works of St. Augustine, and he cited St. Augustine continually in defense of his theory of Satan as the pinnacle of the hierarchy of evil spirits, working for the temporal and eternal suffering of mankind through the inscrutable will of God. The dualism of the Manicheans, it is true, had been defeated in the arena of orthodox belief, but the influence of these and similar dualist beliefs, particularly as they further contributed to illuminating the role of Satan in the world, were to remain a part of Christian doctrine for centuries to come.[6]

That Satan commanded a host or army of subordinate devils was an essential part of late antique and medieval folklore and official doctrine. The major Christian attack upon the pagan gods had anathematized them as evil spirits who deluded mankind. It was in the systematization of these beliefs from 1100 on that the myriads of sub-demons came to hold an essential place in the development of witchcraft doctrines. The book of *Genesis* had told of the "sons of God" who descended to earth and had intercourse with women, producing a race of giants. The book of *Revelation* had described a rebellion in Heaven in which Satan waged war with the forces led by the Archangel Michael and had been cast down to earth with his defeated angels. From these scriptural references later theologians deduced two important concepts: that the earth was infested with a myriad legion of demons (fallen evil spirits) and that these demons could have sexual intercourse with human beings. In the New Testament, Christ often demonstrated his divine powers specifically by exorcising demons, and Scripture held that Christ passed the ability to drive out demons to the Apostles as proof of the divine validity of their mission. The power of exorcism became an essential tool of the later missionary Church:

However many sound social and cultural reasons the historian may find for the expansion of the Christian Church, the fact remains that in all Christian literature from the New Testament onwards, the Christian missionaries advanced principally by revealing the bankruptcy of men's invisible enemies, the demons, through exorcisms and miracles of healing.[7]

Before the work of the scholastic philosophers and systematic theologians in the twelfth and thirteenth centuries, however, the role of the demons in the affairs of man was part of a variegated folklore, and their activities ranged from the horrific and utterly diabolical to a mere impishness and mischievousness, often betraying a whimsical humor. In Aquinas and his contemporaries this folklore became complex and rigorous Church doctrine. The demons were evil angels who had the ability to unite themselves to bodies and to communicate their knowledge and their commands to men. They were a hierarchically organized army in the service of Satan working for the perdition of the faithful. Satan and his hosts could tempt human beings into their service, and these humans became the witches of the theologians, the visible agents of diabolic power. Once the witch had come to be understood in this context, the logic of the witch-hunt and execution became manifest and compelling. There could no longer be simple superstition or simple magic performed by self-proclaimed wizards, wise-women, or sorcerers. There could be only the diabolical witch.

Fear of the Devil and fear of the witch, thus linked by scholastic ontology, increased in importance together from the thirteenth century on, and the changing European perception of the power and triumphs of the Devil clearly became a major factor in the movement toward more intensive witch-scares. In one sense at least, the formulation of beliefs in active witchcraft and the ensuing persecution of witches may be said to have coincided with a new emphasis upon the suffering of God and a "strengthening" of the Devil that emerged in literature and art between the thirteenth and the sixteenth centuries. Historians of art, popular culture, and devotional forms of this period have long noted that the image of the divinity in the early Middle Ages was that of the powerful and ever-triumphant Father of the Old Testament. Before 1100 the Devil was the greatest force of evil, but his power never threatened the power of God in an absolute way: the disproportion between them was clear and unquestionable. After 1100, however, the humanity and suffering of the Christ-God began to receive more emphasis, and with it the human anguish and suffering which Christ had experienced, particularly during the Passion. In the light of a new emphasis upon the human nature of Christ and his capacity for suffering, the powers of the Devil grew more fearsome. No longer was Satan the tempter in the desert who foolishly tried to entice Christ into becoming his servant for mere earthly rewards. No longer was Satan the "feudal" overlord who extended a legitimate claim of death over all men—in this sense, his "vassals"—until he mistakenly extended that claim to Christ himself, thinking him only human, and with this irreparable breach lost forever his absolute rule over the afterlife. Satan became once again, as he had been for St. Augustine, the Great Devourer, the arch-enemy against whose numerous and awesome powers man was utterly helpless without a suffering God's alert and constant aid through the ministry of the Church.[8]

This shift in the human conception of God and Satan is a critical force in the growth of the witch phenomenon, because witch beliefs and persecutions were all based upon the doctrine of the strength and ubiquity of an absolutely hostile, ruthless, and cunning Devil whose capacity for harming mankind had increased greatly. Moreover, all doctrinal authorities agreed that in some mysterious way this was taking place with the permission of God himself. In the face of a clumsily brutal, occasionally stupid, and often bungling Satan, the erring but controlled servant of God, the Church and the faithful could maintain a mutual confidence in their ability to ward off the most serious attacks of the powers of darkness by traditional and unexceptional means: individual moral righteousness and faithful observance of the sacraments in normal times, and exorcisms, particular specialized liturgies, and the invocation of saints' aid in abnormal times. Relics, the wearing of talismans, crosses, or blessed objects, and particular forms of devotion to patron saints all constituted an effective and durable bridge between high theology and popular belief. With the emergence of a more powerful and increasingly effective Satan, however, these ordinary devotional forms often seemed pitifully ineffective. Moreover, the growth of religious reform movements further weakened much popular piety by declaring it mere superstition. In the light of these changes, a stronger and more dramatic response to Satan's threats was necessary.

With the new intensification of the fear of Satan, the figure of the witch, now Satan's servant, became increasingly vile and fearsome. Scholastic philosophers, systematic theologians, and demonologists reached a gradual consensus on the nature and activities of witches. The witch, according to this consensus, had succumbed of his or her own will to Satan's temptation and had entered into a contract or pact with the Devil, one which usually was said to be sealed by an act of carnal intercourse with Satan or the demons.

As a new agent of Satan, the witch was given the power to exceed all human capabilities in working harm upon the faithful. Witches were portrayed as congregating in covens, feasting, and flying through the night air on sticks or beasts to the blasphemous Sabbaths at which they met their master. To be sure, this was only an ideal typology of the witches' activities constructed by learned men whose primary attention had been concentrated upon Satan and his assault on mankind in general, not upon the intermittent complaints of villagers or townsmen who were apprehensive about the supposed malevolence of individual neighbors. The variegated activities of witches throughout Europe came to be made thus homogeneous in the eyes of theologians and ecclesiastical prosecutors, and, whatever the specific accusations against later witches, this ecclesiastical typology soon made its appearance in nearly every case. Once this ideal schema of witch activities had taken shape—by 1450 or thereabouts—the learned Inquisitors and ecclesiastical judges, particularly on the Continent, continued to conceive the fundamental crime of the witch as devil-worship, the necessary act which empowered the witch to commit *maleficia,* evil acts against other humans.[9]

The evil and sufferings—*maleficia*—which men believed the witches inflicted upon mankind soon became a catalogue of all those calamities which men most deeply dreaded, and the witch was seen increasingly as a necessary efficient agent of such events. Intensive anxiety regarding the witches and the nature of the threat they constituted grew and spread through all regions, classes, and conditions of men. The most and the least coherent writers on the subject assigned to the witch an increasingly broader spectrum of crimes that covered the deepest traumatic fears of mankind: the power to cause sudden illness or death; sexual impotence, frigidity, or barrenness; crippling and painful illness; unpredictable climatic or meteorological changes, crop failures, and loss of livestock; involuntary actions, rapid personality changes, and loss of friends; finally, a "demonic possession" in which the individual personality lost its ability to order itself and felt itself given over to all it once believed to be evil and degrading. If mental health may be said to consist of men's confident reliance on the knowledge of the real world which they are certain they possess, the utilization of mental and moral energy to eliminate the causes of trauma and dread, and the attempt to control those forces that most affect their lives, then the witchcraft persecutions, whatever our estimation of their conceptual and noetic components, represented not an insane "aberration," but a desperate attempt to apply a system of putative knowledge towards restoring order in the world.

From the late thirteenth to the late fifteenth century, ecclesiastical pronouncements and judicial decisions reflect both old defenses and, increasingly, an awareness of new dangers. In 1258 Pope Alexander IV issued the first papal letter to empower the Inquisition to deal with witchcraft, but only when witchcraft "manifestly savored of heresy."[10] Pope Alexander's letter was reissued by other popes in 1288 and 1303. As late as 1310 the Council of Treves proposed the withdrawal of the sacraments from those convicted of witchcraft and, for those who nevertheless remained unrepentant, excommunication. But the formal structure of scholastic ontology offered the Inquisitors little choice but to inquire whether the witches were indeed guilty of heresy, and by 1376, the date of publication of the Inquisitor Nicholas Eymeric's handbook of inquisitorial procedure, the *Directorium Inquisitorum*, the connection between witchcraft and heresy was drawn sharply and inflexibly.[11] Once this association was established and the Inquisition was juridically armed against witches, the persecutions followed quickly. In the south of France, long a center of heresy, the early decades of the fourteenth century witnessed the burning of witches as well. Once again the Church asserted its mission to protect the faithful from evil, and those witches it discovered and sentenced to death were remanded to the civil authority for burning with a purely *pro forma* recommendation of mercy. By 1398, supported by scholastic thought—which had by then become derivative and rigid—and papal and conciliar decisions, the intricate judicial theology of such writers as Eymeric, and the evidence of trials, confessions, and recantations of witchcraft, the Faculty of Theology of the University of Paris silenced nearly all doubters with its proof, contained in a twenty-eight-article treatise on demonology, that witchcraft in all of its manifestations could only be heretical.

The juridical and doctrinal developments of the fourteenth century generated a new interest in formal demonology, which manifested itself in a number of new treatises on witchcraft, some of which were exhibited at the Council of Basel in 1437 during the pontificate of Eugenius IV, himself convinced of the pressing danger.[12] The most influential of these treatises was the *Formicarius* (Ant-Heap) by Johann Nider, which brought to bear on any sceptics who might remain the full weight of scriptural, patristic, and scholastic authorities, and gave a full and detailed description of the witches' maleficent powers.[13] In the mid-fifteenth century yet more treatises appeared, all of them stressing urgently and cogently the case for vigorous prosecution and punishment. Finally in 1486 there appeared the single most influential and detailed treatise of all, the *Malleus Maleficarum* (The Hammer of Witches), which not only closed the question in favor of prosecution, but silenced all opposition as well with its rigor and irrefutable weight of authority, offering a ringing affirmative answer to the very first problem which it took up:

Whether the belief that there are such beings as witches is so essential a part of the Catholic faith that obstinately to maintain the opposite opinion manifestly savours of heresy.[14]

Making disbelief, scepticism, or doubt concerning the very reality of witch-craft heretical in itself not only enlarged the scope of possible heretical behavior, but understandably limited unfettered discussion of the nature of witchcraft.

The Protestant Reformation, with its strong emphasis upon the scriptural Satan and its literal obedience to the injunction of *Exodus* 22:18, "Thou shalt not suffer a witch to live," only strengthened the already present fear of diabolism and witchcraft in the lands that reformed the Church. From the mid-fifteenth to the mid-seventeenth century, the witch-beliefs of theologians, philosophers, lawyers, and secular magistrates found a progressively larger and more receptive audience. As H. R. Trevor-Roper has remarked, with much indignation:

Whatever allowance we may make for the mere mutiplication of evidence after the discovery of printing, there can be no doubt that the witch-craze grew, and grew terribly, after the Renaissance. Credulity in high places increased, its engines of expression were made more terrible, more victims were sacrificed to it. The years 1550–1600 were worse than the years 1500–1550, and the years 1600–1650 were worse still. Nor was the craze entirely separable from the intellectual and spiritual life of those years. It was forwarded by the cultivated popes of the Renaissance, by the great Protestant Reformers, by the saints of the Counter-Reformation, by the scholars, lawyers, and churchmen of the age of Scaliger and Lipsius, Bacon and Grotius, Berulle and Pascal.[15]

Nor, one may add, was the "craze" entirely separable from the daily life of these same years. Rural villages, remote mountain farms, and the greatest and most economically advanced cities—with, to be sure, many exceptions and varieties—equally expressed ever greater evidences of shared helplessness and terror. The ensuing malevolence among neighbors and families sustained both suspicion and persecution, sometimes over a period of two or three generations in a single place. No estate, no class, no group, however conceived, was completely exempt from the pervasiveness of belief in witchcraft and the even more dangerous belief that anyone could be a witch and that witches could strike anywhere. The theological and judicial portrait of the witch responded to and inspired in its turn an ever-widening public consensus until scholar and peasant, jurist and artisan, priest and layman, king and merchant, all believed, and believing, feared and called for even more intensive persecution.

In brief, the new intellectual zeal of the fifteenth-century demonologists was more than matched by the increasing anxiety of the general public, and both were reinforced by the increasingly widespread activities—and discoveries of witches—of the inquisitorial and the secular courts. The Church had originally taken the lead in seeking out and persecuting witches, once witch-craft and heresy had been firmly linked. At the outset of the persecutions, the Church often had to threaten to excommunicate those secular authorities who were reluctant to carry out the sentence of death on convicted witches. Soon, however, the Church courts found that civil authorities had grown more cooperative and had even begun to bring witches to trial independently of ecclesiastical procedure. While scepticism was suppressed or dissipated by the general fear inspired by widely circulated horrific tales, by confessions of witchcraft (usually obtained by the more widespread use of torture) and by the spectacular convictions of unsuspected and highly-placed citizens, the number of trials and executions increased at a rapid rate. In the fourteenth century mass burnings had occurred primarily in Provence, the Alpine regions, and Spain. In the fifteenth century they spread across Europe; there were mass trials and executions at Rome (1424), Heidelberg (1446), Cologne (1456), Como (1485), and Metz (1488). By the sixteenth century, Europeans were convinced that the continent was literally swarming with witches, and "burning courts" were established in area after area well into the first half of the seventeenth century. Indeed, it was between 1590 and 1650 that England and Scotland experienced their most intensive, albeit intermittent, witch-hunts and persecutions. It was not uncommon for scores, and occasionally hundreds of witches, contemporaries claimed, to be executed in a single city or region during a period of terror lasting several years.[16] It is impossible to calculate accurately the total number of convicted witches who were burned at the stake or hanged between the fourteenth and seventeenth centuries, but few students begin guessing below the range of fifty to one hundred thousand, and some would double or triple that figure. However great the actual count of victims, witnesses all convey the impression that the witches existed in great numbers and that convictions and executions consumed them in great numbers.

Voices in opposition to the mass persecutions, however, were never entirely silenced. Earlier ecclesiastical insistence, such as that of John of Salisbury in the twelfth century, that night rides and carnal pacts with the devil were illusory, found individual echoes in, for example, the French author of the treatise *Le Songe du Vergier* in the fourteenth century, and the sixteenth-century bishop of Cuenca, Fray Lope de Barrientos, who bluntly remarked that:

Nor should anyone believe such an absurd thing as that these supposed events really take place, other than in dreams or in the imagination. Anyone who believes such things is an infidel and worse than a pagan, to judge the way they conceive such things.[17]

In the mid-sixteenth century the physician Johann Weyer caused a major scandal by publicly denying not, to be sure, that witches existed, but that the particular activities of which they were commonly accused were anything but illusions. Weyer found few followers, but his work is generally regarded as the beginning of extensive theoretical speculation critical of the existence of witches. In the later sixteenth century, Montaigne maintained a scepticism about the certainty of human beliefs which culminated in his dramatic observation that, "after all, it is putting a very high price on one's conjectures to have a man roasted alive because of them."[18] It was, in fact, as unproven "conjectures" that witchcraft beliefs were challenged by many of these early opponents of the witch persecutions. The intentions of the Inquisitors and civil courts, the excessive use of torture, the unremitting concentration upon the poor and defenceless, and the sophisticated psychological techniques of interrogation vitiated for the sceptics much of the theoretical structure of witch beliefs and reduced them to the status of conjectures, still subject to other tests of veracity than those to which they had customarily been submitted. By the end of the sixteenth century, the Englishman Reginald Scot's *Discoverie of Witchcraft* took up the thread of criticism where Weyer's work had left it and constituted a major attack on both the literal existence of witches as men depicted them and the means employed to find them.[19]

Whenever critics of the beliefs or persecutions appeared, however, learned clerics, philosophers, and jurists rushed vigorously to their refutation, and a vast body of literature about witchcraft, pro and con, appeared in the seventeenth century and continued into the eighteenth. Yet from the beginning of the seventeenth century, when the witch beliefs and persecutions appeared to be reaching to new heights, their foundations had already begun to crumble. The collapse of what had been a major intellectual and social force in the life of Europe for three centuries occurred so rapidly that few men at the time were aware of the momentous changes in conceptions and attitudes which underlay its decline. Such philosophical spiritualists and defenders of witchcraft belief and persecution as Henry More and Joseph Glanvil correctly identified them in part as the consequence of a decline in spiritualist and scripturalist explanations of earthly phenomena.[20] In a society undergoing accelerated and fundamental change, almost all of the major new intellectual currents pointed away from an active fear of and belief in witches and the widespread activities of Satan. Anti-scholasticism, scepticism of (and snobbery toward) purely popular traditions, increasing theological optimism concerning the Providence of God, mechanistic explanation of physical events, the separation of spiritual and material causality, empiricism, naturalism, and a critical rationalism began to pervade the realm not only of philosophy and theology, but of the jury and the bench as well. To be sure, defenders of witchcraft beliefs were not wholly silent nor wholly absent from the ranks of men who supported and extended these new strains of thought, but the cumulative impact of the new ideas of natural philosophy and theology was to undermine the conceptions, traditions, and authorities upon which witchcraft beliefs and persecutions had stood. The new patterns of social organization which emerged in the late sixteenth and seventeenth centuries altered or eliminated many of the social relationships and social pressures which had contributed to the emergence of many of the witch scares. The civil community, not the Church or the individual, became responsible for the care of the sick, poor, or insane, and the civil community, abstract and impersonal, was far better able to absorb the fear, hostility and, perhaps, guilt generated by numbers of displaced or useless individuals.

The seventeenth century, then, witnessed both the most intensive expression and the death of witchcraft belief and persecution. Accusations and prosecutions flourished until the 1650's—and, indeed, erupted in Old Salem (now Danvers), Massachusetts, in 1692. Although the last witches were legally burned in Europe as late as the 1780's, there was ultimately no body of educated people able or willing to lead or even to defend such practices. By the dawn of the eighteenth century, the question was no longer whether Christian belief demanded a belief in witchcraft, but whether the system which had generated and compelled such beliefs could continue to hold any authority over the minds and hearts of thinking men. With that question, the men of the eighteenth century led European civilization into another age, and, as Voltaire remarked, the witches and exorcists both, if they remained quiet, would be left in peace.

II. SOURCES

The literature of source-materials and studies dealing with European witchcraft between 1100 and 1700 is vast and diffuse. There is as yet no comprehensive or completely satisfactory history of witchcraft itself during the period, and the study of the social and religious temperament of the society in which the beliefs grew and prospered has only recently begun. The following bibliographical sketch cannot purport to be a thorough guide to source-materials and historiography, but it does offer an account of the best scholarship on the subject and a guide to most of the generally available materials.

The modern study of European witchcraft from 1100 to 1700 may be said to have begun in 1843, when W. G. Soldan published in Stuttgart his *Geschichte der Hexenprozesse*, and J. G. T. Grässe published in Leipzig his monumental bibliography *Bibliotheca Magica et Pneumatica*. Soldan's study was revised by his son-in-law Heinrich Heppe in 1879, and the combined work of Soldan-Heppe was reissued in 1911. Just as the Soldan-Heppe study constituted the first major history of witchcraft, that of Grässe was the first modern attempt to construct a bibliography of witchcraft materials. Grässe's work is still of considerable value; no one has since revised or systematically added to it. With few exceptions, other nineteenth-century studies of witchcraft betray a distinct rationalist disapproval of the ecclesiastical and secular mentality that allowed witchcraft-beliefs to flourish, and added little to the clarification of a major historical problem. In 1889, however, the American historian George Lincoln Burr published what is still the best account of the literature of witchcraft before 1800 in his essay "The Literature of Witchcraft," now available in *George Lincoln Burr: His Life and Selections from His Writings,* edited by Lois Oliphant Gibbons (Ithaca, New York, 1943). The great historian of the Spanish and medieval Inquisitions, Henry Charles Lea, spent the last years of his life compiling materials for a proposed history of witchcraft, but he died before he could begin his work. Lea's collection has been edited by Arthur C. Howland, *Materials toward a History of Witchcraft collected by H. C. Lea,* 3 vols. (Philadelphia, 1938). These volumes constitute a mine of useful citations from hundreds of original sources and are still indispensable to the historian. In 1900 and 1901 the German archivist and historian Joseph Hansen produced two other important volumes: *Zauberwahn, Inquisition und Hexenprozess im Mittelalter* (Munich, 1900) and *Quellen und Untersuchungen zur Geschichte des Hexenwahns und der Hexenverfolgung im Mittelalter* (Bonn, 1901). The first book is a detailed and learned history of late-medieval and Renaissance witchcraft, still the best and most complete work in its field, and the second is an edition of selected Latin, French, and German texts from contemporary documents dealing with the theory and practice of witchcraft. Generally speaking, histories of science and religious thought did not contribute substantially to the study of the witchcraft phenomenon during the first century of modern scholarship on the subject. On the sixteenth-century Reformation there is only Nicholas Paulus, *Hexenwahn und Hexenprozess, vornehmlich im 16. Jahrhundert* (Freiburg-im-Breisgau, 1910).

Since 1930, however, both historians and anthropologists have begun to turn their attention systematically to the problem of witchcraft, and it has been in those rare instances of co-operation between these two disciplines that some of the best recent work has been done. The seminal work of modern anthropological studies in witchcraft is that of E. E. Evans-Pritchard, *Witchcraft, Oracles, and Magic among the Azande* (Oxford, 1937). More recently the short book by Lucy Mair, *Witchcraft* (New York, 1970), offers a model view of the contributions of anthropology to the subject, as does the important book of essays dedicated to Evans-Pritchard and edited by Mary Douglas, *Witchcraft Confessions and Accusations* (London, 1970). The superb study by Alan Macfarlane, *Witchcraft in Tudor and Stuart England* (New York, 1970) is an indispensable work which illustrates vividly the effectiveness of historians' proper use of anthropological methodology. The history of medicine and mental illness has also brought historians' attention to the problems of witchcraft. Gregory Zilboorg, *The Medieval Man and the Witch in the Renaissance* (Baltimore, 1935); Thomas Rogers Forbes, *The Midwife and the Witch* (New

Haven, 1966); George Rosen, *Madness in Society: Chapters in the Historical Sociology of Mental Illness* (New York, 1969) are recent approaches to this little-studied aspect of the witchcraft phenomenon.

The work of modern historians on the subject of witchcraft has been varied. In the field of social and intellectual history, the excellent essay by Lucien Febvre, "Sorcellerie: sottise ou révolution mentale?," *Annales: économies, sociétés, civilizations* (1948), is a good starting-point. The most authoritative study of witchcraft in its social and intellectual setting (chiefly in England) is the superb work of Keith Thomas, *Religion and the Decline of Magic* (New York, 1971), an indispensable aid to the historian and general reader alike, as well as a monumental contribution to the history of Tudor and Stuart England. Julio Caro Baroja, *The World of the Witches*, tr. O. N. V. Glendinning (Chicago, 1965), which discusses European witchcraft from primitive to modern man, is always stimulating and carefully thought-out. H. R. Trevor-Roper, *The European Witch-Craze of the Sixteenth and Seventeenth Centuries* (New York, 1969) offers a sweeping account of the witch-phenomenon as it manifested itself in widespread social conflicts, religious struggles, and cultural change. The study by Robert Mandrou, *Magistrats et sorciers en France au 17e siècle* (Paris, 1968), examines the changing mentality of judges in cases of witchcraft and is a major contribution to the legal history of the phenomenon.

Brief collections of extracts from primary source-materials and scholarship are E. William Monter, *European Witchcraft* (New York, 1969), Barbara Rosen, *Witchcraft* (London, 1970), and Max Marwick, ed., *Witchcraft and Sorcery* (Baltimore, 1970). The most recent general survey of the literature since 1940 is H. C. Erik Midelfort, "Recent Witch-Hunting Research," *Papers of the Bibliographical Society of America* 62 (1968). A recent survey of new work appeared in the (London) *Times Literary Supplement*, No. 3,583, 30 October, 1970.

None of the scholarly disciplines, however, has been able to avoid narrowness, perversity, cant, or aimless witch-fetishism. The lucid discussion of some of the shortcomings of modern scholarship in Eliot Rose, *A Razor for a Goat* (Toronto, 1962), is a helpful tool for the modern student not only of medieval and early-modern European witchcraft but of its more bizarre modern apologists.

III. "ALL THAT HAPPENS VISIBLY IN THIS WORLD CAN BE DONE BY DEMONS": A NOTE ON THE ILLUSTRATIONS

Medieval and early modern artists strove on vellum, wood, and stone to achieve a visual representation of those spiritual forces and events which they believed most affected men's lives. They left the record of their vision in all forms of esoteric and popular art, from the painstakingly illuminated manuscript to the cheap, rough woodcut on a printed broadsheet. The illustrations in this book augment the written sources, for visual representation constituted a significant element in the common perception of the world of demons and witches given substance by scholastic ontology and popular belief. In addition, such representation reflected the particular imagery associated with abstract ideas or common beliefs in different periods of time. Hence, the pictorial sources for the history of witchcraft are a rich and suggestive addition to the written sources.

As the media of visual representation changed from 1100 to 1700, so did the thematic and compositional character of the artistic depiction of witchcraft. Manuscript illuminations, church frescoes, and sculpture were the media most commonly used before the late fifteenth century. While a particular setting or subject might bind the artist to a strictly regulated and theologically determined rendering of spiritual realities (such as the sculptured Last Judgement scenes in Figures 20 and 23), the diversity of regions and sensibilities often allowed for substantial inventiveness in designing the patterns and figures of the forces of evil. The appearance of woodcuts and engravings in the late fifteenth and sixteenth centuries circulated common demonological and witchcraft motifs to larger audiences and increased the tendency (also manifest in the written sources) towards the synthesis, standardization, and repetition of a shared body of witchcraft beliefs, themes, and images. Originality was never wholly lost, for eminent artists often dealt with topics related to witchcraft, and they brought to their works their own unique artistic, aesthetic, and spiritual concerns.

The principles which governed the depiction of witchcraft beliefs were not generically different from those which governed that of other spiritual phenomena, although neither all theologians nor all laymen approved of every detail of that depiction. The concrete representation of demons and witches did not differ from the attempts to portray artistically and dramatically the spiritual population of the Christian universe, terrestrial and celestial, demonic and divine. The medieval and early modern artists sought to bring to the senses of their audiences the hand of God, the rebellion of Satan, the struggle of the angels, and the temptation and perdition of fallen man. The illustration of such phenomena in no way lessened their spiritual reality for the viewer. St. Gregory the Great had called such representations "the scriptures of the unlettered." A twelfth-century theologian had remarked that "the sluggish mind reaches spiritual truths through material objects." Indeed, the vivid imagery enhanced the drama and awesomeness of such forces and events for those unable to read or comprehend the language of the schools. No text illustrates this capacity of religious art in the later middle ages more vividly than does the prayer which the poet François Villon put into the mouth of his illiterate mother:

> I am an old woman, and poor,
> Who knows nothing; I have never read one letter.
> In the church which is my parish church I see
> Paradise painted where there are harps and lutes,
> And a Hell, where the damned are boiled:
> One gives me fear, the other joy, delight.
> Make that joy mine, O Virgin Goddess,
> To whom all sinners, all, must have recourse,
> All filled with faith, no hesitation, weakness there:
> In that faith may I live, may I die.

"That faith," for most Christian Europeans, as for Villon's mother, was forged as much through the pictorial representation of doctrinal truths as through the more formalized written texts of high theology.

Of the very small number of works which contain a series of illustrations of witchcraft beliefs, only two—the late fifteenth-century treatise *De Lamiis* of the jurist Ulrich Molitor of Constance and the early seventeenth-century *Compendium Maleficarum* of the Italian priest Francesco Maria Guazzo— have been drawn upon in this anthology. These two are, however, the most profusely illustrated works on witchcraft before the nineteenth century. Molitor's work, cast as a dialogue between the author and the Archduke Sigismund of Austria (with his judge, Conrad Schatz), presented his moderate defense of traditional and contemporary beliefs concerning witches. Published in 1489, the *De Lamiis* was the fifteenth century's only illustrated treatise on witchcraft. It contained seven woodcuts, four of which are reprinted here. They preserve a remarkable simplicity, directness, and vividness (Figures 38, 39, 46, 52). Guazzo's brief *Compendium Maleficarum* is an unoriginal and confused work written for the Archbishop of Milan and first printed in that city in 1608. It offered a long series of woodcuts that illustrated more aspects of witchcraft and demonology than any previous work. The examples here represent the most important of Guazzo's pictures. Only five of the illustrations are omitted, and these are simple variations of those included in this book.

The eye of the seventeenth century, however, was not the same as that of the twelfth, and Guazzo's depictions of events which twelfth-century writers had described were by no means necessarily similar to the ways in which the earlier writers would have visualized them. In art as in judicial prosecution, it was in the twelfth to the fourteenth centuries that men shaped the basic "vocabulary" of witchcraft themes, but in the fifteenth through the seventeenth centuries that the world and idea became visual image and concrete action most often and most evidently. The sixteenth and seventeenth centuries naturally witnessed far more pictorial representation of witchcraft beliefs than any prior centuries. Figures 1 through 26 thus offer a basic visual lexicon of elements which reappear in Figures 27 through 69.

Representational media reflected, of course, not only the growing sense of immediacy of witchcraft beliefs from the fifteenth century on, but wider cultural and artistic phenomena as well. In his brilliant study *The Waning of the Middle Ages,* the historian J. Huizinga described the fifteenth and early sixteenth centuries as a period of "Religious Thought Crystallizing into Images." The spiritual experience of the late fifteenth century directed its rich and fervid visual imagination into a set of fascinations and emphases radically different from those that had captivated the artists of the twelfth through fourteenth centuries:

Now, whereas.the celestial symbolism of Alain de la Roche seems artificial, his infernal visions are characterized by a hideous actuality. He sees the animals which represent the various sins equipped with horrible genitals, and emitting torrents of fire which obscure the earth with their smoke. He sees the prostitute of apostasy giving birth to apostates, now devouring them and vomiting them forth, now kissing them and petting them like a mother. This is the reverse side of the suave fancies of spiritual love. Human imagination contained, as the inevitable complement of the sweetness of celestial visions, a black mass of demonological conceptions which also sought expression in language of ardent sensuality.

Huizinga's description of the imagery of the visions of Alain de la Roche, a late fifteenth-century Breton mystic and the teacher of Jacob Sprenger, one of the authors of the *Malleus Maleficarum,* describes equally the visual depiction of demons and witches by the artists of the late fifteenth and sixteenth centuries. The direction of the imagination toward the most detailed physical aspects of the relationship between man and Satan produced striking and often terrifying pictorial works. Yet even the most extravagant of these remained within the theological traditions of an earlier period. The fifteenth and sixteenth centuries witnessed the further development and exploitation of a corpus of visual images of witch activities and other elements of diabolism which later periods tended to standardize and repeat.

The late fifteenth and early sixteenth centuries witnessed yet another development of some interest and difficulty to the student of the pictorial sources of witchcraft belief, that of an artist's borrowing conventional images from one group of thematic subjects and applying them to another. The fairy Melusine flying out of the castle window in the shape of a serpent-woman (Figure 50) does not technically belong to the genre of witch-depictions, but the association of flying women with heretics and witches suggests the possibility of a pictorial relationship between two distinct areas of visual consciousness. The illustration of the conception of the wizard Merlin (Figure 14) is a fourteenth-century manuscript illumination belonging to the genre of romances, but the phenomenon of incubism tormented men from the fourteenth to the seventeenth centuries. Finally, witchcraft was a legitimate subject for the representation of nude figures in the sixteenth century, just as were Adam and Eve in the Garden of Eden and the souls of the damned in the twelfth. Many artists' depictions of "witches" may be simply nude studies or, indeed, simply rearrangements of traditional classical figures (e.g., Figure 53) to illustrate a subject of artistic interest.

The quotation which opened this section of the introduction is from Saint Augustine and was repeated by Saint Thomas Aquinas. The graphic demonstration of its thesis was the concern of medieval artists not because they were preoccupied by demonology or witchcraft in and of themselves, but because demons and witches participated in that vast realm of spiritual beings and events whose depiction was the artist's highest goal. The fifteenth and sixteenth centuries, however, with their particular taste for the grotesque and their intense concern with the details of spiritual evil, undertook a much fuller effort to represent the reality of which the saints had spoken. The pictorial history of witchcraft, thus, as in the case of its documentary history, provides a dramatic and informative insight into the development and transition of modern European civilization.

Acknowledgments

The editors would like to express their gratitude and appreciation to Professor John Tallon of the Moore College of Art and Professor James Muldoon of Rutgers University for their assistance in correcting the translations from Latin. The editors, of course, assume joint responsibility for those errors which stubbornly persist in the translations from both Latin and French.

The editors wish to thank Professors Rudolf Hirsch, David Robb, and Charles Minott, and Mr. Alfred J. Marion, of the University of Pennsylvania, for their kind suggestions and assistance. They also wish to thank the Free Library of Philadelphia for its kind permission to reproduce several illuminations from its manuscript 185 of the Lewis Collection. Whatever errors have remained in the visual sources, as in the case of the literary sources, are the editors' responsibility alone.

A.C.K./E.P.

Introduction

Notes to the Introduction

1. A general introduction to the medieval and early modern "world view" may be found in C. S. Lewis, *The Discarded Image* (Cambridge, 1964). Short entries in these notes refer to the discussion of sources, pp. 15-17.

2. A brief account of European intellectual changes in the thirteenth century is the study by John W. Baldwin, *The Scholastic Culture of the Middle Ages, 1000-1300* (Lexington, Mass., 1971). See also R. W. Southern, *The Making of the Middle Ages* (New Haven, Conn., 1961), and F. C. Copleston, *Aquinas* (Baltimore, 1955). On St. Thomas Aquinas and witchcraft, see Charles E. Hopkin, *The Share of Thomas Aquinas in the Growth of the Witchcraft Delusion* (Philadelphia, 1940).

3. See Henry Charles Lea, *The Inquisition of the Middle Ages,* 3 vols. (New York, 1888); abridged edition, ed. Walter Ullmann (New York, 1969).

4. The question of the social context of witchcraft beliefs and persecutions is of the utmost importance. There is a sensitive and broad discussion in Thomas, *Decline of Magic.* See also Macfarlane, *Witchcraft,* and Trevor-Roper, *Witch-Craze.*

5. The older notion of a clear and sufficient causal relationship between the various disasters and crises of the fourteenth and fifteenth centuries—the Black Death, the Hundred Years' War, and recurring famines and pestilences—and witchcraft has largely been rejected. Studies of popular sensibilities to agents of disaster have in fact only begun to lay out a psychological profile of early-modern Europeans. Some excellent studies are those of Séraphine Guerchberg, "The Controversy over the Alleged Sowers of the Black Death in Contemporary Treatises on Plague," in Sylvia Thrupp, ed., *Change in Medieval Society* (New York, 1964); Norman Cohn, *The Pursuit of the Millennium* (3rd ed., New York, 1970); J. Huizinga, *The Waning of the Middle Ages* (New York, n.d.); J. Le Goff, ed., *Hérésies et sociétés dans l'Europe pré-industrielle, 11e-18e siècles* (Paris-La Haye, 1968).

6. On the history of Satan, see any of the standard ecclesiastical encyclopedias, e.g., F. L. Cross, *The Oxford Dictionary of the Christian Church* (London, 1957), *s.v.* Devil, Satan. See also G. Bazin, et al., *Satan* (*Etudes Carmélitaines,* 1948), a partial English translation of which is edited by C. Moeller, *Satan* (New York, 1951). More recently, there is some relevant work in Max Milner, ed., *Entretiens sur l'homme et le diable* (Paris-La Haye, 1965).

7. Peter Brown, *The World of Late Antiquity* (London, 1971), p. 55. See also A. A. Barb, "The Survival of the Magic Arts," in A. Momigliano, ed., *The Conflict Between Paganism and Christianity in the Fourth Century* (Oxford, 1963), pp. 100-125.

8. For the beginning of this process, see Southern, *The Making of the Middle Ages.* On Satan in the *Divine Comedy* of Dante, see A. Valensin, "The Devil in the Divine Comedy," in Moeller, *Satan,* pp. 368-78. The religious sensibility of the fourteenth and fifteenth centuries may be traced in, e.g., the field of art in Millard Meiss, *Painting in Florence and Siena after the Black Death* (New York, 1964), and Huizinga, *The Waning of the Middle Ages.* An excellent, if incomplete, description of the "magical" side of late medieval Christian belief may be found in Thomas, *Decline of Magic,* pp.

3-176. There is a large bibliography in the study by Emile Brouette, "The Sixteenth Century and Satanism," in Moeller, *Satan*, pp. 310-50. For those aspects of medieval religion commonly classified as "folklore," see J. A. McCulloch, *Medieval Faith and Fable* (London, 1932).

9. See, e.g., the remarks in Nicholas Eymeric, *Directorium Inquisitorum* (1376) below, *No.* 14, and the excellent discussion in Thomas, *Decline of Magic*, pp. 435-586.

10. Below, *No.* 11.

11. Below, *No.* 14. In general, see Lea, *Inquisition*.

12. Below, *No.* 16.

13. Below, *No.* 17.

14. *The Hammer of Witches,* tr. Montague Summers (rep. London, 1951), p. 1. Extracts are printed below, *No.* 19.

15. Trevor-Roper, *Witch-Craze*, p. 91.

16. The case of Trier between 1580 and 1593 is striking. See the selections printed below, *No.* 24, and the long study by George Lincoln Burr, "The Fate of Dietrich Flade," reprinted in *George Lincoln Burr: His Life and Selections from His Writings,* ed. Lois Olifant Gibbons (Ithaca, New York, 1943), pp. 190-233.

17. For John of Salisbury, see below, *No.* 3. For witchcraft in later medieval France and *Le Songe due Vergier,* see P. S. Lewis, *Later Medieval France: The Polity* (New York, 1968), pp. 16-27. The quotation from Fray Lope de Barrientos is from Caro Baroja, pp. 276-79; see also pp. 99-111.

18. Below, *No.* 37.

19. The best and most reliable discussion of the real importance of Scot's work is in Thomas, *Decline of Magic,* pp. 578-80. Excerpts are printed below, *No.* 36.

20. Below, *No.* 35.

Witchcraft
in Christendom
1100–1250

Between 1100 and 1250 several important literary genres began to reflect men's view of—and interest in—an increasingly broad spectrum of supernatural events. The chronicles of monastic houses and, later, of individuals, the prolific writing of compendia of theological and legal treatises, and the considerable increase of collections of saints' lives and miracles and moral fables provided curious Europeans with the largest and most varied body of literature since the flourishing of the Roman Empire. It is from this literary "explosion" that we derive our knowledge of attitudes toward witchcraft and sorcery for the period preceding the schematization of dogma and philosophy in the thirteenth century. The chroniclers were interested primarily, of course, in the fortunes of their chief subjects, their own monastic houses, their protectors, or the great men—kings and popes—of their time. Nevertheless, they did not omit curiosities which crossed their paths, and since the events of the invisible world of spirits were at least as important as those of the material world of great powers, they recorded a wide variety of episodes. The compilers of legal treatises—Gratian is an example—brought before their readers texts which ranged in date from the earliest days of the Church to their own times. These they sought to systematize by grouping relevant texts around a number of key problems of law or theology. Whether these compendia were spare and precise—as was Gratian's *Decretum*—or diffuse and rambling—as was Caesarius of Heisterbach's *Dialogue on Miracles*—they all served the function of assembling manageable collections of great scope for the benefit of their readers. It is from these materials that we draw our knowledge of attitudes toward diabolism, witchcraft, and the occult in general before the thirteenth century.

The episodes selected from the twelfth-century chronicles of William of Malmesbury (*No. 2*) and Ralph of Coggeshall (*No. 5*) are inserted in longer histories as singular, isolated episodes which reveal the chronicler's fascination with unusual and striking events rather than a systematic theory of diabolism and witchcraft. Ecclesiastical lawyers, too, lacked systematic categories of diabolism and occult powers. Before the thirteenth century, witchcraft, predicting the future, and the use of demonic powers to achieve earthly objects remained in a traditional juridical framework of ecclesiastical crime which did not attract the attention of either the greatest minds or the strongest civil authorities in early Europe. Before 1250, chroniclers, ecclesiastical lawyers, moralists, and high prelates could record episodes of—and old laws concerning—a number of activities collectively labelled *sortilegia*—magic—without regarding its occurrence as anything other than singular and episodic, simply one more manifestation of Satan's unsuccessful attempts to tempt mankind from orthodox belief and practice.

The first selection printed below (*No. 1*) purports to be a canonical decision handed down by the Council of Ancyra, an ecclesiastical assembly held in 314. It is a famous text in the history of European witchcraft because the well-known collection of ecclesiastical law through which it was passed down in later centuries, Gratian's *Decretum*, became after 1150 the primary body of teaching material for the study of canon law. Moreover, this single text—to which the numerous commentators on Gratian's collection paid remarkably little attention—became the starting-point for all systematic discussions of witchcraft from the fourteenth century on. The first known appearance of the *Canon Episcopi* (as this text is called because of its opening Latin words) was in a canonical collection of the early tenth century compiled by Regino of Prüm, and the text was repeated in the later canonical collections of Burchard of Worms and Ivo of Chartres. Finally, about 1140, the Bolognese monk Gratian incorporated it in his *Concordia Discordantium Canonum* (The Concordance of Discordant Canons), or, as the work came popularly to be called, the *Decretum*.

The *Canon Episcopi* expresses the doctrine that although sorcery and "malefice" come from the Devil, the experiences of sorcerers and magicians are illusory. In the twelfth century, John of Salisbury, in his *Policraticus* (*No. 3*), a compendium of political theory and reflections on the manners and morals of his own time and times past, echoed Gratian's emphasis upon this illusory character. Like Gratian, John of Salisbury did not concern himself extensively with witchcraft, the selection printed below being the only mention of the subject in an otherwise very long and detailed work. In Chapter 17 of Book II, John undertakes a general discussion of whether dreams and their interpretations are to be believed. He discusses the Old Testament dreams of Daniel and Joseph and the famous dream of St. Jerome. He then turns to misleading and false dreams, and in this context he cites the illusions of sorcerers as an example of how simple-minded people are often deceived by their own imaginations and by the wickedness of the Devil.

The extensive literature of semi-learned, popular moral tales of the late twelfth and thirteenth centuries produced a number of works which included accounts of supernatural events related to witchcraft and sorcery. Among the most interesting of these is the *Dialogue on Miracles* (*No. 4*) by Caesarius of Heisterbach, a series of moral tales presented in the format of a discussion by a learned monk and a novice on the topic of Christian belief. Between 1100 and 1250 an increasingly valuable source for information concerning official ecclesiastical views on Church law is the collections of papal letters, some of which themselves were included in later collections of canon law. The letter of Pope Gregory IX to the King of Germany concerning the witches of Stedlingerland (*No. 6*) vividly illustrates the increasing fear of witchcraft in the thirteenth century and the continued emphasis upon its episodic character.

GRATIAN
A Warning to Bishops
The Canon Episcopi
1140

Gratian (fl. 1140) composed his *Concordance of Discordant Canons*, probably at Bologna, around 1140. The principles of its organization were based upon the eleventh- and twelfth-century methods of reconciling the apparent discrepancies often found between two or more equally authoritative sources of law and dogma and upon the recently revived interest in Roman law and its character. Gratian's work, usually called the *Decretum*, contains three parts. One hundred and one *Distinctions* deal with the sources of law and the character of ecclesiastical persons. Thirty-six *Causes* offer hypothetical cases that raise points of law which form the *questions* into which the *Causes* are subdivided. The third part consists of five *Distinctions* on the nature of the sacraments. The excerpt printed below comes from the second part of the *Decretum*. The *Decretum* itself became the primary teaching vehicle of ecclesiastical law until the twentieth century. The twenty-sixth *Causa* of the *Decretum* presents the hypothetical case of a priest, excommunicated by his bishop for being an unrepentent magician and diviner, who is reconciled to the Church at the point of death by another priest, without the bishop's knowledge. This *case* was divided into seven *questions,* each of which consisted of Gratian's introductory and concluding remarks and relevant selections from the writings of ecclesiastical authorities. These last were called *chapters,* and the formal reference to the *Canon Episcopi* is *Causa* 26, *quaestio* 5, *capitulum* 12, or C.26 q.5 c.12 *Episcopi.* In his introduction to *quaestio* 5

Gratian: A Warning to Bishops

Gratian associates divining and sorcery with general idolatry and links the diviner to the avaricious man who makes a god of money. "Those who participate in a cult of idols are to be separated from the communion of the faithful. Hence as the Apostle Paul says in his Epistle to the Corinthians [I *Corinthians*, 5, 9–11] 'If a certain brother is named a fornicator or a miser or a worshipper of idols, do not so much as eat food with him.' " To Gratian, as well as to some later popes and canonists, the magician was simply one member of a category which included fornicators and misers as well.

Gratian, *Decretum*, Part II, C. 26 q.5 c.12 *Episcopi. Corpus Iuris Canonici*, ed. E. Friedberg (Leipzig, 1879), Vol. I, cols. 1030–31. English translation, Lea, *Materials*, Vol. I, pp. 178–80.

*B*ishops and their officials must labor with all their strength to uproot thoroughly from their parishes the pernicious art of sorcery and malefice invented by the Devil, and if they find a man or woman follower of this wickedness to eject them foully disgraced from their parishes. For the Apostle says, "A man that is a heretic after the first and second admonition avoid." Those are held captive by the Devil who, leaving their creator, seek the aid of the Devil. And so Holy Church must be cleansed of this pest. It is also not to be omitted that some wicked women, perverted by the Devil, seduced by illusions and phantasms of demons, believe and profess themselves, in the hours of night, to ride upon certain beasts with Diana, the goddess of pagans, and an innumerable multitude of women, and in the silence of the dead of night to traverse great spaces of earth, and to obey her commands as of their mistress, and to be summoned to her service on certain nights. But I wish it were they alone who perished in their faithlessness and did not draw many with them into the destruction of infidelity. For an innumerable multitude, deceived by this false opinion, believe this to be true, and so believing, wander from the right faith and are involved in the error of the pagans when they think that there is anything of divinity or power except the one God. Wherefore the priests throughout their churches should preach with all insistence to the people that they may know this to be in every way false and that such phantasms are imposed on the minds of infidels and not by the divine but by the malignant spirit. Thus Satan himself, who transfigures himself into an angel of light, when he has captured the mind of a miserable woman and has subjugated her to himself by infidelity and incredulity, immediately transforms himself into the species and similitudes of different personages and deluding the mind which he holds

Figure 1.   The Creation of the Angels and the Fall of Satan.

In these six panels from a manuscript written c. 1400 there is a vivid representation of events from the Book of *Genesis*. The three right-hand panels represent the pride and the fall of Satan. The last panel depicts Satan and his fellow rebellious angels falling into Hell's mouth, all but Satan himself already transformed into monstrous figures.

captive and exhibiting things, joyful or mournful, and persons, known or unknown, leads it through devious ways, and while the spirit alone endures this, the faithless mind thinks these things happen not in the spirit but in the body. Who is there that is not led out of himself in dreams and nocturnal visions, and sees much when sleeping which he had never seen waking? Who is so stupid and foolish as to think that all these things which are only done in spirit happen in the body, when the Prophet Ezekiel saw visions of the Lord in spirit and not in the body, and the Apostle John saw and heard the mysteries of the Apocalypse in the spirit and not in the body, as he himself says "I was in the spirit"? And Paul does not dare to say that he was rapt in the body. It is therefore to be proclaimed publicly to all that whoever believes such things or similar to these loses the faith, and he who has not the right faith in God is not of God but of him in whom he believes, that is, of the Devil. For of our Lord it is written "All things were made by Him." Whoever therefore believes that anything can be made, or that any creature can be changed to better or to worse or be transformed into another species or similitude, except by the Creator himself who made everything and through whom all things were made, is beyond doubt an infidel.

2

WILLIAM of MALMESBURY
The Witch of Berkeley
1140

William of Malmesbury (d. 1142) wrote two important chronicles dealing with the history of England from the fifth to the twelfth century. He is one of the greatest chroniclers of the Middle Ages, and his histories are sprinkled with episodes of curious detail similar to the one printed here. This episode is regarded by William as being of such compelling interest that it interrupts an account of the critical events in England preceding the Norman Conquest in 1066.[1] The year of the event discussed below was 1065.

J. A. Giles, tr., *William of Malmesbury's Chronicle of the Kings of England* (London, 1847), pp. 230–32.

*A*t the same time something similar occurred in England, not by divine miracle, but by infernal craft; which when I shall have related, the credit of the narrative will not be shaken, though the minds of the hearers should be incredulous; for I have heard it from a man of such character, who swore he had seen it, that I should blush to disbelieve. There resided at Berkeley a woman addicted to witchcraft, as it afterwards appeared, and skilled in ancient augury: she was excessively gluttonous, perfectly lascivious, setting no bounds to her debaucheries, as she was not old, though fast

1. For William and the chronicle tradition in general, see J. Bagley, *Historical Interpretation* (Baltimore, 1965).

declining in life. On a certain day, as she was regaling, a jack-daw, which was a very great favourite, chattered a little more loudly than usual. On hearing which the woman's knife fell from her hand, her countenance grew pale, and deeply groaning, "This day," said she, "my plough has completed its last furrow; to-day I shall hear of, and suffer, some dreadful calamity." While yet speaking, the messenger of her misfortunes arrived; and being asked, why he approached with so distressed an air? "I bring news," said he, "from the village," naming the place, "of the death of your son, and of the whole family, by a sudden accident." At this intelligence, the woman, sorely afflicted, immediately took to her bed, and perceiving the disorder rapidly approaching the vitals, she summoned her surviving children, a monk, and a nun, by hasty letters; and, when they arrived, with faltering voice, addressed them thus: "Formerly, my children, I constantly administered to my wretched circumstances by demoniacal arts: I have been the sink of every vice, the teacher of every allurement: yet, while practising these crimes, I was accustomed to soothe my hapless soul with the hope of your piety. Despairing of myself, I rested my expectations on you; I advanced you as my defenders against evil spirits, my safeguards against my strongest foes. Now, since I have approached the end of my life, and shall have those eager to punish, who lured me to sin, I entreat you by your mother's breasts, if you have any regard, any affection, at least to endeavour to alleviate my torments; and, although you cannot revoke the sentence already passed upon my soul, yet you may, perhaps, rescue my body, by these means: sew up my corpse in the skin of a stag; lay it on its back in a stone coffin; fasten down the lid with lead and iron; on this lay a stone, bound round with three iron chains of enormous weight; let there be psalms sung for fifty nights, and masses said for an equal number of days, to allay the ferocious attacks of my adversaries. If I lie thus secure for three nights, on the fourth day bury your mother in the ground; although I fear, lest the earth, which has been so often burdened with my crimes, should refuse to receive and cherish me in her bosom." They did their utmost to comply with her injunctions: but alas! vain were pious tears, vows, or entreaties; so great was the woman's guilt, so great the devil's violence. For on the first two nights, while the choir of priests was singing psalms around the body, the devils, one by one, with the utmost ease bursting open the door of the church, though closed with an immense bolt, broke asunder the two outer chains; the middle one being more laboriously wrought, remained entire. On the third night, about cock-crow, the whole monastery seemed to be overthrown

Figure 2. The Fall of Satan and Adam's and Eve's Expulsion from the Garden of Eden.

The three panels from a Latin manuscript of the Bible written in France in the mid-fifteenth century depict the fall of Satan and the temptation and expulsion of Adam and Eve from the Garden of Eden. Satan and the fallen angels instantly assume horrific aspects and immediately begin to work evil upon human beings.

from its very foundation, by the clamour of the approaching enemy. One devil, more terrible in appearance than the rest, and of loftier stature, broke the gates to shivers by the violence of his attack. The priests grew motionless with fear; their hair stood on end, and they became speechless. He proceeded, as it appeared, with haughty step towards the coffin, and calling on the woman by name, commanded her to rise. She replying that she could not on account of the chains: "You shall be loosed," said he, "and to your cost:" and directly he broke the chain, which had mocked the ferocity of the others, with as little exertion as though it had been made of flax. He also beat down the cover of the coffin with his foot, and taking her by the hand, before them all, he dragged her out of the church. At the doors appeared a black horse, proudly neighing, with iron hooks projecting over his whole back; on which the wretched creature was placed, and, immediately, with the whole party, vanished from the eyes of the beholders; her pitiable cries, however, for assistance, were heard for nearly the space of four miles. No person will deem this incredible, who has read St. Gregory's Dialogues; who tells, in his fourth book, of a wicked man that had been buried in a church, and was cast out of doors again by devils. Among the French also, what I am about to relate is frequently mentioned. Charles Martel, a man of renowned valour, who obliged the Saracens, when they had invaded France, to retire to Spain, was, at his death, buried in the church of St. Denys; but as he had seized much of the property of almost all the monasteries in France for the purpose of paying his soldiers, he was visibly taken away from his tomb by evil spirits, and has nowhere been seen to his day. At length this was revealed to the bishop of Orleans, and by him publicly made known.

3

JOHN of SALISBURY
A Twelfth-Century Sceptic
1154

Episodes of the kind described by William of Malmesbury in the preceding selection were precisely the kind of beliefs that Gratian intended to refute by including the *Canon Episcopi* (above, *No.* 1) in his compilation of Church law. John of Salisbury (d. 1180) was a widely travelled and learned English cleric who had been a friend of St. Thomas à Becket and died as Bishop of Chartres. His compendium on manners, morals, and politics, the *Policraticus,* dealt with a wide range of topics, including the interpretation of dreams and visions, from his discussion of which this selection is taken. John's scepticism of witches' night-rides echoes that of the text in Gratian and may help to cross-illuminate the selections from William of Malmesbury, Ralph of Coggeshall, and Pope Gregory IX.[1]

C. C. J. Webb, ed., *Ioannis Saresberiensis Episcopi Carnotensis Policratici* (Oxford, 1909), Vol. I, Book II, ch. 17, pp. 100–01. Tr. E.P.

*T*he evil spirit, with God's permission, inflicts the excesses of his malice on certain people in such a way that they suffer in the spirit

1. On John's career and work, see Hans Liebeschütz, *Medieval Humanism in the Life and Writings of John of Salisbury* (London, 1950). For a somewhat different store of twelfth-century anecdotes concerning similar phenomena, see Walter Map, *Walter Map's Book "De Nugis Curialium" (Courtiers' Trifles),* tr. M. B. Ogle and Frederick Tupper (London, 1924), pp. 91-101.

things which they erroneously and wretchedly believe they experience in the flesh. It is in this sense that they claim that a *noctiluca*[1] or Herodias or a witch-ruler of the night convokes nocturnal assemblies at which they feast and riot and carry out other rites, where some are punished and others rewarded according to their merits. Moreover, infants are set out for *lamias*[2] and appear to be cut up into pieces, eaten, and gluttonously stuffed into the witches' stomachs. Then, through the mercy of the witch-ruler, they are returned [in one piece] to their cradles. Who could be so blind as not to see in all this a pure manifestation of wickedness created by sporting demons? Indeed, it is obvious from this that it is only poor old women and the simple-minded kinds of men who enter into these credences.

1. The name or substantive *noctiluca* is sometimes, in the work of other writers, synonymous with Diana, the Roman goddess.
2. The *lamia* was considered to be a particular kind of sorceress or witch who sucked the blood of children.

4

CAESARIUS of HEISTERBACH
The Demons and the Knight
1220–1235

Caesarius, Prior of Heisterbach (ca. 1180–1250), a famous Cistercian abbey in the Rhineland, was a well-known theologian and moralist of thirteenth-century Europe. Among his many works, the best-known today is the *Dialogue on Miracles* (ca. 1220–35), from which this selection is taken. The *Dialogue* was a collection of miracle-stories told in the form—widely popular in ecclesiastical circles—of a question-and-answer exchange between a monk and a novice. The book served chiefly as educational moralizing, but Caesarius' literary talent and the vividness of his tales maintained its popularity for centuries.

Caesarius of Heisterbach, *The Dialogue on Miracles,* tr. H. Scott and C. C. Swinton Bland (London, 1929), Vol. I, Book V, ch. 1–2, pp. 313–17.

*O*f *demons, their numbers, their malice and their hostility to man.* It seems fitting that after temptation we should treat of the tempters. Demons are called tempters, because they are either the authors or provokers of all the temptations that draw me into sin. If the devil tempted the first man in Paradise, if he presumed to tempt Christ in the Desert, what man is there in the world that he will leave untempted? To every man there are assigned two angels, the good for protection, the evil for trial.

Novice.—I have no doubt in my mind about the holy angels, because they are often spoken of in the writings of the prophets; but I should like you to show me from the scriptures of either Testament what demons are, how many they are, how wicked, and how appointed to eternal flames.

Monk.—There is abundance of proof of these things. Of Lucifer, that is the devil, so called because of his beauty and his fall, Isaiah says: *How art thou fallen from heaven, O Lucifer, son of the morning* (Isa. xiv. 12). That he became the devil, and that he fell from heaven, the Saviour bears witness, when He says: *I beheld Satan as lightning fall from heaven* (Luke x. 18). Job says of him: *There was a day when the sons of God came to present themselves before the Lord, and Satan came also among them* (Job i. 6); and in the Psalm David, speaking of the traitor Judas, says: *Let Satan stand at his right hand* (Ps. cviv. 5). Also Habakkuk speaking of Christ: *The devil went forth at his feet* (Hab. iii. 5. Vulg.), and in many other places the scripture speaks of the devil. That he was not alone, and that he did not fall alone, John witnesses in the Apocalypse (xii. 78). His malice changed into a dragon the glorious Lucifer, of whose beauty and comeliness is said by Ezekiel: *Thou art the seal of the image of God, full of wisdom and perfect in beauty. Thou hast been in Eden, the garden of God; every precious stone was thy covering* (Ez. xxviii. 12. Vulg.), etc. It is believed that the tenth part of the angels fell, and on account of their multitude the Apostle calls them the *powers of the air* (Eph. ii. 2), for in falling they filled the air. Of their presumption the prophet speaks to Christ in the Psalm (Ps. lxxiv. 24). And the Lord in the gospel says to the Jews: *Ye do the deeds of your father the devil; he was a liar from the beginning and the father of it* (John viii. 41, 44). That he is hostile to men, Job is witness (Job xl. 23). Wherefore the apostle Peter warns us: (1 Pet. v. 8, 9). What is said about one is to be understood of the rest since the singular number is often used for the plural. That they are to be damned eternally is deduced from the words of the Lord, in Matt. xxv. 41. And I think that the fifth book is the right place to treat of the demons, because the philosophers call five the apostate number, since if joined to any other odd number as a multiplier, it always shows itself, perhaps at the beginning, certainly at the end. Thus the devil, withdrawing from the foursquare of eternal stability, is the first to ally himself with wicked men, who are as unequal numbers, and shows himself in his iniquity, often at the beginning, and always at the end of act or speech.

Novice.—I confess that the point wherein I doubted has been proved to me by the testimony of holy scripture; but I do not confess myself satisfied, unless you make these things clear by living examples.

Monk.—That there are demons, that they are many, and that they are wicked, I shall be able to show you by many examples.

> *Of the knight Henry who disbelieved in the existence of demons, and saw them with his own eyes through a necromancer.*

There was a knight, whose name was Henry, who came from the castle of Falkenstein and was butler of our fellow monk, Cæsarius, at that time abbot of Prüm. Now, as I have heard from Cæsarius himself, this knight did not believe in the existence of demons, but looked upon anything that he heard or ever had heard about them as mere frivolous nonsense; and therefore he sent for a certain clerk named Philip, who was most famous for his skill in necromancy, and besought him earnestly to show him some demons. His reply was that demons were both horrible and dangerous to look upon, and that it was not good for all men to see them. But when the knight continued eagerly to urge his request, he went on: "If you will guarantee that I shall receive no harm from your friends or relations, if by chance you shall be deceived or terrified or injured by the demons, I will consent." And he gave him the guarantee.

One day at noon, because demonic power is at its greatest at that hour, Philip took the knight to a cross road, drew a circle round him with a sword, placed him within it, and explained to him the law of circle within circle, and then said: "If you put forth any of your limbs outside this circle before I come back, you will die, because you will immediately be dragged forth by the demons and torn in pieces." He warned him further, that whatever they might beg of him, he must give them nothing, and promise them nothing, and that he should not make the sign of the cross; and added: "The demons will tempt you and terrify you in many ways, but yet they will not be able to hurt you, if you follow carefully my instructions"; and then he left him.

While he sat alone within the circle, lo! he saw coming against him floods of waters, then he heard the grunting of swine, the howling of wind, and many other similar phantasms, with which the demons sought to terrify him. But as an expected javelin does not wound, he found strength in himself to resist all these attacks. Last of all, he saw in a neighbouring wood a figure like a horrible human shadow higher than the tops of the trees, hastening towards him; and he felt at once that this was the devil, as indeed it was. When he reached the circle, he stood still, and asked the knight what he wanted of him. He was in appearance like a gigantic man, very huge and

Figure 3. The Angel of Light Binding the Angel of Darkness.
This capital from the Basilica de la Madeleine at Vézélay depicts the familiar scene of the struggle between angels and devils.

very black, clothed in a dark robe, and so hideous that the knight could not look upon him; but he replied: "You have done well to come, because I wanted to see you." "What for?" he asked. "Because I have heard so much about you." When the devil asked what he had heard about him, the knight replied: "Very little good and much evil." To which the devil said: "Men often judge and condemn me without good cause; I have harmed no one, I never attack anyone unless provoked. Your Master Philip is a good friend of mine, and I of his; ask him if I have ever offended him. I do his pleasure, and he obliges me in all things; it was by his summons that I have come to you now.

Then the knight: "Where were you when he called you?" The demon answered: "As far on the other side of the sea as the sea is from here; and so I think it is fair that you should give me some reward for my trouble." When the knight asked him what he wished for, he replied: "I beg you to give me your cloak." The knight said he would not give it him; and then he demanded his girdle, and then a sheep from his flock. Finding all these requests refused, last of all he asked for the cock that was in his courtyard. Then the knight said: "Why, what use would it be to you?" and the demon answered; "He will sing to me." "But how would you take him?" "You need not trouble about that; all I ask is that you will consent to give him to me."

Then the knight said: "I will not give you anything at all;" and went on: "Tell me, where do you get all your knowledge from?" The demon said: "There is no evil done in all the world that is hidden from me. To show you that this is true, I tell you that it was in such and such a town, and in such and such a house that you lost your innocence, and that in this place and that that you committed such and such sins;" nor was the knight able to deny that he had spoken truth.

Novice.—Surely the knight can never have confessed these sins; for how could the devil know them if they had been confessed?

Monk.—If he had confessed with the intention of sinning again, he would in no degree have taken away the devil's knowledge.

Novice.—I am glad to hear what you say, because I remember you said the same thing in the sixth chapter of the third book.

Monk.—For some time the devil continued to make all kinds of requests, but only met with repeated refusals; and at last he stretched out his arm towards the knight, as if intending to drag him out and carry him off, and so terrified him, that he fell backwards and cried out. Hearing his voice, Philip ran up, and at his coming the phantom immediately disappeared. From that time forward the knight was deathly pale, and never regained his former healthy colour; he lived very carefully, and had no doubts henceforth concerning the existence of demons. He died a little while ago.

5

RALPH of COGGESHALL
The Witch of Rheims
1176–80

Ralph, from 1207 to 1218 Abbot of Coggeshall, a Cistercian monastery in England, wrote his chronicle in the last quarter of the twelfth century. The episode described here reveals clearly the similarity between popular traditions of witchcraft and popular images of heretics.[1]

Walter L. Wakefield and Austin P. Evans, *Heresies of the High Middle Ages: Selected Sources Annotated and Translated,* Records of Civilization: Sources and Studies, No. 81 (New York, 1969), pp. 251–54.

*I*n the time of Louis, king of France, who fathered King Philip, while the error of certain heretics, who are called Publicans in the vernacular, was spreading through several of the provinces of France, a marvelous thing happened in the city of Rheims in connection with an old woman infected with that plague. For one day when Lord William, archbishop of that city and King Philip's uncle, was taking a canter with his clergy outside the city, one of his clerks, Master Gervais of Tilbury by name, noticed a girl walking alone in a vineyard. Urged by the curiosity of hot-blooded youth, he turned aside to her, as we later heard from his own lips when he was a canon. He greeted her and attentively inquired whose daughter she was and what she

1. A fuller discussion of the importance of this selection may be found in Wakefield and Evans, *Heresies of the High Middle Ages,* pp. 249-51.

was doing there alone, and then, after admiring her beauty for a while, he at length in courtly fashion made her a proposal of wanton love. She was much abashed, and with eyes cast down, she answered him with simple gesture and a certain gravity of speech: "Good youth, the Lord does not desire me ever to be your friend or the friend of any man, for if ever I forsook my virginity and my body had once been defiled, I should most assuredly fall under eternal damnation without hope of recall."

As he heard this, Master Gervais at once realized that she was one of that most impious sect of Publicans, who at that time were everywhere being sought out and destroyed, especially by Philip, count of Flanders, who was harassing them pitilessly with righteous cruelty. Some of them, indeed, had come to England and were seized at Oxford, where by command of King Henry II they were shamefully branded on their foreheads with a red-hot key. While the aforesaid clerk was arguing with the girl to demonstrate the error of such an answer, the archbishop approached with his retinue and, learning the cause of the argument, ordered the girl seized and brought with him to the city. When he addressed her in the presence of his clergy and advanced many scriptural passages and reasonable arguments to confute her error, she replied that she had not yet been well enough taught to demonstrate the falsity of such statements but she admitted that she had a mistress in the city who, by her arguments, would very easily refute everyone's objections. So, when the girl had disclosed the woman's name and abode, she was immediately sought out, found, and haled before the archbishop by his officials. When she was assailed from all sides by the archbishop himself and the clergy with many questions and with texts of the Holy Scriptures which might destroy such error, by perverse interpretation she so altered all the texts advanced that it became obvious to everyone that the spirit of all error spoke through her mouth. Indeed, to the texts and narratives of both the Old and New Testaments which they put to her, she answered as easily, as much by memory, as though she had mastered a knowledge of all the Scriptures and had been well trained in this kind of response, mixing the false with the true and mocking the true interpretation of our faith with a kind of perverted insight. Therefore, because it was impossible to recall the obstinate minds of both these persons from the error of their ways by threat or persuasion, or by any arguments or scriptural texts, they were placed in prison until the following day.

On the morrow they were recalled to the archepiscopal court, before the archbishop and all the clergy, and in the presence of the nobility were again confronted with many reasons for renouncing their error publicly. But since they yielded not at all to salutary admonitions but persisted stubbornly in error once adopted, it was unanimously decreed that they be delivered to the flames. When the fire had been lighted in the city and the officials were about to drag them to the punishment decreed, that mistress of vile error exclaimed, "O foolish and unjust judges, do you think now to burn me in your flames? I fear not your judgment, nor do I tremble at the waiting fire!" With these words, she suddenly pulled a ball of thread from her heaving

Figure 4. The Worship of False Gods.
This illumination from a thirteenth-century French Psalter represents the worship of false gods in the Old Testament in terms of Devil-worship.

bosom and threw it out of a large window, but keeping the end of the thread in her hands; then in a loud voice, audible to all, she said "Catch!" At the word, she was lifted from the earth before everyone's eyes and followed the ball out the window in rapid flight, sustained, we believe, by the ministry of the evil spirits who once caught Simon Magus up into the air. What became of that wicked woman, or whither she was transported, the onlookers could in no wise discover. But the girl had not yet become so deeply involved in the madness of that sect; and, since she still was present, yet could be recalled from the stubborn course upon which she had embarked neither by the inducement of reason nor by the promise of riches, she was burned. She caused a great deal of astonishment to many, for she emitted no sigh, not a tear, no groan, but endured all the agony of the conflagration steadfastly and eagerly, like a martyr of Christ. But for how different a cause from the Christian religion, for which they of the past were slaughtered by pagans! People of this wicked sect choose to die rather than be converted from error; but they have nothing in common with the constancy and steadfastness of martyrs for Christ, since it is piety which brings contempt for death to the latter, to the former it is hardness of heart.

These heretics allege that children should not be baptized until they reach the age of understanding; they add that prayers should not be offered for the dead, nor intercession asked of the saints. They condemn marriages; they preach virginity as a cover for their lasciviousness. They abhor milk and anything made thereof and all food which is the product of coition. They do not believe that purgatorial fire awaits one after death but that once the soul is released it goes immediately to rest or to damnation. They accept no scriptures as holy except the Gospels and the canonical letters. They are countryfolk and so cannot be overcome by rational argument, corrected by scriptural texts, or swayed by persuasions. They choose rather to die than to be converted from this most impious sect. Those who have delved into their secrets declare also that these persons do not believe that God administers human affairs or exercises any direction or control over earthly creatures. Instead, an apostate angel, whom they call Luzabel, presides over all the material creation, and all things on earth are done by his will. The body is shaped by the devil, the soul is created by God and infused into the body; whence it comes about that a persistent struggle is always being waged between body and soul. Some also say that in their subterranean haunts they perform execrable sacrifices to their Lucifer at stated times and that there they enact certain sacrilegious infamies.

6

POPE GREGORY IX
The Witches of Stedlingerland
1232

The Decretal letter *Vox in Rama* ("A Voice in Rama") of Pope Gregory IX (1227–41) is addressed to Henry, King of Germany and son of the Emperor Frederick II. It begins with a prologue that, ringing with Biblical imagery, describes the woes which have befallen the Church, the particular occasion of the letter being rumors of witches flourishing in northern Germany. The letter is remarkable in its detail and in the anguish the Pope feels at witnessing this debasement of orthodox Christianity.

E. Martène and U. Durand, *Thesaurus Novus Anecdotorum,* Vol. I (Paris, 1717), col. 950–53. English translation in Caro Baroja, pp. 76–77.

When a novice is to be initiated and is brought before the assembly of the wicked for the first time, a sort of frog appears to him; a toad according to some. Some bestow a foul kiss on his hind parts, others on his mouth, sucking the animal's tongue and slaver. Sometimes the toad is of a normal size, but at others it is as large as a goose or a duck. Usually it is the size of an oven's mouth. The novice comes forward and stands before a man of fearful pallor. His eyes are black and his body so thin and emaciated that he seems to have no flesh and be only skin and bone. The novice kisses him and he is as cold as ice. After kissing him every remnant of faith in the Catholic Church that lingers in the novice's heart leaves him.

Then all sit down to a banquet and when they rise after it is finished, a black cat emerges from a kind of statue which normally stands in the place where these meetings are held. It is as large as a fair-sized dog, and enters backwards with its tail erect. First the novice kises its hind parts, then the Master of Ceremonies proceeds to do the same and finally all the others in turn; or rather all those who deserve the honour. The rest, that is those who are not thought worthy of this favour, kiss the Master of Ceremonies. When they have returned to their places they stand in silence for a few minutes with heads turned towards the cat. Then the Master says: "Forgive us." The person standing behind him repeats this and a third adds, "Lord we know it." A fourth person ends the formula by saying, "We shall obey."

When this ceremony is over the lights are put out and those present indulge in the most loathsome sensuality, having no regard to sex. If there are more men than women, men satisfy one another's depraved appetites. Women do the same for one another. When these horrors have taken place the lamps are lit again and everyone regains their places. Then, from a dark corner, the figure of a man emerges. The upper part of his body from the hips upward shines as brightly as the sun but below that his skin is coarse and covered with fur like a cat. The Master of Ceremonies cuts a piece from the novice's vestments and says to the shining figure: "Master, I have been given this, and I, in my turn, give it to you." To which the other replies: "You have served me well and will serve me yet more in the future. I give into your safekeeping what you have given me." And he disappears as soon as he has spoken these words. Each year at Easter when they receive the body of Christ from the priest, they keep it in their mouths and throw it in the dirt as an outrage against their Saviour. Furthermore, these most miserable of men blaspheme against the Lord of Heaven and in their madness say that the Lord has done evil in casting out Lucifer into the bottomless pit. These most unfortunate people believe in Lucifer and claim that he was the creator of the celestial bodies and will ultimately return to glory when the Lord has fallen from power. Through him and with him they hope to achieve eternal happiness. They confess that they do not believe that one should do God's will but rather what displeases Him. . . .

St. Thomas Aquinas
and the
Nature of Evil

St. Thomas Aquinas (1225–74) was a professor of theology at the University of Paris from 1256 and travelled widely among the academic and religious centers of Christendom during his mature years. In the early part of his academic career he produced a *Commentary on the Sentences of Peter Lombard,* an explication of a work which had become the standard textbook of theology in the late twelfth and early thirteenth century (*No.* 10). The *Summa Contra Gentiles* is a vast attempt to reveal the rational bases of Catholic dogma, not only for the benefit of the "Gentiles" (pagans) but for those who hold different philosophical views as well. The *Summa Theologica* is an immense handbook for those setting out to learn theology. Taken together, these works constitute a great philosophical system, perhaps the most complete and detailed system in history. Although both *summae* were considered extremely controversial in their own day, they later became the foundation of much Catholic thought and were even revived in the nineteenth century. The selections from these works and from the *Quaestiones Quodlibetales* (Questions Dealing with All Kinds of Topics) have been chosen to illustrate Aquinas' systematic ontology, which formed the basis, among other things, of later demonologists' theories.

Aquinas completed in his vast works of theology the long process of summarizing and explicating in infinite detail the character of the relations between man and God, the definition of which had been begun in earnest in the twelfth century. Strongly influenced by both Plato and Aristotle, Aquinas gave a formal structure to Christian philosophy. In his elaborately detailed description of the universe and the powers it contains, he dealt with the problem of evil, with the demons, and with demonic intervention in human affairs. Unlike the chroniclers, moralists, and ecclesiastical lawyers cited in Section I, Aquinas' task was to explain precisely *how* it was possible for demons to influence human actions. The selections below reveal his method: the careful step-by-step description of the nature of reality by constant reference to dogma and to other parts of his elaborately structured work. The excerpts from the *Summa Contra Gentiles* (*No.* 7) deal with the powers of magic in the natural world. Those from the *Summa Theologica* (*No.* 8) deal with the assaults on man made by demons. The brief excerpts which end the selections deal with the effects of witchcraft on marriage (*No.* 9) and the necessity of God's permission for the witch to affect man (*No.* 10). It may be noted that the rigorous logic and the details of the view of the universe found in his work give, as it were, a legitimate intellectual superstructure to the random accounts of chroniclers and the detailed legalism of lawyers. After Thomas, such incidents as those cited above (see *Nos.* 2, 4, and 5) could be regarded not as isolated events to wonder at, but as manifestations of certain truths about the nature of reality which found their explanation in a systematic exposition of Christian dogma.

FROM THE SUMMA
CONTRA GENTILES
Magic and the World of Nature

St. Thomas Aquinas, *The Summa Contra Gentiles,* The Third Book (Part II, ch. CIV–CVI), literally translated by the English Dominican Fathers from the latest Leonine edition (London, 1928), pp. 67–75.

That the works of magicians result not only from the influence of heavenly bodies. Some there were who averred that such works as seem wonderful to us, being wrought by the magic art, are done, not by certain spiritual substances, but by the power of the heavenly bodies. This would seem to be indicated by the fact that those who practise works of this kind, observe the position of the stars: and are assisted by the employment of certain herbs and other corporeal things, for the purpose, as it were, of preparing matter of lower degree to receive the influence of the celestial power.

But this is in contradiction with the apparitions (in the works of magicians). For as it is impossible that an intellect be formed from corporeal principles, as we proved above, it is impossible for effects that are caused exclusively by the intellectual nature, to be produced by the power of a heavenly body. Now in these works of magicians, things appear that are exclusively the work of a rational nature; for instance, answers are given about stolen goods, and the like, and this could not be done except by an intelligence. Therefore it is not true that all such effects are caused by the mere power of a heavenly body.

Further. Speech is an act proper to the rational nature. Now in these works people appear to men and speak to them on various matters. Therefore such things cannot be done by the mere power of heavenly bodies. If, however, someone say that these apparitions are present, not to the sensorial organ, but only to the imagination:—this is, in the first place, apparently untrue. For imaginary forms do not seem real to anyone, unless his external senses be suspended: since it is not possible for a person to look on a likeness as a reality, except the natural judgements of the senses be tied. Now these conversations and apparitions are addressed to those who have free use of their external senses. Therefore these apparitions and speeches cannot be imaginary.

Besides, no imaginary forms can lead a person to intellectual knowledge beyond the natural or acquired faculty of his intellect: this is evident in dreams; since even if they contain some indication of the future, it is not every dreamer that understands the meaning of his dreams. Now, in these apparitions and speeches that occur in the works of magicians, it frequently happens that a person obtains knowledge of things surpassing the faculty of his intelligence, such as the discovery of hidden treasure, the manifestation of the future, and sometimes even true answers are given in matters of science. Either, therefore, these apparitions or speeches are not purely imaginary; or at least it is the work of some higher intelligence, and not only of a heavenly body, that a person obtain the aforesaid knowledge through these imaginings.

Again. That which is done by the power of heavenly bodies, is a natural effect: since they are natural forms that are caused in this lower world by the powers of heavenly bodies. Hence that which cannot be natural to anything, cannot be caused by the power of the heavenly bodies. And yet some such things are stated to be caused by the aforesaid works: for instance, it is averred that at the mere presence of a certain person all doors are unlocked, that a certain man becomes invisible, and many like occurrences are related. Therefore this cannot be done by the power of heavenly bodies.

Further. The reception, through the power of heavenly bodies, of that which follows, implies the reception of what precedes. Now movement of its very nature, is the result of having a soul: since it is proper to animate things to move themselves. Therefore it is impossible for an inanimate being to be moved by itself, through the power of a heavenly body. Yet it is stated that by the magic art an image is made to move of itself, or to speak.

Therefore it is not possible for the effects of the magic art to be caused by a celestial power.

And if it be said that the image in question is endowed with some vital principle by the power of the heavenly bodies; this is impossible. For the

Figure 5. Fallen Human Nature and Observant Demons.

This picture, from one of Albrecht Dürer's woodcuts, expresses the late medieval sense of woman's particular proneness to temptation and sin. Much of the lore concerning female witches derived from woman's allegedly inferior spiritual strength and her predisposition to the sins of pride, lust, and negligence of spiritual affairs. This illustration shows a vain woman being mocked by a grotesque demon.

principle of life in all living things is the substantial form, because, as the Philosopher says (2 *De Anima*, iv.) *in living things to be is to live*. Now, it is impossible for anything to receive anew a substantial form, unless it lose the form which it had previously, since *the generation of one thing is the corruption of another* (3 *Phys.* viii.). But in the making of an image no substantial form is discarded, and there is only a change of shape which is an accident: since the form of copper or something of the kind remains. Therefore the image in question cannot possibly be endowed with the vital principle.

Further. If anything is moved by a principle of life it necessarily has sensation, for the principle of movement is sensation or understanding. But understanding is not found without sensation in things that come to be and pass away. Now there cannot be sensation where there is not the sense of touch; nor the sense of touch without an organ of mean temperature. Such a temperature, however, is not found in the stone or wax or metal out of which the statue is made. It is not possible, therefore, that statues of this sort should be moved by a principle of life.

Besides. Perfect living things are generated not only by a celestial power, but also from seed: for *man and the sun generate man* (2 *Phys.* ii.): and such as are generated by a celestial power alone without seed, are animals formed by putrefaction, and such belong to a lower grade than the others. Accordingly if these images be endowed with the vital principle by a celestial power alone, so as to move themselves, it follows that they belong to the lowest grade of animals. And yet this would be false if they worked by an intrinsic principle of life: since among their operations some are of a high degree, for they give answers about hidden things. Therefore it is not possible that their operations and movements proceed from a principle of life.

Again. We find sometimes a natural effect produced by the power of heavenly bodies without the operation of art: thus, although one may produce frogs, or something of the kind by means of some artifice, frogs do happen to be produced without any artifice. Consequently if these images that are made by necromancy, are endowed with the vital principle by the power of heavenly bodies, it will be possible for them to be formed without the operation of art. But this is not the case. Therefore it is evident that such images have not the principle of life, nor are they moved by the power of heavenly bodies.

Hereby we refute the opinion of Hermes who, according to Augustine (8 *De Civ. Dei* xxiii.) expressed himself thus: *As God is the cause of the heavenly gods, so man fashions the gods that reside in temples, being satisfied to live near men. I refer to those animal images, endowed with sense and spirit, that do great and wonderful things, images gifted with knowledge of the future, and who foretell by dreams and many other things; who afflict men with ailments and heal them, who bring sorrow and joy to them according to their merits.*

This opinion is also refuted by divine authority. For it is said in the Psalm (cxxxiv. 15 *seqq.*): *The idols of the Gentiles are silver and gold, the works of men's hands. They have a mouth but they speak not . . . neither is there any breath in their mouths.*

Yet seemingly we must not absolutely deny the possibility of some kind of efficacy being in these things through the power of the heavenly bodies: but only for such effects as certain lower bodies are able to cause by the power of the heavenly bodies.

Whence the works of magicians derive their efficacy

It remains for us to inquire whence the magic arts derive their efficacy: a question that will present no difficulty if we consider their mode of operation.

For in the practice of their art they make use of certain significative words in order to produce certain definite effects. Now, words, in so far as they signify something, have no power except as derived from some intellect; either of the speaker, or of the person to whom they are spoken. From the intellect of the speaker, as when an intellect is of such great power that it can cause things by its mere thought, the voice serving to convey, as it were, this thought to the things that are to be produced. From the intellect of the person to whom the words are addressed, as when the hearer is induced to do some particular thing, through his intellect receiving the signification of those words. Now, it cannot be said that these significative words uttered by magicians derive efficacy from the intellect of the speaker. For since power follows essence, diversity of power indicates diversity of essential principles. Moreover, man's intellect is invariably of such a disposition that its knowledge is caused by things, rather than that it is able by its mere thought to cause things. Consequently if there be any men that are able of their own power to transform things by words expressive of their thoughts, they will belong to another species, and it would be an equivocation to call them men.

Further. By learning we acquire, not the power to do a thing, but the knowledge of how to do it. Yet some, by learning, are rendered able to perform these magic works. Therefore they must have not only knowledge but also the power to produce these effects.

If someone say that these men, by the influence of the stars, are born with the aforesaid power, while others are excluded from it; so that however much the others, who are born without this power, may be instructed, they

Figure 6. Pride and the Demon.

This woodcut by Albrecht Dürer illustrates Chapter 92 of Sebastian Brandt's moral satire *Das Narrenschiff* ("The Ship of Fools"), a popular compendium of common follies in the late fifteenth and sixteenth centuries. The female figure in the illustration looks into a mirror (cf. Figure 5) and fails to notice that she is sitting on the Devil's trap.

cannot succeed in performing these works; we reply, first that, as shown above, heavenly bodies cannot make an impression on the intellect. Therefore a man's intellect cannot, through the influence of the stars, receive a power whereby the vocal expression of its thoughts is productive of something.

And if it be said that the imagination produces an effect in the utterance of significative words, and that heavenly bodies can work on the imagination, since its operation is performed by a bodily organ:—this does not apply to all the results produced by this art. For we have shown (ch. civ.) that these effects cannot all be produced by the power of the stars. Neither, therefore, can anyone by the power of the stars, receive the power to produce those effects. Consequently it follows that these effects are accomplished by an intellect to whom the discourse of the person uttering these words is addressed. We have an indication of this in the fact that the significative words employed by the magician are *invocations, supplications, adjurations,* or even *commands* as though he were addressing another.

Again. Certain characters and definite figures are employed in the observances of this art. Now a figure cannot be the principle of either action or passion; else, mathematical bodies would be active and passive. Therefore matter cannot, by definite figures, be disposed to receive a certain natural effect. Therefore magicians do not employ figures as dispositions. It remains, then, that they employ them only as signs, for there is no third solution. But we make signs only to other intelligent beings. Therefore the magic arts derive their efficacy from another intelligent being, to whom the magician's words are addressed.

And if someone say that certain figures are appropriate to certain heavenly bodies; and so the lower bodies are determined by certain figures to receive the impressions of certain heavenly bodies:—seemingly this is an unreasonable statement. For the patient is not directed to receive the impression of the agent, except through being in potentiality. Hence those things alone determine it to receive a particular impression, that cause it to be somehow in potentiality. Now figures do not cause matter to be in potentiality to any particular form, because a figure, as such, abstracts from all matter and sensible forms, since it is something mathematical. Therefore a body is not determined by figures or characters to receive the influence of a heavenly body.

Besides. Certain figures are appropriate to heavenly bodies as the effects thereof; for the figures of the lower bodies are caused by heavenly bodies. Now, the aforesaid arts do not use characters or figures as produced by heavenly bodies, in fact they are produced by man in the practice of the art. Therefore the appropriateness of figures to certain heavenly bodies has nothing to do with the question.

Further. As we have shown, matter is nowise disposed to form by means of figures. Hence the bodies on which these figures are impressed, are as capable of receiving the influence of heavenly bodies, as other bodies of the same species. Now, that a thing act on one rather than another of several equally disposed, by reason of something appropriate to be found in it, is a mark of its operating not by natural necessity, but by choice. Hence it is clear that these arts which employ figures in order to produce certain effects, derive their efficacy, not from something that acts by nature, but from some intellectual substance that acts by intelligence. This is also proved by the very name of *character* which they apply to these figures: for a character is a sign. Whereby we are given to understand that they employ these figures merely as signs shown to some intellectual nature.

Since, however, in the products of art figures are like specific forms, someone might say that there is no reason why, through the influence of a heavenly body, some power should not shape the figure that gives an image its species, not indeed as a figure, but as specifying the product of art, which acquires this power from the stars. But as to the letters that form an inscription on an image, and other characters, nothing else can be said of them, but that they are signs: wherefore they are directed to an intelligence only.— This is also proved by the sacrifices, prostrations and other similar practices, which can be nothing else than signs of reverence shown to an intellectual nature.

> *That the intellectual substance which gives*
> *efficacy to the practices of magic*
> *is not good according to virtue*

We must furthermore inquire what is this intellectual nature by whose power these works are done.

And in the first place it is plain that it is not good and praiseworthy: for it is the mark of an ill-disposed mind to countenance things contrary to virtue. Now this is done in these arts: for they are often employed in order to further adultery, theft, murder and like malefices; wherefore those who practise these arts are called *malefics*. Therefore the intellectual nature on whose assistance these arts depend is not well disposed according to virtue.

Again. It is not the mark of a mind well disposed according to virtue, to befriend and assist men of evil life, rather than every upright man. Now those who practise these arts are often men of evil life. Therefore the intellectual nature from whose assistance these arts derive their efficacy is not well disposed according to virtue.

Further. It is the mark of a well disposed mind to guide men towards those goods that are proper to man, namely the goods of reason. Consequently to lead men away from these, and to draw men to goods of the least worth, shows a mind of evil disposition. Now by these arts men progress, not in the goods of reason, which are science and virtue, but in goods of least account, such as the discovery of stolen goods, the capture of thieves, and so forth. Therefore the intellectual substances whose assistance these arts employ, are not well disposed according to virtue.

Moreover. There is a certain deception and unreasonableness in the works of these arts: for they require a man indifferent to lustful pleasure, whereas they are frequently employed to further lustful intercourse. But there is nothing unreasonable or contradictory in the work of a well-disposed mind. Therefore these arts do not employ the assistance of an intellect that is well disposed as to virtue.

Besides. It is an ill-disposed mind that is incited by the commission of crime to lend his assistance to another. But this is done in these arts: for we read of innocent children being slain by those who practise them. Therefore the persons by whose assistance such things are done have an evil mind.

Again. The proper good of the intellect is truth. Since therefore it belongs to good to lead others to good, it belongs to any well-disposed intellect to lead others to truth. In the works of the magicians, however, many things are done by which men are mocked and deceived. The intellect whose help they use, therefore, is not morally well disposed.

Further. A well-disposed intellect is allured by truth in which it takes delight, but not by lies. The magicians, however, in their invocations make use of various lies, whereby they allure those whose help they employ; for they threaten certain impossible things, as for instance that, unless the one who is called upon gives help, he who invokes him will shatter the heavens or displace the stars, as Porphyry narrates in his *Letter to Anebontes*. Those intellectual substances, therefore, with whose help the works of the magicians are performed do not seen to be intellectually well disposed.

Moreover. That a superior should be subject as an inferior to one that commands him; or that an inferior should allow himself to be invoked as a superior, would seem to indicate a person of an ill-disposed mind. Now, magicians call upon those whose assistance they employ, as though these were their superiors: and as soon as they appear they command them as inferiors. In no way therefore are they seemingly of a well-disposed mind.

Hereby we refute the error of pagans who ascribed these works to the gods.

8

FROM THE
SUMMA THEOLOGICA
The Demons and Man

The "Summa Theologica" of St. Thomas Aquinas, literally translated by Fathers of the English Dominican Province, Third Number (CXIV), (London, 1912), pp. 496–505.

O f the assaults of the Demons. (In Five Articles.) We now consider the assaults of the demons. Concerning this we have five points of inquiry: (1) Whether men are assailed by the demons? (2) Whether to tempt is proper to the devil? (3) Whether all the sins of men are to be set down to the assaults or temptations of the demons? (4) Whether they can work real miracles for the purpose of leading men astray? (5) Whether the demons who are overcome by men, are hindered from making further assaults?

First Article
Whether men are assailed by the demons?

We proceed thus to the First Article:—

Objection 1. It seems that men are not assailed by the demons. For angels are sent by God to guard man. But demons are not sent by God: for the demons' intention is the loss of souls; whereas God's is the salvation of souls. Therefore demons are not deputed to assail man.

Obj. 2. Further, it is not a fair fight, for the weak to be set against the strong, and the ignorant against the astute. But men are weak and ignorant, whereas the demons are strong and astute. It is not therefore to be permitted by God, the author of all justice, that men should be assailed by demons.

Obj. 3. Further, the assaults of the flesh and the world are enough for man's exercise. But God permits His elect to be assailed that they may be exercised. Therefore there is no need for them to be assailed by the demons.

On the contrary, The Apostle says (Eph. vi. 12): *Our wrestling is not against flesh and blood; but against principalities and powers, against the rulers of the world of this darkness, against the spirits of wickedness in the high places.*

I answer that, Two things may be considered in the assault of the demons —the assault itself, and the ordering thereof. The assault itself is due to the malice of the demons, who through envy endeavour to hinder man's progress; and through pride usurp a semblance of Divine power, by deputing certain ministers to assail man, as the angels of God in their various offices minister to man's salvation. But the ordering of the assault is from God, Who knows how to make orderly use of evil by ordering it to good. On the other hand, in regard to the angels, both their guardianship and the ordering thereof are to be referred to God as their first author.

Reply Obj. 1. The wicked angels assail men in two ways. Firstly by instigating them to sin; and thus they are not sent by God to assail us, but are sometimes permitted to do so according to God's just judgments. But sometimes their assault is a punishment to man: and thus they are sent by God; as the lying spirit was sent to punish Achab, King of Israel, as is related in 3 Kings (xxii. 20). For punishment is referred to God as its first author. Nevertheless the demons who are sent to punish, do so with an intention other from that for which they are sent; for they punish from hatred or envy; whereas they are sent by God on account of His justice.

Reply Obj. 2. In order that the conditions of the fight be not unequal, there is as regards man the promised recompense, to be gained principally through the grace of God, secondarily through the guardianship of the angels. Wherefore (4 Kings vi. 16), Eliseus said to his servant: *Fear not, for there are more with us than with them.*

Reply Obj. 3. The assault of the flesh and the world would suffice for the exercise of human weakness: but it does not suffice for the demon's malice, which makes use of both the above in assailing men. But by the Divine ordinance this tends to the glory of the elect.

Second Article
Whether to tempt is proper to the devil?

We proceed thus to the Second Article:—

Objection 1. It seems that to tempt is not proper to the devil. For God is said to tempt, according to Genesis xxii. 1, *God tempted Abraham.* Moreover man is tempted by the flesh and the world. Again, man is said to tempt God, and to tempt man. Therefore it is not proper to the devil to tempt.

Obj. 2. Further, to tempt is a sign of ignorance. But the demons know what happens among men. Therefore the demons do not tempt.

Obj 3. Further, temptation is the road to sin. Now sin dwells in the will. Since therefore the demons cannot change man's will, as appears from what has been said above, it seems that it is not in their province to tempt.

On the contrary, It is written (1 Thess. iii. 5): *Lest perhaps he that tempteth should have tempted you:* to which the gloss adds, *that is, the devil, whose office it is to tempt.*

I answer that, To tempt is, properly speaking, to make trial of something. Now we make trial of something in order to know something about it: hence the immediate end of every tempter is knowledge. But sometimes another end, either good or bad, is sought to be acquired through that knowledge; a good end, when, for instance, one desires to know of someone, what sort of a man he is as to knowledge, or virtue, with a view to his promotion; a bad end, when that knowledge is sought with the purpose of deceiving or ruining him.

From this we can gather how various beings are said to tempt in various ways. For man is said to tempt, sometimes indeed merely for the sake of knowing something: and for this reason it is a sin to tempt God; for man, being uncertain as it were, presumes to make an experiment of God's power. Sometimes too he tempts in order to help, sometimes in order to hurt. The devil, however, always tempts in order to hurt by urging man into sin. In this sense it is said to be his proper office to tempt: for though at times man tempts thus, he does this as a minister of the devil. God is said to tempt that He may know, in the same sense as that is said to know which makes others to know. Hence it is written (Deut. xiii. 3): *The Lord your God trieth you, that it may appear whether you love Him.*

The flesh and the world are said to tempt as the instruments or matter of temptations; inasmuch as one can know what sort of a man someone is, according as he follows or resists the desire of the flesh, and according as he despises worldly advantages and adversity: of which things the devil also makes use in tempting.

Thus the reply to the first objection is clear.

Reply Obj. 2. The demons know what happens outwardly among men; but the inward disposition of man God alone knows, Who is the *weigher of spirits* (Prov. xvi. 2). It is this disposition that makes man more prone to one vice than to another: hence the devil tempts, in order to explore this inward disposition of man, so that he may tempt him to that vice to which he is most prone.

Reply Obj. 3. Although a demon cannot change the will, yet, as stated above, he can change the inferior powers of man, in a certain degree: by which powers, though the will cannot be forced, it can nevertheless be inclined.

Third Article

Whether all sins are due to the temptation of the devil?

We proceed thus to the Third Article:—

Objection 1. It seems that all sins are due to the temptation of the devil. For Dionysius says (*Div. Nom.* iv.) that *the multitude of demons is the cause of all evils, both to themselves and to others.* And Damascene says (*De Fide Orth.* ii.) that *all malice and all uncleanness have been devised by the devil.*

Obj. 2. Further, of every sinner can be said what the Lord said of the Jews (John viii. 44): *You are of your father the devil.* But this was in as far as they sinned through the devil's instigation. Therefore every sin is due to the devil's instigation.

Obj. 3. Further, as angels are deputed to guard men, so demons are deputed to assail men. But every good thing we do is due to the suggestion of the good angels: because the Divine gifts are borne to us by the angels. Therefore all the evil we do, is due to the instigation of the devil.

On the contrary, It is written (*De Eccl. Dogmat.*): *Not all our evil thoughts are stirred up by the devil, but sometimes they arise from the movement of our free-will.*

I answer that, One thing can be the cause of another in two ways; directly and indirectly. Indirectly as when an agent is the cause of a disposition to a certain effect, it is said to be the occasional and indirect cause of that effect: for instance, we might say that he who dries the wood is the cause of the wood burning. In this way we must admit that the devil is the cause of all

Figure 7.   The Devil's Instruments: Sensual Music and Temptation.
This capital from the Basilica at Vézélay (cf. Figure 3) depicts the Devil using profane music to tempt a human soul. Throughout the Middle Ages, the demonic use of sensual appeal constituted a commonplace of preachers, theologians, and artists.

our sins; because he it was who instigated the first man to sin, from whose sin there resulted a proneness to sin in the whole human race: and in this sense we must take the words of Damascene and Dionysius.

But a thing is said to be the direct cause of something, when its action tends directly thereunto. And in this way the devil is not the cause of every sin: for all sins are not committed at the devil's instigation, but some are due to the free-will and the corruption of the flesh. For, as Origen says (*Peri Archon* iii.), even if there were no devil, men would have the desire for food and love and suchlike pleasures; with regard to which many disorders may arise unless those desires be curbed by reason, especially if we presuppose the corruption of our natures. Now it is in the power of the free-will to curb this appetite and keep it in order. Consequently there is no need for all sins to be due to the instigation of the devil. But those sins which are due thereto man perpetrates *through being deceived by the same blandishments as were our first parents,* as Isidore says (*De Summo Bono* iii.).

Thus the answer to the first objection is clear.

Reply Obj. 2. When man commits sin without being thereto instigated by the devil, he nevertheless becomes a child of the devil thereby, in so far as he imitates him who was the first to sin.

Reply Obj. 3. Man can of his own accord fall into sin: but he cannot advance in merit without the Divine assistance, which is borne to man by the ministry of the angels. For this reason the angels take part in all our good works: whereas all our sins are not due to the demons' instigation. Nevertheless there is no kind of sin which is not sometimes due to the demons' suggestion.

Fourth Article
Whether demons can lead men astray by means of real miracles?

We proceed thus to the Fourth Article:—

Objection 1. It seems that the demons cannot lead men astray by means of real miracles. For the activity of the demons will show itself especially in the works of Antichrist. But as the Apostle says (2 Thess. ii. 9), his *coming is according to the working of Satan, in all power, and signs, and lying wonders.* Much more therefore at other times do the demons perform only lying wonders.

Obj. 2. Further, true miracles are wrought by some corporeal change. But demons are unable to change the nature of a body; for Augustine says

(*De Civ. Dei* xviii.); *I cannot believe that the human body can receive the limbs of a beast by means of a demon's art or power.* Therefore the demons cannot work real miracles.

Obj. 3. Further, an argument is useless which may prove both ways. If therefore real miracles can be wrought by demons, to persuade one of what is false, they will be useless to confirm the teaching of faith. This is unfitting; for it is written (Mark xvi. 20): *The Lord working withal, and confirming the word with signs that followed.*

On the contrary, Augustine says (*Qq.* 83): *Often by means of the magic art miracles are wrought like those which are wrought by the servants of God.*

I answer that, As is clear from what has been said above, if we take a miracle in the strict sense, the demons cannot work miracles, nor can any creature, but God alone: since in the strict sense a miracle is something done outside the order of the entire created nature, under which order every power of a creature is contained. But sometimes miracle may be taken in a wide sense, for whatever exceeds the human power and experience. And thus demons can work miracles, that is, things which rouse man's astonishment, by reason of their being beyond his power and outside his sphere of knowledge. For even a man by doing what is beyond the power and knowledge of another, leads him to marvel at what he has done, so that in a way he seems to that man to have worked a miracle.

It is to be noted, however, that although these works of demons which appear marvellous to us are not real miracles, they are sometimes nevertheless something real. Thus the magicians of Pharaoh by the demons' power produced real serpents and frogs. *And when fire came down from heaven and at one blow consumed Job's servants and sheep; when the storm struck down his house and with it his children—these were the work of Satan; not phantoms;* as Augustine says (*De Civ. Dei* xx.).

Reply Obj. 1. As Augustine says in the same place, the works of Antichrist may be called lying wonders, *either because he will deceive men's senses by means of phantoms, so that he will not really do what he will seem to do; or because, if he work real prodigies, they will lead those into falsehood who believe in him.*

Reply Obj. 2. As we have said above, corporeal matter does not obey either good or bad angels at their will, so that demons be able by their power to transmute matter from one form to another; but they can employ certain seeds that exist in the elements of the world, in order to produce these effects, as Augustine says (*De Trin.* iii.). Therefore it must be admitted that all the transformations of corporeal things which can be produced by certain natural powers, to which we must assign the seeds above mentioned, can alike be produced by the operation of the demons, by the employment of these seeds; such as the transformation of certain things into serpents or frogs, which can be produced by putrefaction. On the contrary, those transformations which cannot be produced by the power of nature, cannot in reality be effected by the operation of the demons; for instance, that the human body be changed into the body of a beast, or that the body of a dead man return to life. And if at times something of this sort seems to be effected by the operation of demons, it is not real but a mere semblance of reality.

Now this may happen in two ways. Firstly, from within; in this way a demon can work on man's imagination and even on his corporeal senses, so that something seems otherwise than it is, as explained above. It is said indeed that this can be done sometimes by the power of certain bodies. Secondly, from without: for just as he can from the air form a body of any form and shape, and assume it so as to appear in it visibly: so, in the same way he can clothe any corporeal thing with any corporeal form, so as to appear therein. This is what Augustine says (*De Civ. Dei* xviii.): *Man's imagination, which, whether thinking or dreaming, takes the forms of an innumerable number of things, appears to other men's senses, as it were embodied in the semblance of some animal.* This it not to be understood as though the imagination itself or the images formed therein were identified with that which appears embodied to the senses of another man: but that the demon who forms an image in a man's imagination, can offer the same picture to another man's senses.

Reply Obj. 3. As Augustine says (*Qq.* 83): *When magicians do what holy men do, they do it for a different end and by a different right. The former do it for their own glory: the latter, for the glory of God: the former, by certain private compacts: the latter by the evident assistance and command of God, to Whom every creature is subject.*

Fifth Article

Whether a demon who is overcome by man, is for this reason hindered from making further assaults?

We proceed thus to the Fifth Article:—

Objection 1. It seems that a demon who is overcome by a man, is not for that reason hindered from any further assault. For Christ overcame the tempter most effectively. Yet afterwards the demon assailed Him by instigating the Jews to kill Him. Therefore it is not true that the devil when conquered ceases his assaults.

Obj. 2. Further, to inflict punishment on one who has been worsted in a fight, is to incite him to a sharper attack. But this is not befitting God's mercy. Therefore the conquered demons are not prevented from further assaults.

On the contrary, It is written (Matt. iv. 11): *Then the devil left Him, i.e.,* Christ who overcame.

I answer that, some say that when once a demon has been overcome he can no more tempt any man at all, neither to the same nor to any other sin. And others say that he can tempt others, but not the same man. This seems more probable as long as we understand it to be so for a certain definite time: wherefore (Luke iv. 13) it is written: *All temptation being ended, the devil departed from Him for a time.* There are two reasons for this. One is on the part of God's clemency; for as Chrysoston says (*Super Matt. Hom.* v.), *the devil does not tempt man for just as long as he likes, but for as long as God allows; for although He allows him to tempt for a short time, He orders him off on account of our weakness.* The other reason is taken from the astuteness of the devil. As to this, Ambrose says on Luke iv. 13: *The devil is afraid of persisting, because he shrinks from frequent defeat.* That the devil does nevertheless sometimes return to the assault, is apparent from Matthew xii. 44: *I will return into my house from whence I came out.*

From what has been said, the objections can easily be solved.

9

FROM QUODLIBET XI
Witchcraft and Sexual Impotence

St. Thomas Aquinas, *Quodlibet* XI, *Quaestio* IX, *Art.* X, *Utrum maleficia impediant matrimonium,* from St. Thomas Aquinas, *Opera Omnia,* Vol. IX (Parma, 1859), p. 618. Tr. E.P.

Question: Whether the effects of sorcery are an impediment to matrimony.... It would seem that they are not. Since the works of God are stronger than those of the Devil, matrimony being a work of God and sorcery being a work of the Devil, matrimony is therefore stronger than sorcery, and sorcery may not in itself constitute an impediment.

On the other hand, it may be said that the Devil's power is greater than that of man. Since man may impede matrimony, therefore the Devil may also impede it.

I answer that matrimony is a kind of contract. Now by matrimony one person delivers the rights over his body to another for sexual intercourse. We may in fact contend that a contract concerning that which is impossible is no contract at all, since no one may obligate himself to perform the impossible. Hence, when someone obligates himself by matrimony to sexual intercourse, and sexual intercourse is impossible for him, then the marriage does not exist.

But it must be noted that the impossibility of sexual intercourse from any intervening impediment may be considered in two ways. Either the impediment intervenes in a marriage which has already been consummated or in one which has not yet been consummated. If it intervenes after a marriage has already been consummated, then the marriage may not be dissolved. If it occurs before the marriage has been consummated, then the marriage may be dissolved.

One should note, moreover, that impediments of this kind may be either permanent or temporary. If they are permanent, then that marriage is absolutely impeded. If they are temporary, then that marriage is impeded only for a time. This is so in both cases in which the impediment precedes consummation.

Concerning sorcerers, it is known that some say that sorcery has no existence and that it comes simply from lack of belief or superstition, since they wish to prove that demons do not exist except insofar as they are the creatures of man's imagination; insofar as men imagine them to exist, these fantasies afflict the fearful. The catholic faith, on the other hand, insists that demons do indeed exist and that they may impede sexual intercourse by their works. These impediments then, if they precede consummation and are permanent, impede matrimony absolutely.

To the first point I respond that the Devil himself, as well as matrimony, is the work of God. And among the works of God some are stronger than others. One of them may be impeded by another which is stronger. Whence, since the Devil is stronger than matrimony, nothing prevents that through his agency matrimony may be impeded.

10

FROM THE COMMENTARY
ON THE FOUR BOOKS
OF SENTENCES
Witchcraft and Exorcism

St. Thomas Aquinas, *Commentary on the Four Books of Sentences* (Venice, 1481), *Distinctio* XXXIV, *art.* 3 *ad* 3, unnumbered folios. Tr. E.P.

Witchcraft is therefore to be considered permanent[1] because remedy may not be had for it by human agency, although God may impose a remedy either by forcing the Devil or even against the resistance of the Devil. It is never proper that that which is accomplished by witchcraft should be destroyed by yet other witchcraft, as if witchcraft were to testify to its own authenticity. If it were possible to find a remedy by witchcraft, then the effects of witchcraft would nonetheless continue to be permanent, so no one ought by any means to invoke the aid of a demon through witchcraft. Likewise, it is not proper that if, on account of our sins, a certain power over our person is given to the demon, the power should cease when the sin ceases, because the punishment remains, although the sin has gone. Thus, even the exorcisms of the Church are not always efficacious in driving out demons, insofar as the divine judgement requires [them] for all punishments of the body. Exorcisms are always efficacious, however, against those specific infestations against which they were first instituted.

1. That is to say that reason ostensibly compels the belief that the effects of witchcraft cannot be removed by any natural agency and hence must be considered to be permanent effects. [Editor's note]

74

Figure 8. The Wise Men and the Temptation of Herod.
The representation of the Devil tempting Herod is a thirteenth-century visualization
of the New Testament scene. See Figure 9.

Figure 9. The Massacre of the Innocents.
This illustration follows in the manuscript those in Figure 8. The Devil tempts Herod
to massacre the Holy Innocents. From a thirteenth-century French Psalter.

The Papacy,
the Inquisition,
and the Early Witch-Finders
1250–1484

The complex mechanisms and ontology of the spiritual and material universe, which the writings of St. Thomas Aquinas and his fellow scholastic philosophers had described in overwhelming and persuasive detail, afforded men of the late thirteenth and fourteenth centuries a convincing and, indeed, irrefutable rationale for approaching the problems of diabolism, heresy, and witchcraft. The papacy, the investigative institutions of the Church—particularly the Inquisition—and local preachers and theologians all reflected in their writings the slow process by which isolated cases of witchcraft and possession came to be conceived as being similar reflections of a systematic assault on man by Satan and his followers, the demons and witches. In 1258 the Inquisition asked Pope Alexander IV (1254–61) for permission to add witchcraft to those ecclesiastical offenses of which it could take judicial cognizance. Pope Alexander refused the Inquisition's request, but he left an important opening for later action. In his decretal letter *Quod super nonullis* of the same year (No. 11), Alexander allowed that the Inquisition could try witches only if there was evidence of manifest heresy in their cases. It remained for the Inquisitors and theologians and canon lawyers to find the means of identifying witchcraft with heresy. In the 1320's Pope John XXII (1316–34) expressed a particular horror of witches and claimed that he feared for his own life at their hands. In his and others' letters concerning the witches (Nos. 12–13) Pope John's remarks reveal a widespread acceptance of the existence and danger of witchcraft, its association with the Devil, and its relation to heresy.

Yet another approach was taken by the Inquisition itself. In the genre known as *Inquisitors' Handbooks,* writers such as Bernard Gui and Nicholas Eymeric laid down in painstaking detail the categories of heresy and the methods for discovering, judging, and punishing it. Eymeric's *Directorium Inquisitorum,* completed in 1376 (*No.* 14), reflects particularly the systematic and detailed assimilation of witchcraft to Biblical, patristic, and legal tradition. By the mid-fourteenth century, witch trials were becoming more frequent, and in a trial of that time there occurs the first documented account of the Witches' Sabbath, the regular nocturnal perversion of church-going which was to become a characteristic aspect of witches' activity in the sixteenth and seventeenth centuries (*No.* 15). In 1437, Pope Eugenius IV (1431–39) expressed the growing feeling that the threat from witches was increasing (*No.* 16), and at about the same time a book in defense of the faith, the *Formicarius* (Ant-Heap) by the Dominican professor of theology Johann Nider (*No.* 17) offered a wealth of anecdotes about the well-known and terrible activities of the witches.

By the end of the fifteenth century, witchcraft had been assimilated to heresy, been pronounced against by the highest and most powerful ecclesiastical authorities, and had served as the grounds of accusation in a large number of political and religious trials. Diabolism, the Sabbath, and undeviating hostility toward Christian society had become the mark of all "witches"—and all witches had become fellow servants of Satan.

11

POPE ALEXANDER IV
Magic and the Inquisition
1258

Hansen, *Quellen*, p. 1; *Liber Sextus*, V.2.8 *Corpus Iuris Canonici*, ed. E. Friedberg (Leipzig, 1877), Vol. II, col. 1071–72. The Ordinary Gloss on this passage is in *Sextum Decretalium Liber* (Venice, 1567), pp. 339–41. Tr. E.P.

Rubric: The Inquisitors, deputed to investigate heresy, must not intrude into investigations of divination or sorcery without knowledge of manifest heresy involved.[1]

It is reasonable that those charged with the affairs of the faith, which is the greatest of privileges, ought not thereby to intervene in other matters. The inquisitors of pestilential heresy, commissioned by the apostolic see, ought not intervene in cases of divination or sorcery unless these *clearly savour* of manifest heresy. Nor should they punish those who are engaged in these things, but leave them to other judges for punishment.

Ordinary Gloss: "clearly savour . . ." as in praying at the altars of idols, to offer sacrifices, to consult demons, to elicit responses from them . . . or if they associate themselves publicly with heretics in order to predict the future by means of the Body and Blood of Christ, etc.

1. It should be noted that Pope Alexander's intention in this excerpt, as well as the intentions of the compilers of the *Liber Sextus* in 1298, was rather to define the province of the Inquisition than to contribute to the literature of witchcraft. The very next text after the one cited here, for example, raises the question of whether the Inquisition should deal with usurers.

[Editors' Note]

12

WILLIAM, CARDINAL OF SANTA SABINA
Magic and the Inquisition
1320

The pontificate of John XXII (1316–34) witnessed a number of striking changes in the medieval Church. Pope John was a brilliant organizer and administrator and had a taste for ruling. The papacy was located at the imperial city of Avignon (now in southern France) during his pontificate, and John attempted to restore some of the prestige which the papacy and the Church had lost in the preceding two decades. Yet he also experienced several attempts on his life, one of which appears to have been an attempted assassination by poison and sorcery; hence his and Cardinal William of Santa Sabina's letters denouncing a danger which both suddenly felt to be at once immediate and threatening.[1]

William, Cardinal of Santa Sabina, Letter of 22 August, 1320, to the Inquisitors of Carcassonne and Toulouse. Latin text in Hansen, *Quellen,* pp. 4–5. Tr. E.P.

Our most holy father and lord, by divine providence Pope John XXII, fervently desires that the witches, the infectors of God's flock, flee from the midst of the House of God. He ordains and commits to you that, by his authority against them who make sacrifice to demons or adore them, or do homage unto them by giving them as a sign a written pact or other token; or who make certain binding pacts with them, or who make or

1. On John XXII's pontificate and the affair of assassination, see Guy Mollatt, *The Popes at Avignon, 1305-1378,* tr. J. Love (New York, 1965).

80

have made for them certain images or other things which bind them to demons, or by invoking the demons plan to perpetrate whatever sorceries they wish; or who, abusing the sacrament of baptism, themselves baptize or cause to be baptized an image of wax or some other material; and who themselves make these things or have them made in order to invoke the demons; or if knowingly they have baptism, orders, or confirmation repeated; then, concerning sorcerers and witches, who abuse the sacrament of the eucharist or the consecrated host and other sacraments of the Church by using them or things like them in their witchcraft and sorcery, you can investigate and otherwise proceed against them by whatever means available, which are canonically assigned to you concerning the proceeding against heretics. Indeed, our same lord amplifies and extends the power given to Inquisitors by law as much as the office of the inquisition against heretics and, by his certain knowledge, likewise the privileges in all and singular cases mentioned above.

13

POPE JOHN XXII
Magic and the Inquisition
1326

Pope John XXII, the Decretal *Super illius specula*. Latin text in Hansen, *Quellen*, 5–6. Tr. E.P.

Grievingly we observe . . . that many who are Christians in name only . . . sacrifice to demons, adore them, make or have made images, rings, mirrors, phials, or other things for magic purposes, and bind themselves to demons. They ask and receive responses from them and to fulfill their most depraved lusts ask them for aid. Binding themselves to the most shameful slavery for the most shameful of things, they allay themselves with death and make a pact with hell. By their means a most pestilential disease, besides growing stronger and increasingly serious, grievously infests the flock of Christ throughout the world. By this edict we warn in perpetuity, guided by the sound counsel of our brothers, all and singular who have been reborn at the baptismal font. In virtue of holy obedience and under threat of anathema we warn them in advance that none of them ought dare to teach or learn anything at all concerning these perverse dogmas, or, what is even more execrable, to use any of them by whatever means for whatever purpose. . . . We hereby promulgate the sentence of excommunication upon all and singular who against our most charitable warnings and orders presume to engage in these things, and we desire that they incur this sentence *ipso facto*.

Figure 10. Temptation.

No aspect of theology was more frequently alluded to in religious tracts nor more frequently depicted in pictures than the varieties of temptation. In the fifteenth century, these depictions became progressively more horrific and grotesque. This late fifteenth-century painting portrays the temptations of St. Antony, one of the founders of monasticism in the third century.

14

NICHOLAS EYMERIC
Heresy, Witchcraft, and the Inquisition
1376

Nicholas Eymeric became the Inquisitor of the Kingdom of Aragon in 1356. "Trained in varied learning, and incessant in industry . . . he systematized the procedure of his beloved institution [i.e., the Inquisition], giving the principles and details which should guide the inquisitor in all his acts. The book [the *Directorium Inquisitorium*] remained an authority to the last, and formed the basis of all subsequent compilations."[1] Eymeric's handbook for Inquisitors was reprinted late in the sixteenth century with an extended commentary by the canon lawyer Francesco Peña.

Nicholas Eymeric, *Directorium Inquisitorium,* 1376. Latin text in the edition of Rome, 1587, Part II, *Quaestio* XLII *De Sortilegis et Divinatoribus,* pp. 335–36; *Quaestio* XLIII *De Invocantibus Daemones,* pp. 338–43. Tr. E.P.

*T*he forty-second question asks whether magicians and diviners are to be considered heretics or as those suspected of heresy and whether they are to be subjected to the judgment of the Inquisitor of heretics. To this we answer that there are two things to be seen here, just as there are really two things asked in this question. The first is, whether magicians and diviners are subject to the judgment of the Inquisitor of heretics. The sec-

1. Henry C. Lea, *The Inquisition of the Middle Ages,* abr. Margaret Nicholson (New York, 1961), pp. 354-55.

ond, posed thusly, is whether they are to be considered as heretics or as those suspected of heresy.

1. The first thing to be considered, just as in the last *Quaestio* different kinds of blasphemers were distinguished, is that diviners and magicians must be distinguished; that is, there are two kinds of diviners and magicians.

2. Some are to be considered magicians and diviners just as are those who act purely according to the technique of chiromancy, who divine things from the lineaments of the hand and judge natural effects and the condition of men from this. . . .

3. Some others, however, are magicians and diviners who are not pure chiromantics, but are contracted to heretics, as are those who show the honor of *latria*[1] or *dulia*[2] to the demons, who rebaptize children and do other similar things. And they do these things in order to foresee the future or penetrate to the innermost secrets of the heart. These people are guilty of manifest heresy. And such magicians and diviners do not evade the judgment of the Inquisitor, but are punished according to the laws pertaining to heretics.

*T*he Forty-third question asks whether those who invoke demons, either magicians or heretics or those suspected of heresy, are subject to the judgment of the Inquisitor of heretics. . . .

2. It appears to the Inquisitors from the above-mentioned books and from other books that certain invokers of demons manifestly show the honor of *latria* to the demons they invoke, inasmuch as they sacrifice to them, adore them, offer up horrible prayers to them, vow themselves to the service of the demons, promise them their obedience, and otherwise commit themselves to the demons, swearing by the name of some superior demon whom they invoke. They willingly celebrate the praises of the demon or sing songs in his honor and genuflect or prostrate themselves before him. They observe chastity out of reverence for the demon or abstain upon his instructions or they lacerate their own flesh. Out of reverence for the demon or by his instructions they wear white or black vestments. They worship him by signs and characters and unknown names. They burn candles or incense to him or aromatic spices. They sacrifice animals and birds, catching their blood

---

1. *Latria* is that form of adoration which must be shown only to God; hence, *idolatria* is worship shown to idols which ought to be shown only to God.
2. *Dulia* is a form of veneration to be shown only to saints, holy men, and to God's vicars on earth.

Figure 11. Spiritually Negligent Women and Observant Demons.

A popular element in ecclesiastical and moral satire in the later middle ages was inattention at divine services. Here the devils enter the church itself to record the sins of the negligent women.

as a curative agent, or they burn them, throwing salt in the fire and making a holocaust in this manner. All of these things and many more evil things are found in consulting and desiring things from demons, in all of which and in whichever the honor of *latria*, if the above things are considered intelligently, is clearly shown to the demons. If, note well, the sacrifices to God according to the old and the new law are considered, it is found there that these acts are true sacrifices only when exhibited to God, and not to the demons. This, then, is the case with the first category of those who invoke or speak on behalf of demons. . . . And by this manner the priests used to invoke Baal, offering their own blood and that of animals, as one reads in 4 *Kings*, 18.

3. Certain other invokers of demons show to the demons they invoke not the honor of *latria*, but that of *dulia*, in that they insert in their wicked prayers the names of demons along with those of the Blessed or the Saints, making them mediators in their prayers heard by God. They bow down before images of wax, worshipping God by their names or qualities. These things and many other wretched things are found described in the afore-mentioned books in which the honor of *dulia* is shown to demons. If, indeed, the means of praying to the Saints which the Church has diligently instituted are considered, it will clearly be seen that these prayers are to be said, not to demons, but only to the Saints and the Blessed. This, then, is the case of the second category of those who invoke demons. And in this manner the Saracens invoke Mohammed as well as God and the Saints and certain Beghards invoke Petrus Johannis and others condemned by the Church.

4. Yet certain other invokers of demons make a certain kind of invocation in which it does not appear clearly that the honor either of *latria* or *dulia* is shown to the demons invoked, as, in tracing a circle on the ground, placing a child in the circle, setting a mirror, a sword, an amphora, or something else in the way before the boy, holding their book of necromancy, reading it, and invoking the demon and other suchlike, as is taught by that art and proved by the confessions of many. This, then, is the third way of invoking demons. And by this means Saul invoked the spirit of the python through the Pythoness. In Saul's invocation, it is seen, no honor was done, neither *dulia* nor *latria*, as one reads in 1 *Kings*, 26.

It seems, therefore, that the means of invoking demons vary in three ways. These conclusions pose in turn three cases or conclusions according to which the invokers of demons ought to be distinguished from one another in three ways.

5.   First, the case or conclusion is that if the invokers of demons show to the demons they invoke the honor of *latria* by whatever means and if they are clearly and judicially convicted of this, or if they confess, then they are to be held by the judgment of the Church not as magicians, but as heretics, and if they recant and abjure heresy they are to be perpetually immured as penitent heretics. If, however, they do not wish to desist or if they say they wish to desist and repent but do not wish to abjure, or if they do abjure and afterwards relapse, they are to be relinquished to the secular arm, punished by the ultimate torture according to all the canonical sanctions which judge other heretics.

This conclusion may be deduced in three ways: first from the sayings of the saints and doctors of theology, second from the sayings of the doctors of canon law, and third from the decisions of the Church.

First, from the sayings of the theologians, Blessed St. Augustine in Book 10 of *The City of God,* speaking of sacrifices shown only to God and not to Demons, says this: "We see that it is observed in each republic that men honor the highest leader by a singular sign which, if it is offered to someone else, would be the hateful crime of *lèse-majesté.* And thus it is written in the divine law under pain of death to those who offer divine honors to others. Exterior deeds are signs of interior deeds, just as spoken words are the signs of things; we direct our voices signifying prayers or praises to him, to whom we offer the same things in our hearts which we say, so we know that in sacrificing a visible sacrifice is to be offered to him to whom in our hearts we ought to offer ourselves as an invisible sacrifice. . . ."

By these words Augustine shows clearly that such sacrifice ought to be offered to God alone, and when it is offered to another than God, then by that deed one shows oneself to believe that that person is higher than God, which is heresy. Whoever, therefore, offers sacrifice to demons considers the demon as God and shows himself to believe the demon to be the true God by offering external signs. By which deeds they are to be considered heretics. . . .

Superstition is a vice opposed to the Christian religion or Christian worship. Therefore, it is heresy in a Christian, and as a consequence those who sacrifice to demons are to be considered heretics.

6.   St. Thomas, in a commentary on Isaiah (1 *Isaiah,* 3) . . . poses the question whether it is illicit to seek the future through augury, and at the end of his commentary says, concerning demonology and what the demons are able to know, that it is always a sin to inquire of them as well as an apostasy from faith. As says Augustine, so says blessed Thomas.

The same St. Thomas [in his commentary to Peter Lombard's] *Sentences*, in Book 2, *distinctio* 7, asks whether it is a sin to use the aid of a demon and answers . . . that that which is beyond the faculties of human nature is to be asked only of God, and, just as they gravely sin who, through the cult of *latria* to an idol, impute that which is only God's to a creature of God, so indeed do they gravely sin who implore the aid of a demon in those things which are only to be asked of God. And in this way is seeing into the future [to be considered]. . . .

7. Indeed, the same is to be said of other magical works in which the accomplishment of the task is anticipated by the aid of the devil. In all these there is apostasy from the faith because of the compact made with the demon or because of a promise if the compact is already in existence or by any other deed, even if sacrifice is not performed. Man may not serve two masters, as says St. Matthew in Chapter 8, and St. Thomas. From these things it is shown clearly that to invoke and consult demons, even without making sacrifice to them, is apostasy from the faith and, as a consequence, heresy. It is much worse if a sacrifice is involved. . . .

Peter of Tarentaise, who later was Pope Innocent V, holds . . . that although a man may be asked about a book which is lost, a demon may not, because the demon, when asked about such things, will not respond unless a pact is made with him, or illicit veneration, adjuration, or invocation. . . .

8. Our conclusion is also proved by the sayings of the Canon lawyers. . . .

Thirdly, our conclusion is also proved by the decisions of the Church. Indeed, Causa XXVI q.5 c.[12] *Episcopi* says this: "Bishops and their officials should labor with all their strength. . . ."[1]

And from this it appears that those who share and exercise the magical art are to be considered heretics and avoided. . . .

And from this it appears that the said evil women, persevering in their wickedness, have departed from the right way and the faith and the devils delude them. If, therefore, these same women, concerning whom it is not contested that they offer sacrifices to the demons they invoke, are perfidious and faithless and deviate from the right way as the said canon from the Council of Ancyra makes clear, then, as a consequence, if they have been baptized they are to be considered heretics; since for a Christian to deviate from the right way and faith and to embrace infidelity is properly to hereticize. How much more, then, are Christians, who show the honor of *latria* to demons and sacrifice to the demons they invoke, to be said and

1. Eymeric here gives the *Canon Episcopi* (above, *No.* 1).

considered to be perfidious, deviants from the right way, and faithless in the love of Christians, which is heresy—and by consequence to be considered heretics? . . .

Indeed, the further a creature is separated from divine perfection, the greater the fault it is to show him the honor of *latria*. And since the demons (not on account of their nature, but on account of their guilt) are the most separated from God of all creatures, so much the worse is it to adore them. And to number them among the Angels is wicked heresy. Those who count Angels among the heretics show manifest heresy by so counting them, adoring them, or by any way sacrificing to them. And as a consequence, those who perpetrate this kind of wickedness are to be judged as heretics by the Church.

9. The Constitution of Pope John XXII against magicians and magical superstitions. . . .[2]

10. . . . Whoever invokes the aid of Mohammed, even if he does nothing else, falls into manifest heresy. So does anyone who in his honor constructs an altar to him. In similar cases the same thing may be said of invoking any demon, building him an altar, sacrificing to him, etc. These are the acts of *latria*, which ought to be given only to God. . . .

11. In the second case the conclusion is that if those who invoke the demons do not show to the demons they invoke the honor of *latria*, but do show them the honor of *hyperdulia* or that of *dulia* in the manner described before and have clearly confessed to this judicially or have been convicted of it, such are to be considered by the judgment of the Church not magicians, but heretics, and as a consequence if they recant and abjure heresy they are to be perpetually immured as penitent heretics. If, however, they do not recant, they are to be treated as impenitent heretics; likewise if they abjure and then relapse, they are to suffer punishment like other heretics.

12. . . . *Dulia* may be expressed in two ways, or rather in two kinds of case. The first is as a sign of sanctity. This is the case of Abraham, Lot [and others]. . . . This case is that of Angels and saints who are in the heavenly fatherland and are adored by us and celebrated by the honor of *dulia*.

13. The second case is a sign of governance, jurisdiction, and power. This is the case with the prophet Nathan, and *Bersabee* the mother of Solomon who adored David the King, as it says in 3 *Kings*, 1. This is also the case with Popes, Kings, and others who lawfully wield power, as vice-

2. Eymeric here gives the constitution of Pope John XXII (above, *No.* 13).

Figure 12. Devil and Woman.

In this late fifteenth-century woodcut illustrating a moral tract, the woman leaves the altar with a demon riding the tail of her cloak.

gerents of God in authority and rule. If, therefore, anyone should show to them the honor of *dulia* then he shows himself to believe that person to whom he displays the honor of *dulia* to be a saint and a friend of God, or a governor or a rector duly constituted by God, and thus that God ought to be honored in him, his vicar. Now when the honor of *dulia* is shown to a saint, God is principally adored by the honor of *latria* through the saint. And when a Pope, King, or any other person who wields power is revered by the honor of *dulia*, God is venerated by the honor of *latria* through his Vicar. And thus by these kinds of honors which are shown to the saints and to the rectors of the Church and to the princes of this world, it is not themselves, but God in them who is principally venerated. Therefore, showing the honor of *dulia* to a demon who has been invoked by these means and by exterior actions, is to reveal oneself in heart and mind as believing inwardly that the demon is above the saints and the friend of God and is to be venerated as if saintly, or that he is above the rectors of this world and the governors duly constituted by God and therefore is to be revered as having jurisdiction and power. In both senses this is heretical and perverse, since it is contrary to the holy scriptures and against the decisions of the Church. The Demon is neither a saint nor the friend of God, chiefly since he is obstinate in his sin and wickedness. Nor is he one of God's governors in this world duly constituted, but he is the captured slave, the falsifier and deceiver, as the sacred canons and all that we have said above clearly shows. Therefore, those who are convicted of showing the demon the honor of *dulia* are to be treated not as magicians, but as heretics. . . .

15

THE INQUISITION
OF TOULOUSE
The Witches' Sabbath
Fourteenth Century

This text is taken from depositions in the archive of the Inquisition at Toulouse. The key description of the witches' assembly, the Sabbath, marks the first record we possess of the juridical recognition of the reality of these meetings. These declarations are the forerunners of thousands of confessions of witchcraft taken by ecclesiastical and civil courts between the fourteenth and the eighteenth centuries.

Text in Caro Baroja, pp. 84–86. French text in Hansen, *Quellen*, pp. 450–53.

Anne Marie de Georgel and Catherine, the wife of Delort, both from Toulouse and advanced in years, have declared in their confessions to the legal authorities that they have been members of the numberless hosts of Satan for about twenty years, and have given themselves to him for this life and the next. Frequently on Friday nights they have attended the Sabbath which is held sometimes in one place, sometimes in another. There, in company with other men and women who are equally sacrilegious, they commit all manner of excesses, whose details are horrible to tell. Each of them has been interrogated separately and they have given explanations which have entirely convinced us of their guilt.

Anne Marie de Georgel declares that one morning when she was wash-

Figure 13. Albrecht Dürer, *The Knight, Death, and the Devil.*
Dürer's famous engraving epitomizes the visual proximity of Death and the Devil to the highest type of idealized human figure. The grotesque Devil illustrates graphically the increasing fascination with repulsive demonic shapes and features (cf. Figure 10, above).

ing clothes near Pech-David above the town, she saw a man of huge stature coming towards her across the water. He was dark-skinned and his eyes burned like living coals; he was dressed in the hides of beasts. This monster asked her if she would give herself to him and she said yes. Then he blew into her mouth and from the Saturday following she was borne to the Sabbath, simply because it was his will. There she found a huge he-goat and after greeting him she submitted to his pleasure. The he-goat in return taught her all kinds of secret spells; he explained poisonous plants to her and she learned from him words for incantations and how to cast spells during the night of the vigil of St. John's day, Christmas Eve, and the first Friday in every month. He advised her to make sacrilegious communion if she could, offending God and honouring the Devil. And she carried out these impious suggestions.

Anne Marie de Georgel then admitted that she had not ceased to do evil, practising all manner of filthiness during the years which passed from the time of her initiation to that of her imprisonment. The fear of Our Lord did not stay her hand. She boiled together in a cauldron, over an accursed fire, poisonous herbs and substances taken from the bodies of animals or humans which she had sacrilegiously and foully taken from the consecrated ground of cemeteries to use for her spells; she frequented the gallows-trees by night stealing shreds of clothing from the hanged, or taking the rope by which they were hanging, or laying hold of their hair, their nails or flesh. Like a true daughter of Satan, in answer to questions about the symbols of the Apostles and the faith which true believers have in our Holy Religion, she averred that God and the Devil were completely equal, the former reigning over the *sky* and the latter the *earth*; all souls which the Devil managed to seduce were lost to the Most High God and lived perpetually on earth or in the air, going every night to visit the houses in which they had lived and trying to inspire in their children and relatives a desire to serve the Devil rather than God.

She also told us that the struggle between God and the Devil had gone on since eternity and would have no end. Sometimes one is victorious, sometimes the other, and at this time the situation was such that Satan was sure to triumph. At first, after she had been taken prisoner, having been denounced by respectable persons who had good reason to complain of her spells, she denied the abominable pact she had made and would not confess in spite of the requests of others as well as ourselves. But when she had been justly forced to give an account of herself, she finally admitted a series of crimes which deserved the most horrible punishment. She has sworn she repents, and has asked for reconciliation with the Church which has been granted her. Nevertheless, she must still be handed over to the secular arm which will realise the penalties she must pay.

Catherine, the wife of Pierre Delort of Toulouse, stands convicted on her own declarations and on the evidence of trustworthy persons, of meeting a shepherd in the field of the Parish of Quint and having a relationship with him contrary to the law. He, abusing his power over her, obliged her to make a pact with the Devil. This loathsome ceremony took place at midnight at the edge of a wood at a place where two roads meet. She let some blood from her left arm and allowed it to flow on to a fire made of human bones which had been stolen from the parish cemetery. She pronounced certain strange words which she no longer remembers and the Devil Berit appeared to her in the form of a violet flame. Since then she has made certain harmful concoctions and potions which cause men and beasts to die.

Every Friday night she fell into a strange sleep during which she was carried to the Sabbath. Asked where this took place she answered: on the slopes of Pech-David in the wood at Bouconne, in the middle of the open country between Toulouse and Montauban. Sometimes further away still, on the top of the Black Mountains of the Pyrenees, and in countries quite unknown to her. There she worshipped the he-goat and served his pleasure and that of all those who were present at that loathsome feast. The corpses of newly-born children were eaten by them; they had been stolen from their nurses during the night; all manner of revolting liquids were drunk and there was no savour in any of the food.

Asked whether she had seen any of those of her acquaintance at the Sabbath she replied that she had frequently. She did not name them; some of them had died in their wickedness, others have been taken into custody thanks to our vigilance; a few have escaped, but the vengeance of the Lord will be upon them.

Catherine, forced to confess by the means we have power to use to make people speak the truth, was convicted of all the crimes we suspected her of committing, although she protested her innocence for a long time and made several false declarations. She made hail fall on the fields of her enemies, caused their wheat to rot by means of a pestilential fog, and damaged the vineyards with frost. She caused the oxen and sheep of her neighbours to sicken and die for the advantages this might bring her. For the same motives she caused her aunts, whose heir she was, to die, by heating waxen figures dressed in one of their blouses over a slow fire, so that their unfortunate lives wasted away as the waxen figures melted in the brazier.

Figure 14. The Incubus: The Begetting of Merlin.
This illumination from a fourteenth-century French manuscript depicts the conception of the legendary wizard Merlin by a demon and a mortal woman. The *incubus*, the demon who impregnates women, was an important element in the complex sexual associations of witch beliefs between the fourteenth and the eighteenth centuries.

16

POPE EUGENIUS IV
Two Letters on the Pressing Danger
1434-37

Pope Eugenius IV (1431–47) was an austere and devout man whose pontificate was troubled by his bad relations with the Council of Basel and his opposition to the antipope Felix V. During his pontificate, the ecclesiastical reform movement which had been begun in Bohemia by John Hus had turned into a major civil war, and the city of Rome itself was troubled by rebellion and opposition to the pope. It was in the particularly troubled early years of his pontificate that Pope Eugenius turned his attention briefly to the problem of witchcraft, a question that troubled him particularly because of his intense interest in genuine piety and the reform of the clergy.

Latin texts in Hansen, *Quellen,* pp. 17–18. Tr. E.P.

A Letter to the Inquisitor Pontus Fougeyron,
1434.

Among many heretics there are found also many Christian and Jewish magicians, diviners, invokers of demons, bewitchers [*carminatores*], conjurers, superstitious people, augurs, those who use nefarious and forbidden arts, through whose efforts the Christian people, or at least a numerous and simple-minded part of them, are stained and perverted.

98

Figure 15. The Saintly Exorcist.
This bronze panel from the cathedral doors at Verona depicts Saint Zeno exorcising the demon from the daughter of Gallienus.

Figure 16. The Saintly Exorcist.
Although not all aspects of demonic temptations were continually illustrated in the Middle Ages, the ritual of exorcism, especially in representations of individual saint's lives, was a popular motif. This bronze panel from the cathedral doors of Gniezno, Poland, depicts St. Adalbert driving out a demon from a possessed man.

Pope Eugenius IV: The Pressing Danger

A Letter to All Inquisitors of Heretical Depravity, 1437.

The news has reached us, not without great bitterness of spirit, that the prince of darkness makes many who have been bought by the blood of Christ partakers in his own fall and damnation, bewitching them by his cunning arts in such a way that these detestable persuasions and illusions make them members of his sect. They sacrifice to demons, adore them, seek out and accept responses from them, do homage to them, and make with them a written agreement or another kind of pact through which, by a single word, touch, or sign, they may perform whatever evil deeds or sorcery they wish and be transported to or away from wherever they wish. They cure diseases, provoke bad weather, and make pacts concerning other evil deeds. Or, so that they may achieve these purposes, the reckless creatures make images or have images made in order to constrain the demons, or by invoking them perpetrate more sorcery. In their sorcery they are not afraid to use the materials of Baptism, the Eucharist, and other sacraments. They make images of wax or other materials which by their invocations they baptize or cause to be baptized. Sometimes they make a reversal of the Holy Cross, upon which our Savior hanged for us. Not honoring the mysteries, they sometimes inflict upon the representations and other signs of the cross various shameful things by execrable means.

17

JOHANNES NIDER
The Formicarius,
Folklore and Theology
1437

Johannes Nider, a Dominican theologian, wrote his long treatise on theology, the *Formicarius (Ant-Heap)*, in 1437. The work takes the form of a dialogue between a theologian and a doubter, and the fifth book deals with the nature and practice of witchcraft.

Text in Burr, *The Witch-Persecutions*, pp. 6–7. Burr's translation is based on the Latin edition of Augsburg, 1476, Lib. V, ch. 3.

I will relate to you some examples, which I have gained in part from the teachers of our faculty, in part from the experience of a certain upright secular judge, worthy of all faith, who from the torture and confessions of witches and from his experiences in public and private has learned many things of this sort—a man with whom I have often discussed this subject broadly and deeply—to wit, Peter, a citizen of Bern, in the diocese of Lausanne, who has burned many witches of both sexes, and has driven others out of the territory of the Bernese. I have moreover conferred with one Benedict, a monk of the Benedictine order, who, although now a very devout cleric in a reformed monastery at Vienna, was a decade ago, while still in the world, a necromancer, juggler, buffoon, and strolling player, well-known as an expert among the secular nobility. I have likewise heard certain of the

Figure 17. Christ Driving Out Demons from the Possessed Son.

The bottom panel of this illumination from a thirteenth-century French Psalter depicts Christ exorcising the demon, which issues from the mouth of the possessed man. Cf. Figures 15 and 16.

following things from the Inquisitor of Heretical Pravity at Autun, who was a devoted reformer of our order in the convent at Lyons, and has convicted many of witchcraft in the diocese of Autun. . . .

The same procedure was more clearly described by another young man, arrested and burned as a witch, although, as I believe, truly, penitent, who had earlier, together with his wife, a witch invincible to persuasion, escaped the clutches of the aforesaid judge, Peter. The aforesaid youth, being again indicted at Bern, with his wife, and placed in a different prison from hers, declared: "If I can obtain absolution for my sins, I will freely lay bare all I know about witchcraft, for I see that I have death to expect." And when he had been assured by the scholars that, if he should truly repent, he would certainly be able to gain absolution for his sins, then he gladly offered himself to death, and disclosed the methods of the primeval infection.

The ceremony, he said, of my seduction was as follows: First, on a Sunday before the holy water is consecrated, the future disciple with his masters must go into the church, and there in their presence must renounce Christ and his faith, baptism, and the church universal. Then he must do homage to the *magisterulus*, that is, to the little master (for so, and not otherwise, they call the Devil). Afterward he drinks from the aforesaid flask; and, this done, he forthwith feels himself to conceive and hold within himself an image of our art and the chief rites of this sect. After this fashion was I seduced; and my wife also, whom I believe of so great pertinacity that she will endure the flames rather than confess the least whit of truth; but, alas, we are both guilty. What the young man had said was found in all respects the truth. For, after confession, the young man was seen to die in great contrition. His wife, however, though convicted by the testimony of witnesses, would not confess the truth even under the torture or in death; but, when the fire was prepared for her by the executioner, uttered in most evil words a curse upon him, and so was burned.

The Hammer
of *Witches*

The growing apprehension on the part of high Church officials, Inquisitors, and the clergy in general that witchcraft was not only extant and dangerous, but a clearly recognizable part of Satan's concerted attack on all mankind, produced at the end of the fifteenth century two remarkable documents which, from all sides, represent the climax of earlier witch-theories and the chief shaping force of later persecutions. In 1484, at the instance of two German Inquisitors, Pope Innocent VIII issued his famous letter *Summis Desiderantes* (No. 18), a document in which the fears of Pope John XXII and the activity of Pope Eugenius IV are brought to a summary conclusion, formalized and accepted in their totality, and a plan of action against the world-wide conspiracy of the witches and Satan, their master, finally laid down. Two years later, as if to justify the letter's strong terms in retrospect, the same two Dominican Inquisitors, Jacob Sprenger and Heinrich Krämer (Institor) produced a book, somewhat on the model of the earlier Inquisitors' Handbooks, solely on the subject of witchcraft, the *Malleus Maleficarum*, the *Hammer of Witches* (No. 19). The *Malleus* instantly became the chief source of information about witches' activities and, to the surprise of no one, it was precisely those characteristics of witchcraft to which the *Malleus* paid most attention that appeared all over Europe during the sixteenth and seventeenth centuries. All later handbooks of witch-theory, however "scientific" or "anti-Catholic," looked back to the *Malleus* as their chief inspiration, as their "encyclopedia." The *Malleus* further inspired more papal activity, and the letter of Pope Alexander VI, a man not generally marked by excessive concern for the salvation of mankind, reflects the attack on the witches as a permanent aspect of papal policy after 1500 (*No. 20*).

The *Malleus* is divided into three parts. The first part establishes that disbelief in witches is manifest heresy, offers a kind of census of the effects of witchcraft, and explains why it is that women are witches more frequently than men. The second part offers a typology of witchcraft as well as a typology for its investigation. The third part treats in infinite detail the nature of the legal proceedings against witches, and justifies all its deviations from orthodox civil and ecclesiastical legal procedures with careful citations of Scripture, the Church Fathers, and more recent theologians and ecclesiastical lawyers. The excerpts from the *Malleus* given below are by no means an attempt to summarize or offer "highlights" of the work. It is a tightly-knit book, each argument and dogma carefully drawn from the conclusions of the preceding arguments and dogmas, and it is excerpted only reluctantly. The force of the *Malleus* is its comprehensive character, and the selections made below offer only representative samplings of its intricate design. A reading of the whole work is well worth the effort, and it is only with this cautionary note that the editors have excerpted as much as they have.

18

POPE INNOCENT VIII
Summis desiderantes
The "Witch-Bull"
1484

Pope Innocent VIII (1484–92) was moved by the complaints of two Dominican Inquisitors, Heinrich Krämer and Jacob Sprenger, that local ecclesiastical authorities in Germany refused to aid them in their pursuit of heretical witchcraft. Sprenger and Krämer described some of their cases to the pope and elicited from him the famous Bull called, from its opening Latin words, *Summis desiderantes*. The similarity in terminology of this and earlier papal letters on the subject is certainly striking, and its purpose is clearly to remove the juridical obstacles preventing Krämer and Sprenger from carrying out their witch-hunt. This document has traditionally been considered the "beginning" of the witch-persecutions, but its likeness to other papal documents, its particular emphasis upon preaching, and its lack of dogmatic pronouncement on the subject of witchcraft place it squarely in the tradition of papal concern for heresy and disbelief. Its circulation with Sprenger and Krämer's later handbook, the *Malleus Maleficarum* (No. 19), gave it both a wider circulation and a more direct role in subsequent witch persecutions than it might otherwise have had.

Latin text in Hansen, *Quellen*, pp. 24–27. English translation from Burr, *The Witch-Persecutions*, pp. 7–10.

Desiring with supreme ardor, as pastoral solicitude requires, that the catholic faith in our days everywhere grow and flourish as much as possible, and that all heretical pravity be put far from the territories of the faithful, we freely declare and anew decree this by which our pious desire may be fulfilled, and, all errors being rooted out by our toil as with the hoe of a wise laborer, zeal and devotion to this faith may take deeper hold on the hearts of the faithful themselves.

It has recently come to our ears, not without great pain to us, that in some parts of upper Germany, as well as in the provinces, cities, territories, regions, and dioceses of Mainz, Köln, Trier, Salzburg, and Bremen, many persons of both sexes, heedless of their own salvation and forsaking the catholic faith, give themselves over to devils male and female, and by their incantations, charms, and conjurings, and by other abominable superstitions and sortileges, offences, crimes, and misdeeds, ruin and cause to perish the off-spring of women, the foal of animals, the products of the earth, the grapes of vines, and the fruits of trees, as well as men and women, cattle and flocks and herds and animals of every kind, vineyards also and orchards, meadows, pastures, harvests, grains and other fruits of the earth; that they afflict and torture with dire pains and anguish, both internal and external, these men, women, cattle, flocks, herds, and animals, and hinder men from begetting and women from conceiving, and prevent all consummation of marriage; that, moreover, they deny with sacrilegious lips the faith they received in holy baptism; and that, at the instigation of the enemy of mankind, they do not fear to commit and perpetrate many other abominable offences and crimes, at the risk of their own souls, to the insult of the divine majesty and to the pernicious example and scandal of multitudes. And, although our beloved sons Henricus Institoris and Jacobus Sprenger, of the order of Friars Preachers, professors of theology, have been and still are deputed by our apostolic letters as inquisitors of heretical pravity, the former in the afore-said parts of upper Germany, including the provinces, cities, territories, dioceses, and other places as above, and the latter throughout certain parts of the course of the Rhine; nevertheless certain of the clergy and of the laity of those parts, seeking to be wise above what is fitting, because in the said letter of deputation the aforesaid provinces, cities, dioceses, territories, and other places, and the persons and offences in question were not individually and specifically named, do not blush obstinately to assert that these are not at all included in the said parts and that therefore it is illicit for the afore-said inquisitors to exercise their office of inquisition in the provinces, cities, dioceses, territories, and other places aforesaid, and that they ought not to be permitted to proceed to the punishment, imprisonment, and correction

Figure 18. The Moment of Death.

This woodcut from a late fifteenth-century handbook on *Ars moriendi* ("The Art of Dying") depicts a common late medieval visualization of the moment of death. Angels and demons contend for the soul of the dying man, the demons bearing the names of sins particularly characteristic of the eve of death.

109

of the aforesaid persons for the offences and crimes above named. Wherefore in the provinces, cities, dioceses, territories, and places aforesaid such offences and crimes, not without evident damage to their souls and risk of eternal salvation, go unpunished.

We therefore, desiring, as is our duty, to remove all impediments by which in any way the said inquisitors are hindered in the exercise of their office, and to prevent the taint of heretical pravity and of other like evils from spreading their infection to the ruin of others who are innocent, the zeal of religion especially impelling us, in order that the provinces, cities, dioceses, territories, and places aforesaid in the said parts of upper Germany may not be deprived of the office of inquisition which is their due, do hereby decree, by virtue of our apostolic authority, that it shall be permitted to the said inquisitors in these regions to exercise their office of inquisition and to proceed to the correction, imprisonment, and punishment of the aforesaid persons for their said offences and crimes, in all respects and altogether precisely as if the provinces, cities, territories, places, persons, and offences aforesaid were expressly named in the said letter. And, for the greater sureness, extending the said letter and deputation to the provinces, cities, dioceses, territories, places, persons, and crimes aforesaid, we grant to the said inquisitors that they or either of them, joining with them our beloved son Johannes Gremper, cleric of the diocese of Constance, master of arts, their present notary, or any other notary public who by them or by either of them shall have been temporarily delegated in the provinces, cities, dioceses, territories, and places aforesaid, may exercise against all persons, of whatsoever condition and rank, the said office of inquisition, correcting, imprisoning, punishing, and chastising, according to their deserts, those persons whom they shall find guilty as aforesaid.

And they shall also have full and entire liberty to propound and preach to the faithful the word of God, as often as it shall seem to them fitting and proper, in each and all the parish churches in the said provinces, and to do all things necessary and suitable under the aforesaid circumstances, and likewise freely and fully to carry them out.

And moreover we enjoin by apostolic writ on our venerable brother, the Bishop of Strasburg, that, either in his own person or through some other or others solemnly publishing the foregoing wherever, whenever, and how often soever he may deem expedient or by these inquisitors or either of them may be legitimately required, he permit them not to be molested or

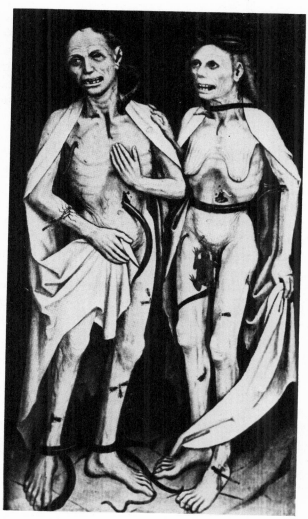

Figure 19. The Dead.

The theological contrast between fallen, corruptible nature and revivifying grace led to artistic representation of grotesque aspects of death, often contrasting the dead and the living and often concentrating upon the state in death of those who had made much of the delights of the flesh in life. This example depicts dead lovers, a favorite theme of moral philosophers and painters.

hindered in any manner whatsover by any authority whatsoever in the matter of the aforesaid and of this present letter, threatening all opposers, hinderers, contradictors, and rebels, of whatever rank, state, decree, eminence, nobility, excellence, or condition they may be, and whatever privilege of exemption they may enjoy, with excommunication, suspension, interdict, and other still more terrible sentences, censures, and penalties, as may be expedient, and this without appeal and with power after due process of law of aggravating and reaggravating these penalties, by our authority, as often as may be necessary, to this end calling in the aid, if need be, of the secular arm.

And this, all other apostolic decrees and earlier decisions to the contrary notwithstanding; or if to any, jointly or severally, there has been granted by this apostolic see exemption from interdict, suspension, or excommunication, by apostolic letters not making entire, express, and literal mention of the said grant of exemption; or if there exist any other indulgence whatsoever, general or special, of whatsoever tenor, by failure to name which or to insert it bodily in the present letter the carrying out of this privilege could be hindered or in any way put off,—or any of whose whole tenor special mention must be made in our letters. Let no man, therefore, dare to infringe this page of our declaration, extension, grant, and mandate, or with rash hardihood to contradict it. If any presume to attempt this, let him know the he incurs the wrath of almighty God and of the blessed apostles Peter and Paul.

Given in Rome, at St. Peter's, in the year of Our Lord's incarnation 1484, on the nones of December, in the first year of our pontificate.

19

HEINRICH KRÄMER
and JACOB SPRENGER
The *Malleus Maleficarum*
1486

The *Malleus Maleficarum* (The Hammer of Witches), written in 1486 by the
Dominican Inquisitors Heinrich Krämer (more commonly called Institoris, the
Latinized form of Krämer), and Jacob Sprenger, became the first "encyclopedia" of witch-beliefs, and was constantly cited in support of those beliefs
by Catholics and Protestants down to the eighteenth century. Its form is
similar to that of other works in the same genre; it springs from the handbook for investigating heretics, some examples of which were in fact called
"Hammers of Heretics." Krämer and Sprenger were the Inquisitors in Upper
Germany; their book was prefaced by Pope Innocent VIII's Bull *Summis
desiderantes,* and contained as an appendix an alleged decision in its favor
by the Faculty of Theology of the University of Cologne. With such claims
to the sanction of authority, the *Malleus* exhaustively analyzed the entire
problem of witch-beliefs and set out meticulously the ways by which witches
could be found, convicted, and executed. The unrelenting thoroughness of
Krämer and Sprenger served, in a sense, to sum up the entire history of recent
witch-beliefs and to present Christian Europe with a complete, persuasive,
massively documented, and duly authorized description of the witches in
its midst.

From the *Malleus Maleficarum,* tr. Montague Summers (London, 1928), Pt. I,
Qu. VI, XI: Pt. II, Qu. I, ch. II, IV, VII; Pt. III, Intro., Qu. V, IX, X,

XIII, XIV, XV, XVIII, XXXI, XXXIV (pp. 41–47, 66, 99–101, 109–13, 118–22, 204, 209–10, 216–18, 222–30, 235, 258–61, 268–71).

Why it is that Women are chiefly addicted to Evil Superstitions.

*T*here is also, concerning witches who copulate with devils, much difficulty in considering the methods by which such abominations are consummated. On the part of the devil: first, of what element the body is made that he assumes; secondly, whether the act is always accompanied by the injection of semen received from another; thirdly, as to time and place, whether he commits this act more frequently at one time than at another; fourthly, whether the act is invisible to any who may be standing by. And on the part of the women, it has to be inquired whether only they who were themselves conceived in this filthy manner are often visited by devils; or secondly, whether it is those who were offered to devils by midwives at the time of their birth; and thirdly, whether the actual venereal delectation of such is of a weaker sort. But we cannot here reply to all these questions, both because we are only engaged in a general study, and because in the second part of this work they are all singly explained by their operations, as will appear in the fourth chapter, where mention is made of each separate method. Therefore let us now chiefly consider women; and first, why this kind of perfidy is found more in so fragile a sex than in men. And our inquiry will first be general, as to the general conditions of women; secondly, particular, as to which sort of women are found to be given to superstition and witchcraft; and thirdly, specifically with regard to midwives, who surpass all others in wickedness.

Why Superstition is chiefly found in Women.

As for the first question, why a greater number of witches is found in the fragile feminine sex than among men; it is indeed a fact that it were idle to contradict, since it is accredited by actual experience, apart from the verbal testimony of credible witnesses. And without in any way detracting from a sex in which God has always taken great glory that His might should be spread abroad, let us say that various men have assigned various reasons for this fact, which nevertheless agree in principle. Wherefore it is good, for the admonition of women, to speak of this matter; and it has often been proved by experience that they are eager to hear of it, so long as it is set forth with discretion.

For some learned men propound this reason; that there are three things in nature, the Tongue, an Ecclesiastic, and a Woman, which know no moderation in goodness or vice; and when they exceed the bounds of their condition they reach the greatest heights and the lowest depths of goodness and vice. When they are governed by a good spirit, they are most excellent

Figure 20. Judgement.

The moment of death, the judgement of souls, and the final disposition of the dead preoccupied much of medieval thought and frequently found visual expression. This picture shows not the judgement of souls immediately after death, but the somber Last Judgement, a common representation found over the doors of churches.

in virtue; but when they are governed by an evil spirit, they indulge the worst possible vices.

This is clear in the case of the tongue, since by its ministry most of the kingdoms have been brought into the faith of Christ; and the Holy Ghost appeared over the Apostles of Christ in tongues of fire. Other learned preachers also have had as it were the tongues of dogs, licking the wounds and sores of the dying Lazarus. As it is said: With the tongues of dogs ye save your souls from the enemy.

For this reason S. Dominic, the leader and father of the Order of Preachers, is represented in the figure of a barking dog with a lighted torch in his mouth, that even to this day he may by his barking keep off the heretic wolves from the flock of Christ's sheep.

It is also a matter of common experience that the tongue of one prudent man can subdue the wrangling of a multitude; wherefore not unjustly Solomon sings much in their praise, in *Proverbs* x: In the lips of him that hath understanding wisdom is found. And again, The tongue of the just is as choice silver: the heart of the wicked is little worth. And again, The lips of the righteous feed many; but fools die for want of wisdom. For this cause he adds in chapter xvi, The preparations of the heart belong to man; but the answer of the tongue is from the Lord.

But concerning an evil tongue you will find in *Ecclesiasticus* xxviii: A backbiting tongue hath disquieted many, and driven them from nation to nation: strong cities hath it pulled down, and overthrown the houses of great men. And by a backbiting tongue it means a third party who rashly or spitefully interferes between two contending parties.

Secondly, concerning Ecclesiastics, that is to say, clerics and religious of either sex, S. John Chrysostom speaks on the text, He cast out them that bought and sold from the temple. From the priesthood arises everything good, and everything evil. S. Jerome in his epistle to Nepotian says: Avoid as you would the plague a trading priest, who has risen from poverty to riches, from a low to a high estate. And Blessed Bernard in his 23rd Homily *On the Psalms* says of clerics: If one should arise as an open heretic, let him be cast out and put to silence; if he is a violent enemy, let all good men flee from him. But how are we to know which ones to cast out or to flee from? For they are confusedly friendly and hostile, peaceable and quarrelsome, neighbourly and utterly selfish.

And in another place: Our bishops are become spearmen, and our pastors shearers. And by bishops here is meant those proud Abbots who impose heavy labours on their inferiors, which they would not themselves touch with their little finger. And S. Gregory says concerning pastors: No one does more harm in the Church than he who, having the name or order of sanctity, lives in sin; for no one dares to accuse him of sin, and therefore the sin is widely spread, since the sinner is honoured for the sanctity of his order. Blessed Augustine also speaks of monks to Vincent the Donatist: I freely confess to your charity before the Lord our God, which is the witness of my soul from the time I began to serve God, what great difficulty I have experienced in the fact that it is impossible to find either worse or better men that those who grace or disgrace the monasteries.

Now the wickedness of women is spoken of in *Ecclesiasticus* xxv: There is no head above the head of a serpent: and there is no wrath above the wrath of a woman. I had rather dwell with a lion and a dragon than to keep house with a wicked woman. And among much which in that place precedes and follows about a wicked woman, he concludes: All wickedness is but little to the wickedness of a woman. Wherefore S. John Chrysostom says on the text, It is not good to marry (*S. Matthew* xix): What else is woman but a foe to friendship, an unescapable punishment, a necessary evil, a natural temptation, a desirable calamity, a domestic danger, a delectable detriment, an evil of nature, painted with fair colours! Therefore if it be a sin to divorce her when she ought to be kept, it is indeed a necessary torture; for either we commit adultery by divorcing her, or we must endure daily strife. Cicero in his second book of *The Rhetorics* says: The many lusts of men lead them into one sin, but the one lust of women leads them into all sins; for the root of all woman's vices is avarice. And Seneca says in his *Tragedies:* A woman either loves or hates; there is no third grade. And the tears of a woman are a deception, for they may spring from true grief, or they may be a snare. When a woman thinks alone, she thinks evil.

But for good women there is so much praise, that we read that they have brought beatitude to men, and have saved nations, lands, and cities; as is clear in the case of Judith, Debbora, and Esther. See also 1 *Corinthians* vii: If a woman hath a husband that believeth not, and he be pleased to dwell with her, let her not leave him. For the unbelieving husband is sanctified by the believing wife. And *Ecclesiasticus* xxvi: Blessed is the man who has a virtuous wife, for the number of his days shall be doubled. And throughout that chapter much high praise is spoken of the excellence of good women; as also in the last chapter of *Proverbs* concerning a virtuous woman.

And all this is made clear in the New Testament concerning women and

Figure 21. The Judgement of Souls.

This illumination from a thirteenth-century Psalter shows clearly the devils' devices for gaining souls by unfairly tilting the scales of justice against them (top) and the graphic difference between damnation and salvation (bottom).

Figure 22. The Saved and the Damned.

The same ecclesiastical and secular ranks are found in Heaven and Hell. The angels lead the saved, the demons bind the lost.

virgins and other holy women who have by faith led nations and kingdoms away from the worship of idols to the Christian religion. Anyone who looks at Vincent of Beauvais (*in Spe. Histor.*, XXVI. 9) will find marvellous things of the conversion of Hungary by the most Christian Gilia, and of the Franks by Clotilda, the wife of Clovis. Wherefore in many vituperations that we read against women, the word woman is used to mean the lust of the flesh. As it is said: I have found a woman more bitter than death, and a good woman subject to carnal lust.

Others again have propounded other reasons why there are more superstitious women found than men. And the first is, that they are more credulous; and since the chief aim of the devil is to corrupt faith, therefore he rather attacks them. See *Ecclesiasticus* xix: He that is quick to believe is light-minded, and shall be diminished. The second reason is, that women are naturally more impressionable, and more ready to receive the influence of a disembodied spirit; and that when they use this quality well they are very good, but when they use it ill they are very evil.

The third reason is that they have slippery tongues, and are unable to conceal from their fellow-women those things which by evil arts they know; and, since they are weak, they find an easy and secret manner of vindicating themselves by witchcraft. See *Ecclesiasticus* as quoted above: I had rather dwell with a lion and a dragon than to keep house with a wicked woman. All wickedness is but little to the wickedness of a woman. And to this may be added that, as they are very impressionable, they act accordingly.

There are also others who bring forward yet other reasons, of which preachers should be very careful how they make use. For it is true that in the Old Testament the Scriptures have much that is evil to say about women, and this because of the first temptress, Eve, and her imitators; yet afterwards in the New Testament we find a change of name, as from Eva to Ave (as S. Jerome says), and the whole sin of Eve taken away by the benediction of Mary. Therefore preachers should always say as much praise of them as possible.

But because in these times this perfidy is more often found in women than in men, as we learn by actual experience, if anyone is curious as to the reason, we may add to what has already been said the following: that since they are feebler both in mind and body, it is not surprising that they should come more under the spell of witchcraft.

For as regards intellect, or the understanding of spiritual things, they seem to be of a different nature from men; a fact which is vouched for by the logic of the authorities, backed by various examples from the Scriptures. Terence says: Women are intellectually like children. And Lactantius (*Institutiones*, III): No woman understood philosophy except Temeste. And *Proverbs* xi, as it were describing a woman, says: As a jewel of gold in a swine's snout, so is a fair woman which is without discretion.

But the natural reason is that she is more carnal than a man, as is clear from her many carnal abominations. And it should be noted that there was a defect in the formation of the first woman, since she was formed from a bent rib, that is, a rib of the breast, which is bent as it were in a contrary direction to a man. And since through this defect she is an imperfect animal, she always deceives. For Cato says: When a woman weeps she weaves snares. And again: When a woman weeps, she labours to deceive a man. And this is shown by Samson's wife, who coaxed him to tell her the riddle he had propounded to the Philistines, and told them the answer, and so deceived him. And it is clear in the case of the first woman that she had little faith; for when the serpent asked why they did not eat of every tree in Paradise, she answered: Of every tree, etc.—lest perchance we die. Thereby she showed that she doubted, and had little faith in the word of God. And all this is indicated by the etymology of the word; for *Femina* comes from *Fe* and *Minus*, since she is ever weaker to hold and preserve the faith. And this as regards faith is of her very nature; although both by grace and nature faith never failed in the Blessed Virgin, even at the time of Christ's Passion, when it failed in all men.

Therefore a wicked woman is by her nature quicker to waver in her faith, and consequently quicker to abjure the faith, which is the root of witchcraft.

And as to her other mental quality, that is, her natural will; when she hates someone whom she formerly loved, then she seethes with anger and impatience in her whole soul, just as the tides of the sea are always heaving and boiling. Many authorities allude to this cause. *Ecclesiasticus* xxv: There is no wrath above the wrath of a woman. And Seneca (*Tragedies*, VIII): No might of the flames or of the swollen winds, no deadly weapon is so much to be feared as the lust and hatred of a woman who has been divorced from the marriage bed.

This is shown too in the woman who falsely accused Joseph, and caused him to be imprisoned because he would not consent to the crime of adultery with her (*Genesis* xxx). And truly the most powerful cause which contributes to the increase of witches is the woeful rivalry between married

Figure 23. The Torments of the Damned.
This sculptural relief depicts in grotesque and vivid detail the torments of those souls condemned to hell at the hands of active and ferocious demons.

folk and unmarried women and men. This is so even among holy women, so what must it be among the others? For you see in *Genesis* xxi how impatient and envious Sarah was of Hagar when she conceived: how jealous Rachel was of Leah because she had no children (*Genesis* xxx): and Hannah, who was barren, of the fruitful Peninnah (I. *Kings* i): and how Miriam (*Numbers* xii) murmured and spoke ill of Moses, and was therefore stricken with leprosy: and how Martha was jealous of Mary Magdalen, because she was busy and Mary was sitting down (*S. Luke* x). To this point is *Ecclesiasticus* xxxvii: Neither consult with a woman touching her of whom she is jealous. Meaning that it is useless to consult with her, since there is always jealousy, that is, envy, in a wicked woman. And if women behave thus to each other, how much more will they do so to men.

Valerius Maximus tells how, when Phoroneus, the king of the Greeks, was dying, he said to his brother Leontius that there would have been nothing lacking to him of complete happiness if a wife had always been lacking to him. And when Leontius asked how a wife could stand in the way of happiness, he answered that all married men well knew. And when the philosopher Socrates was asked if one should marry a wife, he answered: If you do not, you are lonely, your family dies out, and a stranger inherits; if you do, you suffer perpetual anxiety, querulous complaints, reproaches concerning the marriage portion, the heavy displeasure of your relations, the garrulousness of a mother-in-law, cuckoldom, and no certain arrival of an heir. This he said as one who knew. For S. Jerome in his *Contra Iouinianum* says: This Socrates had two wives, whom he endured with much patience, but could not be rid of their contumelies and clamorous vituperations. So one day when they were complaining against him, he went out of the house to escape their plaguing, and sat down before the house; and the women then threw filthy water over him. But the philosopher was not disturbed by this, saying, "I knew that the rain would come after the thunder."

There is also a story of a man whose wife was drowned in a river, who, when he was searching for the body to take it out of the water, walked up the stream. And when he was asked why, since heavy bodies do not rise but fall, he was searching against the current of the river, he answered: "When that woman was alive she always, both in word and deed, went contrary to my commands; therefore I am searching in the contrary direction in case even now she is dead she may preserve her contrary disposition."

And indeed, just as through the first defect in their intelligence they are more prone to abjure the faith; so through their second defect of inordinate affections and passions they search for, brood over, and inflict various vengeances, either by witchcraft, or by some other means. Wherefore it is no wonder that so great a number of witches exist in this sex.

Women also have weak memories; and it is a natural vice in them not to be disciplined, but to follow their own impulses without any sense of what is due; this is her whole study, and all that she keeps in her memory. So Theophrastus says: If you hand over the whole management of the house to her, but reserve some minute detail to your own judgement, she will think that you are displaying a great want of faith in her, and will stir up strife; and unless you quickly take counsel, she will prepare poison for you, and consult seers and soothsayers; and will become a witch.

But as to domination by women, hear what Cicero says in the *Paradoxes*. Can he be called a free man whose wife governs him, imposes laws on him, orders him, and forbids him to do what he wishes, so that he cannot and dare not deny her anything that she asks? I should call him not only a slave, but the vilest of slaves, even if he comes of the noblest family. And Seneca, in the character of the raging Medea, says: Why do you cease to follow your happy impulse; how great is that part of vengeance in which you rejoice? Where he adduces many proofs that a woman will not be governed, but will follow her own impulse even to her own destruction. In the same way we read of many women who have killed themselves either for love or sorrow because they were unable to work their vengeance.

S. Jerome, writing of Daniel, tells a story of Laodice, wife of Antiochus king of Syria; how, being jealous lest he should love his other wife, Berenice, more than her, she first caused Berenice and her daughter by Antiochus to be slain, and then poisoned herself. And why? Because she would not be governed, but would follow her own impulse. Therefore S. John Chrysostom says not without reason: O evil worse than all evil, a wicked woman, whether she be poor or rich. For if she be the wife of a rich man, she does not cease night and day to excite her husband with hot words, to use evil blandishments and violent importunations. And if she have a poor husband she does not cease to stir him also to anger and strife. And if she be a widow, she takes it upon herself everywhere to look down on everybody, and is inflamed to all boldness by the spirit of pride.

If we inquire, we find that nearly all the kingdoms of the world have been overthrown by women. Troy, which was a prosperous kingdom, was, for the rape of one woman, Helen, destroyed, and many thousands of Greeks slain. The kingdom of the Jews suffered much misfortune and

Figure 24. The Jaws of Hell.

The great sea-monster Leviathan, mentioned in the Book of Job, became for medieval biblical commentators a symbol of Satan and the model for the jaws of Hell. These monstrous jaws were frequently depicted in manuscript illuminations and became one of the most frequently used stage-sets for medieval morality plays.

destruction through the accursed Jezebel, and her daughter Athaliah, queen of Judah, who caused her son's sons to be killed, that on their death she might reign herself; yet each of them was slain. The kingdom of the Romans endured much evil through Cleopatra, Queen of Egypt, that worst of women. And so with others. Therefore it is no wonder if the world now suffers through the malice of women.

And now let us examine the carnal desires of the body itself, whence has arisen unconscionable harm to human life. Justly may we say with Cato of Utica: If the world could be rid of women, we should not be without God in our intercourse. For truly, without the wickedness of women, to say nothing of witchcraft, the world would still remain proof against innumerable dangers. Hear what Valerius said to Rufinus: You do not know that woman is the Chimaera, but it is good that you should know it; for that monster was of three forms; its face was that of a radiant and noble lion, it had the filthy belly of a goat, and it was armed with the virulent tail of a viper. And he means that a woman is beautiful to look upon, contaminating to the touch, and deadly to keep.

Let us consider another property of hers, the voice. For as she is a liar by nature, so in her speech she stings while she delights us. Wherefore her voice is like the song of the Sirens, who with their sweet melody entice the passers-by and kill them. For they kill them by emptying their purses, consuming their strength, and causing them to forsake God. Again Valerius says to Rufinus: When she speaks it is a delight which flavours the sin; the flower of love is a rose, because under its blossom there are hidden many thorns. See *Proverbs* v, 3–4: Her mouth is smoother than oil; that is, her speech is afterwards as bitter as absinthium. [Her throat is smoother than oil. But her end is as bitter as wormwood.]

Let us consider also her gait, posture, and habit, in which is vanity of vanities. There is no man in the world who studies so hard to please the good God as even an ordinary woman studies by her vanities to please men. An example of this is to be found in the life of Pelagia, a worldly woman who was wont to go about Antioch tired and adorned most extravagantly. A holy father, named Nonnus, saw her and began to weep, saying to his companions, that never in all his life had he used such diligence to please God; and much more he added to this effect, which is preserved in his orations.

It is this which is lamented in *Ecclesiastes* vii, and which the Church even now laments on account of the great multitude of witches. And I have found a woman more bitter than death, who is the hunter's snare, and her heart is a net, and her hands are bands. He that pleaseth God shall escape from her; but he that is a sinner shall be caught by her. More bitter than death, that is, than the devil: *Apocalypse* vi, 8, His name was Death. For though the devil tempted Eve to sin, yet Eve seduced Adam. And as the sin of Eve would not have brought death to our soul and body unless the sin had afterwards passed on to Adam, to which he was tempted by Eve, not by the devil, therefore she is more bitter than death.

More bitter than death, again, because that is natural and destroys only the body; but the sin which arose from woman destroys the soul by depriving it of grace, and delivers the body up to the punishment for sin.

More bitter than death, again, because bodily death is an open and terrible enemy, but woman is a wheedling and secret enemy.

And that she is more perilous than a snare does not speak of the snare of hunters, but of devils. For men are caught not only through their carnal desires, when they see and hear women: for S. Bernard says: Their face is a burning wind, and their voice the hissing of serpents: but they also cast wicked spells on countless men and animals. And when it is said that her heart is a net, it speaks of the inscrutable malice which reigns in their hearts. And her hands are as bands for binding; for when they place their hands on a creature to bewitch it, then with the help of the devil they perform their design.

To conclude. All witchcraft comes from carnal lust, which is in women insatiable. See *Proverbs* xxx: There are three things that are never satisfied, yea, a fourth thing which says not, It is enough; that is, the mouth of the womb. Wherefore for the sake of fulfilling their lusts they consort even with devils. More such reasons could be brought forward, but to the understanding it is sufficiently clear that it is no matter for wonder that there are more women than men found infected with the heresy of witchcraft. And in consequence of this, it is better called the heresy of witches than of wizards, since the name is taken from the more powerful party. And blessed be the Highest Who has so far preserved the male sex from so great a crime: for since He was willing to be born and to suffer for us, therefore He has granted to men this privilege.

That Witches who are Midwives in Various
Ways Kill the Child Conceived in the Womb,
and Procure an Abortion; or if they do not this
Offer New-born Children to Devils.

Figure 25. The Model of Salvation.

This illumination from a thirteenth-century Psalter presents a dramatically schematized conception of salvation and damnation. Note the tonsures and crowns among the damned, reminding humans that earthly status is no bar to damnation, and the jaws of Hell.

128

Here is set forth the truth concerning four horrible crimes which devils commit against infants, both in the mother's womb and afterwards. And since the devils do these things through the medium of women, and not men, this form of homicide is associated rather with women than with men. And the following are the methods by which it is done.

The Canonists treat more fully than the Theologians of the obstructions due to witchcraft; and they say that it is witchcraft, not only when anyone is unable to perform the carnal act, of which we have spoken above; but also when a woman is prevented from conceiving, or is made to miscarry after she has conceived. A third and fourth method of witchcraft is when they have failed to procure an abortion, and then either devour the child or offer it to a devil.

There is no doubt concerning the first two methods, since, without the help of devils, a man can by natural means, such as herbs, savin for example, or other emmenagogues, procure that a woman cannot generate or conceive, as has been mentioned above. But with the other two methods it is different; for they are effected by witches. And there is no need to bring forward the arguments, since very evident instances and examples will more readily show the truth of this matter.

The former of these two abominations is the fact that certain witches, against the instinct of human nature, and indeed against the nature of all beasts, with the possible exception of wolves, are in the habit of devouring and eating infant children. And concerning this, the Inquisitor of Como, who has been mentioned before, has told us the following: that he was summoned by the inhabitants of the County of Barby to hold an inquisition, because a certain man had missed his child from its cradle, and finding a congress of women in the night-time, swore that he saw them kill his child and drink its blood and devour it. Also, in one single year, which is the year now last passed, he says that forty-one witches were burned, certain others taking flight to the Lord Archduke of Austria, Sigismund. For confirmation of this there are certain writings of John Nider in his *Formicarius*, of whom, as of those events which he recounts, the memory is still fresh in men's minds; wherefore it is apparent that such things are not incredible. We must add that in all these matters witch midwives cause yet greater injuries, as penitent witches have often told to us and to others, saying: No one does more harm to the Catholic Faith than midwives. For when they do not kill children, then, as if for some other purpose, they take them out of the room and, raising them up in the air, offer them to devils. But the method which they observe in crimes of this sort will be shown in the Second Part, which we must soon approach. But first one more question must be inquired into, namely, that of the Divine permission. For it was said at the beginning that three things are necessary for the effecting of witchcraft: the devil, a witch, and the Divine permission.

Of the Way whereby a Formal Pact with Evil is made.

The method by which they profess their sacrilege through an open pact of fidelity to devils varies according to the several practices to which different witches are addicted. And to understand this it first must be noted that there are, as was shown in the First Part of this treatise, three kinds of witches; namely, those who injure but cannot cure; those who cure but, through some strange pact with the devil, cannot injure; and those who both injure and cure. And among those who injure, one class in particular stands out, which can perform every sort of witchcraft and spell, comprehending all that all the others individually can do. Wherefore, if we describe the method of profession in their case, it will suffice also for all the other kinds. And this class is made up of those who, against every instinct of human or animal nature, are in the habit of eating and devouring the children of their own species.

And this is the most powerful class of witches, who practise innumerable other harms also. For they raise hailstorms and hurtful tempests and lightnings; cause sterility in men and animals; offer to devils, or otherwise kill, the children whom they do not devour. But these are only the children who have not been re-born by baptism at the font, for they cannot devour those who have been baptized, nor any without God's permission. They can also, before the eyes of their parents, and when no one is in sight, throw into the water children walking by the water side; they make horses go mad under their riders; they can transport themselves from place to place through the air, either in body or in imagination; they can affect Judges and Magistrates so that they cannot hurt them; they can cause themselves and others to keep silence under torture; they can bring about a great trembling in the hands and horror in the minds of those who would arrest them; they can show to others occult things and certain future events, by the information of devils, though this may sometimes have a natural cause (see the question: *Whether devils can foretell the future*, in the *Second Book of Sentences*); they can see absent things as if they were present; they can

Figure 26.   The Torments of the Damned.
The torments of the damned remained a vivid inspirational source to artists until well into the sixteenth century. This fifteenth-century painting by the Netherlands artist Terry Bouts (1420–75) depicts these torments in as vivid detail as that of the sculptural scenes at Conques, three hundred years earlier.

turn the minds of men to inordinate love or hatred; they can at times strike whom they will with lightning, and even kill some men and animals; they can make of no effect the generative desires, and even the power of copulation, cause abortion, kill infants in the mother's womb by a mere exterior touch; they can at times bewitch men and animals with a mere look, without touching them, and cause death; they dedicate their own children to devils; and in short, as has been said, they can cause all the plagues which other witches can only cause in part, that is, when the Justice of God permits such things to be. All these things this most powerful of all classes of witches can do, but they cannot undo them.

But it is common to all of them to practise carnal copulation with devils; therefore, if we show the method used by this chief class in their profession of their sacrilege, anyone may easily understand the method of the other classes.

There were such witches lately, thirty years ago, in the district of Savoy, towards the State of Berne, as Nider tells in his *Formicarius*. And there are now some in the country of Lombardy, in the domains of the Duke of Austria, where the Inquisitor of Como, as we told in the former Part, caused forty-one witches to be burned in one year; and he was fifty-five years old, and still continues to labour in the Inquisition.

Now the method of profession is twofold. One is a solemn ceremony, like a solemn vow. The other is private, and can be made to the devil at any hour alone. The first method is when witches meet together in conclave on a set day, and the devil appears to them in the assumed body of a man, and urges them to keep faith with him, promising them worldly prosperity and length of life; and they recommend a novice to his acceptance. And the devil asks whether she will abjure the Faith, and forsake the holy Christian religion and the worship of the Anomalous Woman (for so they call the Most Blessed Virgin Mary), and never venerate the Sacraments; and if he finds the novice or disciple willing, then the devil stretches out his hand, and so does the novice, and she swears with upraised hand to keep that covenant. And when this is done, the devil at once adds that this is not enough; and when the disciple asks what more must be done, the devil demands the following oath of homage to himself: that she give herself to him, body and soul, for ever, and do her utmost to bring others of both sexes into his power. He adds, finally, that she is to make certain unguents from the bones and limbs of children, especially those who have been baptized; by all which means she will be able to fulfil all her wishes with his help.

We Inquisitors had credible experience of this method in the town of Breisach in the diocese of Basel, receiving full information from a young girl witch who had been converted, whose aunt also had been burned in the diocese of Strasburg. And she added that she had become a witch by the method in which her aunt had first tried to seduce her.

For one day her aunt ordered her to go upstairs with her, and at her command to go into a room where she found fifteen young men clothed in green garments after the manner of German knights. And her aunt said to her: Choose whom you wish from these young men, and I will give him to you, and he will take you for his wife. And when she said she did not wish for any of them, she was sorely beaten and at last consented, and was initiated according to the aforesaid ceremony. She said also that she was often transported by night with her aunt over vast distances, even from Strasburg to Cologne.

This is she who occasioned our inquiry in the First Part into the question whether witches are truly and bodily transported by devils from place to place: and this was on account of the words of the Canon (6, q. 5, *Episcopi*), which seem to imply that they are only so carried in imagination; whereas they are at times actually and bodily transported.

For when she was asked whether it was only in imagination and phantastically that they so rode, through an illusion of devils, she answered that they did so in both ways; according to the truth which we shall declare later of the manner in which they are transferred from place to place. She said also that the greatest injuries were inflicted by midwives, because they were under an obligation to kill or offer to devils as many children as possible; and that she had been severely beaten by her aunt because she had opened a secret pot and found the heads of a great many children. And much more she told us, having first, as was proper, taken an oath to speak the truth.

And her account of the method of professing the devil's faith undoubtedly agrees with what has been written by that most eminent Doctor, John Nider, who even in our times has written very illuminatingly; and it may be especially remarked that he tells us the following, which he had from an Inquisitor of the diocese of Edua, who held many inquisitions on witches in that diocese, and caused many to be burned.

For he says that this Inquisitor told him that in the Duchy of Lausanne certain witches had cooked and eaten their own children, and that the following was the method in which they became initiated into such practices. The witches met together and, by their art, summoned a devil in the form of a man, to whom the novice was compelled to swear to deny the Christian religion, never to adore the Eucharist, and to tread the Cross underfoot whenever she could do so secretly.

Here is another example from the same source. There was lately a general report, brought to the notice of Peter the Judge in Boltingen, that thirteen infants had been devoured in the State of Berne; and public justice exacted full vengeance on the murderers. And when Peter asked one of the captive witches in what manner they ate children, she replied: "This is the manner of it. We set our snares chiefly for unbaptized children, and even for those that have been baptized, especially when they have not been protected by the sign of the Cross and prayers" (reader, notice that, at the devil's command, they take the unbaptized chiefly, in order that they may not be baptized), "and with our spells we kill them in their cradles or even when they are sleeping by their parents' side, in such a way that they afterwards are thought to have been overlain or to have died some other natural death. Then we secretly take them from their graves, and cook them in a cauldron, until the whole flesh comes away from the bones to make a soup which may easily be drunk. Of the more solid matter we make an unguent which is of virtue to help us in our arts and pleasures and our transportations; and with the liquid we fill a flask or skin, whoever drinks from which, with the addition of a few other ceremonies, immediately acquires much knowledge and becomes a leader in our sect."

Here is another very clear and distinct example. A young man and his wife, both witches, were imprisoned in Berne; and the man, shut up by himself apart from her in a separate tower, said: "If I could obtain pardon for my sins, I would willingly declare all that I know about witchcraft; for I see that I ought to die." And when he was told by the learned clerks who were there that he could obtain complete pardon if he truly repented, he joyfully resigned himself to death, and laid bare the method by which he had first been infected with his heresy. "The following," he said, "is the manner in which I was seduced. It is first necessary that, on a Sunday before the consecration of Holy Water, the novice should enter the church with the masters, and there in their presence deny Christ, his Faith, baptism, and the whole Church. And then he must pay homage to the Little Master, for so and not otherwise do they call the devil." Here it is to be noted that this method agrees with those that have been recounted; for it is immaterial whether the devil is himself present or not, when homage is offered to him.

Figure 27. Pope
Innocent VIII.
Author of the bull
*Summis desider-
antes* (IV.18.). The
text in this eigh-
teenth-century
German engraving
reads: "Innocent
VIII. The Pope of
Rome, the man who
raised up the witch
trials in Germany."

135

For this he does in his cunning, perceiving the temperament of the novice, who might be frightened by his actual presence into retracting his vows, whereas he would be more easily persuaded to consent by those who are known to him. And therefore they call him the Little Master when he is absent, that through seeming disparagement of his Master the novice may feel less fear. "And then he drinks from the skin, which has been mentioned, and immediately feels within himself a knowledge of all our arts and an understanding of our rites and ceremonies. And in this manner was I seduced. But I believe my wife to be so obstinate that she would rather go straight to the fire than confess the smallest part of the truth; but, alas! we are both guilty." And as the young man said, so it happened in every respect. For the young man confessed and was seen to die in the greatest contrition; but the wife, though convicted by witnesses, would not confess any of the truth, either under torture or in death itself; but when the fire had been prepared by the gaoler, cursed him in the most terrible words, and so was burned. And from these examples their method of initiation in solemn conclave is made clear.

The other private method is variously performed. For sometimes when men or women have been involved in some bodily or temporal affliction, the devil comes to them, at times in person, and at times speaking to them through the mouth of someone else; and he promises that, if they will agree to his counsels, he will do for them whatever they wish. But he starts from small things, as was said in the first chapter, and leads gradually to the bigger things. We could mention many examples which have come to our knowledge in the Inquisition, but, since this matter presents no difficulty, it can briefly be included with the previous matter.

Here follows the Way whereby Witches copulate with those Devils known as Incubi.

As to the method in which witches copulate with Incubus devils, six points are to be noted. First, as to the devil and the body which he assumes, of what element it is formed. Second, as to the act, whether it is always accompanied with the injection of semen received from some other man. Third, as to the time and place, whether one time is more favourable than another for this practice. Fourth, whether the act is visible to the women, and whether only those who were begotten in this way are so visited by devils. Fifth, whether it applies only to those who were offered to the devil at birth by midwives. Sixth, whether the actual venereal pleasure is greater or less in this act. And we will speak first of the matter and quality of the body which the devil assumes.

It must be said that he assumes an aerial body, and that it is in some respects terrestrial, in so far as it has an earthly property through condensation; and this is explained as follows. The air cannot of itself take definite shape, except the shape of some other body in which it is included. And in that case it is not bound by its own limits, but by those of something else; and one part of the air continues into the next part. Therefore he cannot simply assume an aerial body as such.

Know, moreover, that the air is in every way a most changeable and fluid matter: and a sign of this is the fact that when any have tried to cut or pierce with a sword the body assumed by a devil, they have not been able to; for the divided parts of the air at once join together again. From this it follows that air is in itself a very competent matter, but because it cannot take shape unless some other terrestrial matter is joined with it, therefore it is necessary that the air which forms the devil's assumed body should be in some way inspissated, and approach the property of the earth, while still retaining its true property as air. And devils and disembodied spirits can effect this condensation by means of gross vapours raised from the earth, and by collecting them together into shapes in which they abide, not as defilers of them, but only as their motive power which gives to that body the formal appearance of life, in very much the same way as the soul informs the body to which it is joined. They are, moreover, in these assumed and shaped bodies like a sailor in a ship which the wind moves.

So when it is asked of what sort is the body assumed by the devil, it is to be said that with regard to its material, it is one thing to speak of the beginning of its assumption, and another thing to speak of its end. For in the beginning it is just air; but in the end it is inspissated air, partaking of some of the properties of earth. And all this the devils, with God's permission, can do of their own nature; for the spiritual nature is superior to the bodily. Therefore the bodily nature must obey the devils in respect of local motion, though not in respect of the assumption of natural shapes, either accidental or substantial, except in the case of some small creatures (and then only with the help of some other agent, as has been hinted before). But as to local motion, no shape is beyond their power; thus they can move them as they wish, in such circumstances as they will.

From this there may arise an incidental question as to what should be thought when a good or bad Angel performs some of the functions of life

Figure 28. Invoking the Devil: The Magic Circle.

This seventeenth-century engraving is a most ornate and detailed depiction of the magician invoking a demon from the protective circle, in this case one marked by burning candles. The elements of the circle, as may be seen in the following two illustrations, illustrate a commonly held belief. See the scene described by Caesarius of Heisterbach, above, I.4.

Figure 29. The Seventeenth-Century Circle.

This engraving is much simpler in detail than the preceding one, although the figure of the old woman and the grotesque demon are generically similar to those in Figure 28.

138

by means of true natural bodies, and not in aerial bodies; as in the case of Balaam's ass, through which the Angel spoke, and when devils take possession of bodies. It is to be said that those bodies are not called assumed, but occupied. See S. Thomas, II. 8, Whether Angels assume bodies. But let us keep strictly to our argument.

In what way is it to be understood that devils talk with witches, see them, hear them, eat with them, and copulate with them? And this is the second part of this first difficulty.

For the first, it is to be said that three things are required for true conversation: namely, lungs to draw in the air; and this is not only for the sake of producing sound; but also to cool the heart; and even mutes have this necessary quality.

Secondly, it is necessary that some percussion be made of a body in the air, as a greater or less sound is made when one beats wood in the air, or rings a bell. For when a substance that is susceptible to sound is struck by a sound-producing instrument, it gives out a sound according to its size, which is received in the air and multiplied to the ears of the hearer, to whom, if he is far off, it seems to come through space.

Thirdly, a voice is required; and it may be said that what is called Sound in inanimate bodies is called Voice in living bodies. And here the tongue strikes the respirations of air against an instrument or living natural organ provided by God. And this is not a bell, which is called a sound, whereas this is a voice. And this third requisite may clearly be exemplified by the second; and I have set this down that preachers may have a method of teaching the people.

And fourthly, it is necessary that he who forms the voice should mean to express by means of that voice some concept of the mind to someone else, and that he should himself understand what he is saying; and so manage his voice by successively striking his teeth with his tongue in his mouth, by opening and shutting his lips, and by sending the air struck in his mouth into the outer air, that in this way the sound is reproduced in order in the ears of the hearer, who then understands his meaning.

To return to the point. Devils have no lungs or tongue, though they can show the latter, as well as teeth and lips, artificially made according to the condition of their body; therefore they cannot truly and properly speak. But since they have understanding, and when they wish to express their meaning, then, by some disturbance of the air included in their assumed body, not of air breathed in and out as in the case of men, they produce, not voices, but sounds which have some likeness to voices, and send them articulately through the outside air to the ears of the hearer. And that the likeness of a voice can be made without the respiration of air is clear from the case of other animals which do not breathe, but are said to make a sound, as do also certain other instruments, as Aristotle says in the *de Anima*. For certain fishes, when they are caught, suddenly utter a cry outside the water, and die.

All this is applicable to what follows, so far as the point where we treat of the generative function, but not as regards good Angels. If anyone wishes to inquire further into the matter of devils speaking in possessed bodies, he may refer to S. Thomas in the *Second Book of Sentences*, dist. 8, art. 5. For in that case they use the bodily organs of the possessed body; since they occupy those bodies in respect of the limits of their corporeal quantity, but not in respect of the limits of their essence, either of the body or of the soul. Observe a distinction between substance and quantity, or accident. But this is impertinent.

For now we must say in what manner they see and hear. Now sight is of two kinds, spiritual and corporeal, and the former infinitely excels the latter; for it can penetrate, and is not hindered by distance, owing to the faculty of light of which it makes use. Therefore it must be said that in no way does an Angel, either good or bad, see with the eyes of its assumed body, nor does it use any bodily property as it does in speaking, when it uses the air and the vibration of the air to produce sound which becomes reproduced in the ears of the hearer. Wherefore their eyes are painted eyes. And they freely appear to men in these likenesses that they may manifest to them their natural properties and converse with them spiritually by these means.

For with this purpose the holy Angels have often appeared to the Fathers at the command of God and with His permission. And the bad angels manifest themselves to wicked men in order that men, recognizing their qualities, may associate themselves with them, here in sin, and elsewhere in punishment.

S. Dionysius, at the end of his *Celestial Hierarchy*, says: In all parts of the human body the Angel teaches us to consider their properties: concluding that since corporeal vision is an operation of the living body through a bodily organ, which devils lack, therefore in their assumed bodies, just as they have the likeness of limbs, so they have the likeness of their functions.

And we can speak in the same way of their hearing, which is far finer than that of the body; for it can know the concept of the mind and the conversation of the soul more subtly than can a man by hearing the mental concept through the medium of spoken words. See S. Thomas, the *Second Book of Sentences*, dist. 8. For if the secret wishes of a man are read in his face, and physicians can tell the thoughts of the heart from the heart-beats and the state of the pulse, all the more can such things be known by devils.

And we may say as to eating, that in the complete act of eating there are four processes. Mastication in the mouth, swallowing into the stomach, digestion in the stomach, and fourthly, metabolism of the necessary nutriment and ejection of what is superfluous. All Angels can perform the first two processes of eating in their assumed bodies, but not the third and fourth; but instead of digesting and ejecting they have another power by which the food is suddenly dissolved in the surrounding matter. In Christ the process of eating was in all respects complete, since He had the nutritive and metabolistic powers; not, be it said, for the purpose of converting the food into His own body, for those powers were, like His body, glorified; so that the food was suddenly dissolved in His body, as when one throws water on to fire.

How in Modern Times Witches perform the Carnal Act with Incubus Devils, and how they are Multiplied by this Means.

But no difficulty arises out of what has been said, with regard to our principal subject, which is the carnal act which Incubi in an assumed body perform with witches: unless perhaps anyone doubts whether modern witches practise such abominable coitus; and whether witches had their origin in this abomination.

In answering these two doubts we shall say, as to the former of them, something of the activities of the witches who lived in olden times, about 1400 years before the Incarnation of Our Lord. It is, for example, unknown whether they were addicted to these filthy practices as modern witches have been since that time; for so far as we know history tells us nothing on this subject. But no one who reads the histories can doubt that there have always been witches, and that by their evil works much harm has been done to men, animals, and the fruits of the earth, and that Incubus and Succubus devils have always existed; for the traditions of the Canons and the holy Doctors have left and handed down to posterity many things concerning them through many hundreds of years. Yet there is this difference, that in times long past the Incubus devils used to infest women against their wills; as is often shown by Nider in his *Formicarius,* and by Thomas of Brabant in his book on the *Universal Good,* or on *Bees.*

But the theory that modern witches are tainted with this sort of diabolic filthiness is not substantiated only in our opinion, since the expert testimony of the witches themselves has made all these things credible; and that they do not now, as in times past, subject themselves unwillingly, but willingly embrace this most foul and miserable servitude. For how many women have we left to be punished by secular law in various dioceses, especially in Constance and the town of Ratisbon, who have been for many years addicted to these abominations, some from their twentieth and some from their twelfth or thirteenth year, and always with a total or partial abnegation of the Faith? All the inhabitants of those places are witnesses of it. For without reckoning those who secretly repented, and those who returned to the Faith, no less than forty-eight have been burned in five years. And there was no question of credulity in accepting their stories because they turned to free repentance; for they all agreed in this, namely, that they were bound to indulge in these lewd practices in order that the ranks of their perfidy might be increased. But we shall treat of these individually in the Second Part of this work, where their particular deeds are described; omitting those which came under the notice of our colleague the Inquisitor of Como in the County of Burbia, who in the space of one year, which was the year of grace 1485, caused forty-one witches to be burned; who all publicly affirmed, as it is said, that they had practised these abominations with devils. Therefore this matter is fully substantiated by eye-witnesses, by hearsay, and the testimony of credible witnesses.

As for the second doubt, whether witches had their origin from these abominations, we may say with S. Augustine that it is true that all the superstitious arts had their origin in a pestilent association of men with devils. For he says so in his work *On the Christian Doctrine:* All this sort of practices, whether of trifling or of noxious superstition, arose from some pestilent association of men with devils, as though some pact of infidel and guileful friendship had been formed, and they are all utterly to be repudiated. Notice here that it is manifest that, as there are various kinds of superstition or magic arts, and various societies of those who practise them; and as among the fourteen kinds of that art the species of witches is the worst, since they have not a tacit but an overt and expressed pact with the devil, and more than this, have to acknowledge a form of devil-worship through abjuring

Figure 30. The Seventeenth-Century Circle.

This early seventeenth-century woodcut, from Guazzo's *Compendium Maleficarum*, depicts a number of witches of both sexes invoking the demon from the circle.

the Faith; therefore it follows that witches hold the worst kind of association with devils, with especial reference to the behaviour of women, who always delight in vain things.

Notice also S. Thomas, the *Second Book of Sentences* (dist. 4, art. 4), in the solution of an argument, where he asks whether those begotten in this way by devils are more powerful than other men. He answers that this is the truth, basing his belief not only on the text of Scripture in *Genesis* vi: And the same became the mighty men which were of old; but also on the following reason. Devils know how to ascertain the virtue in semen: first, by the temperament of him from whom the semen is obtained; secondly, by knowing what woman is most fitted for the reception of that semen; thirdly, by knowing what constellation is favourable to that corporeal effect; and we may add, fourthly, from their own words we learn that those whom they beget have the best sort of disposition for devils' work. When all these causes so concur, it is concluded that men born in this way are powerful and big in body.

Therefore, to return to the question whether witches had their origin in these abominations, we shall say that they originated from some pestilent mutual association with devils, as is clear from our first knowledge of them. But no one can affirm with certainty that they did not increase and multiply by means of these foul practices, although devils commit this deed for the sake not of pleasure but of corruption. And this appears to be the order of the process. A Succubus devil draws the semen from a wicked man; and if he is that man's own particular devil, and does not wish to make himself an Incubus to a witch, he passes that semen on to the devil deputed to a woman or witch; and this last, under some constellation that favours his purpose that the man or woman so born should be strong in the practice of witchcraft, becomes the Incubus to the witch.

And it is no objection that those of whom the text speaks were not witches but only giants and famous and powerful men; for, as was said before, witchcraft was not perpetrated in the time of the law of Nature, because of the recent memory of the Creation of the world, which left no room for Idolatry. But when the wickedness of man began to increase, the devil found more opportunity to disseminate this kind of perfidy. Nevertheless, it is not to be understood that those who were said to be famous men were necessarily so called by reason of their good virtues.

Whether the Relations of an Incubus Devil with a Witch are always accompanied by the Injection of Semen.

To this question it is answered that the devil has a thousand ways and means of inflicting injury, and from the time of his first Fall has tried to destroy the unity of the Church, and in every way to subvert the human race. Therefore no infallible rule can be stated as to this matter, but there is this probable distinction: that a witch is either old and sterile, or she is not. And if she is, then he naturally associates with the witch without the injection of semen, since it would be of no use, and the devil avoids superfluity in his operations as far as he can. But if she is not sterile, he approaches her in the way of carnal delectation which is procured for the witch. And should she be disposed to pregnancy, then if he can conveniently possess the semen extracted from some man, he does not delay to approach her with it for the sake of infecting her progeny.

But if it is asked whether he is able to collect the semen emitted in some nocturnal pollution in sleep, just as he collects that which is spent in the carnal act, the answer is that it is probable that he cannot, though others hold a contrary opinion. For it must be noted that, as has been said, the devils pay attention to the generative virtue of the semen, and such virtue is more abundant and better preserved in semen obtained by the carnal act, being wasted in the semen that is due to nocturnal pollutions in sleep, which arises only from the superfluity of the humours and is not emitted with so great generative virtue. Therefore it is believed that he does not make use of such semen for the generation of progeny, unless perhaps he knows that the necessary virtue is present in that semen.

But this also cannot altogether be denied, that even in the case of a married witch who has been impregnated by her husband, the devil can, by the commixture of another semen, infect that which has been conceived.

How, as it were, they Deprive Man of his Virile Member.

We have already shown that they can take away the male organ, not indeed by actually despoiling the human body of it, but by concealing it with some glamour, in the manner which we have already declared. And of this we shall instance a few examples.

In the town of Ratisbon a certain young man who had an intrigue with a girl, wishing to leave her, lost his member; that is to say, some glamour was cast over it so that he could see or touch nothing but his smooth body. In his worry over this he went to a tavern to drink wine; and after he had sat there for a while he got into conversation with another woman who was there, and told her the cause of his sadness, explaining everything, and demonstrating in his body that it was so. The woman was astute, and asked whether he suspected anyone; and when he named such a one, unfolding the whole matter, she said: "If persuasion is not enough, you must use some violence, to induce her to restore to you your health." So in the evening the young man watched the way by which the witch was in the habit of going, and finding her, prayed her to restore to him the health of his body. And when she maintained that she was innocent and knew nothing about it, he fell upon her, and winding a towel tightly round her neck, choked her, saying: "Unless you give me back my health, you shall die at my hands." The she, being unable to cry out, and with her face already swelling and growing black, said: "Let me go, and I will heal you." The young man then relaxed the pressure of the towel, and the witch touched him with her hand between the thighs, saying: "Now you have what you desire." And the young man, as he afterwards said, plainly felt, before he had verified it by looking or touching, that his member had been restored to him by the mere touch of the witch.

A similar experience is narrated by a certain venerable Father from the Dominican House of Spires, well known in the Order for the honesty of his life and for his learning. "One day," he says, "while I was hearing confessions, a young man came to me and, in the course of his confession, woefully said that he had lost his member. Being astonished at this, and not being willing to give it easy credence, since in the opinion of the wise it is a mark of light-heartedness to believe too easily, I obtained proof of it when I saw nothing on the young man's removing his clothes and showing the place. Then, using the wisest counsel I could, I asked whether he suspected anyone of having so bewitched him. And the young man said that he did suspect someone, but that she was absent and living in Worms. Then I said: 'I advise you to go to her as soon as possible and try your utmost to soften her with gentle words and promises'; and he did so. For he came back after a few days and thanked me, saying that he was whole and had recovered everything. And I believed his words, but again proved them by the evidence of my eyes."

But there are some points to be noted for the clearer understanding of what has already been written concerning this matter. First, it must in no way be believed that such members are really torn right away from the body, but that they are hidden by the devil through some prestidigitatory art so that they can be neither seen nor felt. And this is proved by the authorities and by argument; although it has been treated of before, where Alexander of Hales says that a Prestige, properly understood, is an illusion of the devil, which is not caused by any material change, but exists only in the perceptions of him who is deluded, either in his interior or exterior senses.

With reference to these words it is to be noted that, in the case we are considering, two of the exterior senses, namely, those of sight and touch, are deluded, and not the interior senses, namely, common-sense, fancy, imagination, thought, and memory. (But S. Thomas says they are only four, as has been told before, reckoning fancy and imagination as one; and with some reason, for there is little difference between imagining and fancying. See S. Thomas, I, 79.) And these senses, and not only the exterior senses, are affected when it is not a case of hiding something, but of causing something to appear to a man either when he is awake or asleep.

As when a man who is awake sees things otherwise than as they are; such as seeing someone devour a horse with its rider, or thinking he sees a man transformed into a beast, or thinking that he is himself a beast and must associate with beasts. For then the exterior senses are deluded and are employed by the interior senses. For by the power of devils, with God's permission, mental images long retained in the treasury of such images, which is the memory, are drawn out, not from the intellectual understanding in which such images are stored, but from the memory, which is the repository of mental images, and is situated at the back of the head, and are presented to the imaginative faculty. And so strongly are they impressed on that faculty that a man has an inevitable impulse to imagine a horse or a beast, when the devil draws from the memory an image of a horse or a beast; and so he is compelled to think that he sees with his external eyes such a beast when there is actually no such beast to see; but it seems to be so by reason of the impulsive force of the devil working by means of those images.

And it need not seem wonderful that devils can do this, when even a natural defect is able to effect the same result, as is shown in the case of frantic and melancholy men, and in maniacs and some drunkards, who are unable to discern truly. For frantic men think they see marvellous things, such as beasts and other horrors, when in actual fact they see nothing. See above, in the question, Whether witches can turn the minds of men to love and hatred; where many things are noted.

And, finally, the reason is self-evident. For since the devil has power over inferior things, except only the soul, therefore he is able to effect certain changes in those things, when God allows, so that things appear to be otherwise than they are. And this he does, as I have said, either by confusing and deluding the organ of sight so that a clear thing appears cloudy: just as after weeping, owing to the collected humours, the light appears different from what it was before. Or by operating on the imaginative faculty by a transmutation of mental images, as has been said. Or by some agitation of various humours, so that matters which are earthy and dry seem to be fire or water: as some people make everyone in the house strip themselves naked under the impression that they are swimming in water.

It may be asked further with reference to the above method of devils, whether this sort of illusions can happen indifferently to the good and to the wicked: just as other bodily infirmities can, as will be shown later, be brought by witches even upon those who are in a state of grace. To this question, following the words of Cassian in his *Second Collation* of the Abbot Sirenus, we must answer that they cannot. And from this it follows that all who are deluded in this way are presumed to be in deadly sin. For he says, as is clear from the words of S. Antony: The devil can in no way enter the mind or body of any man, nor has the power to penetrate into the thoughts of anybody, unless such a person has first become destitute of all holy thoughts, and is quite bereft and denuded of spiritual contemplation.

Figures 31–38.
The Creation of Witches.

Figure 31. The Devil's Court.

The enthroned demon in this illustration from Guazzo's *Compendium Maleficarum* receives the homage of those who have given themselves to him. Giving homage was not only necessary to bind a witch to his or her master, but had been recognized by theologians and inquisitors as constituting the offense of *dulia*, a heresy when offered to demons, thus bringing witches under the jurisdiction of the Inquisition. See the description of Nicholas Eymeric (III.14) in the text above.

Figure 32. Baptizing a Witch.

The theological and liturgical framework of witch beliefs insisted that the agreements which bound a witch to Satan were a perversion of those rites which bound a soul to God—hence the frequent mention of perverted sacraments and offenses committed upon religious objects. The ritual perversion of Baptism was widely believed of witches from the fourteenth to the eighteenth centuries. This illustration is from Guazzo's *Compendium Maleficarum*, but see the fourteenth- and fifteenth-century references in III.12, 13, and 16 above.

148

This agrees with Boethius where he says in the *Consolation of Philosophy:* We had given you such arms that, if you had not thrown them away, you would have been preserved from infirmity.

Also Cassian tells in the same place of two Pagan witches, each in his own way malicious, who by their witchcraft sent a succession of devils into the cell of S. Antony for the purpose of driving him from there by their temptations; being infected with hatred for the holy man because a great number of people visited him every day. And though these devils assailed him with the keenest of spurs to his thoughts, yet he drove them away by crossing himself on the forehead and breast, and by prostrating himself in earnest prayer.

Therefore we may say that all who are so deluded by devils, not reckoning any other bodily infirmities, are lacking in the gift of divine grace. And so it is said in *Tobias* vi: The devil has power against those who are subject to their lusts.

This is also substantiated by what we told in the First Part in the question, Whether witches can change men into the shapes of beasts. For we told of a girl who was turned into a filly, as she herself and, except S. Macharius, all who looked at her were persuaded. But the devil could not deceive the senses of the holy man; and when she was brought to him to be healed, he saw a true woman and not a horse, while on the other hand everyone else exclaimed that she seemed to be a horse. And the Saint, by his prayers, freed her and the others from that illusion, saying that this had happened to her because she had not attended sufficiently to holy things, nor used as she should Holy Confession and the Eucharist. And for this reason, because in her honesty she would not consent to the shameful proposal of a young man, he had caused a Jew who was a witch to bewitch the girl so that, by the power of the devil, he turned her into a filly.

We may summarize our conclusions as follows:—Devils can, for their profit and probation, injure the good in their fortunes, that is, in such exterior things as riches, fame, and bodily health. This is clear from the case of the Blessed Job, who was afflicted by the devil in such matters. But such injuries are not of their own causing, so that they cannot be led or driven into any sin, although they can be tempted both inwardly and outwardly in the flesh. But the devils cannot afflict the good with this sort of illusions, either actively or passively.

Not actively, by deluding their senses as they do those of others who are not in a state of grace. And not passively, by taking away their male

Figure 33. Trampling upon the Cross.
This symbolically powerful act was yet another in the series of ritual perversions of sacraments and sacramentals that witches were believed to perform. See above, III.16.

Figure 34. Tokens of Witchcraft.
The belief that the witch gave garments to the Devil as a token of submission was widespread. Sometimes, these garments were particularly enchanted and returned to the giver to cement the bond between the witch and Satan yet more fully. This illustration is from Guazzo, *Compendium Maleficarum.*

organs by some glamour. For in these two respects they could never injure Job, especially the passive injury with regard to the venereal act; for he was of such continence that he was able to say: I have vowed a vow with my eyes that I shall never think about a virgin, and still less about another man's wife. Nevertheless the devil knows that he has great power over sinners (see *S. Luke* xi: When a strong man armed keepeth his palace, his goods are in peace).

But it may be asked, as to illusions in respect of the male organ, whether, granted that the devil cannot impose this illusion on those in a state of grace in a passive way, he cannot still do so in an active sense: the argument being that the man in a state of grace is deluded because he ought to see the member in its right place, when he who thinks it has been taken away from him, as well as other bystanders, does not see it in its place; but if this is conceded, it seems to be contrary to what has been said. It can be said that there is not so much force in the active as in the passive loss; meaning by active loss, not his who bears the loss, but his who sees the loss from without, as is self-evident. Therefore, although a man in a state of grace can see the loss of another, and to that extent the devil can delude his senses; yet he cannot passively suffer such loss in his own body, as, for example, to be deprived of his member, since he is not subject to lust. In the same way the converse is true, as the Angel said to Tobias: Those who are given to lust, the devil has power over them.

And what, then, is to be thought of those witches who in this way some-times collect male organs in great numbers, as many as twenty or thirty members together, and put them in a bird's nest, or shut them up in a box, where they move themselves like living members, and eat oats and corn, as has been seen by many and is a matter of common report? It is to be said that it is all done by devil's work and illusion, for the senses of those who see them are deluded in the way we have said. For a certain man tells that, when he had lost his member, he approached a known witch to ask her to restore it to him. She told the afflicted man to climb a certain tree, and that he might take which he liked out of a nest in which there were several members. And when he tried to take a big one, the witch said: You must not take that one; adding, because it belonged to a parish priest.

All these things are caused by devils through an illusion or glamour, in the manner we have said, by confusing the organ of vision by transmuting the mental images in the imaginative faculty. And it must not be said that these members which are shown are devils in assumed members, just as they sometimes appear to witches, and men in assumed aerial bodies, and converse with them. And the reason is that they effect this thing by an easier method, namely, by drawing out an inner mental image from the repository of the memory, and impressing it on the imagination.

And if anyone wishes to say that they could go to work in a similar way, when they are said to converse with witches and other men in assumed bodies; that is, that they could cause such apparitions by changing the mental images in the imaginative faculty, so that when men thought the devils were present in assumed bodies, they were really nothing but an illusion caused by such a change of the mental images in the inner perceptions.

It is to be said that, if the devil had no other purpose than merely to show himself in human form, then there would be no need for him to appear in an assumed body, since he could effect his purpose well enough by the aforesaid illusion. But this is not so; for he has another purpose, namely, to speak and eat with them, and to commit other abominations. Therefore it is necessary that he should himself be present, placing himself actually in sight in an assumed body. For, as S. Thomas says, Where the Angel's power is, there he operates.

And it may be asked, if the devil by himself and without any witch takes away anyone's virile member, whether there is any difference between one sort of deprivation and the other. In addition to what has been said in the First Part of this work on the question, Whether witches can take away the male organ, it can be said that, when the devil by himself takes away a member, he does actually take it away, and it is actually restored when it has to be restored. Secondly, as it is not taken away without injury, so it is not without pain. Thirdly, that he never does this unless compelled by a good Angel, for by so doing he cuts off a great source of profit to him; for he knows that he can work more witchcraft on that act than on other human acts. For God permits him to do more injury to that than to other human acts, as has been said. But none of the above points apply when he works through the agency of a witch, with God's permission.

And if it is asked whether the devil is more apt to injure men and creatures by himself than through a witch, it can be said that there is no comparison between the two cases. For he is infinitely more apt to do harm through the agency of witches. First, because he thus gives greater offence to God, by usurping to himself a creature dedicated to Him. Secondly, because when God is the more offended, He allows him the more power

Figure 35. Desecrating the Dead.

The witches were frequently alleged to use the bodies of the dead in their rites. This illustration from Guazzo's *Compendium Maleficarum* indicates ritual disinterment, disemboweling, and gallows-robbing. One of the most frequently levelled charges against witches was their use of corpses (particularly those of the unbaptized or the recently dead) in sealing their pacts with Satan or working magic against others.

Figure 36. The Devils and Illness.

This picture is used by Guazzo in the *Compendium Maleficarum* to illustrate the demons' power to inflict and cure illness, although the grouping of children, young people, and adults indicates its equal value in depicting the devils' selection of witches.

of injuring men. And thirdly, for his own gain, which he places in the perdition of souls.

Introduction to Part III

Therefore in answer to the arguments, it is clear that witches and sorcerers have not necessarily to be tried by the Inquisitors. But as for the other arguments which seek to make it possible for the Bishops in their turn to be relieved from the trial of witches, and leave this to the Civil Court, it is clear that this is not so easy in their case as it is in that of the Inquisitors. For the Canon Law (c. *ad abolendam,* c. *uergentis,* and c. *excommunicamus utrumque*) says that in a case of heresy it is for the ecclesiastical judge to try and to judge, but for the secular judge to carry out the sentence and to punish; that is, when a capital punishment is in question, though it is otherwise with other penitential punishments.

It seems also that in the heresy of witches, though not in the case of other heresies, the Diocesans also can hand over to the Civil Courts the duty of trying and judging, and this for two reasons: first because, as we have mentioned in our arguments, the crime of witches is not purely ecclesiastical, being rather civil on account of the temporal injuries which they commit; and also because special laws are provided for dealing with witches.

Finally, it seems that in this way it is easiest to proceed with the extermination of witches, and that the greatest help is thus given to the Ordinary in the sight of that terrible Judge who, as the Scriptures testify, will exact the strictest account from and will most hardly judge those who have been placed in authority. Accordingly we will proceed on this understanding, namely, that the secular Judge can try and judge such cases, himself proceeding to the capital punishment, but leaving the imposition of any other penitential punishment to the Ordinary.

Whether Mortal Enemies may be Admitted as Witnesses.

But if it is asked whether the Judge can admit the mortal enemies of the prisoner to give evidence against him in such a case, we answer that he cannot; for the same chapter of the Canon says: You must not understand that in this kind of charge a mortal personal enemy may be admitted to give evidence. Henry of Segusio also makes this quite clear. But it is mortal enemies that are spoken of; and it is to be noted that a witness is not necessarily to be disqualified because of every sort of enmity. And a mortal enmity is constituted by the following circumstances: when there is a death feud or vendetta between the parties, or when there has been an attempted homicide, or some serious wound or injury which manifestly shows that there is mortal hatred on the part of the witness against the prisoner. And in such a case it is presumed that, just as the witness has tried to inflict temporal death on the prisoner by wounding him, so he will also be willing to effect his object by accusing him of heresy; and just as he wished to take away his life, so he would be willing to take away his good name. Therefore the evidence of such mortal enemies is justly disqualified.

But there are other serious degrees of enmity (for women are easily provoked to hatred), which need not totally disqualify a witness, although they render his evidence very doubtful, so that full credence cannot be placed in his words unless they are substantiated by independent proofs, and other witnesses supply an indubitable proof of them. For the Judge must ask the prisoner whether he thinks that he has any enemy who would dare to accuse him of that crime out of hatred, so that he might compass his death; and if he says that he has, he shall ask who that person is; and then the Judge shall take note whether the person named as being likely to give evidence from motives of malice has actually done so. And if it is found that this is the case, and the Judge has learned from trustworthy men the cause of that enmity, and if the evidence in question is not substantiated by other proofs and the words of other witnesses, then he may safely reject such evidence. But if the prisoner says that he hopes he has no such enemy, but admits that he has had quarrels with women; or if he says that he has

Figure 37. The Infamous Kiss.
Like the perversion of sacraments and the desecrating of the dead, the kiss on the Devil's posterior was widely held to be an essential element in the making of a witch. In many illustrations the posterior itself contains a face, and in many others, the Devil is kissed in the shape of a toad or other animal.

an enemy, but names someone who, perhaps, has not given evidence, in that case, even if other witnesses say that such a person has given evidence from motives of enmity, the Judge must not reject his evidence, but admit it together with the other proofs.

There are many who are not sufficiently careful and circumspect, and consider that the depositions of such quarrelsome women should be altogether rejected, saying that no faith can be placed in them, since they are nearly always actuated by motives of hatred. Such men are ignorant of the subtlety and precautions of magistrates, and speak and judge like men who are colour-blind. But these precautions are dealt with in Questions XI and XII.

What is to be done after the Arrest,
and whether the Names of the Witnesses
should be made Known to the Accused.
This is the Fourth Action.

There are two matters to be attended to after the arrest, but it is left to the Judge which shall be taken first; namely, the question of allowing the accused to be defended, and whether she should be examined in the place of torture, though not necessarily in order that she should be tortured. The first is only allowed when a direct request is made; the second only when her servants and companions, if she has any, have first been examined in the house.

But let us proceed in the order as above. If the accused says that she is innocent and falsely accused, and that she wishes to see and hear her accusers, then it is a sign that she is asking to defend herself. But it is an open question whether the Judge is bound to make the deponents known to her and bring them to confront her face to face. For here let the Judge take note that he is not bound either to publish the names of the deponents or to bring them before the accused, unless they themselves should freely and willingly offer to come before the accused and lay their depositions in her presence. And it is by reason of the danger incurred by the deponents that the Judge is not bound to do this. For although different Popes have had different opinions on this matter, none of them has ever said that in such a case the Judge is bound to make known to the accused the names of the informers or accusers (but here we are not dealing with the case of an accuser). On the contrary, some have thought that in no case ought he to do so, while others have thought that he should in certain circumstances.

Figure 38. The Demon Lover.
The Devil often appeared to witches in forms similar to this, and no witchcraft text fails to mention the Devil's amorousness and the witch's lust.

But, finally, Boniface VIII decreed as follows: If in a case of heresy it appears to the Bishop or Inquisitor that grave danger would be incurred by the witnesses or informers on account of the powers of the persons against whom they lay their depositions, should their names be published, he shall not publish them. But if there is no danger, their names shall be published just as in other cases.

Here it is to be noted that this refers not only to a Bishop or Inquisitor, but to any Judge conducting a case against witches with the consent of the Inquisitor or Bishop; for, as was shown in the introductory Question, they can depute their duties to a Judge. So that any such Judge, even if he be secular, has the authority of the Pope, and not only of the Emperor.

Also a careful Judge will take notice of the powers of the accused persons; for these are of three kinds, namely, the power of birth and family, the power of riches, and the power of malice. And the last of these is more to be feared than the other two, since it threatens more danger to the witnesses if their names are made known to the accused. The reason for this is that it is more dangerous to make known the names of the witnesses to an accused person who is poor, because such a person has many evil accomplices, such as outlaws and homicides, associated with him, who venture nothing but their own persons, which is not the case with anyone who is nobly born or rich, and abounding in temporal possessions. And the kind of danger which is to be feared is explained by Pope John XXII as the death or cutting off of themselves or their children or kindred, or the wasting of their substance, or some such matter.

Further, let the Judge take notice that, as he acts in this matter with the authority of the Supreme Pontiff and the permission of the Ordinary, both he himself and all who are associated with him at the depositions, or afterwards at the pronouncing of the sentence, must keep the names of the witnesses secret, under pain of excommunication. And it is in the power of the Bishop thus to punish him or them if they do otherwise. Therefore he should very implicitly warn them not to reveal the names from the very beginning of the process.

Wherefore the above decree of Pope Boniface VIII goes on to say: And that the danger to those accusers and witnesses may be the more effectively met, and the inquiry conducted more cautiously, we permit, by the authority of this statute, that the Bishop or Inquisitors (or, as we have said, the Judge) shall forbid all those who are concerned in the inquiry to reveal without their permission any secrets which they have learned from the Bishop or Inquisitors, under pain of excommunication which they may incur by violating such secrets.

It is further to be noted that just as it is a punishable offence to publish the names of witnesses indiscreetly, so also it is to conceal them without good reason from, for instance, such people as have a right to know them, such as the lawyers and assessors whose opinion is to be sought in proceeding to the sentence; in the same way the names must not be concealed when it is possible to publish them without risk of any danger to the witnesses. On this subject the above decree speaks as follows, towards the end: We command that in all cases the Bishop or Inquisitors shall take especial care not to suppress the names of the witnesses as if there were danger to them when there is perfect security; nor conversely to decide to publish them when there is some danger threatened, the decision in this matter resting with their own conscience and discretion. And it has been written in comment on these words: Whoever you are who are a Judge in such a case, mark those words well, for they do not refer to a slight risk but to a grave danger; therefore do not deprive a prisoner of his legal rights without very good cause, for this cannot but be an offence to Almighty God.

The reader must note that all the process which we have already described, and all that we have yet to describe, up to the methods of passing sentence (except the death sentence), which it is in the province of the ecclesiastical Judge to conduct, can also, with the consent of the Diocesans, be conducted by a secular Judge. Therefore the reader need find no difficulty in the fact that the above Decree speaks of an ecclesiastical and not a secular Judge; for the latter can take his method of inflicting the death sentence from that of the Ordinary in passing sentence of penance.

What Kind of Defence may be Allowed, and of the Appointment of an Advocate. This is the Fifth Action.

If, therefore, the accused asks to be defended, how can this be admitted when the names of the witnesses are kept altogether secret? It is to be said that three considerations are to be observed in admitting any defence. First, that an Advocate shall be allotted to the accused. Second, that the names of the witnesses shall not be made known to the Advocate, even under an oath of secrecy, but that he shall be informed of everything contained in the depositions. Third, the accused shall as far as possible be given the benefit of every doubt, provided that this involves no scandal to the faith nor is in any way detrimental to justice, as will be shown. And in like manner the prisoner's procurator shall have full access to the whole process, only the names of the witnesses and deponents being suppressed; and the Advocate can act also in the name of procurator.

As to the first of these points: it should be noted that an Advocate is not to be appointed at the desire of the accused, as if he may choose which Advocate he will have; but the Judge must take great care to appoint neither a litigious nor an evil-minded man, nor yet one who is easily bribed (as many are), but rather an honourable man to whom no sort of suspicion attaches.

And the Judge ought to note four points, and if the Advocate be found to conform to them, he shall be allowed to plead, but not otherwise. For first of all the Advocate must examine the nature of the case, and then if he finds it a just one he may undertake it, but if he finds it unjust he must refuse it; and he must be very careful not to undertake an unjust or desperate case. But if he has unwittingly accepted the brief, together with a fee, from someone who wishes to do him an injury, but discovers during the process that the case is hopeless, then he must signify to his client (that is, the accused) that he abandons the case, and must return the fee which he has received. This is the opinion of Godfrey of Fontaines, which is wholly in conformity with the Canon *de jud.* 1, *rem non novam*. But Henry of Segusio holds an opposite view concerning the return of the fee in a case in which the Advocate has worked very hard. Consequently if an Advocate has wittingly undertaken to defend a prisoner whom he knows to be guilty, he shall be liable for the costs and expenses (*de admin. tut.* 1, *non tamen est ignotum*).

The second point to be observed is that in his pleading he should conduct himself properly in three respects. First, his behaviour must be modest and free from prolixity or pretentious oratory. Secondly, he must abide by the truth, not bringing forward any fallacious arguments or reasoning, or calling false witnesses, or introducing legal quirks and quibbles if he be a skilled lawyer, or bringing counter-accusations; especially in cases of this sort, which must be conducted as simply and summarily as possible. Thirdly, his fee must be regulated by the usual practice of the district.

But to return to our point; the Judge must make the above conditions clear to the Advocate, and finally admonish him not to incur the charge of defending heresy, which would make him liable to excommunication.

And it is not a valid argument for him to say to the Judge that he is not defending the error, but the person. For he must not by any means so conduct his defence as to prevent the case from being conducted in a plain and summary manner, and he would be doing so if he introduced any complications or appeals into it; all which things are disallowed altogether. For it is granted that he does not defend the error; for in that case he would be more damnably guilty than the witches themselves, and rather a heresiarch than a heretical wizard. Nevertheless, if he unduly defends a person already suspect of heresy, he makes himself as it were a patron of that heresy, and lays himself under not only a light but a strong suspicion, in accordance with the manner of his defence; and ought publicly to abjure that heresy before the Bishop.

We have put this matter at some length, and it is not to be neglected by the Judge, because much danger may arise from an improper conducting of the defence by an Advocate or Procurator. Therefore, when there is any objection to the Advocate, the Judge must dispense with him and proceed in accordance with the facts and the proofs. But when the Advocate for the accused is not open to any objection, but is a zealous man and a lover of justice, then the Judge may reveal to him the names of the witnesses, under an oath of secrecy.

> *Of the Points to be Observed by the Judge*
> *before the Formal Examination in the*
> *Place of Detention and Torture.*
> *This is the Eighth Action.*

The next action of the Judge is quite clear. For common justice demands that a witch should not be condemned to death unless she is convicted by her own confession. But here we are considering the case of one who is judged to be taken in manifest heresy for one of the other two reasons set down in the First Question, namely, direct or indirect evidence of the fact, or the legitimate production of witnesses; and in this case she is to be exposed to questions and torture to extort a confession of her crimes.

And to make the matter clear we will quote a case which occurred at Spires and came to the knowledge of many. A certain honest man was bargaining with a woman, and would not come to terms with her about the price of some article; so she angrily called after him, "You will soon wish you had agreed." For witches generally use this manner of speaking, or something like it, when they wish to bewitch a person by looking at him. Then he, not unreasonably being angry with her, looked over his shoulder to see with what intention she had uttered those words; and behold! he was suddenly bewitched so that his mouth was stretched sideways as far as his ears in a horrible deformity, and he could not draw it back, but remained so deformed for a long time.

We put the case that this was submitted to the Judge as direct evidence of the fact; and it is asked whether the woman is to be considered as manifestly taken in the heresy of witchcraft. This should be answered from the words of S. Bernard which we have quoted above. For there are three ways in which a person may be judged to be so taken, and they not so closely conjoined as though it were necessary for all three to agree in one conclusion, but each one by itself, namely, the evidence of the fact, or the legitimate production of witnesses, or her own confession, is sufficient to prove a witch to be manifestly taken in that heresy.

But indirect evidence of the fact is different from direct evidence; yet though it is not so conclusive, it is still taken from the words and deeds of witches, as was shown in the Seventh Question, and it is judged from witch-craft which is not so immediate in its effect, but follows after some lapse of time from the utterance of the threatening words. Wherefore may we conclude that this is the case with such witches who have been accused and have not made good their defence (or have failed to defend themselves because this privilege was not granted them; and it was not granted because they did not ask for it). But what we are to consider now is what action the Judge should take, and how he should proceed to question the accused with a view to exorting the truth from her so that sentence of death may finally be passed upon her.

And here, because of the great trouble caused by the stubborn silence of witches, there are several points which the Judge must notice, and these are dealt with under their several heads.

And the first is that he must not be too quick to subject a witch to examination, but must pay attention to certain signs which will follow. And he must not be too quick for this reason: unless God, through a holy Angel, compels the devil to withhold his help from the witch, she will be so insensible to the pains of torture that she will sooner be torn limb from limb than confess any of the truth.

But the torture is not to be neglected for this reason, for they are not all equally endowed with this power, and also the devil sometimes of his own will permits them to confess their crimes without being compelled by a holy Angel. And for the understanding of this the reader is referred to that which is written in the Second Part of this work concerning the homage which they offer to the devil.

For there are some who obtain from the devil a respite of six or eight or ten years before they have to offer him their homage, that is, devote themselves to him body and soul; whereas others, when they first profess their abjuration of the faith, at the same time offer their homage. And the reason why the devil allows that stipulated interval of time is that, during that time, he may find out whether the witch has denied the faith with her lips only but not in her heart, and would therefore offer him her homage in the same way.

For the devil cannot know the inner thoughts of the heart except conjecturally from outward indications, as we showed in the First Part of this work where we dealt with the question whether devils can turn the minds of men to hatred or love. And many have been found who, driven by some necessity or poverty, have been induced by other witches, in the hope of ultimate forgiveness in confession, to become either total or partial apostates from the faith. And it is such whom the devil deserts without any compulsion by a holy Angel; and therefore they readily confess their crimes, whereas others, who have from their hearts bound themselves to the devil, are protected by his power and preserve a stubborn silence.

And this provides a clear answer to the question how it comes about that some witches readily confess, and others will by no means do so. For in the case of the former, when the devil is not compelled by God, he still deserts them of his own will, in order that by temporal unhappiness and a horrible death he may lead to despair those over whose hearts he could never obtain the mastery. For it is evident from their sacramental confessions that they have never voluntarily obeyed the devil, but have been compelled by him to work witchcraft.

And some also are distinguished by the fact that, after they have admitted their crimes, they try to commit suicide by strangling or hanging themselves. And they are induced to do this by the Enemy, lest they should obtain pardon from God through sacramental confession. This chiefly happens in the case of those who have not been willing agents of the devil; although it may also happen in the case of willing agents, after they have confessed their crimes: but then it is because the devil has been compelled to desert the witch.

In conclusion we may say that it is as difficult, or more difficult, to compel a witch to tell the truth as it is to exorcize a person possessed of the devil. Therefore the Judge ought not to be too willing or ready to proceed to such examination, unless, as has been said, the death penalty is involved. And in this case he must exercise great care, as we shall show; and first we shall speak of the method of sentencing a witch to such torture.

Of the Method of Sentencing the Accused
to be Questioned: and How she must
be Questioned on the First Day; and
Whether she may be Promised her Life.
The Ninth Action.

Secondly, the Judge must take care to frame his sentence in the following manner.

We, the Judge and assessors, having attended to and considered the details of the process enacted by us against you N. of such a place in such a Diocese, and having diligently examined the whole matter, find that you are equivocal in your admissions; as for example, when you say that you used such threats with no intention of doing an injury, but nevertheless there are various proofs which are sufficient warrant for exposing you to the question and torture. Wherefore, that the truth may be known from your own mouth, and that henceforth you may not offend the ears of the Judges, we declare, judge and sentence that on this present day at such an hour you be placed under the question and torture. This sentence was given, etc.

Alternatively, as has been said, the Judge may not be willing to deliver the accused up to be questioned, but may punish her with imprisonment with the following object in view. Let him summon her friends and put it to them that she may escape the death penalty, although she will be punished in another way, if she confesses the truth, and urge them to try to persuade her to do so. For very often meditation, and the misery of imprisonment, and the repeated advice of honest men, dispose the accused to discover the truth.

And we have found that witches have been so strengthened by this sort of advice that, as a sign of their rebellion, they have spat on the ground as if it were in the devil's face, saying, "Depart, cursed devil; I shall do what is just"; and afterwards they have confessed their crimes.

But if, after keeping the accused in a state of suspense, and continually postponing the day of examination, and frequently using verbal persuasions, the Judge should truly believe that the accused is denying the truth, let them question her lightly without shedding blood; knowing that such questioning is fallacious and often, as has been said, ineffective.

And it should be begun in this way. While the officers are preparing for the questioning, let the accused be stripped; or if she is a woman, let her first be led to the penal cells and there stripped by honest women of good reputation. And the reason for this is that they should search for any instrument of witchcraft sewn into her clothes; for they often make such instruments, at the instruction of devils, out of the limbs of unbaptized children, the purpose being that those children should be deprived of the beatific vision. And when such instruments have been disposed of, the Judge shall use his own persuasions and those of other honest men zealous for the faith to induce her to confess the truth voluntarily; and if she will not, let him order the officers to bind her with cords, and apply her to some engine of torture; and then let them obey at once but not joyfully, rather appearing to be disturbed by their duty. Then let her be released again at someone's earnest request, and taken on one side, and let her again be persuaded; and in persuading her, let her be told that she can escape the death penalty.

Here it is asked whether, in the case of a prisoner legally convicted by her general bad reputation, by witnesses, and by the evidence of the fact, so that the only thing lacking is a confession of the crime from her own mouth, the Judge can lawfully promise her her life, whereas if she were to confess the crime she would suffer the extreme penalty.

We answer that different people have various opinions on this question. For some hold that if the accused is of a notoriously bad reputation, and gravely suspected on unequivocal evidence of the crime; and if she is herself a great source of danger, as being the mistress of other witches, then she may be promised her life on the following conditions: that she be sentenced to

Figures 39–46. Witches' Acts Against Mankind.

Figure 39. Witchcraft and Natural Disasters.

The most popular common accusation against the witches was that they caused natural disasters. This woodcut from Molitor's *De Lamis* depicts the ritual calling down of rain.

imprisonment for life on bread and water, provided that she supply evidence which will lead to the conviction of other witches. And she is not to be told, when she is promised her life, that she is to be imprisoned in this way; but should be led to suppose that some other penance, such as exile, will be imposed on her as punishment. And without doubt notorious witches, especially such as use witches' medicines and cure the bewitched by superstitious means, should be kept in this way, both that they may help the bewitched, and that they may betray other witches. But such a betrayal by them must not be considered of itself sufficient ground for a conviction, since the devil is a liar, unless it is also substantiated by the evidence of the fact, and by witnesses.

Others think that, after she has been consigned to prison in this way, the promise to spare her life should be kept for a time, but that after a certain period she should be burned.

A third opinion is that the Judge may safely promise the accused her life, but in such a way that he should afterwards disclaim the duty of passing sentence on her, deputing another Judge in his place.

There seems to be some advantage in pursuing the first of these courses on account of the benefit which may accrue from it to those who are bewitched; yet it is not lawful to use witchcraft to cure witchcraft, although (as was shown in the First and Introductory Question to this Third Part) the general opinion is that it is lawful to use vain and superstitious means to remove a spell. But use and experience and the variety of such cases will be of more value to Judges than any art or text-book; therefore this is a matter which should be left to the Judges. But it has certainly been very often found by experience that many would confess the truth if they were not held back by the fear of death.

But if neither threats nor such promises will induce her to confess the truth, then the officers must proceed with the sentence, and she must be examined, not in any new or exquisite manner, but in the usual way, lightly or heavily according as the nature of her crimes demands. And while she is being questioned about each several point, let her be often and frequently exposed to torture, beginning with the more gentle of them; for the Judge should not be too hasty to proceed to the graver kind. And while this is being done, let the Notary write all down, how she is tortured and what questions are asked and how she answers.

And note that, if she confesses under torture, she should then be taken to

Figure 40. Witchcraft and Natural Disasters.
Here the witches call down storms at sea, causing shipwreck. From Olaus Magnus,
Historia de gentibus septentrionalibus.

Figure 41. Witchcraft and Natural Disasters.
This woodcut from Guazzo, *Compendium Maleficarum,* depicts a witch, riding a great
beast through the sky, causing a rain of fire to descend.

another place and questioned anew, so that she does not confess only under the stress of torture.

The next step of the Judge should be that, if after being fittingly tortured she refuses to confess the truth, he should have other engines of torture brought before her, and tell her that she will have to endure these if she does not confess. If then she is not induced by terror to confess, the torture must be continued on the second or third day, but not repeated at that present time unless there should be some fresh indication of its probable success.

Let the sentence be pronounced in her presence in the following manner: We the aforesaid Judge, as above, assign to you N. such a day for the continuation of your questioning, that the truth may be heard from your own mouth. And the Notary shall write all down in the process.

And during the interval before that assigned time the Judge himself or other honest men shall do all in their power to persuade her to confess the truth in the manner we have said, giving her, if it seems expedient to them, a promise that her life will be spared.

The Judge should also take care that during that interval there should always be guards with her, so that she is never left alone, for fear lest the devil will cause her to kill herself. But the devil himself knows better than anyone can set down in writing whether he will desert her of his own will, or be compelled to do so by God.

Of the Continuing of the Torture, and of the
Devices and Signs by which the Judge can
Recognize a Witch; and how he ought to Protect
himself from their Spells. Also how they are
to be Shaved in those Parts where they use to
Conceal their Devil's Masks and Tokens
together with the due Setting Forth of
Various Means of Overcoming their Obstinacy
in Keeping Silence and Refusal to Confess.
And it is the Tenth Action.

The Judge should act as follows in the continuation of the torture. First he should bear in mind that, just as the same medicine is not applicable to all the members, but there are various and distinct salves for each several member, so not all heretics or those accused of heresy are to be subjected to the same method of questioning, examination and torture as to the charges laid against them; but various and different means are to be employed according to their various natures and persons. Now a surgeon cuts off rotten limbs; and mangy sheep are isolated from the healthy; but a prudent Judge will not consider it safe to bind himself down to one invariable rule in his method of dealing with a prisoner who is endowed with a witch's power of taciturnity, and whose silence he is unable to overcome. For if the sons of darkness were to become accustomed to one general rule they would provide means of evading it as a well-known snare set for their destruction.

Therefore a prudent and zealous Judge should seize his opportunity and choose his method of conducting his examination according to the answers or depositions of the witnesses, or as his own previous experience or native wit indicates to him, using the following precautions.

If he wishes to find out whether she is endowed with a witch's power of preserving silence, let him take note whether she is able to shed tears when standing in his presence, or when being tortured. For we are taught both by the words of worthy men of old and by our own experience that this is a most certain sign, and it has been found that even if she be urged and exhorted by solemn conjurations to shed tears, if she be a witch she will not be able to weep: although she will assume a tearful aspect and smear her cheeks and eyes with spittle to make it appear that she is weeping; wherefore she must be closely watched by the attendants.

In passing sentence the Judge or priest may use some such method as the following in conjuring her to true tears if she be innocent, or in restraining false tears. Let him place his hand on the head of the accused and say: I conjure you by the bitter tears shed on the Cross by our Saviour the Lord Jesus Christ for the salvation of the world, and by the burning tears poured in the evening hour over His wounds by the most glorious Virgin Mary, His Mother, and by all the tears which have been shed here in this world by the Saints and Elect of God, from whose eyes He has now wiped away all tears, that if you be innocent you do now shed tears, but if you be guilty that you shall by no means do so. In the name of the Father, and of the Son, and of the Holy Ghost, Amen.

And it is found by experience that the more they are conjured the less are they able to weep, however hard they may try to do so, or smear their cheeks with spittle. Nevertheless it is possible that afterwards, in the absence of the Judge and not at the time or in the place of torture, they may be able to weep in the presence of their gaolers.

And as for the reason for a witch's inability to weep, it can be said that the grace of tears is one of the chief gifts allowed to the penitent; for S. Bernard tells us that the tears of the humble can penetrate to heaven and conquer the unconquerable. Therefore there can be no doubt that they are displeasing to the devil, and that he uses all his endeavour to restrain them, to prevent a witch from finally attaining to penitence.

But it may be objected that it might suit with the devil's cunning, with God's permission, to allow even a witch to weep; since tearful grieving, weaving and deceiving are said to be proper to women. We may answer that in this case, since the judgements of God are a mystery, if there is no other way of convicting the accused, by legitimate witnesses or the evidence of the fact, and if she is not under a strong or grave suspicion, she is to be discharged; but because she rests under a slight suspicion by reason of her reputation to which the witnesses have testified, she must be required to abjure the heresy of witchcraft, as we shall show when we deal with the second method of pronouncing sentence.

A second precaution is to be observed, not only at this point but during the whole process, by the Judge and all his assessors; namely, that they must not allow themselves to be touched physically by the witch, especially in any contact of their bare arms or hands; but they must always carry about them some salt consecrated on Palm Sunday and some Blessed Herbs. For these can be enclosed together in Blessed Wax and worn round the neck, as we showed in the Second Part when we discussed the remedies against illnesses and diseases caused by witchcraft; and that these have a wonderful protective virtue is known not only from the testimony of witches, but from the use and practice of the Church, which exorcizes and blesses such objects for this very purpose, as is shown in the ceremony of exorcism when it is said, For the banishing of all the power of the devil, etc.

But let it not be thought that physical contact of the joints or limbs is the only thing to be guarded against; for sometimes, with God's permission, they are able with the help of the devil to bewitch the Judge by the mere sound of the words which they utter, especially at the time when they are exposed to torture.

And we know from experience that some witches, when detained in prison, have importunately begged their gaolers to grant them this one thing, that they should be allowed to look at the Judge before he looks at them; and by so getting the first sight of the Judge they have been able so to alter the minds of the Judge or his assessors that they have lost all their anger against them and have not presumed to molest them in any way, but have allowed them to go free. He who knows and has experienced it gives this true testimony; and would that they were not able to effect such things!

Let judges not despise such precautions and protections, for by holding them in little account after such warning they run the risk of eternal damnation. For our Saviour said: If I had not come, and spoken to them, they would not have sin; but now they have no excuse for their sin. Therefore let the judges protect themselves in the above manner, according to the provisions of the Church.

And if it can conveniently be done, the witch should be led backward into the presence of the Judge and his assessors. And not only at the present point, but in all that has preceded or shall follow it, let him cross himself and approach her manfully, and with God's help the power of that old Serpent will be broken. And no one need think that it is superstitious to lead her in backwards; for, as we have often said, the Canonists allow even more than this to be done for the protection against witchcraft, and always say that it is lawful to oppose vanity with vanity.

The third precaution to be observed in this tenth action is that the hair should be shaved from every part of her body. The reason for this is the same as that for stripping her of her clothes, which we have already mentioned; for in order to preserve their power of silence they are in the habit of hiding some superstitious object in their clothes or in their hair, or even in the most secret parts of their bodies which must not be named.

But it may be objected that the devil might, without the use of such charms, so harden the heart of a witch that she is unable to confess her crimes; just as it is often found in the case of other criminals, no matter how great the tortures to which they are exposed, or how much they are convicted by the evidence of the facts and of witnesses. We answer that it is true that the devil can effect such taciturnity without the use of such charms; but he prefers to use them for the perdition of souls and the greater offence to the Divine Majesty of God.

This can be made clear from the example of a certain witch in the town of Hagenau, whom we have mentioned in the Second Part of this work. She used to obtain this gift of silence in the following manner: she killed a newly-born first-born male child who had not been baptized, and having roasted it in an oven together with other matters which it is not expedient to mention, ground it to powder and ashes; and if any witch or criminal carried about him some of this substance he would in no way be able to confess his crimes.

Here it is clear that a hundred thousand children so employed could not of their own virtue endow a person with such a power of keeping silence; but any intelligent person can understand that such means are used by the devil for the perdition of souls and to offend the Divine Majesty.

Again, it may be objected that very often criminals who are not witches exhibit the same power of keeping silence. In answer to this it must be said that this power of taciturnity can proceed from three causes. First, from a natural hardness of heart; for some are soft-hearted, or even feeble-minded, so that at the slightest torture they admit everything, even some things which are not true; whereas others are so hard that however much they are tortured the truth is not to be had from them; and this is especially the case with those who have been tortured before, even if their arms are suddenly stretched and twisted.

Secondly, it may proceed from some instrument of witchcraft carried about the person, as has been said, either in the clothes or in the hairs of the body. And thirdly, even if the prisoner has no such object secreted about her person, they are sometimes endowed with this power by other witches, however far they may be removed from them. For a certain witch at Issbrug used to boast that, if she had no more than a thread from the garments of any prisoner, she could so work that however much that prisoner were tortured, even to death, she would be unable to confess anything. So the answer to this objection is clear.

But what is to be said of a case that happened in the Diocese of Ratisbon? Certain heretics were convicted by their own confession not only as impenitent but as open advocates of that perfidy; and when they were condemned to death it happened that they remained unharmed in the fire. At length their sentence was altered to death by drowning, but this was no more effective. All were astonished, and some even began to say that their heresy must be true; and the Bishop, in great anxiety for his flock, ordered a three days' fast. When this had been devoutly fulfilled, it came to the knowledge of someone that those heretics had a magic charm sewed between the skin and the flesh under one arm; and when this was found and removed, they were delivered to the flames and immediately burned. Some say that a certain necromancer learned this secret during a consultation with a devil, and betrayed it; but however it became known, it is probable that the devil, who is always scheming for the subversion of the faith, was in some way compelled by Divine power to reveal the matter.

From this it may be seen what a Judge ought to do when such a case happens to him: namely, that he should rely upon the protection of God, and by the prayers and fasting of devout persons drive away this sort of devil's work from witches, in those cases where they cannot be made to confess under torture even after their clothes have been changed and all their hair has been shaved off and abraded.

Now in the parts of Germany such shaving, especially of the secret parts, is not generally considered delicate, and therefore we Inquisitors do not use it; but we cause the hair of their head to be cut off, and placing a morsel of Blessed Wax in a cup of Holy Water and invoking the most Holy Trinity, we give it them to drink three times on a fasting stomach, and by the grace of God we have by this means caused many to break their silence. But in other countries the Inquisitors order the witch to be shaved all over her body. And the Inquisitor of Como has informed us that last year, that is, in 1485, he ordered forty-one witches to be burned, after they had been shaved all over. And this was in the district and country of Burbia, commonly called Wormserbad, in the territory of the Archduke of Austria, towards Milan.

But it may be asked whether, in a time of need, when all other means of breaking a witch's silence have failed, it would be lawful to ask the advice in this matter of sorceresses who are able to cure those who are bewitched. We answer that, whatever may have been done in that matter at Ratisbon, it is our earnest admonition in the Lord that no one, no matter how great may be the need, should consult with sorceresses on behalf of the State; and this because of the great offence which is thereby caused to the Divine Majesty, when there are so many other means open to us which we may use either in their own proper form or in some equivalent form, so that the truth will be had from their own mouths and they can be consigned to the flames; or failing this, God will in the meantime provide some other death for the witch.

For there remain to us the following remedies against this power of silence. First, let a man do all that lies in his own power by the exercise of his own qualities, persisting often with the methods we have already mentioned, and especially on certain days, as will be shown in the following Question. See II. *Corinthians* ix: That ye may abound in all good works.

Secondly, if this should fail, let him consult with other persons; for perhaps they may think of some means which has not occurred to him, since there are various methods of counteracting witchcraft.

Thirdly, if these two fail, let him have recourse to devout persons, as it is said in *Ecclesiasticus* xxxvii: Be continually with a godly man, whom thou knowest to keep the commandments of the Lord. Also let him invoke the Patron Saints of the country. But if all these fail, let the Judge and all the people at once put their trust in God with prayers and fasting, that the witchcraft may be removed by reason of their piety. For so Josaphat prayed in II. *Paralipomenon* xx: When we know not what we should do, we have this one refuge, that we should turn our eyes to Thee. And without doubt God will not fail us in our need.

To this effect also S. Augustine speaks (26, q. 7, *non obseruabitis*): Whosoever observes any divinations or auguries, or attends to or consents to such as observe them, or gives credit to such by following after their works, or goes into their houses, or introduces them into his own house, or asks questions of them, let him know that he has perverted the Christian faith and his baptism and is a pagan and apostate and enemy of God, and runs grave danger of the eternal wrath of God, unless he is corrected by ecclesiastical penances and is reconciled with God. Therefore let the Judge not fail always to use the lawful remedies, as we have said, together with these following final precautions.

Of the Manner of Pronouncing a Sentence which is Final and Definitive.

In proceeding to treat of those cases in which the secular Judge by himself can arrive at a judgement and pronounce sentence without the co-operation of the Diocesan and Ordinaries, we necessarily presuppose that not only is it consistent with the protection of the faith and of justice that we Inquisitors should be relieved of the duty of passing sentence in these cases, but in the same sincerity of spirit we endeavour to relieve the Diocesans also from that duty; not in any desire to detract from their authority and jurisdiction, for if they should elect to exercise their authority in such matters, it would follow that we Inquisitors must also concur in it.

It must be remembered, also, that this crime of witches is not purely ecclesiastic; therefore the temporal potentates and Lords are not debarred from trying and judging it. At the same time we shall show that in some cases they must not arrive at a definitive judgement without the authorisation of the Diocesans.

But first we must consider the sentence itself: secondly, the nature of its pronouncement; and thirdly, in how many ways it is to be pronounced. With regard to the first of these questions, S. Augustine says that we must not pronounce sentence against any person unless he has been proved guilty, or has confessed. Now there are three kinds of sentence—interlocutory, definitive, and preceptive. These are explained as follows by S. Raymund. An interlocutory sentence is one which is given not on the main issue of the case but on some other side issues which emerge during the hearing of a case; such as a decision whether or not a witness is to be disallowed, or whether some digression is to be admitted, and such matters as that. Or it may perhaps be called interlocutory because it is delivered simply by word of mouth without the formality of putting it in writing.

A definitive sentence is one which pronounces a final decision as to the main issue of the case.

A preceptive sentence is one which is pronounced by a lower authority on the instruction of a higher. But we shall be concerned with the first two of these, and especially with the definitive sentence.

Now it is laid down by law that a definitive sentence which has been arrived at without a due observance of the proper legal procedure in trying a case is null and void in law; and the legal conduct of a case consists in two things. One concerns the basis of the judgement; for there must be a due provision for the hearing of arguments both for the prosecution and the defence, and a sentence arrived at without such a hearing cannot stand. The other is not concerned with the basis of the judgement, but provides that the sentence must not be conditional; for example, a claim for possession should not be decided conditionally upon some subsequent claim of property; but where there is no question of such an objection the sentence shall stand.

But in the case we are considering, which is a process on behalf of the faith against a charge of heresy (though the charge is a mixed one), the procedure is straightforward and summary. That heretic, and as truly such to be delivered and abandoned to the secular Court: wherefore by this sentence we cast you away as an impenitent heretic from our ecclesiastical Court, and deliver or abandon you to the power of the secular Court: praying the said Court to moderate or temper its sentence of death against you. This sentence was given, etc.

Of one Taken and Convicted, but Denying Everything.

The twelfth method of finishing and concluding a process on behalf of the faith is used when the person accused of heresy, after a diligent examination of the merits of the process in consultation with skilled lawyers, is found to be convicted of heresy by the evidence of the facts or by the legitimate production of witnesses, but not by his own confession. That is to say, he may be convicted by the evidence of the facts, in that he has publicly practised heresy; or by the evidence of witnesses against whom he can take no legitimate exception; yet, though so taken and convicted, he firmly and constantly denies the charge. See Henry of Segusio *On Heresy*, question 34.

The procedure in such a case is as follows. The accused must be kept in strong durance fettered and chained, and must often be visited by the officers, both in a body and severally, who will use their own best endeavours and those of others to induce him to discover the truth; telling him that if he does so and confesses his error, and abjures that vile heresy, he will be admitted to mercy; but that if he refuses and persists in his denial, he will in the end be abandoned to the secular law, and will not be able to escape temporal death.

But if he continues for a long time in his denials, the Bishop and his officers, now in a body and now severally, now personally and now with the assis-

Figure 42. The Witches Burn a Town.
Witches were most frequently blamed for precisely those natural and man-made disasters to which fifteenth- and sixteenth-century society was most prone. The frightfulness and destructiveness of fires in the closely packed and badly protected early modern cities insured that the charge of burning buildings would be a common one against witches.

176

Figure 43. The Bewitched Stableboy.
Natural disasters and personal afflictions accounted for much popular resentment of witches. In Hans Baldung Grien's 1544 woodcut "The Bewitched Stableboy" the witch may be seen at the right.

tance of other honest and upright men, shall summon before them now one witness, now another, and warn him to attend strictly to what he has deposed, and to be sure whether or not he has told the truth; that he should beware lest in damning another temporally he damn himself eternally; that if he be afraid, let him at least tell them the truth in secret, that the accused should not die unjustly. And let them be careful to talk to him in such a way that they may see clearly whether or not his depositions have been true.

But if the witnesses, after this warning, adhere to their statements, and the accused maintains his denials, let not the Bishop and his officers on that account be in any haste to pronounce a definitive sentence and hand the prisoner over to secular law; but let them detain him still longer, now persuading him to confess, now yet again urging the witnesses (but one at a time) to examine their consciences well. And let the Bishop and his officers pay particular attention to that witness who seems to be of the best conscience and the most disposed to good, and let them more insistently charge him on his conscience to speak the truth whether or not the matter was as he had deposed. And if they see any witness vacillate, or there are any other indications that he has given false evidence, let them attest him according to the counsel of learned men, and proceed as justice shall require.

For it is very often found that after a person so convicted by credible witnesses has long persisted in his denials, he has at length relented, especially on being truly informed that he will not be delivered to the secular Court, but be admitted to mercy if he confesses his sin, and he has then freely confessed the truth which he has so long denied. And it is often found that the witnesses, actuated by malice and overcome by enmity, have conspired together to accuse an innocent person of the sin of heresy; but afterwards, at the frequent entreaty of the Bishop and his officers, their consciences have been stricken with remorse and, by Divine inspiration, they have revoked their evidence and confessed that they have out of malice put that crime upon the accused. Therefore the prisoner in such a case is not to be sentenced hastily, but must be kept for a year or more before he is delivered up to the secular Court.

When a sufficient time has elapsed, and after all possible care has been taken, if the accused who has been thus legally convicted has acknowledged his guilt and confessed in legal form that he hath been for the period stated ensnared in the crime of heresy, and has consented to abjure that and every heresy, and to perform such satisfaction as shall seem proper to the Bishop and Inquisitor for one convicted of heresy both by his own confession and the legitimate production of witnesses; then let him as a penitent heretic publicly abjure all heresy, in the manner which we have set down in the eighth method of concluding a process on behalf of the faith.

But if he has confessed that he hath fallen into such heresy, but nevertheless obstinately adheres to it, he must be delivered to the secular Court as an impenitent, after the manner of the tenth method which we have explained above.

But if the accused has remained firm and unmoved in his denial of the charges against him, but the witnesses have withdrawn their charges, revoking their evidence and acknowledging their guilt, confessing that they had put so great a crime upon an innocent man from motives of rancour and hatred, or had been suborned or bribed thereto; then the accused shall be freely discharged, but they shall be punished as false witnesses, accusers or informers. This is made clear by Paul of Burgos in his comment on the Canon c. *multorum*. And sentence or penance shall be pronounced against them as shall seem proper to the Bishop and Judges; but in any case such false witnesses must be condemned to perpetual imprisonment on a diet of bread and water, and to do penance for all the days of their life, being made to stand upon the steps before the church door, etc. However, the Bishops have power to mitigate or even to increase the sentence after a year or some other period, in the usual manner.

But if the accused, after a year or other longer period which has been deemed sufficient, continues to maintain his denials, and the legitimate witnesses abide by their evidence, the Bishop and Judges shall prepare to abandon him to the secular Court; sending to him certain honest men zealous for the faith, especially religious, to tell him that he cannot escape temporal death while he thus persists in his denial, but will be delivered up as an impenitent heretic to the power of the secular Court. And the Bishop and his officers shall give notice to the Bailiff or authority of the secular Court that on such a day at such an hour and in such a place (not inside a church) he should come with his attendants to receive an impenitent heretic whom they will deliver to him. And let him make public proclamation in the usual places that all should be present on such a day at such an hour and place to hear a sermon preached on behalf of the faith, and that the Bishop and his officer will hand over a certain obstinate heretic to the secular Court.

On the appointed day for the pronouncement of sentence the Bishop and his officer shall be in the place aforesaid, and the prisoner shall be placed on high before the assembled clergy and people so that he may be seen by all, and the secular authorities shall be present before the prisoner. Then sentence shall be pronounced in the following manner:

We, N., by the mercy of God Bishop of such city, or Judge in the territories of such Prince, seeing that you, N., of such a place in such a Diocese, have been accused before us of such heresy (naming it); and wishing to be more certainly informed whether the charges made against you were true, and whether you walked in darkness or in the light; we proceeded to inform ourselves by diligently examining the witnesses, by often summoning and questioning you on oath, and admitting an Advocate to plead in your defence, and by proceeding in every way as we were bound by the canonical decrees.

And wishing to conclude your trial in a manner beyond all doubt, we convened in solemn council men learned in the Theological faculty and in the Canon and Civil Laws. And having diligently examined and discussed each circumstance of the process and maturely and carefully considered with the said learned men everything which has been said and done in this present case, we find that you, N., have been legally convicted of having been infected with the sin of heresy for so long a time, and that you have said and done such and such (naming them) on account of which it manifestly appears that you are legitimately convicted of the said heresy.

But since we desired, and still desire, that you should confess the truth and renounce the said heresy, and be led back to the bosom of Holy Church and to the unity of the Holy Faith, that so you should save your soul and escape the destruction of both your body and soul in hell; we have by our own efforts and those of others, and by delaying your sentence for a long time, tried to induce you to repent; but you being obstinately given over to wickedness have scorned to agree to our wholesome advice, and have persisted and do persist with stubborn and defiant mind in your contumacious and dogged denials; and this we say with grief, and grieve and mourn in saying it. But since the Church of God has waited so long for you to repent and acknowledge your guilt, and you have refused and still refuse, her grace and mercy can go no farther.

Wherefore that you may be an example to others and that they may be kept from all such heresies, and that such crimes may not remain unpunished: We the Bishop and Judges named on behalf of the faith, sitting in tribunal as Judges judging, and having before us the Holy Gospels that our judgement may proceed as from the countenance of God and our eyes see with equity, and having before our eyes only God and the glory and honour

Figure 44.　The Witch Invokes Destructive Spirits.
This woodcut from Olaus Magnus' *Historia de gentibus septentrionalibus* illustrates the powers that aided the witch in inflicting harm and even death on individuals.

Figure 45.　Witch-Induced Stupors.
This woodcut from Guazzo's *Compendium Maleficarum* illustrates one of the varieties of stupor that witches could induce, both by drugs and enchantments.

of the Holy Faith, we judge, declare and pronounce sentence that you standing here in our presence on this day at the hour and place appointed for the hearing of your final sentence, are an impenitent heretic, and as such to be delivered or abandoned to secular justice; and as an obstinate and impenitent heretic we have by this sentence cast you off from the ecclesiastical Court and deliver and abandon you to secular justice and the power of the secular Court. And we pray that the said secular Court may moderate its sentence of death upon you. This sentence was given, etc.

The Bishop and Judges may, moreover, arrange that just men zealous for the faith, known to and in the confidence of the secular Court, shall have access to the prisoner while the secular Court is performing its office, in order to console him and even yet induce him to confess the truth, acknowledge his guilt, and renounce his errors.

But if it should happen that after the sentence, and when the prisoner is already at the place where he is to be burned, he should say that he wishes to confess the truth and acknowledge his guilt, and does so; and if he should be willing to abjure that and every heresy; although it may be presumed that he does this rather from fear of death than for love of the truth, yet I should be of the opinion that he may in mercy be received as a penitent heretic and be imprisoned for life. See the gloss on the chapters *ad abolendam* and *excommunicamus*. Nevertheless, according to the rigour of the law, the Judges ought not to place much faith in a conversion of this sort; and furthermore, they can always punish him on account of the temporal injuries which he has committed.

Of the Method of passing Sentence upon a Witch who Annuls Spells wrought by Witchcraft; and of Witch Midwives and Archer-Wizards.

The fifteenth method of bringing a process on behalf of the faith to a definitive sentence is employed when the person accused of heresy is not found to be one who casts injurious spells of witchcraft, but one who removes them; and in such a case the procedure will be as follows. The remedies which she uses will either be lawful or unlawful; and if they are lawful, she is not to be judged a witch but a good Christian. But we have already shown at length what sort of remedies are lawful.

Unlawful remedies, on the other hand, are to be distinguished as either absolutely unlawful, or in some respect unlawful. If they are absolutely unlawful, these again can be divided into two classes, according as they do or do not involve some injury to another party; but in either case they are always accompanied by an expressed invocation of devils. But if they are only in some respect unlawful, that is to say, if they are practised with only a tacit, and not an expressed, invocation of devils, such are to be judged rather vain than unlawful, according to the Canonists and some Theologians, as we have already shown.

Therefore the Judge, whether ecclesiastical or civil, must not punish the first and last of the above practices, having rather to commend the first and tolerate the last, since the Canonists maintain that it is lawful to oppose vanity with vanity. But he must by no means tolerate those who remove spells by an expressed invocation of devils, especially those who in doing so bring some injury upon a third party; and this last is said to happen when the spell is taken off one person and transferred to another. And we have already made it clear in a former part of this work that it makes no difference whether the person to whom the spell is transferred be herself a witch or not, or whether or not she be the person who cast the original spell, or whether it be a man or any other creature.

It may be asked what the Judge should do when such a person maintains that she removes spells by lawful and not unlawful means; and how the Judge can arrive at the truth of such a case. We answer that he should summon her and ask her what remedies she uses; but he must not rely only upon her word, for the ecclesiastical Judge whose duty it is must make diligent inquiry, either himself or by means of some parish priest who shall examine all his parishioners after placing them upon oath, as to what remedies she uses. And if, as is usually the case, they are found to be superstitious remedies, they must in no way be tolerated, on account of the terrible penalties laid down by the Canon Law, as will be shown.

Again, it may be asked how the lawful remedies can be distinguished from the unlawful, since they always assert that they remove spells by certain prayers and the use of herbs. We answer that this will be easy, provided that a diligent inquiry be made. For although they must necessarily conceal their superstitious remedies, either that they may not be arrested, or that they may the more easily ensnare the minds of the simple, and therefore make great show of their use of prayers and herbs; yet they can be manifestly convicted by four superstitious actions as sorceresses and witches.

For there are some who can divine secrets, and are able to tell things which they could only know through the revelation of evil spirits. For example: when the injured come to them to be healed, they can discover and make known the cause of their injury; as that it arose from some quarrel with a neighbour or some other cause; and they can perfectly know this and tell it to those who consult them.

Secondly, they sometimes undertake to cure the injury or spell of one person, but will have nothing to do with that of another. For in the Diocese of Spires there is a witch in a certain place called Zunhofen who, although she seems to heal many persons, confesses that she can in no way heal certain others; and this is for no other reason than, as the inhabitants of the place assert, that the spells cast on such persons have been so potently wrought by other witches with the help of devils that the devils themselves cannot remove them. For one devil cannot or will not always yield to another.

Thirdly, it sometimes happens that they know that they must make some reservation or exception in their cure of such injuries. Such a case is known to have occurred in the town of Spires itself. An honest woman who had been bewitched in her shins sent for a diviner of this sort to come and heal her; and when the witch had entered her house and looked at her, she made such an exception. For she said: If there are no scales and hairs in the wound, I could take out all the other evil matter. And she revealed the cause of the injury, although she had come from the country from a distance of two miles, saying: You quarrelled with your neighbour on such a day, and therefore this has happened to you. Then, having extracted from the wound many other matters of various sorts, which were not scales or hairs, she restored her to health.

Fourthly, they sometimes themselves observe, or cause to be observed, certain superstitious ceremonies. For instance, they fix some such time as before sunrise for people to visit them; or say that they cannot heal injuries which were caused beyond the limits of the estate on which they live; or that they can only heal two or three persons in a year. Yet they do not heal them, but only seem to do so by ceasing to injure them.

We could add many other considerations as touching the condition of such persons: as that, after the lapse of a certain time they have incurred the reputation of leading a bad and sinful life, or that they are adulteresses, or the survivors from covens of other witches. Therefore their gift of healing is not derived from God on account of the sanctity of their lives.

Here we must refer incidentally to witch midwives, who surpass all other witches in their crimes, as we have shown in the First Part of this work. And the number of them is so great that, as has been found from their

Figure 46. The Archer-Witch.

This illustration from Molitor's *De Lamis* illustrates yet another frightful potential talent of the witch. The Archer-Witch inflicted pain and injury by shooting her victim with enchanted arrows.

confessions, it is thought that there is scarcely any tiny hamlet in which at least one is not to be found. And that the magistrates may in some degree meet this danger, they should allow no midwife to practise without having been first sworn as a good Catholic; at the same time observing the other safeguards mentioned in the Second Part of this work.

Here too we must consider archer-wizards, who constitute the graver danger to the Christian religion in that they have obtained protection on the estates of nobles and Princes who receive, patronize, and defend them. But that all such receivers and protectors are more damnable than all witches, especially in certain cases, is shown as follows. The Canonists and Theologians divide into two classes the patrons of such archer-wizards, according as they defend the error or the person. They who defend the error are more damnable than the wizards themselves, since they are judged to be not only heretics but heresiarchs (24, quest. 3). And the laws do not make much special mention of such patrons, because they do not distinguish them from other heretics.

But there are others who, while not excusing the sin, yet defend the sinner. These, for example, will do all in their power to protect such wizards (or other heretics) from trial and punishment at the hands of the Judge acting on behalf of the Faith.

Similarly there are those in public authority, that is to say, public persons such as temporal Lords, and also spiritual Lords who have temporal jurisdiction, who are, either by omission or commission, patrons of such wizards and heretics.

They are their patrons by omission when they neglect to perform their duty in regard to such wizards and suspects, or to their followers, receivers, defenders and patrons, when they are required by the Bishops or Inquisitors to do this: that is, by failing to arrest them, by not guarding them carefully when they are arrested, by not taking them to the place within their jurisdiction which has been appointed for them, by not promptly executing the sentence passed upon them, and by other such derelictions of their duty.

They are their patrons by commission when, after such heretics have been arrested, they liberate them from prison without the licence or order of the Bishop or Judge; or when they directly or indirectly obstruct the trial, judgement, and sentence of such, or act in some similar way. The penalties for this have been declared in the Second Part of this work, where we treated of archer-wizards and other enchanters of weapons.

It is enough now to say that all these are by law excommunicated, and incur the twelve great penalties. And if they continue obstinate in that excommunication for a year, they are then to be condemned as heretics.

Who, then, are to be called receivers of such; and are they to be reckoned as heretics? All they, we answer, who receive such archer-wizards, enchanters of weapons, necromancers, or heretic witches as are the subject of this whole work. And such receivers are of two classes, as was the case with the defenders and patrons of such.

For there are some who do not receive them only once or twice, but many times and often; and these are well called in Latin *receptatores*, from the frequentative form of the verb. And receivers of this class are sometimes blameless, since they act in ignorance and there is no sinister suspicion attaching to them. But sometimes they are to blame, as being well aware of the sins of those whom they receive; for the Church always denounces these wizards as the most cruel enemies of the faith. And if nevertheless temporal Lords receive, keep and defend them, etc., they are and are rightly called receivers of heretics. And with regard to such, the laws say that they are to be excommunicated.

But others there are who do not often or many times receive such wizards or heretics, but only once or twice; and these are not properly called *receptatores*, but *receptores*, since they are not frequent receivers. (Yet the Archdeacon disagrees with this view; but it is no great matter, for we are considering not words but deeds.)

But there is this difference between *receptatores* and *receptores:* those temporal Princes are always *receptatores* who simply will not or cannot drive away such heretics. But *receptores* may be quite innocent.

Finally, it is asked who are they who are said to be obstructors of the duty of Inquisitors and Bishops against such heretics; and whether they are to be reckoned as heretics. We answer that such obstructors are of two kinds. For there are some who cause a direct obstruction, by rashly on their own responsibility releasing from gaol those who have been detained on a charge of heresy, or by interfering with the process of the Inquisition by wreaking some injury to witnesses on behalf of the Faith because of the evidence they have given; or it may be that the temporal Lord issues an order that none but himself may try such a case, and that anyone charged with this crime should be brought before no one but himself, and that the evidence should be given only in his presence, or some similar order. And such, according to Giovanni d'Andrea, are direct obstructors. They who directly obstruct the process, judgement or sentence on behalf of the Faith, or help, advise or favour others in doing so, although they are guilty of great sin, are not on that account to be judged heretics, unless it appears in other ways that they are obstinately and willfully involved in such heresies of witches. But they are to be smitten with the sword of excommunication; and if they stubbornly endure that excommunication for a year, then are they to be condemned as heretics.

But others are indirect obstructors. These, as Giovanni d'Andrea explains, are those who give such orders as that no one shall bear arms for the capture of heretics except the servants of the said temporal Lord. Such are less guilty than the former, and are not heretics; but they, and also any who advise, help or patronize them in such actions, are to be excommunicated; and if they obstinately remain in that excommunication for a year, they are then to be condemned as if they were heretics. And here it is to be understood that they are in such a way to be condemned as heretics that, if they are willing to return, they are received back to mercy, having first abjured their error; but if not, they are to be handed over to the secular Court as impenitents.

To sum up. Witch-midwives, like other witches, are to be condemned and sentenced according to the nature of their crimes; and this is true also of those who, as we have said, remove spells of witchcraft superstitiously and by the help of devils; for it can hardly be doubted that, just as they are able to remove them, so can they inflict them. And it is a fact that some definite agreement is formed between witches and devils whereby some shall be able to hurt and others to heal, that so they may more easily ensnare the minds of the simple and recruit the ranks of their abandoned and hateful society. Archer-wizards and enchanters of weapons, who are only protected by being patronized, defended and received by temporal Lords, are subject to the same penalties; and they who patronize them, etc., or obstruct the officers of justice in their proceedings against them, are subject to all the penalties to which the patrons of heretics are liable, and are to be excommunicated. And if after they have obstinately endured that excommunication for a year they wish to repent, let them abjure that obstruction and patronage, and they can be admitted to mercy; but if not, they must be handed over as impenitents to the secular Court. And even if they have not endured their excommunication for a year, such obstructors can still be proceeded against as patrons of heretics.

And all that has been said with regard to patrons, defenders, receivers, and obstructors in the case of archer-wizards, etc., applies equally in respect of all other witches who work various injuries to men, animals, and the fruits of the earth. But even the witches themselves, when in the court of conscience with humble and contrite spirit they weep for their sins and make clean confession asking forgiveness, are taken back to mercy. But when they are known, those whose duty it is must proceed against them, summoning, examining, and detaining them, and in all things proceeding in accordance with the nature of their crimes to a definitive and conclusive sentence, as has been shown, if they wish to avoid the snare of eternal damnation by reason of the excommunication pronounced upon them by the Church when they deliberately fail in their duty.

20

POPE ALEXANDER VI
The Pursuit of Witches in Lombardy
1501

The increased attention which fifteenth-century popes had paid to the appearance of witchcraft cases in different parts of Christendom had culminated in Pope Innocent VIII's privilege to the Dominican Inquisitors Krämer and Sprenger (*No.* 18) and the Inquisitors' encyclopedia of witchcraft, the *Malleus Maleficarum* (*No.* 19). The papal privilege, printed as an introduction to the *Malleus* in all subsequent editions, offered a rationale for persecution by both ecclesiastical and civil tribunals. The privilege and the *Malleus,* however, applied primarily to southern Germany and Switzerland. Shortly after their publication, Pope Alexander VI issued the following letter to Angelo of Verona, the Inquisitor of Lombardy; his concern was possibly inspired by the evils the *Malleus* had palpably demonstrated, and certainly by the notorious reluctance of northern Italian prelates to allow the authority of the Inquisition into their districts.

Pope Alexander VI, the Bull *Cum acceperimus,* 1501. Latin text in Hansen, *Quellen, p. 31.* Tr. E.P.

*A*s we have learned that in the province of Lombardy many people of both sexes give themselves over to diverse incantations and devilish superstitions in order to procure many wicked things by their venery and vain rites, to destroy men, beasts, and fields, to spread great scandal, and to induce grievous errors, we decree, in order both to fulfill our pastoral office from our high commission and to restrain these evils, scandals, and errors, that they shall cease. That is the reason why we send to you, commit to you, and order you and your successors appointed in Lombardy our full confidence in the Lord, that you may seek out diligently those people of both sexes (either by yourself or with the aid of a company which you shall choose) and secure and punish them through the medium of justice. And so that you may be better able to fulfill this commission, we give to you against them full and sufficient powers, notwithstanding all other constitutions and apostolic orders, indulgences, and ordinary concessions which have been accorded at other times, and notwithstanding all other orders to the contrary of these, whatever they may be.

The Witch-Persecutions
of the Sixteenth Century

The central theological event of the sixteenth century was the Protestant Reformation. Its effect upon witchcraft-belief, however, was surprisingly small. While Protestants on the whole were intensely critical of the Catholic system of ecclesiastical courts and shifted persecution of the witch primarily to the civil criminal courts, Protestant theology generally reaffirmed its belief in the presence and evil operations of fallen men and women in contractual service to Satan.

Martin Luther, relying upon the scriptural bases for such belief, dramatically reasserted the reality of the Devil in search of men's souls, citing his own personal encounters with the Evil One, and warned that the world of the flesh and much of the world of the spirit was under Satan's sway; the witchcraft of which St. Paul spoke in his *Epistle to the Galatians* seemed to Luther to exist all about men in the contemporary world. Indeed, by suggesting not merely that witchcraft was a heresy, but that all heresy and false Biblical interpretation was witchcraft, Luther extended the scope of persecution (No. 21).

Jean Calvin cited with equal assurance the scriptural warnings against Satan and his host of demons, and attacked all attempts at metaphorical interpretation of man's relationships with the Powers of Darkness. Calvin insisted that the Bible had either literally described men possessed by or in service to Satan, or offered meaningless statements about the nature of God's universe; the latter, of course, was unacceptable. Furthermore, Calvin's analysis of the will reaffirmed the concept of the *voluntary* surrender of a soul to the Devil, a concept central to continued witchcraft-belief and prosecution (*No.* 22).

Leading Catholic thinkers conceded nothing to the reformers in their commitment to ridding the world of Satan's legions. Jean Bodin reminded princes that the crime of the witch was *lèse-majesté* against God, a crime infinitely more heinous than any earthly criminal act. The laws against witches were divine, not secular, and no prince had the power to avoid prosecuting or to pardon such an offender. For Bodin, it was better that a few unfortunate innocents should burn than that a witch should go unpunished (*No.* 23).

In Catholic areas of Western Germany, witch persecutions reached new heights of intensity in the second half of the sixteenth century. Contemporary accounts of witch-hunts and of the systematic crushing of opposition to such trials, such as those at the cathedral city of Trèves (Trier), offer a sense of the increased ardor of certain officials and populaces (*No.* 24).

In many Protestant areas, the new religious fervor occasioned by the Reformation raised the fear of witches to a great pitch in areas where such phenomena had been relatively rare. Thus, in Scotland (*No.* 25) and in England (*No.* 26), the sixteenth century witnessed the beginning of major persecutions that were to intensify well into the seventeenth century, when they would reach their zenith.

By the end of the sixteenth century, Nicholas Rémy, systematically re-synthesizing the components of witchcraft-belief and vividly portraying for his readers the horrific evils effected by the witch, spoke for a Europe, Catholic and Protestant, still singularly resolved upon its task of fulfilling its scriptural obligation, "Thou shall not suffer a witch to live" (*No.* 27).

21

MARTIN LUTHER
Witchcraft and the Reformation

Martin Luther (1483–1546) shattered forever the ostensible unity of the Christian Church and of Christian theology in Catholic Europe, but he shared and reinforced the witchcraft-beliefs of the culture that produced him. There is nothing singular in his demonological thought, but his testimonies of the Devil's physical and spiritual assaults upon him indicate how personal and intense a matter the work of Satan and his hosts was for the great reformer. His writings and his correspondence make frequent reference to the evil and harmful actions of witches, among which he often included the deeds of his opponents. Although Luther had total faith in the omnipotence of Christ over the Devil and his legions, he saw the power of witches as indeed awesome, and once wrote: "I should have no compassion on these witches; I would burn all of them."[1]

Martin Luther, *A Commentary on St. Paul's Epistle to the Galatians* (Philadelphia, 1875), pp. 287–90, 590–91.

*W*ho hath bewitched you, that you should not believe the *truth?* Here have ye another commendation of this goodly righteousness of the law, and of our own righteousness, namely, that it maketh us to

1. *The Table Talk of Martin Luther*, tr. William Hazlitt (London, 1872), p. 251.

Figures 47–49. The Witches, Demons, and Children.

Figure 47. The Devil Carries off a Child.
This woodcut by Dürer from the fifteenth-century *Ritter von Turn* depicts the Devil carrying off a child promised to it by the child's parents.

196

contemn the truth: It bewitcheth us in such sort, that we do not believe nor obey the truth, but rebel against it.

Of the bodily and spiritual witchcraft

Paul calleth the Galatians foolish and bewitched, comparing them to children, to whom witchcraft doth much harm. As though he should say: It happeneth to you as it doth to children, whom witches, sorcerers, and enchanters are wont to charm by their enchantments, and by the illusions of the devil. Afterwards, in the fifth chapter, he rehearseth sorcery among the works of the flesh, which is a kind of witchcraft, whereby he plainly testifieth, that indeed such witchcraft and sorcery there is, and that it may be done. Moreover, it cannot be denied but that the devil liveth, yea, and reigneth throughout the whole world. Witchcraft and sorcery therefore are the works of the devil; whereby he doth not only hurt men, but also, by the permission of God, he sometimes destroyeth them. Furthermore, we are all subject to the devil, both in body and goods; and we be strangers in this world, whereof he is the prince and god. Therefore the bread which we eat, the drink which we drink, the garments which we wear, yea, the air, and whatsoever we live by in the flesh, is under his dominion.

But he doth not only bewitch men after this gross manner, but also after a more subtle sort, and much more dangerous; wherein he is a marvellous cunning workman. And hereof it cometh that Paul applieth the bewitching of the senses to the bewitching of the spirit. For by this spiritual witchcraft that old serpent bewitcheth not men's senses, but their minds with false and wicked opinions: which opinions, they that are so bewitched, do take to be true and godly. Briefly, so great is the malice of this sorcerer the devil, and his desire to hurt, that not only he deceiveth those secure and proud spirits with his enchantments, but even those also which are professors of true Christianity, and well affected in religion: yea, as touching myself, to say the truth, he sometimes assaileth me so mightily, and oppresseth me with such heavy cogitations, that he utterly shadoweth my Saviour Christ from me, and in a manner taketh him clean out of my sight. To be brief, there is none of us all which is not oftentimes bewitched by false persuasions: that is to say, which doth not fear, trust, or rejoice where he ought not, or doth not sometimes think otherwise of God, of Christ, of faith, of his vocation, &c., than he should do.

Let us therefore learn to know the subtle sleights of this sorcerer, lest if he find us sleeping in security he deceive us by his enchantments. True it is, that by his sorcery he can do no hurt to our ministry: yet is he with us in spirit. Day and night he rangeth about, seeking how he may devour every one of us alone, and unless he find us sober, and armed with spiritual weapons, that is to say, with the word of God and faith, he will devour us.

This is the cause that he oftentimes stirreth up new battles against us. And indeed it is very profitable for us that he thus assaileth us, and by his subtle trains exerciseth us; for by this means he confirmeth our doctrine, he stirreth up and increaseth faith in us. Indeed, we have been many times cast down, and yet still are cast down in this conflict, but we perish not: for Christ hath always triumphed, and doth triumph through us. Wherefore we hope assuredly, that we shall also hereafter by Jesus Christ obtain the victory against the devil. And this hope bringeth unto us sure consolation, so that in the midst of our temptations we take courage and say: Behold, Satan hath heretofore tempted us, and by his false illusions hath provoked us to infidelity, to the contempt of God, despair, &c., yet hath he not prevailed, nor shall he prevail hereafter. "He is greater that is in us, than he that is in the world." 1 John iv. 4. Christ is stronger, who hath and doth overcome that strong one in us, and shall overcome him forever. Notwithstanding the devil sometimes overcometh us in the flesh, that we may have experience of the power of a stronger against that strong one, and may say, with Paul, "When I am weak, then am I strong."

Let no man think therefore that the Galatians only were bewitched of the devil: but let every man think that he himself might have been, and yet may be bewitched by him. There is none of us so strong that he is able to resist him, and especially if he attempt to do it by his own strength. "Job was an upright and a just man, fearing God, and there was none like unto him upon the earth." Job i. 8. But what power had he against the devil, when God withdrew his hand? Did not this holy man horribly fall? Therefore this enchanter was not only mighty in the Galatians, but he goeth about continually to deceive, if not all men, yet as many as he can, with his illusions and false persuasions: "For he is a liar, and the father of lies." John viii. 44.

Verse 1. Who hath bewitched you?

Here Paul excuseth the Galatians, and layeth the fault upon the false apostles. As though he should say, I see that ye are not fallen through willfulness or malice; but the devil hath sent the enchanting false apostles, his children, amongst you, and they do so bewitch you, in teaching you that ye are justified by the law, that now ye think otherwise of Christ than ye did afore, when ye heard the gospel preached by me. But we labour, both by preaching and writing unto you, to uncharm that sorcery wherewith the false apostles have bewitched you, and to set at liberty those which are snared therewith.

So we also at this day labour by the word of God against those fantastical opinions of the Anabaptists, that we may set at liberty those that are entangled therewith, and reduce them to the pure doctrine of faith, and there hold them. And this our labour is not altogether in vain; for we have called back many whom they have bewitched, and have delivered them out of their snares. Notwithstanding such there are, as will not suffer themselves to be taught, especially the chief sorcerers and authors of this witchery. They will hear no reason, nor admit the Scripture: yea, they abuse and corrupt the Scripture, and avoid such places as are alleged against them, with their false glosses and devilish dreams, clean contrary to the Scripture; which is a manifest sign that they are bewitched of the devil. Wherefore they are nothing amended by our admonitions, but are much more hardened and more obstinate than they were before. And surely I could never have believed, but that I have good experience thereof at this day, that the power of the devil is so great, that he is able to make falsehood so like the truth. Moreover, (which is yet much more horrible,) when he goeth about to overwhelm sorrowful consciences with overmuch heaviness, he can so cunningly and so lively change himself into the likeness of Christ, that it is impossible for the poor tempted and afflicted soul to perceive it: whereby many simple and ignorant persons are deceived and driven down to desperation, and some also to destroy themselves; for they are so bewitched of the devil, that they believe this to be a most certain truth, that they are tempted and accused, not of the devil, but of Christ himself.

Such a thing of late happened to that miserable man Dr. Kraws of Halle, which said, "I have denied Christ, and therefore he standeth now before his Father and accuseth me." He being blinded with the illusion of the devil, hath so strongly conceived in his mind this imagination, that by no exhortation, no consolation, no promises of God he could be brought from it; whereupon he despaired, and so miserably destroyed himself. This was a mere lie, a bewitching of the devil, and a fantastical definition of a strange Christ, whom the Scripture knoweth not. For the Scripture setteth forth Christ, not as a judge, a tempter, an accuser; but a reconciler, a mediator, a comforter, and a throne of grace.

But the poor man, deluded by the devil, could not then see this; and therefore, against all Scripture, he thinketh this to be an undoubted truth: "Christ accuseth thee before his Father: he standeth not for thee, but against thee; therefore thou art damned." And this temptation is not of man, but of the devil, which that ·enchanter most strongly imprinteth in the heart of the tempted. But unto us which are led and taught by another spirit, it is a cursed lie, and a bewitching of the devil. But unto those that are thus bewitched, it is so certain a truth, that none can be more certain.

Seeing then that the devil is able to print in our heart so manifest a lie, that we would swear a thousand times it were an undoubted truth, we must not be proud, but walk in fear and humility, calling upon the Lord Jesus, that we be not led into temptation. Worldly and secure men, which, having heard the gospel once or twice preached, do by-and-by imagine that they have received abundance of the Spirit, fall at length in like manner, because they fear not God, they are not thankful unto him, but persuade themselves that they are able, not only to hold and defend the doctrine of true religion, but also to stand against the devil in any assault or conflict, be it ever so great. Such are meet instruments for the devil to bewitch and to throw down to desperation.

On the other side, say not then, I am perfect; I cannot fall, but humble thyself, and fear, lest, if thou stand to-day, tomorrow thou be overthrown. I myself, although I be a doctor of divinity, and have now preached Christ, and fought against the devil in his false teachers a great while, by mine own experience have found how hard a matter this is. For I cannot shake off Satan as I desire: neither can I so apprehend Christ as the Scripture setteth him forth: but oftentimes the devil setteth before mine eyes a false Christ. But, thanks be to God who keepeth us in the word, in faith, and in prayer, that we may walk before him in humility and fear, and not presume of our own wisdom, righteousness, and strength, but trust in the power of Christ, who is strong when we are weak, and by us weak and feeble creatures continually overcometh and triumpheth; to whom be glory forever.

This bewitching then, and this sorcery, is nothing else but a plain illusion of the devil, printing in the heart a false opinion of Christ and against Christ, and he that is deluded with this opinion, is bewitched. They therefore that have this opinion, that they are justified by the works of the law, or by the traditions of men, are bewitched; for this opinion is against faith and against Christ. Paul useth this word [bewitching] in contempt of the false apostles, which so vehemently urged the doctrine of the law and works. As if he should say, What a devilish bewitching is this? For as the senses are perverted by bodily witchcraft, so are the minds of men also deluded by this spiritual witchcraft. . . .

Witchcraft

Of witchcraft I have spoken before, in the third chapter. This vice was very common in these our days, before the light and truth of the gospel was revealed. When I was a child, there were many witches and sorcerers, which bewitched both cattle and men, but specially children, and did great harm also otherwise; but now, in the light of the gospel, these things be not so commonly heard of, for the gospel thrusteth the devil out of his seat, with all his illusions. But now he bewitcheth men much more horribly, namely, with spiritual sorcery and witchcraft.

Paul reckoneth witchcraft among the works of the flesh, which notwithstanding, as all men know, is not a work of fleshly lust or lechery, but a kind of idolatry. For witchcraft covenanteth with the devil; superstition or idolatry covenanteth with God: albeit, not with the true God, but with a counterfeit god. Wherefore idolatry is, indeed, a spiritual witchcraft. For as witches do enchant cattle and men, so idolaters, that is to say, all justiciaries, or justifiers of themselves, go about to bewitch God, and to make him such a one as they do imagine. Now they imagine him to be such a one as will justify them, not of his mere grace and mercy, and through faith in Christ, but in respect of their will-worshippings, and works of their own choosing, and in recompence thereof will give them righteousness and life everlasting. But whilst they go about to bewitch God, they bewitch themselves: for if they continue in this wicked opinion which they conceive of God, they shall die in their idolatry and be damned. The works of the flesh are well known for the most part, therefore they shall not need any further declaration.

22

JEAN CALVIN
Witchcraft and the Reformation

Jean Calvin (1509–64) brought the remarkable rigor and logic of his mind, the clarity and forcefulness of his prose, and the total commitment of his soul to the service of the Protestant Reformation; these same qualities are all manifest in his treatment of demonology as well. The role and power of Satan is critical to the concept of witchcraft as it had evolved in Christian Europe, as is the concept of the pact between Devil and witch. Both of these areas are clarified by Calvin in a manner which more than justified the concern with witchcraft and the persecutions which the sixteenth century sustained and intensified. By elaborating the scriptural bases of demonological belief, Calvin insured that the Reformation would not tamper with Church dogma on these matters. He frequently referred his readers to a passage of the New Testament, *Ephesians* vi:11–12, which starkly summed up their sense of the predicament: "Put on the whole armour of God, that ye may be able to stand against the wiles of the Devil. For we wrestle not against flesh and blood, but against principalities, against powers, against the rulers of the darkness of this world."

Jean Calvin, *Institutes of the Christian Religion*, ed. John T. McNeill, tr. Ford Lewis Battles, Library of Christian Classics, Vol. XX (Philadelphia, 1960), Book I, ch. XIV, 13–19, pp. 172–79; Book II, ch. IV, 1–2, pp. 309–11.

Jean Calvin

*T*he devils in the purposes of God: Scripture forearms us against the adversary. All that Scripture teaches concerning devils aims at arousing us to take precaution against their stratagems and contrivances, and also to make us equip ourselves with those weapons which are strong and powerful enough to vanquish these most powerful foes. For when Satan is called the god [II Cor. 4:4] and prince [John 12:31] of this world, when he is spoken of as a strong armed man [Luke 11:21; cf. Matt. 12:29], the spirit who holds power over the air [Eph. 2:2], a roaring lion [I Peter 5:8], these descriptions serve only to make us more cautious and watchful, and thus more prepared to take up the struggle. This also sometimes is noted explicitly: for Peter, after he has said that the devil "prowls around like a roaring lion seeking someone to devour" [I Peter 5:8], immediately subjoins the exhortation that with faith we steadfastly resist him [I Peter 5:9]. And Paul, after he has warned us that our struggle is not with flesh and blood, but with the princes of the air, with the powers of darkness, and spiritual wickedness [Eph. 6:12], forthwith bids us put on that armour capable of sustaining so great and dangerous a contest [Eph. 6:13 ff.]. We have been forewarned that an enemy relentlessly threatens us, an enemy who is the very embodiment of rash boldness, of military prowess, of crafty wiles, of untiring zeal and haste, of every conceivable weapon and of skill in the science of warfare. We must, then, bend our every effort to this goal: that we should not let ourselves be overwhelmed by carelessness or faintheartedness, but on the contrary, with courage rekindled stand our ground in combat. Since this military service ends only at death, let us urge ourselves to perseverance. Indeed, conscious of our weakness and ignorance, let us especially call upon God's help, relying upon him alone in whatever we attempt, since it is he alone who can supply us with counsel and strength, courage and armor.

The realm of wickedness

Moreover, in order that we may be aroused and exhorted all the more to carry this out, Scripture makes known that there are not one, not two, nor a few foes, but great armies, which wage war against us. For Mary Magdalene is said to have been freed from seven demons by which she was possessed [Mark 16:9; Luke 8:2], and Christ bears witness that usually after a demon has once been cast out, if you make room for him again, he will take with him seven spirits more wicked than he and return to his empty possession [Matt. 12:43–45]. Indeed, a whole legion is said to have assailed one man [Luke 8:30]. We are therefore taught by these examples that we have to wage war against an infinite number of enemies, lest, despising their fewness, we should be too remiss to give battle, or, thinking that we are sometimes afforded some respite, we should yield to idleness.

But the frequent mention of Satan or the devil in the singular denotes the empire of wickedness opposed to the Kingdom of Righteousness. For as the church and fellowship of the saints has Christ as Head, so the faction of the impious and impiety itself are depicted for us together with their prince who holds supreme sway over them. For this reason, it was said: "Depart, . . . you cursed, into the eternal fire, prepared for the devil and his angels" [Matt. 25:41].

An irreconcilable struggle

The fact that the devil is everywhere called God's adversary and ours also ought to fire us to an unceasing struggle against him. For if we have God's glory at heart, as we should have, we ought with all our strength to contend against him who is trying to extinguish it. If we are minded to affirm Christ's Kingdom as we ought, we must wage irreconcilable war with him who is plotting its ruin. Again, if we care about our salvation at all, we ought to have neither peace nor truce with him who continually lays traps to destroy it. So, indeed, is he described in Gen., ch. 3, where he seduces man from the obedience owed to God, that he may simultaneously deprive God of his due honor and hurl man himself into ruin [vs. 1–5]. So, also, in the Evangelists, where he is called "an enemy" [Matt. 13:28, 39], and is said to sow weeds in order to corrupt the seed of eternal life [Matt. 13:25]. In sum, we experience in all of Satan's deeds what Christ testifies concerning him, that "from the beginning he was a murderer . . . and a liar" [John 8:44]. For he opposes the truth of God with falsehoods, he obscures the light with darkness, he entangles men's minds in errors, he stirs up hatred, he kindles contentions and combats, everything to the end that he may overturn God's Kingdom and plunge men with himself into eternal death. From this it appears that he is in nature depraved, evil, and malicious. For there must be consummate depravity in that disposition which devotes itself to assailing God's glory and man's salvation. This, also, is what John means in his letter, when he writes that "the devil has sinned from the beginning" [I John 3:8]. Indeed, he considers him as the author, leader, and architect of all malice and iniquity.

Figure 48. The Witches Offer Children to the Devil.

This woodcut illustrated a tract on the witchcraft trial of Agnes Sampson in 1591. Here, the witches voluntarily bring their children to Satan—a variation of the Dürer figures in the preceding illustration.

Figure 49. The Dismemberment of a Child-Victim.

In this illustration from Guazzo's *Compendium Maleficarum* a child is to be killed, cooked, and ritually dismembered to be used as part of the witches demonic pharmacopeia.

The devil is a degenerate creation of God

Yet, since the devil was created by God, let us remember that this malice, which we attribute to his nature, came not from his creation but from his perversion. For, whatever he has that is to be condemned he has derived from his revolt and fall. For this reason, Scripture warns us lest, believing that he has come forth in his present condition from God, we should ascribe to God himself what is utterly alien to him. For this reason, Christ declares that "when Satan lies, he speaks according to his own nature" and states the reason, because "he abode not in the truth" [John 8:44]. Indeed, when Christ states that Satan "abode not in the truth," he hints that he was once in it, and when he makes him "the father of lies," he deprives him of imputing to God the fault which he brought upon himself.

But although these things are briefly and not very clearly stated, they are more than enough to clear God's majesty of all slander. And what concern is it to us to know anything more about devils or to know it for another purpose? Some persons grumble that Scripture does not in numerous passages set forth systematically and clearly that fall of the devils, its cause, manner, time, and character. But because this has nothing to do with us, it was better not to say anything, or at least to touch upon it lightly, because it did not befit the Holy Spirit to feed our curiosity with empty histories to no effect. And we see that the Lord's purpose was to teach nothing in his sacred oracles except what we should learn to our edification. Therefore, lest we ourselves linger over superfluous matters, let us be content with this brief summary of the nature of devils: they were when first created angels of God, but by degeneration they ruined themselves, and were made the instruments of ruin for others. Because this is profitable to know, it is plainly taught in Peter and Jude. God did not spare those angels who sinned [II Peter 2:4] and kept not their original nature, but left their abode [Jude 6]. And Paul, in speaking of the "elect angels" [I Tim. 5:21], is no doubt tacitly contrasting them with the reprobate angels.

The devil stands under God's power

As for the discord and strife that we say exists between Satan and God, we ought to accept as a fixed certainty the fact that he can do nothing unless God wills and assents to it. For we read in the history of Job that he presented himself before God to receive his commands [Job 1:6; 2:1], and did not dare undertake any evil act without first having obtained permission [chs. 1:12; 2:6]. Thus, also, when Ahab was to be deceived, Satan took upon himself to become a spirit of falsehood in the mouth of all the prophets; and commissioned by God, he carried out his task [I Kings 22:20–22]. For this reason, too, the spirit of the Lord that troubled Saul is called "evil" because the sins of the impious king were punished by it as by a lash [I Sam. 16:14; 18:10]. And elsewhere it is written that the plagues were inflicted upon the Egyptians by God "through evil angels" [Ps. 78:49]. According to these particular examples Paul generally testifies that the blinding of unbelievers is God's work [II Thess. 2:11], although he had before called it the activity of Satan [II Thess. 2:9; cf. II Cor. 4:4; Eph. 2:2]. Therefore Satan is clearly under God's power, and is so ruled by his bidding as to be compelled to render him service. Indeed, when we say that Satan resists God, and that Satan's works disagree with God's works, we at the same time assert that this resistance and this opposition are dependent upon God's sufferance. I am not now speaking of Satan's will, nor even of his effort, but only of his effect. For inasmuch as the devil is by nature wicked, he is not at all inclined to obedience to the divine will, but utterly intent upon contumacy and rebellion. From himself and his own wickedness, therefore, arises his passionate and deliberate opposition to God. By this wickedness he is urged on to attempt courses of action which he believes to be most hostile to God. But because with the bridle of his power God holds him bound and restrained, he carries out only those things which have been divinely permitted to him; and so he obeys his Creator, whether he will or not, because he is compelled to yield him service wherever God impels him.

Assurance of victory!

Now, because God bends the unclean spirits hither and thither at will, he so governs their activity that they exercise believers in combat, ambush them, invade their peace, beset them in combat, and also often weary them, rout them, terrify them, and sometimes wound them; yet they never vanquish or crush them. But the wicked they subdue and drag away; they exercise power over their minds and bodies, and misuse them as if they were slaves for every shameful act. As far as believers are concerned, because they are disquieted by enemies of this sort, they heed these exhortations: "Give no place to the devil" [Eph. 4:27]. "The devil your enemy goes about as a roaring lion, seeking someone to devour; resist him, be firm in your faith" [I Peter 5:8–9], and the like. Paul admits that he was not free from this sort of strife when he writes that, as a remedy to tame his pride, he was given an angel of Satan to humble him [II Cor. 12:7]. Therefore this exercise is common to all the children of God. But because that promise to crush Satan's head [Gen. 3:15] pertains to Christ and all his members in common, I deny that believers can ever be conquered or overwhelmed by him. Often, indeed, are they distressed, but not so deprived of life as not to recover; they fall under violent blows, but afterward they are raised up; they are wounded, but not fatally; in short, they so toil throughout life that at the last they obtain a victory.

Yet I do not confine this to individual acts. For we know that by God's just vengeance David was for a time given over to Satan, that at his prompting he should take a census of the people [II Sam. 24:1]. And Paul does not abandon hope of pardon as impossible, even if men are ensnared in the devil's net [II Tim. 2:25–26]. In another passage Paul shows that the promise mentioned above begins to have effect in this life, wherein we must struggle; and that after the struggle it is fulfilled. As he puts it, "The God of peace will soon crush Satan under your feet." [Rom. 16:20.] In our Head, indeed, this victory always fully existed, for the prince of the world had nothing in him [John 14:30]. Moreover, it now appears in part in us, who are his members; it will be completed when we shall have put off our flesh, in respect to which we are as yet subject to infirmity, and will be filled with the power of the Holy Spirit.

To the extent that Christ's Kingdom is upbuilt, Satan with his power falls; as the Lord himself says, "I saw Satan fall like lightning from heaven" [Luke 10:18]. For, by this answer he confirms what the apostles had related concerning the power of their preaching. Likewise: "When a prince occupies his own palace, all his possessions are undisturbed. But when one stronger than he overcomes him, he is cast out," etc. [Luke 11:21–22 p.]. And Christ, by dying, conquered Satan, who had "the power of death" [Heb. 2:14], and triumphed over all his forces, to the end that they might not harm the church. Otherwise, at every moment they would do away with it a hundred times over. For, such is our weakness and such is the power of his fury, how could we stand even in the slightest against his manifold and continuous attacks, unless we relied upon the victory of our leader? Therefore God does not allow Satan to rule over the souls of believers, but gives over only the impious and unbelievers, whom he deigns not to regard as members of his own flock, to be governed by him. For the devil is said to occupy this world unchallenged until he is cast out by Christ [cf. Luke 11:21]. Likewise, he is said to blind all those who do not believe in the gospel [II Cor. 4:4].

Again, to carry out his "work in the sons of disobedience" [Eph. 2:2], and rightly, for all the impious are vessels of wrath. Hence, to whom would they be subjected but to the minister of divine vengeance? Finally, they are said to be of their father the devil [John 8:44]; for, as believers are recognized as the children of God because they bear his image, so are those rightly recognized to be the children of Satan from his image, into which they have degenerated [I John 3:8–10].

Devils are not thoughts, but actualities

Inasmuch as we have before refuted that trifling philosophy about the holy angels which teaches that they are nothing but good inspirations or impulses which God arouses in men's minds, so also in this place ought those men to be refuted who babble of devils as nothing else than evil emotions or perturbations which come upon us from our flesh. We shall be able to do this briefly because there are not a few testimonies of Scripture clear enough on this matter. First, when those who have degenerated from their original state [Jude 6] are called unclean spirits and apostate angels [Matt. 12:43], the names themselves sufficiently express, not impulses or affections of minds, but rather what are called minds or spirits endowed with sense perception and understanding. Likewise, when the children of God are compared with the children of the devil both by Christ and by John [John 8:44; I John 3:10], would this comparison not be pointless if the name "devil" signified nothing but evil inspirations? And John adds something even clearer, that "the devil has sinned from the beginning" [I John 3:8]. So, also, when Jude introduces "the archangel Michael, as contending with the devil" [Jude 9], he surely sets against the good angel an evil and rebellious one. What we read in the history of Job agrees with this, that Satan appeared with the holy angels in God's presence [Job 1:6; 2:1]. Moreover, clearest of all are those passages which make mention of the punishment, which the devils have begun to feel from God's judgment, and will especially feel at the resurrection. "O Son" of David, why "have you come to torment us before the time?" [Matt. 8:29]. Likewise: "Depart, you cursed ones, into the eternal fire prepared for the devil and his angels." [Matt. 25:41.] Also: "If he spared not his own angels, but cast them bound with chains into darkness to be kept for eternal damnation," etc. [II Peter 2:4.]

How meaningless would these expressions be, that the devils are destined for eternal judgment, that fire has been prepared for them, that they are now tormented and tortured by Christ's glory, if devils were nonexistent!

But this matter does not require discussion among those who have faith in the Lord's Word, while among these empty speculators, indeed, to whom nothing is pleasing unless it be new, there is little profit in the testimonies of Scripture. It seems to me, therefore, that I have accomplished what I meant to do, namely, to equip godly minds against such delusions, with which uneasy men confound themselves and others more simple-minded than they. But it was worth-while to touch upon this point, also, lest any persons, entangled in that error, while thinking themselves without an enemy, become more slack and heedless about resisting.

How God Works in Men's Hearts

> Man under Satan's control: but Scripture shows God making use
> of Satan in hardening the heart of the reprobate. Man stands under
> the devil's power, and indeed willingly.

Unless I am mistaken, we have sufficiently proved that man is so held captive by the yoke of sin that he can of his own nature neither aspire to good through resolve nor struggle after it through effort. Besides, we posited a distinction between compulsion and necessity from which it appears that man, while he sins of necessity, yet sins no less voluntarily. But, while he is bound in servitude to the devil, he seems to be actuated more by the devil's will than by his own. It consequently remains for us to determine the part of the devil and the part of man in the action. Then we must answer the question whether we ought to ascribe to God any part of the evil works in which Scripture signifies that some action of his intervenes.

Somewhere Augustine compares man's will to a horse awaiting its rider's command, and God and the devil to its riders. "If God sits astride it," he says, "then as a moderate and skilled rider, he guides it properly, spurs it if it is too slow, checks it if it is too swift, restrains it if it is too rough or too wild, subdues it if it balks, and leads it into the right path. But if the devil saddles it, he violently drives it far from the trail like a foolish and wanton rider, forces it into ditches, tumbles it over cliffs, and goads it into obstinacy and fierceness." Since a better comparison does not come to mind, we shall be satisfied with this one for the present. It is said that the will of the natural man is subject to the devil's power and is stirred up by it. This does not mean that, like unwilling slaves rightly compelled by their masters to obey, our will, although reluctant and resisting, is constrained to take orders from the devil. It means rather that the will, captivated by Satan's wiles, of necessity obediently submits to all his leading. For those whom the Lord does not make worthy to be guided by his Spirit he abandons, with just judgment, to Satan's action. For this reason the apostle says that "the god of this world has blinded the minds of the unbelievers," who are destined to destruction, that they may not see the light of the gospel [II Cor. 4:4]; and in another place that he "is . . . at work in the disobedient sons" [Eph. 2:2]. The blinding of the impious and all iniquities following from it are called "the works of Satan." Yet their cause is not to be sought outside man's will, from which the root of evil springs up, and on which rests the foundation of Satan's kingdom, that is, sin.

God, Satan, and man active in the same event

Far different is the manner of God's action is such matters. To make this clearer to us, we may take as an example the calamity inflicted by the Chaldeans upon the holy man Job, when they killed his shepherds and in enmity ravaged his flock [Job 1:17]. Now their wicked act is perfectly obvious; nor does Satan do nothing in that work, for the history states that the whole thing stems from him [Job 1:12].

But Job himself recognizes the Lord's work in it, saying that He has taken away what had been seized through the Chaldeans [Job 1:21]. How may we attribue this same work to God, to Satan, and to man as author, without either excusing Satan as associated with God, or making God the author of evil? Easily, if we consider first the end, and then the manner, of acting. The Lord's purpose is to exercise the patience of His servant by calamity; Satan endeavors to drive him to desperation; the Chaldeans strive to acquire gain from another's property contrary to law and right. So great is the diversity of purpose that already strongly marks the deed. There is no less difference in the manner. The Lord permits Satan to afflict His servant; He hands the Chaldeans over to be impelled by Satan, having chosen them as His ministers for this task. Satan with his poison darts arouses the wicked minds of the Chaldeans to execute that evil deed. They dash madly into injustice, and they render all their members guilty and befoul them by the crime. Satan is properly said, therefore, to act in the reprobate over whom he exercises his reign, that is, the reign of wickedness. God is also said to act in His own manner, in that Satan himself, since he is the instrument of God's wrath, bends himself hither and thither at His beck and command to execute His just judgments. I pass over here the universal activity of God whereby all creatures, as they are sustained, thus derive the energy to do anything at all. I am speaking only of that special action which appears in every particular deed. Therefore we see no inconsistency in assigning the same deed to God, Satan, and man; but the distinction in purpose and manner causes God's righteousness to shine forth blameless there, while the wickedness of Satan and of man betrays itself by its own disgrace.

23

JEAN BODIN
The Witches and the Law
1580

Jean Bodin is best known as the author of one of the most influential works in the history of political theory, *Six Livres de la République* (1576). A study of the concept of sovereignty, this work went through twenty-eight editions within a generation, and ranked its author with Machiavelli as one of Europe's two leading political theorists in the sixteenth century. Bodin was a learned and humane scholar and statesman, and one of the earliest defenders of toleration in a century of religious hatreds and bloodshed.

On the subject of witchcraft, however, Bodin was a traditionalist and an implacable enemy of all who would question the justice and legitimacy of the witch-hunt-and-execution. To his *Démonomanie des Sorciers* (1580), one of the most widely-read demonological treatises of his day, he appended a victorious and closely-reasoned critique of Johann Weyer's assault upon contemporary views. So inconceivable was it to Bodin that an educated man could dissent from the clear theological and empirical truth of witchcraft that he accused Weyer of being himself a witch and called for his prosecution.

Jean Bodin, *De la Démonomanie des Sorciers* (Paris, 1580), Bk. IV, ch. V. From Burr, *Witch Persecutions*, pp. 5–6.

*T*here are two means by which states are maintained in their weal and greatness—reward and penalty: the one for the good, the other

Figure 50. The Fairy Melusine and Medieval Legend.
Although this fifteenth-century woodcut does not depict a witch proper, it does describe activities that later would be attributed to witches and would form one of the most familiar aspects of witch belief: the witch's supernatural means of locomotion. The Fairy Melusine here transforms herself into a serpent-woman and flies from her locked chamber.

214

for the bad. And, if the distribution of these two be faulty, nothing else is to be expected than the inevitable ruin of the state. . . .

But those greatly err who think that penalties are established only to punish crime. I hold that this is the least of the fruits which accrue therefrom to the state. For the greatest and the chief is the appeasing of the wrath of God, especially if the crime is directly against the majesty of God, as is this one. . . . Now, if there is any means to appease the wrath of God, to gain his blessing, to strike awe into some by the punishment of others, to preserve some from being infected by others, to diminish the number of evil-doers, to make secure the life of the well-disposed, and to punish the most detestable crimes of which the human mind can conceive, it is to punish with the utmost rigor the witches. . . .[1] Now, it is not within the power of princes to pardon a crime which the law of God punishes with the penalty of death—such as are the crimes of witches. Moreover, princes do gravely insult God in pardoning such horrible crimes committed directly against his majesty, seeing that the pettiest prince avenges with death insults against himself. Those too who let the witches escape, or who do not punish them with the utmost rigor, may rest assured that they will be abandoned by God to the mercy of the witches. And the country which shall tolerate this will be scourged with pestilences, famines, and wars; and those which shall take vengeance on the witches will be blessed by him and will make his anger to cease. Therefore it is that one accused of being a witch ought never to be fully acquitted and set free unless the calumny of the accuser is clearer than the sun, inasmuch as the proof of such crimes is so obscure and so difficult that not one witch in a million would be accused or punished if the procedure were governed by the ordinary rules.

1. Bodin then proceeds to enumerate fifteen distinct crimes, all horrid, of which every witch is guilty, and argues that, in default of proof, violent presumption should suffice for the sentence of witches to death. [Burr's note]

24

1581–93
The Persecutions at Trier

Witch-fears and witch-persecutions of great intensity flared sporadically throughout Europe in the late sixteenth century. One of the most striking lasted for almost twelve years, with varying degrees of activity, in the lands of the Elector-Archbishop of Trier (Trèves), centered in the cathedral city of Trier. The following account was written years after the events by an eye-witness to the persecutions, the canon Linden. Despite its brevity, it offers a wealth of illuminating details: the involvement of notables as well as com-moners, the pervasiveness of the fear, the severity of the judicial process, and the ability of men to profit from the agonies of their brothers.[1]

A persecution such as that at Trier demands a population that believes in the efficacy of the process by which the witch is identified and extermi-nated. Sceptics were dangerous dissenters, intolerable to those who saw the need to mobilize an area against the servants of evil. When such a sceptic arose at Trier, he not only had to be silenced, but, in the end, brought to add his voice to the consensus for persecution.

From Burr, *The Witch-Persecutions,* pp. 13–18.

---

1. Further texts from the Trier persecutions may be found in George L. Burr, "The Fate of Dietrich Flade," in L. O. Gibbons, ed., *George Lincoln Burr: His Life and Selections from His Writings* (Ithaca, N.Y., 1943).

*I*nasmuch as it was popularly believed that the continued sterility of many years was caused by witches through the malice of the Devil, the whole country rose to exterminate the witches. This movement was promoted by many in office, who hoped wealth from the persecution. And so, from court to court throughout the towns and villages of all the diocese, scurried special accusers, inquisitors, notaries, jurors, judges, constables, dragging to trial and torture human beings of both sexes and burning them in great numbers. Scarcely any of those who were accused escaped punishment. Nor were there spared even the leading men in the city of Trier. For the Judge, with two Burgomasters, several Councilors and Associate Judges, canons of sundry collegiate churches, parish-priests, rural deans, were swept away in this ruin. So far, at length, did the madness of the furious populace and of the courts go in this thirst for blood and booty that there was scarcely anybody who was not smirched by some suspicion of this crime.

Meanwhile notaries, copyists, and innkeepers grew rich. The executioner rode a blooded horse, like a noble of the court, and went clad in gold and silver; his wife vied with noble dames in the richness of her array. The children of those convicted and punished were sent into exile; their goods were confiscated; plowman and vintner failed—hence came sterility. A direr pestilence or a more ruthless invader could hardly have ravaged the territory of Trier than this inquisition and persecution without bounds: many were the reasons for doubting that all were really guilty. This persecution lasted for several years; and some of those who presided over the administration of justice gloried in the multitude of the stakes, at each of which a human being had been given to the flames.

At last, though the flames were still unsated, the people grew impoverished, rules were made and enforced restricting the fees and costs of examinations and examiners, and suddenly, as when in war funds fail, the zeal of the persecutors died out.

And, finally, as I have made mention of Losæus Callidius*, who tried by a

---

*It was during this persecution at Trier that Cornelius Loos, a scholar of Dutch birth who held a professorship in the university of that city, dared to protest against both the persecution itself and the superstitions out of which it grew. Failing in his appeals to the authorities, he wrote a book to set forth his views; but the manuscript was seized in the hands of the printer, and Loos himself thrown into prison. Thence he was brought out, in the spring of 1593, and, before the assembled church dignitaries of the place, pronounced a solemn recantation. This recantation has been preserved by the Jesuit Delrio in the great work which in 1599-1600 he published in support of the persecution. [Burr's note]

thousand arts to make public the book which he had written in defence of the witches (and some fear that even yet some evil demon may bring this about), I have brought for an antidote the Recantation signed by him. Its authentic and so-called original copy is in the possession of a devout and most honorable man, Joannes Baxius, J. U. Lic. (whose energy and zeal against this nefarious heresy God will some day reward), from whom I have received the following transcript, certified by a notary:

I, Cornelius Losæus Callidius, born at the town of Gouda in Holland, but now (on account of a certain treatise *On True and False Witchcraft*, rashly and presumptuously written without the knowledge and permission of the superiors of this place, shown by me to others, and then sent to be printed at Cologne) arrested and imprisoned in the Imperial Monastery of St. Maximin, near Trier, by order of the Most Reverend and Most Illustrious Lord, the Papal Nuncio, Octavius, Bishop of Tricarico: whereas I am informed of a surety that in the aforesaid book and also in certain letters of mine on the same subject sent clandestinely to the clergy and town council of Trier, and to others (for the purpose of hindering the execution of justice against the witches, male and female), are contained many articles which are not only erroneous and scandalous, but also suspected of heresy and smacking of the crime of treason, as being seditious and foolhardy, against the common opinion of theological teachers and the decisions and bulls of the Supreme Pontiffs, and contrary to the practice and to the statutes and laws of the magistrates and judges, not only of this Archdiocese of Trier, but of other provinces and principalities, I do therefore revoke, condemn, reject, and repudiate the said articles, in the order in which they are here subjoined.

1. In the first place, I revoke, condemn, reject, and censure the idea (which both in words and writing I have often and before many persons pertinaciously asserted, and which I wished to be the head and front of this my disputation) that the things which are written about the bodily transportation or translation of witches, male and female, are altogether fanciful and must be reckoned the figments of an empty superstition; [and this I recant] both because it smacks of rank heresy and because this opinion partakes of sedition and hence savors of the crime of treason.

2. For (and this in the second place I recant), in the letters which I have clandestinely sent to sundry persons, I have pertinaciously, without solid reasons, alleged against the magistracy that the [aerial] flight of witches is false and imaginary; asserting, moreover, that the wretched creatures are

compelled by the severity of the torture to confess things which they have never done, and that by cruel butchery innocent blood is shed and by a new alchemy gold and silver coined from human blood.

3. By these and by other things of the same sort, partly in private conversations among the people, partly in sundry letters addressed to both the magistracies,[1] I have accused of tyranny to their subjects the superiors and the judges.

4. And consequently, inasmuch as the Most Reverend and Most Illustrious Archbishop and Prince-Elector of Trier not only permits witches, male and female, to be subjected in his diocese to deserved punishment, but has also ordained laws regulating the method and costs of judicial procedure against witches, I have with heedless temerity tacitly insinuated the charge of tyranny against the aforesaid Elector of Trier.

5. I revoke and condemn, moreover, the following conclusions of mine, to wit: that there are no witches who renounce God, pay worship to the Devil, bring storms by the Devil's aid, and do other like things, but that all these things are dreams.

6. Also, that magic (*magia*) ought not to be called witchcraft (*maleficium*), nor magicians (*magi*) witches (*malefici*), and that the passage of Holy Scripture, "Thou shalt not suffer a witch to live" (*Maleficos non patieris vivere*)[2] is to be understood of those who by a natural use of natural poisons inflict death.

7. That no compact does or can exist between the Devil and a human being.

8. That devils do not assume bodies.

9. That the life of Hilarion written by St. Jerome is not authentic.

10. That there is no sexual intercourse between the Devil and human beings.

11. That neither devils nor witches can raise tempests, rain-storms, hail-storms, and the like, and that the things said about these are mere dreams.

12. That spirit and form apart from matter cannot be seen by man.

13. That it is rash to assert that whatever devils can do, witches also can do through their aid.

14. That the opinion that a superior demon can cast out an inferior is erroneous and derogatory to Christ.[3]

1. i.e., both lay and spiritual. [Burr's note]
2. Exodus, xxi, 18. [Burr's note]
3. A marginal note here cites Luke, xi. [Burr's note]

Figure 51.
The witch travelling on a monster. From Guazzo, *Compendium Malefi-carum.*

Figure 52. Witches Transformed into Beasts Riding.

This woodcut from Molitor's *De Lamis* is one of the earliest representations of the witches' ability to transform themselves into animals. Their vehicle is the stick, much older than the legendary broom.

220

15. That the Popes in their bulls do not say that magicians and witches perpetrate such things (as are mentioned above).

16. That the Roman Pontiffs granted the power to proceed against witches, lest if they should refuse they might be unjustly accused of magic, just as some of their predecessors had been justly accused of it.

These assertions, all and singular, with many calumnies, falsehoods, and sycophancies, toward the magistracy, both secular and ecclesiastical, spitefully, immodestly, and falsely poured forth, without cause, with which my writings on magic teem, I hereby expressly and deliberately condemn, revoke, and reject, earnestly beseeching the pardon of God and of my superiors for what I have done, and solemnly promising that in future I will neither in word nor in writing, by myself or through others, in whatsoever place it may befall me to be, teach, promulgate, defend, or assert any of these things. If I shall do to the contrary, I subject myself thenceforward, as if it were now, to all the penalties of the law against relapsed heretics, recusants, seditious offenders, traitors, backbiters, sycophants, who have been openly convicted, and also to those ordained against perjurers. I submit myself also to arbitrary correction, whether by the Archbishop of Trier or by any other magistrates under whom it may befall me to dwell, and who may be certified of my relapse and of my broken faith, that they may punish me according to my deserts, in honor and reputation, property and person.

In testimony of all which I have, with my own hand, signed this my recantation of the aforesaid articles, in presence of notary and witnesses.

(Signed)

CORNELIUS LOOSÆUS CALLIDIUS

(and attested)

Done in the Imperial Monastery of St. Maximin, outside the walls of Trier, in the abbot's chamber, in presence of the Reverend, Venerable, and Eminent Sirs, Peter Binsfeld,[4] Bishop of Azotus, vicar-general in matters spiritual of the Most Reverend Archbishop of Trier, our most clement lord, and Reinerus, abbot of the said monastery, Bartholomæus van Bodeghem, of Delft, J. U. L., Official of the Ecclesiastical Court of Trier, Georgius von

4. Binsfeld, suffragan bishop and real head of ecclesiastical affairs in the diocese, was doubtless the prime mover in the punishment of Loos. He had himself written a book, *De confessionibus maleficorum et sagarum* (Trier, 1589), to prove that the confessions of witches were worthy of all faith. [Burr's note]

Helffenstein, Doctor of Theology, Dean of the Collegiate Church of St. Simeon in the city of Trier, and Joannes Colmann, J. U. D., Canon of the said church and Seal-Bearer of the Court of Trier,[5] etc., in the year of Our Lord 1592 *more Trev.*,[6] on Monday, March 15th, in the presence of me the notary undersigned and of the worthy Nicolaus Dolent and Daniel Maier, secretary and copyist respectively of the Reverend Lord Abbot, as witnesses specially called and summoned to this end.

(*Signed*) ADAMUS HEC TECTONIUS, Notary

(*And below*)

Compared with its original and found to agree, by me the undersigned Secretary of the town of Antwerp,

G. KIEFFEL

Here you have the Recantation in full. And yet afterwards again at Brussels, while serving as curate in the church of Notre Dame de la Chapelle, he was accused of relapse, and was released only after a long imprisonment, and being again brought into suspicion (whence you may understand the pertinacity of his madness) escaped a third indictment through a premature death; but (much the pity!) left behind not a few partisans, men so imperfectly versed in medicine and sound theology as to share this stupid error. Would that they might be wise, and seriously realize at last how rash and noxious it is to prefer the ravings of a single heretic, Weyer, to the judgment of the Church!

5. i.e., the ecclesiastical court, of which Bodeghem was the head (the Official). [Burr's note]
6. 1593, according to our calendar; according to the *Mos Trevirense* the year began on March 25th. [Burr's note]

25

1591
The Persecution in Scotland

As is true in our own time, individual criminal cases could excite the public interest and contribute to popular conceptions as much as any general considerations of crime and the nature of the criminal. The following account of the trial for witchcraft of Dr. Fian was circulated in a contemporary pamphlet, *Newes from Scotland* (1591). Of particular interest is the denunciation of one alleged witch extracted under torture from another accused witch, indicating by what means a persecution could grow and flourish.

From Burr, *The Witch Persecutions,* pp. 19–23.

Within the towne of Trenent, in the kingdome of Scotland, there dwelleth one David Seaton, who, being deputie bailiffe in the said towne, had a maid called Geillis Duncane, who used secretlie to absent and lie forth of hir maister's house every other night: This Geillis Duncane tooke in hand to helpe all such as were troubled or grieved with anie kinde of sicknes or infirmitie, and in short space did perfourme many matters most miraculous; which things, for asmuche as she began to do them upon a sodaine, having never done the like before, made her maister and others to be in great admiration, and wondered thereat: by means whereof, the saide Davide Seaton had his maide in great suspition that shee did not those things by naturall and lawful waies, but rather supposed it to bee done by some extraordinarie and unlawfull meanes. Whereupon, her maister began to grow verie inquisitive, and examined hir which way and by what means shee was able to performe matters of so great importance; whereat shee gave him no aunswere: nevertheless, her maister, to the intent that hee might the better trie and finde out the truth of the same, did with the help of others torment her with the torture of the pilliwinkes[1] upon her fingers, which is a grievous torture; and binding or wrinching her head with a cord or roape, which is a most cruell torment also; yet would she not confess anie thing; whereuppon, they suspecting that she had beene marked by the Devill (as commonly witches are), made diligent search about her, and found the enemies mark to be in her fore crag, or fore part of her throate; which being found, she confessed that al her doings was done by the wicked allurements and entisements of the Devil, and that she did them by witchcraft. After this her confession, she was committed to prison, where shee continued a season, where immediately shee accused these persons following to bee notorious witches, and caused them forthwith to be apprehended, one after another, viz. Agnes Sampson the eldest witche of them all, dwelling in Haddington; Agnes Tompson of Edenbrough; Doctor Fian alias John Cuningham, master of the schoole at Saltpans in Lowthian, of whose life and strange acts you shal heare more largely in the end of this discourse. These were by the saide Geillis Duncane accused, as also George Motts wife, dwelling in Lowthian; Robert Grierson, skipper; and Jannet Blandilands; with the potter's wife of Seaton: the smith at the Brigge Hallis, with innumerable others in those parts, and dwelling in those bounds aforesaid; of whom some are alreadie executed, the rest remaine in prison to receive the doome of judgment at the Kinges Majesties will and pleasure.

The saide Geillis Duncane also caused Ewphame Mecalrean to bee apprehended, who conspired and performed the death of her godfather, and who used her art upon a gentleman, being one of the Lordes and Justices of the Session, for bearing good will to her daughter. Shee also caused to be apprehended one Barbara Naper, for bewitching to death Archibalde lait Earle of Angus, who languished to death by witchcraft, and yet the same was not suspected; but that hee died of so straunge a disease as the Phisition knewe not how to cure or remedie the same. But of all other the said witches, these two last before recited, were reputed for as civill honest

---

1. An instrument of torture similar to the thumbscrews later in use. [Burr's note]

women as anie that dwelled within the cittie of Edenbrough, before they were apprehended. Many other besides were taken dwelling in Lieth, who are detayned in prison untill his Majesties further will and pleasure be knowne. . . .[2]

As touching the aforesaide Doctor Fian alias John Cunningham, the examination of his actes since his apprehension, declareth the great subtletie of the Divell, and therefore maketh thinges to appeare the more miraculous; for beeing apprehended by the accusation of the saide Geillis Duncane aforesaide, who confessed he was their Regester, and that there was not one man suffered to come to the Divels readinges but onely hee: the saide Doctor was taken and imprisoned, and used with the accustomed paine provided for those offences, inflicted upon the rest, as is aforesaide. First, By thrawing of his head with a rope, whereat he would confess nothing. Secondly, Hee was perswaded by faire meanes to confesse his follies, but that would prevaile as little. Lastly, Hee was put to the most severe and cruell paine in the worlde, called the bootes;[3] who after he had received three strokes, being inquired if he would confesse his damnable actes and wicked life, his toong would not serve him to speake; in respect whereof the rest of the witches willed to search his toong, under which was founde two pinnes, thrust up into the heade; whereupon the witches did say, Now is the charme stinted; and shrewed, that those charmed pinnes were the cause he could not confesse any thing: Then was he immediately released of the bootes, brought before the King,[4] his confession was taken, and his own hand willingly set thereunto. . . .[5]

---

2. Then follows an account of the torture and confession of Agnes Sampson. [Burr's note]

3. "The boots, or *bootikens*," says Pitcairn in his note on this passage, "were chiefly made use of in extreme cases, such as High Treason, Witchcraft, etc. This horrid instrument extended from the ankles to the knee, and at each stroke of a large hammer (which forced the wedges closer), the question was repeated. In many instances, the bones and flesh of the leg were crushed and lacerated in a shocking manner before confession was made." [Burr's note]

4. The personal interest taken in these trials by King James is explained by the fact that one of the crimes which the witches were made to confess was that they had gone to sea in sieves and there raised the contrary wind which distressed His Majesty's ship on his return from Denmark, whither he had gone to fetch his bride. It was, perhaps, the experience thus gained in the persecution which impelled King James later to compose a book on witchcraft (*Daemonologie*, Edinburgh, 1597); and which led him, on his ascent of the English throne in 1603, not only to bring out at London a fresh edition of this treatise, but to inspire a new and sterner English statute against the witches. Under this statute of James was carried on the later witch-persecution in England; and it formed a basis for that in the colonies. [Burr's note]

5. Then follows a summary of his confession and an account of his commission to a solitary cell. What is next printed is alleged to have happened on the morrow. [Burr's note]

Figure 53. Witch, Goat, and *Putti.*
This classical engraving by Albrecht Dürer reflects the popular belief that witches rode their demonic mounts facing backwards.

Thus, all the daie, this Doctor Fian continued very solitarie, and seemed to have a care of his owne soule, and would call uppon God, shewing himselfe penitent for his wicked life; neverthless, the same night, hee found such meanes that he stole the key of the prison doore and chamber in which he was, which in the night hee opened and fled awaie to the Saltpans, where hee was always resident, and first apprehended. Of whose sodaine departure, when the Kings Majestie had intelligence, hee presently commanded diligent inquirie to bee made for his apprehension; and for the better effecting thereof, hee sent publike proclamations into all partes of his lande to the same effect. By meanes of whose hot and harde pursuite he was agayn taken, and brought to prison; and then, being called before the Kings Highnes, hee was re-examined, as well touching his departure, as also touching all that had before happened. But this Doctor, notwithstanding that his owne confession appeareth, remaining in recorde under his owne hande writting, and the same thereunto fixed in the presence of the Kings Majestie and sundrie of his Councell, yet did he utterly denie the same.

Whereupon the Kings Majestie, perceiving his stubborne willfulnesse, conceived and imagined, that in the time of his absence, hee had entered

Figure 54. The Witches' Procession.
This engraving by Agostino Veneziano (1515–33) depicts a procession of witches in terms recognizably characteristic of formal processions in early sixteenth-century art. The nude figures and heroic poses are combined with popular witch lore to produce a striking, but uncharacteristic depiction of the witches' travels.

227

into newe conference and league with the Devill his maister; and that hee had beene again newly marked, for the which he was narrowly searched; but it coulde not in anie waie be founde; yet for more tryall of him, to make him confesse, hee was commaunded to have a most strange torment, which was done in this manner following. His nailes upon all his fingers were riven and pulled off with an instrument called in Scottish a Turkas, which in England wee call a payre of pincers, and under every nayle there was thrust in two needels over even up to the heads. At all which torments notwithstanding, the Doctor never shronke anie whit; neither woulde he then confesse it the sooner, for all the tortures inflicted upon him. Then was hee, with all convenient speede, by commandement, convaied againe to the torment of the bootes, wherein hee continued a long time, and did abide so many blowes in them, that his legges were crusht and beaten together as small as might be; and the bones and flesh so brused, that the bloud and marrow spouted forth in great abundance; whereby, they were made unserviceable for ever. And notwithstanding all these grievous paines and cruell torments, he would not confesse anie things; so deeply had the Devill entered into his heart, that hee utterly denied all that which he before avouched; and would saie nothing thereunto, but this, that what hee had done and sayde before, was onely done and sayde, for fear of paynes which he had endured.

Upon great consideration, therefore, taken by the Kings Majestie and his Councell, as well for the due execution of justice uppon such detestable malefactors, as also for example sake, to remayne a terrour to all others heerafter, that shall attempt to deale in the lyke wicked and ungodlye actions as witchcraft, sorcerie, conjuration, and such lyke; the saide Doctor Fian was soon after arraigned, condemned and adjudged by the law to die, and then to be burned according to the lawe of that lande provided in that behalfe. Whereupon hee was put into a carte, and beeing first strangled, hee was immediately put into a great fire, being readie provided for that purpose, and there burned in the Castle Hill of Edenbrough, on a Saterdaie, in the ende of Januarie last past, 1591.

26

1566
The Confessions of the Chelmsford Witches
England

What proved the efficacy of the witch-persecutions to contemporaries above all else was the success of the courts in securing confessions from so many of the accused. Here was tangible proof of the intentions, the diabolical pact, and the unnatural powers of the witch, uttered by his or her own tongue and signed by his or her own hand. Why did they confess? Was it simply a question of torture and the fear of torture? Did the courts strike some sense of guilt whereby the "witch" was led to see herself as the prosecutor described her? Did the accused actually believe herself to possess these traits and powers before being brought to trial, and call attention upon herself by her subsequent actions? The data from which to construct answers to these questions are painfully inadequate to the task. The effect of the confessions, however, is less unclear: they spread both fear of the witch and confidence in the courts.

From Charles Williams, *Witchcraft* (London, 1941), pp. 194–201.

*E*lizabeth Francis, the first to be examined, deposed as follows:
"First she learned this art of witchcraft at the age of twelve years of her grandmother, whose name was Mother Eve of Hatfield Peverell, deceased. Item, when she taught it her, she counselled her to renounce God and his word and to give of her blood to Satan (as she termed it), which she delivered her in the likeness of a white spotted cat, and taught her to feed

Figures 55–58. The Witches' Sabbath.

Figure 55.
From Guazzo, *Compendium Maleficarum.*

Figure 56. The Sabbath Feast.
This woodcut from Guazzo's *Compendium Maleficarum* depicts the well-known diabolical feast that the witches attended in the presence of their master. The menus varied
from country to country, and many writers remarked that the food had no taste.

the said cat with bread and milk, and she did so, also she taught her to call it by the name of Satan and to keep it in a basket.

"When this Mother Eve had given her the Cat Satan, then this Elizabeth desired first of the said Cat (calling it Satan) that she might be rich and to have goods, and he promised her she should—asking her what she would have, and she said sheep (for this Cat spake to her as she confessed in a strange hollow voice, but such as she understood by use) and this Cat forthwith brought sheep into her pasture to the number of eighteen, black and white, which continued with her for a time, but in the end did all wear away she knew not how.

"Item, when she had gotten these sheep, she desired to have one Andrew Byles to her husband, which was a man of some wealth, and the Cat did promise she should, but that he said she must first consent that this Andrew should abuse her, and she so did.

"And after when this Andrew had thus abused her he would not marry her, wherefore she willed Satan to waste his goods, which he forthwith did, and yet not being contented with this, she willed him to touch his body which he forthwith did whereof he died.

"Item, that every time that he did anything for her, she said that he required a drop of blood, which she gave him by pricking herself, sometime in one place and then in another, and where she pricked herself there remained a red spot which was still to be seen.

"Item, when this Andrew was dead, she doubting herself with child, willed Satan to destroy it, and he bade her take a certain herb and drink it, which she did, and destroyed the child forthwith.

"Item, when she desired another husband he promised her another, naming this Francis whom she now hath, but said he is not so rich as the other, willing her to consent unto that Francis in fornication which she did, and thereof conceived a daughter that was born within a quarter of a year after they were married.

"After they were married they lived not so quietly as she desired, being stirred (as she said) to much unquietness and moved to swearing and cursing, wherefore she willed Satan her Cat to kill the child, being about the age of half a year old, and he did so, and when she yet found not the quietness that she desired, she willed it to lay a lameness in the leg of this Francis her husband, and it did in this manner. It came in a morning to this Francis' shoe, lying in it like a toad, and when he perceived it putting on his shoe, and had touched it with his foot, he being suddenly amazed asked of her what it was, and she bad him kill it and he was forthwith taken with a lameness whereof he cannot be healed.

"After all this when she had kept this Cat by the space of fifteen or sixteen years, and as some say (though untruly) being weary of it, she came to one Mother Waterhouse her neighbour (a poor woman) when she was going to the oven and desired her to give her a cake, and she would give her a thing that she should be the better for so long as she lived, and this Mother Waterhouse gave her a cake, whereupon she brought her this cat in her apron and taught her as she was instructed before by her grandmother Eve, telling her that she must call him Satan and give him of her blood and bread and milk as before, and at this examination would confess no more."

Agnes Waterhouse, who was said to have received the cat, was presently examined "before Justice Southcote and M. Gerard the Queen's attorney." She was a woman of sixty-four; her daughter Joan was examined also, and the chief evidence against them was that of a child of twelve. The account is as follows:

> *The Confession of Agnes Waterhouse the*
> *xxvii day of July in Anno 1566 at Chelmsford*
> *before Justice Southcote and M. Gerard*
> *the Queen's attorney.*

"First being demanded whether that she were guilty or not guilty upon her arraignment of the murdering of a man, she confessed that she was guilty, and then upon the evidence given against her daughter Joan Waterhouse, she said that she had a white Cat, and willed her Cat that he should destroy many of her neighbours' cattle, and also that he should kill a man, and so he did, and then after she must go two or three miles from her house, and then she took thought how to keep her Cat, then she and her Cat concluded that he the said Cat would become a Toad, and then she should keep him in a close house, and give him milk, and so he would continue till she came home again, and then being gone forth, her daughter having been at a neighbour's house there by, required of one Agnes Brown, of the age of twelve years or more, a piece of bread and cheese, and the said Agnes said that she had none, and that she had not the key of the milkhouse door, and then the said Joan went home and was angry with the said Agnes Brown and she said that she remembered that her mother was wont to go up and down in her house and to call Satan Satan she said she would prove the like, and then she went up and down the house and called Satan, and then there came a black Dog to her and asked her what she would have, and then she said she was afraid and said, I would have thee to make one Agnes Brown afraid, and then he asked her what she would give him and she said she would give him a red cock, and he said he would have none of that, and she asked him what he would have then, and he said he would have her body and soul, and so upon request and fear together she gave him her body and soul (and then said the queen's attorney *How wilt thou do before God?* O my Lord, I trust God will have mercy upon me, and then he said *thou sayest well*), and then he departed from her, and then she said that she heard that he made the said Agnes Brown afraid.

"The said Agnes Brown was then demanded and called for, and then she came in, and being asked what age she was of she said she thought she was twelve years old, and then the queen's attorney asked her what she could say, and then she said that at such a day, naming the day certain, she was churning of butter and there came to her a thing like a black Dog with a face like an ape, a short tail, a chain and a silver whistle (to her thinking) about his neck, and a pair of horns on his head, and brought in his mouth the key of the milkhouse door, and then my lord she said, I was afraid, for he skipped and leaped to and fro, and sat on the top of a nettle, and then I asked him what he would have, and he said he would have butter, and I said I had none for him and then he said he would have some or he went, and then he did run to put the key into the lock of the milkhouse door, and I said he should have none, and he said he would have some, and then he opened the door and went upon the shelf, and there upon a new cheese laid down the key, and being a while within he came out again, and locked the door and said that he had made flap butter for me, and so departed, and then she said she told her aunt of it, and then she sent for the priest, and when he came he bade her to pray to God, and call on the name of Jesus, and so the next day my lord he came again to me with the key of our milk-house door in his mouth, and then I said in the name of Jesus what hast thou there, and then he laid down the key and said that I spake evil words in speaking of that name, and then he departed, and so my aunt took up the key, for he had kept it from us two days and a night, and then we went into the milkhouse and there we did see the print of butter upon the cheese, and then within a few days after he came again with a bean pod in his mouth, and then the queen's attorney asked what that was, and so the other Justices declared, and then she said my lord I said in the name of Jesus what hast thou there, and so then he laid it down and said I spake evil words and departed and came again by and by with a piece of bread in his mouth, and I asked him what he would have, and he said butter it was that he would have, and so he departed, and my lord I did not see him no more till Wednesday last, which was the 28th day of July, why said the queen's attorney was he with thee on Wednesday last, yes she said, what did he then to thee said he, my lord said she he came with a knife in his mouth and asked me if I were not dead, and I said No I thanked God, and then he said if I would not die that he would thrust his knife to my heart but he would make me to die, and then I said in the name of Jesus lay down thy knife, and he said he would not depart from his sweet dame's knife as yet, and then I asked of him who was his dame, and then he nodded and wagged his head to your house Mother Waterhouse, then the queen's attorney asked of the said Agnes Waterhouse what she said to it, then she demanded what manner knife that it was and Agnes Brown said that it was a dagger knife, there thou liest said Agnes Waterhouse, why, quoth the queen's attorney, marry my lord (quoth she) she saith it is a dagger knife and I have none such in my house, but a great knife, and therein she lieth, yea yea, my lord quoth Joan Waterhouse she lieth in that she saith it had a face like an ape, for this that came to me was like a dog, well said the queen's attorney, well, can you make it come before us now, if ye can we will dispatch you out of prison by and by, no faith said Agnes Waterhouse I cannot, for in faith if I had let him go as my daughter did I could make him come by and by, but now I have no more power over him, then said the queen's attorney, Agnes Waterhouse when did thy Cat suck of thy blood never said she, no said he, let me see, and then the jailer lifted up her kerchief on her head, and there was divers spots in her face and one on her nose, then said the queen's attorney, in good faith Agnes when did he suck of thy blood last, by my faith my lord said she, not this fortnight, and so the jury went together for that matter."

The end and last confession
of mother Waterhouse at her death,
which was the 29th day of July, Anno 1566.

"First (being ready prepared to receive her death) she confessed earnestly that she had been a witch and used such execrable sorcery the space of fifteen years, and had done many abominable deeds, the which she repented earnestly and unfeignedly, and desired almighty God's forgiveness in that she had abused his most holy name by her devilish practises, and trusted to be saved by his most unspeakable mercy. And being demanded of the bystanders, she confessed that she sent her Satan to one Wardol, a neighbour of hers, being a tailor (with whom she was offended) to hurt and destroy him and his goods. And this her Satan went thereabout for to have done her will, but in the end he returned to her again, and was not able to do this mischief, she asked the cause, and he answered because the said Wardol was so strong in faith that he had no power to hurt him, yet she sent him divers and sundry times (but all in vain) to have mischieved him. And being demanded whether she was accustomed to go to church to the common prayer or divine service, she said yea, and being required what she did there she said she did as other women do, and prayed right heartily there, and when she was demanded what prayer she said, she answered the Lord's prayer, the Ave Maria, and the Belief, and then they demanded whether in Latin or in English, and she said in Latin, and they demanded why she said it not in English but in Latin, seeing that it was set out by public authority and according to God's word that all men should pray in the English and mother tongue that they best understand, and she said that Satan would at no time suffer her to say it in English, but at all times in Latin: for these and many other offences which she hath committed, done and confessed, she bewailed, repented, and asked mercy of God, and all the world forgiveness, and thus she yielded up her soul, trusting to be in joy with Christ her Saviour, which dearly had bought her with his most precious blood. Amen."

27

NICOLAS RÉMY
The Evidence of Witchcraft
1595

Nicolas Rémy, statesman, jurist, and man of letters, was privy counsellor to the Duke of Lorraine and a judge involved in witchcraft cases for more than fifteen years. When an epidemic drove him from the court at Nancy to a country estate where he enjoyed a long stretch of leisure time, Rémy compiled a demonological treatise based primarily upon his own courtroom experience. It enjoyed a great reputation, being reprinted eight times, including two German translations. Rémy dealt learnedly and systematically with the formal confessions of his victims, producing a book that seemed irrefutable both as sound Christian scholarship and for its clear natural evidence.

Nicolas Rémy, *Demonolatry*, tr. E. A. Ashby (London, 1930), Bk. I, ch. I–III, pp. 1–7.

The Inducements by which Men may first be led astray by Demons, and so falling become Dealers in Magic. Experience itself, to our own great loss and bane, affords us sad proof that Satan seizes as many opportunities of deceiving and destroying mankind as there are different moods and affections natural to the human character. For such as are given over to their lusts and to love he wins by offering them the hope of gaining their desires: or if they are bowed under the load of daily poverty, he allures them by some large and ample promise of riches: or he tempts them by showing them the means of avenging themselves when they have been angered by some injury or hurt received: in short, by whatever other corruption or luxury they have been depraved, he draws them into his power and holds them as it were bound to him. But it is not our purpose to discuss here what are those blind passions and desires by which men may be led into sin; for it would be a waste of time and an abuse of learning to involve ourselves in the much-worn controversy between Prometheus and Epimetheus, reason and appetite. That we pass by, and say that Satan assails mankind not only through their secret and domestic affections and (if I may so express it) by burrowing into their very hearts, but also openly and in declared warfare, as it is called. For he openly addresses them by word of mouth, and appears in visible person to converse with them, as he did when he contended with the Saviour in the wilderness (*S. Matthew* iv). But this he does the more easily when he finds a man weakened by the hardships and cares of life; for then he suggests to the man that he is grieved at his misfortunes and is willing to come to help him. But not even so can he aid and assist any man unless that man has broken his baptismal pledge and agreed to transfer his allegiance to him and acknowledge him as his Master. But if he cannot gain his object in this way by mere persuasion, then Satan employs those allurements and temptations which I have already mentioned: he fabricates some fair and delectable body and offers it for a man's enjoyment: or he can do much by means of a false display of riches: or by providing drugs to poison those upon whom a man wishes to be avenged, or to heal those to whom a man owes a debt of gratitude: often, indeed, the Demons forcibly drive and compel men into compliance by fierce threats and revilings, or by the fear of the lash or prison. For men may just as easily be led by violence to practise sorcery as by coaxing and blandishment, though I shall not here adduce examples to substantiate this statement, since this matter will be considered more fully in its due place: for the present I am content to say that I have found it to be the rarer case for a sorcerer to be driven by force into his abominable practices.

The truth is that, when Satan cannot move a man by fair words, he compels him by fear and threats of danger. When Claude Morèle, who was convicted of witchcraft at Serre (5th Dec., 1586), was asked what was the chief inducement that had first led him to give himself to the Demon, he answered that he had withstood the temptation of all the Demon's fair words, and had only yielded when Satan had threatened to kill his wife and children. At Guermingen, 19th Dec., 1589, Antoine Welch no longer dared to oppose the Demon in anything after he had threatened to twist his neck unless he obeyed his commands, for he seemed on the very point of fulfilling his threat. At Harécourt, 10th Nov., 1586, when he could by no promises persuade Alexée Driget to dedicate herself to him, the Demon at last threatened to destroy the house in which she lived: and this misfortune indeed befell her not long afterwards; but it will be more convenient to discuss elsewhere whether he was the actual cause of it, or whether he merely foresaw that it would happen. Certainly there are many examples in the pagan histories of houses being cast down, the destruction of the crops, chasms in the earth, fiery blasts and other such disastrous tempests stirred up by Demons for the destruction of men for no other purpose than to bind their minds to the observance of some new cult and to establish their mastery more and more firmly over them.

Therefore we may first conclude that it is no mere fable that witches meet and converse with Demons in very person. Secondly, it is clear that Demons use the two most powerful weapons of persuasion against the feeble wills of mortals, namely, hope and fear, desire and terror; for they well know how to induce and inspire such emotions.

> *How Demons prepare, for those whom they*
> *have won, by their Cunning, Drugged Powders,*
> *Wands, Ointments and Various Venoms*
> *of the sort: some of which cause Death, some*
> *only Sickness, and some even Healing. And how*
> *these things are not always, or for all Men,*
> *poisonous: since there may be found some who*
> *are uninjured by frequent Applications of them,*
> *notably they whose Office and Business it is*
> *to condemn Witches to Death.*

From the very beginning the Devil was a murderer (*S. John* viii), and never has he ceased to tempt the impious to commit slaughter and parricide. Therefore it is no wonder that, once he has caught men in his toils, his first care is to furnish them with the implements and instruct them in the practices of witchcraft. And lest the business should be delayed or hindered through lack of poison or difficulty in administering it, he provides them at the very first with a fine powder which must infallibly cause the sickness or death of those against whom it is used: nor does its harmfulness of

Figure 57.   The Sabbath.
This seventeenth-century panorama of witch activities is an example of a popular pictorial genre.

necessity depend upon its being mingled with a man's food or drink, or applied to his bare flesh; for it is enough if but his clothes be lightly dusted with it. The powder which kills is black; that which only causes sickness is ashen, or sometimes reddish in colour. And since witches are often led by fear or bribery, and sometimes even by pity (of which they claim that they are not entirely destitute), to heal those who have been stricken in this manner, they are not without a remedy to their hand; for they are given a third powder, white in colour, with which they dust the sick, or mix it with their food or drink, and so the sickness is dispersed. And these drugs of varying properties and virtue are distinguishable only by their colour. Claude Fellet (at Mazières, 9th Nov., 1584), Jeanne le Ban (at Masmunster, 3rd Jan., 1585), Colette Fischer (at Gerbeville, 7th May, 1585), and nearly all the women of their fellowship, record that they always found the effects of their powders such as we have said. But this distinction in the colours is not so much to ensure the selection of the required poison (for the drugs owe their potency to the Demon, not to any inherent properties of their own), as a visible sign of the pact between the witch and the Demon, and a guarantee of faith. Matteole Guilleraea (at Mazières, 4th Dec., 1584) and Jeanne Alberte (at S. Pierre-Mont, 8th Nov., 1581) add that although the ashen-coloured powder does not as a rule cause a fatal sickness, it has nevertheless the power to kill when it is first received by witches after their enlistment in that army of wickedness; for that initial step has a kind of preference.

But it is a matter of no small wonder that witches not only impregnate with such poisons articles of which the purpose and use is to drive away Demons, but even make use of them during the very time of prayer and the performance of the Sacraments. At Seaulx, 11th Oct., 1587, Jacobeta Weher was envious of the lover of the daughter of her fellow-countryman Pétrone, but could not injure her as she wished; for the girl had emphatically bidden her beware of trying to harm her. But at last, under pretext of doing something else, she infected an asperge with the poison powder and sprinkled the girl with it as she was praying in church: and at once she was stricken with a mortal sickness and soon after died. At Blainville, 16th Jan., 1587, the whole neighbourhood, except Alexée Belheure, had been invited to a feast given by a noble knight named Darnielle on the occasion of his son's baptism. Ill brooking this slight, she evaded the observation of those who were carrying the newly baptized child and, sprinkling it with a poison powder of this kind, killed it.

And since it is not convenient for them always to keep this powder ready in their hand to throw, they have also wands imbued with it or smeared with some unguent or other venemous matter, which they commonly carry as if for driving cattle. With these they often, as it were in joke, strike the men or the cattle which they wish to injure: and that this is no vain or innocent touch is testified by the confessions of François Fellet (at Mazières, 19th Dec., 1583), Marguereta Warner (at Ronchamp, 1st Dec., 1586), Matteole Guilleret (at Pagny-sur-Moselle, 1584), and Jacobeta Weher whom I have just mentioned.

Yet there are those who, thanks to some singular blessing from Heaven, are immune from such attacks; for witches have not always unlimited power against all men, as Jeanne Gransaint (at Condé-sur-l'Escaut, July, 1582) and Catharina Ruffe (at Ville-sur-Moselle, 28th July, 1587) have recorded that they were more than once informed by their Demons. I remember questioning that woman of Nancy called Lasnier (Asinaria), from her husband the ass-driver, upon the statements of the witnesses, and especially concerning this particular point; and she spoke with great indignation as follows: "It is well for you Judges that we can do nothing against you! For there are none upon whom we would more gladly work our spite than you who are always harrying us folk with every torture and punishment." Jaqueline Xaluëtia (at Grand-Bouxières-sous-Amance, 29th April, 1588), freely and without any previous questioning, acknowledged the same. This woman, having long been suspected of witchcraft, was put in chains; but after a little she was liberated by order of the Judge, because she had endured all the torture of her questioning in an obstinate silence. After much turning of the matter over in her mind, she could not rest until she had worked some evil upon the Judge who had treated her with such severity; for the filthy rabble of witches is commonly desirous of revenge. Therefore she ceased not to pester her Demon to find some safe and easy way for her to vent her spite: but he, knowing her folly towards herself in this matter, kept pleading different excuses for postponing the affair and inventing reasons why he should not comply with her wish. But at length, since Xaluëtia did not cease to importune him, he told her in shame and grief that, in place of that fortune which he had often foretold for her, her own folly and impotence would be exposed and would betray her. "I have always, my Xaluëtia," he said, "endured very hardly the unbridled severity of those executioners towards you, and often in the past have I had a mind to be revenged: but I openly admit that all my attempts come to nothing.

For they are in His guardianship and protection who alone can oppose my designs. But I can repay these officers for their persecutions by causing them to share in a common disaster, and will strike the crops and the fields far and wide with a tempest and lay them waste as much as I am able."

This is not unlike the statement of Nicole Morèle (at Serre, 24th Jan., 1587), that Demons are impregnated and seared with an especial hatred towards those who put into operation the law against witches, but that it is in vain that they attempt or seek to wreak any vengeance against them. See

Figure 58. The Witches at Work.
This little-known painting by Michael Herr is another version of the popular seventeenth-century image of groups of witches and demons conducting their variety of diabolical rites.

how God defends and protects the authority of those to whom He has given the mandate of His power upon earth, and how He has therefore made them partakers of His prerogative and honour, calling them Gods even as Himself (*Ps. lxxxii*): so that without doubt they are sacrosanct and, by reason of their duty and their office, invulnerable even to the spells of witches. Indeed they are not even bound in the least by the commands of the Demons themselves, even though they may have previously vowed allegiance to them and have been touched with the stain of that oath. For that witches benefit by the protection of the sanctity of a Magistrate's office (at least for as long as they hold such office), so that they are free from all the most importunate complaints and instigations of their Little Masters, who testified by Didier Finance (at Saint-Dié, 14th July, 1581), who said that during the whole period of his magistracy he never once saw his familiar spirit, who at all other times had been his most sedulous adviser on every occasion. Therefore let the Magistrate undertake his duties with confidence, knowing that he is pursuing a vocation in which he will always have God as his champion and protector. By reason of a like sanctity Marcus, in the *De Operatione Daemonum* of Psellus, tells that his Demon uttered no sound upon the days when the Crucifixion and Resurrection are commemorated, although he strove his utmost to do so. Moreover, the poisons which Demons give to witches are thus harmless only to those Judges whom I have just mentioned: for there can be no doubt that the poisons which they gather and concoct with their own hands are equally injurious to all men else and are imbued with equal venom against all. It has, moreover, often been proved by experience that witches also have their own laboratories stuffed full of animals, plants and metals endowed with some natural poison; and these are so numerous and various that they may be reckoned as many as those which Agamede in Homer (*Iliad*, xi. 741) is said to have known:

> Who knew all poisons that the wide earth breeds.

For they are in the discipline and service of that Master who is ignorant of nothing which has power to destroy men.

But I would rather that such matters remain hidden in the bosom of Nature than that, through my naming them, they should come to any man's knowledge. And it is for this reason that I have always been led, whenever I have found such things written down in the examination of prisoners, to have them altogether suppressed: or at least I would advise, or rather admonish, the actuary to omit them when he reads out such examinations in public. For in Lorraine it is the custom to refer the judgement of capital crimes to the votes of the ignorant and excited multitude, giving them full power, and having no regard to the provocation caused by a public exhibition of the accused; although this is contrary to the recommendation of the Duumvirs of Nancy, to whom the whole matter should first be referred. Would that these matters were not now so publicly known! But it has indeed come to pass after the wont of mankind, who with impetuous rashness thrust into the light those matters which should more particularly be kept hidden; and the memory of such things lives longer and is often more curious and pleasant to dwell upon than that of natural human happenings. In this way the Scholiast of Theocritus wrote that after many ages he saw with wonder at Mount Selinus in Sicily the very mortars in which Circe and Medea brewed their poisons. And if men have so prized the mere implements, as if they were the earthen lamp of Epictetus, what must we think they would have done if they had found the actual poisons, or the secret rule of compounding them inscribed upon some monument?

That Witches can with safety anoint their
Hands and their entire Bodies with their Magic
Ointments: yet if they but touch the Edge
of a Person's Garment it will at once prove fatal
to such a one, provided that it is the Witch's
intent to Hurt. For otherwise such Contact
is harmless and does not injure.

Witches have another most treacherous manner of applying their poison; for, having their hands smeared with it, they take hold of the very ends of a man's garment as it were to entreat and propitiate him. Thus it is hardly possible for you to be on your guard and avoid them, since the action has an appearance of kindness rather than of injury. Nevertheless, it is a most instant poison to the body, as has been made manifest by frequent experience: and it is the more marvellous because the witch's bare hand endures with complete safety the poison which thus penetrates even several folds of clothing. You may say that there have been men who have transmitted the infection of the plague to others although they themselves were free from it; but this is not a parallel case. For, as will be explained elsewhere, this touch of a witch is noxious and fatal only to those whom the witch wishes to injure: whereas the infection of the plague strikes those whom you least wish to harm. And this forces me to believe that, in the case we are considering, something is due to the hidden ministry of the Demon, which does not appear but works in secret; and that the unguent is merely the outward symbol of the wretched witch's complicity in the crime under the guidance and advice of the Demon. Indeed we know from experience that the poison can with impunity be handled and touched by anybody after the witches have been thrown into prison and have renounced their partnership with the Demon; and the officers who are sent to search for their boxes of poison are able to bring them back in their hands with safety.

This was proved not long since (2nd Sept., 1589) at Furscheim, a village in German Lorraine. Marie Alberte and Catharina Praevotte, just before they were sentenced for witchcraft, were asked to say whether they had left any of their evil poisons at home, so that after they were dead these venoms might not be a danger to any. They at once told where the poison could be found; and the searchers brought two earthenware vessels containing bitumen spotted with yellow and white and glistening here and there with specks of metal. Otillia Kelvers and Anguel Yzarts (6th and 7th Aug., 1589) of the same town, and several other witches in other towns, were found to have done the same. Some may think that the witches give such information in order to curry favour with their Judges, and that they cunningly indicate some unguent which they have prepared for some other and ordinary domestic use instead of the true poison; but this is not the case, and there are many clear proofs that there is no pretence or simulation in this matter.

For, in the first place, if these unguents are put upon the fire they flare and splutter and glitter as nothing else can. Jeanne Michaëlis of Etival (2nd June, 1590) has testified to this fact. Again, there have been seen cases of witches who as soon as the Judge has given them permission to rub or anoint themselves with the unguent, have at once been carried aloft and have disappeared. Lucius Apuleius (Bk. III, *de Asino Aureo*) tells of Pamphile that she in the same way applied such an unguent to herself and, after a few tentative leaps from the ground, flew up and away in full flight. And however much witches may differ concerning other matters, they are all, when questioned, agreed about the magic use, properties and powers of this ointment. They are even particular in describing its colour; and this provides further proof that the matter is no dream, but visible and perceptible to the eyes. At St. Dominique, 2nd Dec., 1586, Jeanne Gallée tells that the Demon gave it to her wrapped in oak leaves, and that its colour was white: and that she nearly always had her hands smeared with it that she might never be without the means of doing an injury on any occasion. At Haraucourt, 2nd Nov., 1586, Alexée Drigie agrees with this, except that she declared hers was reddish in colour: and she adds that when, at the instigation of the Demon, she anointed with it her husband who was lying asleep by her side he very soon died in great agony, writhing and contorting all his limbs.

Witchcraft in the
Seventeenth Century

The seventeenth century witnessed many new outbreaks of witchcraft trials and a steady stream of old and new rationales for them. The opening of the secular courts to witch-persecutions, which had occurred in the second half of the sixteenth century, placed the proceedings in the hands of judges who were often far less subtle jurists than their ecclesiastical counterparts and far more susceptible to local pressures. The dramatic area-wide persecutions at Würzburg (*No. 29*) and Bamberg (*No. 30*) were spectacular examples of wholesale extermination, but the striking individual case of the Devils of Loudun (*No. 31*) and the small-scale persecution surrounding the case of Suzanne Gaudry (*No. 32*) illustrate the fact that accusations of witchcraft could flare up suddenly and in relative isolation. The letter of Father Surin, the exorcist in the Loudun affair, and the crudeness of the judges of Suzanne Gaudry reveal the varieties of spiritual and psychological extremes which the persecutions of the seventeenth century produced.

In the second half of the century, the witch-fears spread to the British colonies in North America, and Cotton Mather's sermon on witchcraft (*No. 33*) indicates the intellectual and emotional temper which soon led to the trials at Salem, Massachusetts. Theoretical demonological and witchcraft studies continued to affirm and develop the traditional concepts, even in the last decades of the seventeenth century, as is demonstrated by Richard Bovet's *Pandaemonium* of 1684 (*No. 34*); the evidence supporting witchcraft continued to be accumulated, as is shown by the letter of Henry More and the essay by Joseph Glanvil (*No. 35*). Glanvil and More, among the most highly respected thinkers of the seventeenth century, maintained a philosophical spiritualism which predisposed them not only to belief in witchcraft, but also to affirmation of its existence by the presentation of "natural data" that offer tantalizing views of social as well as intellectual history.

28

ca. 1630
The Persecution at Bonn

This letter from Pastor Duren of the village of Alfter, near Bonn, to Count Werner von Salm purports to describe the witch-persecutions in that city. But the authenticity of this document is unverifiable because the putative manuscript source is no longer extant, and the events it describes are corroborated by no other documents or references. George Lincoln Burr translated and reprinted it in his *Witch Persecutions,* and thus it has been made a well-known part of that small body of "primary sources" with which the English-speaking student of the history of witchcraft is familiar. What Burr apparently overlooked, however, was the remarkable similarity of this "Bonn letter" to the authenticated letter of the Chancellor of the Prince-Bishop of Würzburg of August, 1629, describing the prosecutions in that city (*No. 29*). Thus, the chief interest of this document is historiographical rather than historical. The problem of fraudulent accounts of witch persecutions has not yet received historians' full attention. In some cases, possibly including this one at Bonn, the derivative character of our only source raises the question of the reliability of the data it contains. Yet its circulation no doubt contributed to current popular fears, and hence it does offer insights into one aspect of the witch-literature of the seventeenth century.

From Burr, *The Witch Persecutions,* pp. 18–19.

*T*hose burned are mostly male witches of the sort described. There must be half the city implicated: for already professors, law-students, pastors, canons, vicars, and monks have here been arrested and burned. His Princely Grace has seventy wards who are to become pastors, one of whom, eminent as a musician, was yesterday arrested; two others were sought for, but have fled. The Chancellor and his wife and the Private Secretary's wife are already executed. On the eve of Our Lady's Day there was executed here a maiden of nineteen who bore the name of being the fairest and the most blameless of all the city, and who from her childhood had been brought up by the Bishop himself. A canon of the cathedral, named Rotenhahn, I saw beheaded and burned. Children of three or four years have devils for their paramours. Students and boys of noble birth, of nine, ten, eleven, twelve, thirteen, fourteen years, have here been burned. In fine, things are in such a pitiful state that one does not know with what people one may talk and associate.

29

1629
The Persecutions at Würzburg

In the 1620's, a particularly intensive witch-hunt developed in the area in and around the cathedral city of Würzburg. This contemporary account was written in August, 1629, by the Prince-Bishop's Chancellor in a letter to a friend. It is preserved in the *Codex German* of the municipal library in Munich. As in the persecutions at Trier (*No. 24*), the victims included notables, and the terror was apparently all-pervasive.

From Burr, *The Witch-Persecutions,* pp. 28–29.

As to the affair of the witches, which Your Grace thinks brought to an end before this, it has started up afresh, and no words can do justice to it. Ah, the woe and the misery of it—there are still four hundred in the city, high and low, of every rank and sex, nay, even clerics, so strongly accused that they may be arrested at any hour. It is true that, of the people of my Gracious Prince here, some out of all offices and faculties must be executed: clerics, electoral councilors and doctors, city officials, court assessors, several of whom Your Grace knows. There are law students to be arrested. The Prince-Bishop has over forty students who are soon to be pastors; among them thirteen or fourteen are said to be witches. A few days ago a Dean was arrested; two others who were summoned have fled.

The notary of our Church consistory, a very learned man, was yesterday arrested and put to the torture. In a word, a third part of the city is surely involved. The richest, most attractive, most prominent, of the clergy are already executed. A week ago a maiden of nineteen was executed, of whom it is everywhere said that she was the fairest in the whole city, and was held by everybody a girl of singular modesty and purity. She will be followed by seven or eight others of the best and most attractive persons. . . . And thus many are put to death for renouncing God and being at the witch-dances, against whom nobody has ever else spoken a word.

To conclude this wretched matter, there are children of three and four years, to the number of three hundred, who are said to have had intercourse with the Devil. I have seen put to death children of seven, promising students of ten, twelve, fourteen, and fifteen. Of the nobles—but I cannot and must not write more of this misery. There are persons of yet higher rank, whom you know, and would marvel to hear of, nay, would scarcely believe it; let justice be done. . . .

P.S.—Though there are many wonderful and terrible things happening, it is beyond doubt that, at a place called the Fraw-Rengberg, the Devil in person, with eight thousand of his followers, held an assembly and celebrated mass before them all, administering to his audience (that is, the witches) turnip-rinds and parings in place of the Holy Eucharist. There took place not only foul but most horrible and hideous blasphemies, whereof I shudder to write. It is also true that they all vowed not to be enrolled in the Book of Life, but all agreed to be inscribed by a notary who is well known to me and my colleagues. We hope, too, that the book in which they are enrolled will yet be found, and there is no little search being made for it.

30

1628
The Persecutions at Bamberg

The archives of the municipal library of the cathedral city of Bamberg contain the minutes of a very famous trial in the history of European witchcraft, that of the burgomaster, or mayor, himself, Johannes Junius. This trial is of particular interest not only because of the light it sheds on the process of accusation, but also because included among its documents is the letter which Junius smuggled out of prison to his daughter, indicating that the official court-documents upon which we so depend for our understanding of witchcraft can cover a multitude of virtues and sufferings that are too often unseen in our histories.

From Burr, *The Witch-Persecutions*, pp. 23–28.

On Wednesday, June 28, 1628, was examined without torture Johannes Junius, Burgomaster at Bamberg, on the charge of witchcraft: how and in what fashion he had fallen into that vice. Is fifty-five years old, and was born at Niederwaysich in the Wetterau. Says he is wholly innocent, knows nothing of the crime, has never in his life renounced God; says that he is wronged before God and the world, would like to hear of a single human being who has seen him at such gatherings [as the witch-sabbaths].

Confrontation of Dr. Georg Adam Haan. Tells him to his face he will stake his life on it, that he saw him, Junius, a year and a half ago at a witch-gathering in the electoral council-room, where they ate and drank. Accused denies the same wholly.

Confronted with Hopffens Elsse. Tells him likewise that he was on Haupts-moor at a witch-dance; but first the holy wafer was desecrated. Junius denies. Hereupon he was told that his accomplices had confessed against him and was given time for thought.

On Friday, June 30, 1628, the aforesaid Junius was again without torture exhorted to confess, but again confessed nothing, whereupon, . . . since he would confess nothing, he was put to the torture, and first the

Thumb-screws were applied. Says he has never denied God his Saviour nor suffered himself to be otherwise baptized;[1] will again stake his life on it; feels no pain in the thumb-screws.

Leg-screws. Will confess absolutely nothing; knows nothing about it. He has never renounced God; will never do such a thing; has never been guilty of this vice; feels likewise no pain.

Is stripped and examined; on his right side is found a bluish mark, like a clover leaf, is thrice pricked therein, but feels no pain and no blood flows out.

Strappado. He has never renounced God; God will not forsake him; if he were such a wretch he would not let himself be so tortured; God must show some token of his innocence. He knows nothing about witchcraft. . . .

On July 5, the above named Junius is without torture, but with urgent persuasions, exhorted to confess, and at last begins and confesses:

When in the year 1624 his law-suit at Rothweil cost him some six hundred florins, he had gone out, in the month of August, into his orchard at Fried-richsbronnen; and, as he sat there in thought, there had come to him a woman like a grass-maid, who had asked him why he sat there so sorrowful; he had answered that he was not despondent, but she had led him by seductive speeches to yield him to her will. . . . And thereafter this wench had changed into the form of a goat, which bleated and said, "Now you see with whom you have had to do. You must be mine or I will forthwith break your neck." Thereupon he had been frightened, and trembled all over for fear. Then the transformed spirit had seized him by the throat and demanded that he should renounce God Almighty, whereupon Junius said, "God

---

1. "Otherwise baptized" is the usual phrase for the rite, a parody of baptism, by which the Devil was believed to initiate his followers. [Burr's note]

forbid," and thereupon the spirit vanished through the power of these words. Yet it came straightway back, brought more people with it, and persistently demanded of him that he renounce God in Heaven and all the heavenly host, by which terrible threatening he was obliged to speak this formula: "I renounce God in Heaven and his host, and will henceforward recognize the Devil as my God."

After the renunciation he was so far persuaded by those present and by the evil spirit that he suffered himself to be otherwise baptized in the evil spirit's name. The Morhauptin had given him a ducat as dower-gold, which afterward became only a potsherd.

He was then named Krix. His paramour he had to call Vixen. Those present had congratulated him in Beelzebub's name and said that they were now all alike. At this baptism of his there were among others the aforesaid Christiana Morhauptin, the young Geiserlin, Paul Glaser, [and others]. After this they had dispersed.

At this time his paramour had promised to provide him with money, and from time to time to take him to other witch-gatherings. . . .

Whenever he wished to ride forth [to the witch-sabbath] a black dog had come before his bed, which said to him that he must go with him, whereupon he had seated himself upon the dog and the dog had raised himself in the Devil's name and so had fared forth.

About two years ago he was taken to the electoral council-room, at the left hand as one goes in. Above at a table were seated the Chancellor, the Burgomaster Neydekher, Dr. Georg Haan, [and many others]. Since his eyes were not good, he could not recognize more persons.

More time for consideration was now given him. On July 7, the aforesaid Junius was again examined, to know what further had occurred to him to confess. He confesses that about two months ago, on the day after an execution was held, he was at a witch-dance at the Black Cross, where Beelzebub had shown himself to them all and said expressly to their faces that they must all be burned together on this spot, and had ridiculed and taunted those present. . . .

Of crimes. His paramour had immediately after his seduction demanded that he should make away with his younger son Hans Georg, and had given him for this purpose a gray powder; this, however, being too hard for him, he had made away with his horse, a brown, instead.

His paramour had also often spurred him on to kill his daughter, . . . and

Figures 59–60. The Devil Carries off a Witch.

Figure 59.
This woodcut from Conrad Lycosthenus' *Prodigiorum ac Ostentorum Chronicon* ("The Chronicle of Prodigies and Curiosities"), printed at Basel in 1577, illustrates the events described in the selection from William of Malmesbury, the twelfth-century chronicler, in section I.2, above. The motif of the Devil carrying off a witch to Hell became a common one, its most famous instance being that of the Faust Legend.

Figure 60.
The theme of this woodcut from Olaus Magnus, *Historia de gentibus septentrionalibus*, has its roots in the vivid belief that demons carry the damned, particularly those who have served them on earth, to Hell.

256

because he would not do this he had been maltreated with blows by the evil spirit.

Once at the suggestion of his paramour he had taken the holy wafer out of his mouth and given it to her. . . .

A week before his arrest as he was going to St. Martin's church the Devil met him on the way, in the form of a goat, and told him that he would soon be imprisoned, but that he should not trouble himself—he would soon set him free. Besides this, by his soul's salvation, he knew nothing further; but what he had spoken was the pure truth; on that he would stake his life. On August 6, 1628, there was read to the aforesaid Junius this his confession, which he then wholly ratified and confirmed, and was willing to stake his life upon it. And afterward he voluntarily confirmed the same before the court.[2]

Many hundred thousand good-nights, dearly beloved daughter Veronica. Innocent have I come into prison, innocent have I been tortured, innocent must I die. For whoever comes into the witch prison must become a witch or be tortured until he invents something out of his head and—God pity him —bethinks him of something. I will tell you how it has gone with me. When I was the first time put to the torture, Dr. Braun, Dr. Kötzendörffer, and two strange doctors were there. Then Dr. Braun asks me, "Kinsman, how come you here?" I answer, "Through falsehood, through misfortune." "Hear, you," he says, "you are a witch; will you confess it voluntarily? If not, we'll bring in witnesses and the executioner for you." I said "I am no witch, I have a pure conscience in the matter; if there are a thousand witnesses, I am not anxious, but I'll gladly hear the witnesses." Now the chancellor's son was set before me . . . and afterward Hoppfens Elsse. She had seen me dance on Haupts-moor. . . . I answered: "I have never renounced God, and will never do it—God graciously keep me from it. I'll rather bear whatever I must." And then came also—God in highest Heaven have mercy—the executioner, and put the thumb-screws on me, both hands bound together, so that the blood ran out at the nails and everywhere, so that for four weeks I could not use my hands, as you can see from the writing. . . . Thereafter they first stripped me, bound my hands behind me, and drew me up in the

2. So ended the trial of Junius, and he was accordingly burned at the stake. But it so happens that there is also preserved in Bamberg a letter, in quivering hand, secretly written by him to his daughter while in the midst of his trial (July 24, 1628). [Burr's note]

torture.[3] Then I thought heaven and earth were at an end; eight times did they draw me up and let me fall again, so that I suffered terrible agony. . . .

And this happened on Friday, June 30, and with God's help I had to bear the torture. . . . When at last the executioner led me back into the prison, he said to me: "Sir, I beg you, for God's sake confess something, whether it be true or not. Invent something, for you cannot endure the torture which you will be put to; and, even if you bear it all, yet you will not escape, not even if you were an earl, but one torture will follow after another until you say you are a witch. Not before that," he said, "will they let you go, as you may see by all their trials, for one is just like another. . . ."

And so I begged, since I was in wretched plight, to be given one day for thought and a priest. The priest was refused me, but the time for thought was given. Now, my dear child, see in what hazard I stood and still stand. I must say that I am a witch, though I am not,—must now renounce God, though I have never done it before. Day and night I was deeply troubled, but at last there came to me a new idea. I would not be anxious, but, since I had been given no priest with whom I could take counsel, I would myself think of something and say it. It were surely better that I just say it with mouth and words, even though I had not really done it; and afterwards I would confess it to the priest, and let those answer for it who compel me to do it. . . . And so I made my confession, as follows; but it was all a lie.

Now follows, dear child, what I confessed in order to escape the great anguish and bitter torture, which it was impossible for me longer to bear. . . .

Then I had to tell what people I had seen [at the witch-sabbath]. I said that I had not recognized them. "You old rascal, I must set the executioner at you. Say—was not the Chancellor there?" So I said yes. "Who besides?" I had not recognized anybody. So he said: "Take one street after another; begin at the market, go out on one street and back on the next." I had to name several persons there. Then came the long street. I knew nobody. Had to name eight persons there. Then the Zinkenwert—one person more. Then over the upper bridge to the Georgthor, on both sides. Knew nobody again. Did I know nobody in the castle—whoever it might be, I should speak without fear. And thus continuously they asked me on all the streets, though I could not and would not say more. So they gave me to the executioner,

3. This torture of the strappado, which was that in most common use by the courts, consisted of a rope, attached to the hands of the prisoner (bound behind his back) and carried over a pulley at the ceiling. By this he was drawn up and left hanging. To increase the pain, weights were attached to his feet or he was suddenly jerked up and let drop. [Burr's note]

told him to strip me, shave me all over, and put me to the torture. "The rascal knows one on the market-place, is with him daily, and yet won't name him." By that they meant Dietmayer: so I had to name him too.

Then I had to tell what crimes I had committed. I said nothing. . . . "Draw the rascal up!" So I said that I was to kill my children, but I had killed a horse instead. It did not help. I had also taken a sacred wafer, and had desecrated it. When I had said this, they left me in peace.

Now, dear child, here you have all my confession, for which I must die. And they are sheer lies and made-up things, so help me God. For all this I was forced to say through fear of the torture which was threatened beyond what I had already endured. For they never leave off with the torture till one confesses something; be he never so good, he must be a witch. Nobody escapes, though he were an earl. . . .

Dear child, keep this letter secret so that people do not find it, else I shall be tortured most piteously and the jailers will be beheaded. So strictly is it forbidden. . . . Dear child, pay this man a dollar. . . . I have taken several days to write this: my hands are both lame. I am in a sad plight. . . .

Good night, for your father Johannes Junius will never see you more. July 24, 1628.

Dear child, six have confessed against me at once: the Chancellor, his son, Neudecker, Zaner, Hoffmaisters Ursel, and Hoppfens Elsse—all false, through compulsion, as they have all told me, and begged my forgiveness in God's name before they were executed. . . . They know nothing but good of me. They were forced to say it, just as I myself was. . . .[4]

---

4. The last paragraph was added to the margin of the letter. [Burr's note]

31

1636
The Devils of Loudun

No single witchcraft trial of any individual is better known to us today, in all its details, than that of Urbain Grandier, a priest of Loudun, France, tortured and burned at the stake in 1636. The context, machinations, pathology, and ultimate tragedy of the case have been clearly and movingly portrayed in Aldous Huxley's *The Devils of Loudun*. The Sentence of the Royal Commissioners is noteworthy for its dramatic and well-staged effects, calculated to impress upon all minds the gravity of the crimes of this priest convicted of bewitching a convent. More remarkable is the letter of Father Surin who, sent to exorcise the demons Grandier was accused of summoning, found himself possessed as well, and offered, in a rambling letter to his friend and spiritual advisor, a startling description of the symptomology of witchcraft in terms meaningful to a devout Christian of the seventeenth century.

From J. Aubin, *Les diables de Loudun* (Amsterdam, 1693), pp. 154–55, 218–21. Tr. A. C. K.

The Sentence of the Royal Commissioners Against Urbain Grandier (1636). We have decreed and shall decree the said Urbain Grandier duly arraigned and convicted of the crime of Wizardry, Sorcery and Possessions occurring by his deed, in the persons of several Ursuline Nuns of this town of Loudun, and other members of the Secular Clergy;

together with other incidents and crimes resulting from this. For expiation of which, we have condemned and shall condemn this Grandier to make honorable repentance, bare-headed, a rope around his neck, bearing in his hand a burning torch weighing two pounds, before the main door of the Church of Saint Pierre du Marché, and before that of Saint Ursula of this said town, and there, upon his knees, to ask pardon of God, of the King and of Justice; and this accomplished, to be taken to the public square of Sainte Croix, to be attached to a stake upon a pyre, which will be constructed at the said square for this purpose, and there to be burned alive with the pacts and the signs of Sorcery lying on the pyre, together with his Manuscript Book against priestly celibacy, and his ashes scattered to the wind. We have decreed and shall decree each and every of his possessions to be acquired and confiscated by the King, out of which the sum of one-hundred and fifty *livres* initially will be taken, to be used to purchase a copper lamp, upon which extracts of this present Sentence will be engraved, this being installed in a prominent place in the said Church of the Ursulines, to remain there in perpetuity. And prior to proceeding to the execution of the present Sentence, we order that the said Grandier will be subjected to ordinary and extraordinary Torture. . . . Pronounced at Loudun before the said Grandier, and executed the eighteenth of August, 1636.

Letter of Father Surin, Jesuit, exorcist of the
Ursuline Sisters of Loudun, to his Friend Father
Datichi, Jesuit, at Rennes; written from
Loudun, May 3, 1635.

Pax Christi.

To my Reverend Father,

There is scarcely anyone to whom it is more of a pleasure to relate my adventures than to your Reverence, who hears them willingly, and who formulates thoughts on them that do not come easily to other men, who do not know me as you do. Since my last letter I have fallen into a state of things far beyond my foresight, but most in conformity with the Providence of God for my soul: I am no longer at Marennes, but at Loudun, where I have just received your letter. I am in perpetual conversation with the Devils, in which I have had encounters which would be too lengthy to elaborate for you, and which have given me more reasons to know and admire the goodness of God than I have ever had. I want to tell you something, and I would tell you more of it if you were more close-mouthed.

Eigentliche Abbildung der ehemaligen
Probe und Reinigung der Hexen
auf dem kalten Waßer.

Figure 61. The Water Test.

One of the quasi-judicial tests to determine whether or not the accused was a witch
was to immerse her in water. If the water rejected the victim, guilt was taken as
proven. This and other tests aroused the anger of some lawyers and judges for their
violation of recognized legal procedure, but these objections only provoked the greater
zeal of those judges who argued that extraordinary crimes required extraordinary
judicial investigations. The character of evidence derived from such trials as this ultimately drew the attack of large numbers of lawyers and judges, whose views finally
prevailed in the seventeenth century.

262

I have entered into combat with four of the most powerful and malicious Demons of Hell. Me, I say, whose infirmities you know; God has permitted the combats to be so violent, and the contacts so frequent, that the least of the battlefields was the exorcism, for the enemies have announced themselves under cover, day and night, in a thousand different ways. You can imagine what a pleasure there is in finding oneself at the mercy of God alone. I will not say more on it; it is enough that knowing my state, you decide to pray for me. All the more because for three and a half months, I am never without a Devil at my side, exerting himself. Things have gone so far that God has permitted, for my sins, I think, something never seen, perhaps, in the Church: that during the exercise of my ministry, the Devil passes from the body of the possessed person, and coming into mine, assaults me and overturns me, shakes me, and visibly travels through me, possessing me for several hours like an energumen. I would not know how to explain to you what occurs inside of me during this time, and how this Spirit unites with mine, without depriving me either of the knowledge or the liberty of my soul, while nevertheless making himself like another me, and how it is as if I had two souls, one of which is deprived of its body, of the use of its organs, and stands apart, watching the actions of the one which has entered. The two Spirits battle on the same field, which is the body, and the soul is as if it were divided; following one part of itself, it is the subject of diabolical impressions; following the other, of movements which are its own, or which God gives to it. At the same time, I feel a great peace, under the absolute will of God; and without my knowing how, there comes an extreme rage, and aversion to Him, which becomes almost violent trying to separate itself from the other feeling, which astounds those who see it; on the one hand a great joy and *douceur,* and on the other, a sadness which reveals itself by lamentations and cries similar to those of the Demons: I feel the state of damnation and am frightened by it, and I feel as if I were pierced by sharp points of despair in this foreign soul which seems to be mine, and the other soul, which is full of confidence, makes light of such feelings, and in full liberty curses the one which causes them; verily, I feel that the same cries which leave my mouth come equally from these two souls, and I am hard-pressed to discern if it is the mirth which produces them, or the extreme fury which fills me. The tremblings which overcome me when the Holy Sacrament is bestowed upon me come equally, it seems to me, from horror at its presence, which is unbearable to me, and from a sweet and gentle reverence, without my being able to attribute them more to one than to the other, and without its being in my power to restrain them. When one of these two souls moves me to want to make the sign of the cross on my mouth, the other turns my hand away with great speed, and seizes my finger with my teeth, in order to gnaw on it in a rage. I almost never find prayer easier and more tranquil than during these agitations; while my body rolls on the ground, and the Ministers of the Church speak to me as if to a Devil, and accuse me of maledictions, I could not tell you the joy that I feel, having become a Devil not out of rebellion to God, but by virtue of the distress which depicts ingenuously for me the state to which sin has reduced me; so that appropriating to myself all of the maledictions which are offered to me, my soul has cause to sink in its nothingness. When the other possessed persons see me in this state, it is a pleasure to see their triumph, and how the Devils make fun of me, saying, Doctor, heal thyself, and go preach now from the pulpit; how nice it will be to see him preach, after he has rolled on the ground; *Tentaverunt, subsannaverunt me subsannatione, frenduerunt super me dentibus suis.* What a cause of benediction to see oneself made the Devil's plaything, and how the Justice of God in this world makes sense of my sins! what a blessing to experience the state from which Jesus Christ has drawn me, no longer by hearsay, but by the sensation of that very state; and how good it is to have at one and the same time the ability to enter into that misery and to give thanks to the goodness which has delivered us from it with so many efforts! That is how things stand with me at this time, almost every day. Great disputes are emerging over this, and *factus sum magna quaestio*, if it is a Possession or not, if it is possible that Ministers of the Gospel come to such great harm. Some say that it is a chastisement from God upon me, as punishment for some illusion; others say something quite different; as for me, I hold fast where I am, and would not exchange my fate for anyone's, being firmly convinced that there is nothing better than to be reduced to such great extremities. The one in which I find myself is such that I have few free actions: when I want to speak, my words are blocked; at Mass, I am paralyzed; at the table, I cannot carry a bite to my mouth; at Confession, I suddenly forget my sins; and I feel the Devil come and go inside of me as if it were his home. From the moment I awake, he is there: at prayer, he snatches my thought away whenever he wants; when my heart begins to swell with God, he fills it with fury; he puts me to sleep when I want to stay awake; and publicly, out of the mouth of the Possessed Woman, he boasts that he is my master: to which

I have nothing to retort. Having the reproach of my conscience, and the sentence pronounced upon sinners on my head, I must submit to it, and worship the order of Divine Providence, to which every creature must submit. There is not just one Demon who works on me, but two ordinarily; one of them is Leviathan, the opposite of the Holy Ghost, in as much as they have said here that they have a Trinity in Hell that the Witches worship, *Lucifer, Beelzebub,* and *Leviathan,* who is the third Person of Hell, and several authors have remarked and written on this heretofore. Now, the actions of this false Paraclete are completely the opposite of the true one, and they impart a desolation that one could never describe adequately. He is the leader of the entire group of our Demons, and he is the supervisor of the whole affair, which is one of the strangest that perhaps has ever been seen. In this same location, we see Paradise and Hell; nuns who are, taken in one sense, like St. Ursulas, and taken in another, worse than the most damned in all sorts of dissoluteness, obscenity, blasphemy and frenzy. I do not want your Reverence to make my letter public, if it please you. You are the sole person, outside of my Confessor and my Superiors, to whom I have wanted to tell so much, and only in order to provide some communication which helps us to glorify God, in Whom I am your most humble servant,

Jean-Joseph Surin

32

1652
The Trial of Suzanne Gaudry

The trial of Suzanne Gaudry, preserved in the oddly meticulous and syntactically disordered court records, offers a view of a case close to the modern age's traditional stereotype of witchcraft persecutions: the pathetic and illiterate old woman, the sabbath, the nocturnal flights, the carnal love of the devil, the effective use of terror and torture to obtain a confession, the recantation and burning at the stake, all brought together in a judicial atmosphere composed half of orderly interrogation and half of frightful insinuation and contradiction. The "leading questions," drawn from the "experience" of past centuries, show how a local secular court coordinated its activities to the more general traditions, and make clearer how the content of confessions remained so constant throughout the period of persecutions.

From J. Français, *L'Eglise et la Sorcellerie* (Paris, 1910), pp. 236–51. Tr. A. C. K.

*A*t Ronchain, 28 May, 1652. . . . *Interrogation of Suzanne Gaudry, prisoner at the court of Rieux.* Questioned about her age, her place of origin, her mother and father.

—Said that she is named Suzanne Gaudry, daughter of Jean Gaudry and Marguerite Gerné, both natives of Rieux, but that she is from Esgavans, near Odenarde, where her family had taken refuge because of the wars, that she was born the day that they made bonfires for the Peace between

France and Spain, without being able otherwise to say her age.

Asked why she has been taken here.

—Answers that it is for the salvation of her soul.

—Says that she was frightened of being taken prisoner for the crime of witchcraft.

Asked for how long she has been in the service of the devil.

—Says that about twenty-five or twenty-six years ago she was his lover, that he called himself Petit-Grignon, that he would wear black breeches, that he gave her the name Magin, that she gave him a pin with which he gave her his mark on the left shoulder, that he had a little flat hat; said also that he had his way with her two or three times only.

Asked how many times she has been at the nocturnal dance.

—Answers that she has been there about a dozen times, having first of all renounced God, Lent and baptism; that the site of the dance was at the little marsh of Rieux, understanding that there were diverse dances. The first time, she did not recognize anyone there, because she was half blind. The other times, she saw and recognized there Noelle and Pasquette Gerné, Noelle the wife of Nochin Quinchou and the other of Paul Doris, the widow Marie Nourette, not having recognized others because the young people went with the young people and the old people with the old. And that when the dance was large, the table also was accordingly large.

Questioned what was on the table.

—Says that there was neither salt nor napkin, that she does not know what there was because she never ate there. That her lover took here there and back.

Asked if her lover had never given her some powder.

—Answers that he offered her some, but that she never wanted to take any, saying to her that it was to do with what she wanted, that this powder was gray, that her lover told her she would ruin someone but good, and that he would help her, especially that she would ruin Elisabeth Dehan, which she at no time wanted to do, although her lover was pressing her to do it, because this Elisabeth had battered his crops with a club.

Interrogated on how and in what way they danced.

—Says that they dance in an ordinary way, that there was a guitarist and some whistlers who appeared to be men she did not know; which lasted about an hour, and then everyone collapsed from exhaustion.

Figure 62. The Witch-Finder General.
This illustration depicts Matthew Hopkins, the famous "Witch-Finder Generall" of mid seventeenth-century England, investigating two witches and their familiars.

The Trial of Suzanne Gaudry

Inquired what happened after the dance.

—Says that they formed a circle, that there was a king with a long black beard dressed in black, with a red hat, who made everyone do his bidding, and that after the dance he made a . . . [the word is missing in the text], and then everyone disappeared. . . .

Interrogated on how long it has been since she has seen Grignon, her lover.

—Says that it has been three or four days.

Questioned if she has abused the Holy Communion.

—Says no, never, and that she has always swallowed it. Then says that her lover asked her for it several times, but that she did not want to give it to him.

After several admonitions were sent to her, she has signed this

Mark
X
Suzanne Gaudry

Second Interrogation, May 29, 1652, in the presence of the afore-mentioned.

This prisoner, being brought back into the chamber, was informed about the facts and the charges and asked if what she declared and confessed yesterday is true.

—Answers that if it is in order to put her in prison it is not true; then after having remained silent said that it is true.

Asked what is her lover's name and what name has he given himself.

—Said that his name is Grinniou and that he calls himself Magnin.

Asked where he found her the first time and what he did to her.

—Answers that it was in her lodgings, that he had a hide, little black breeches, and a little flat hat; that he asked her for a pin, which she gave to him, with which he made his mark on her left shoulder. Said also that at the time she took him oil in a bottle and that she had thoughts of love.

Asked how long she has been in subjugation to the devil.

—Says that it has been about twenty-five or twenty-six years, that her lover also then made her renounce God, Lent, and baptism, that he has known her carnally three or four times, and that he has given her satisfaction. And on the subject of his having asked her if she wasn't afraid of having a baby, says that she did not have that thought.

Asked how many times she found herself at the nocturnal dance and carol and who she recognized there.

—Answers that she was there eleven or twelve times, that she went there on foot with her lover, where the third time she saw and recognized Pasquette and Noelle Gerné, and Marie Homitte, to whom she never spoke, for the reason that they did not speak to each other. And that the sabbat took place at the little meadow. . . .

Interrogated on how long it is since she saw her lover, and if she also did not see Marie Hourie and her daughter Marie at the dance.

—Said that it has been a long time, to wit, just about two years,[1] and that she saw neither Marie Hourie nor her daughter there; then later said, after having asked for some time to think about it, that it has been a good fifteen days or three weeks [since she saw him], having renounced all the devils of hell and the one who misled her.

Asked what occurred at the dance and afterwards.

—Says that right after the dance they put themselves in order and approached the chief figure, who had a long black beard, dressed also in black, with a red hat, at which point they were given some powder, to do with it what they wanted; but that she did not want to take any.

Charged with having taken some and with having used it evilly.

—Says, after having insisted that she did not want to take any, that she took some, and that her lover advised her to do evil with it; but that she did not want to do it.

Asked if, not obeying his orders, she was beaten or threatened by him, and what did she do with this powder.

—Answers that never was she beaten; she invoked the name of the Virgin [and answered] that she threw away the powder that she had, not having wanted to do any evil with it.

Pressed to say what she did with this powder. Did she not fear her lover too much to have thrown it away?

—Says, after having been pressed on this question, that she made the herbs in her garden die at the end of the summer, five to six years ago, by means of the powder, which she threw there because she did not know what to do with it.

---

1. Compare to first interrogation. [Editor's note]

Asked if the devil did not advise her to steal from Elisabeth Dehan and to do harm to her.

—Said that he advised her to steal from her and promised that he would help her; but urged her not to do harm to her; and that is because she [Elisabeth Dehan] had cut the wood in her [Suzanne Gaudry's] fence and stirred up the seeds in her garden, saying that her lover told her that she would avenge herself by beating her.

Charged once more with having performed some malefice with this powder, pressed to tell the truth.

—Answers that she never made any person or beast die; then later said that she made Philippe Cornié's red horse die, about two or three years ago, by means of the powder, which she placed where he had to pass, in the street close to her home.

Asked why she did that and if she had had any difficulty with him.

—Says that she had had some difficulty with his wife, because her cow had eaten the leeks.

Interrogated on how and in what way they dance in the carol.

—Says that they dance in a circle, holding each others' hands, and each one with her lover at her side, at which she says that they do not speak to each other, or if they speak that she did not hear it, because of her being hard-of-hearing. At which there was a guitarist and a piper, whom she did not know; then later says that it is the devils who play.

After having been admonished to think of her conscience, was returned to prison after having signed this

Mark

X

Suzanne Gaudry

Deliberation of the Court of Mons—June 3, 1652

The under-signed advocates of the Court of Mons have seen these interrogations and answers. They say that the aforementioned Suzanne Gaudry confesses that she is a witch, that she has given herself to the devil, that she has renounced God, Lent, and baptism, that she has been marked on the shoulder, that she has cohabited with him and that she has been to the dances, confessing only to have cast a spell upon and caused to die a beast of Philippe Cornié; but there is no evidence for this, excepting a prior statement. For this reason, before going further, it will be necessary to become acquainted with, to examine and to probe the mark, and to hear Philippe Cornié on the death of the horse and on when and in what way he died. . . .

Deliberation of the Court of Mons—June 13, 1652

[The Court] has reviewed the current criminal trial of Suzanne Gaudry, and with it the trial of Antoinette Lescouffre, also a prisoner of the same office.

It appeared [to the Court] that the office should have the places probed where the prisoners say that they have received the mark of the devil, and after that, they must be interrogated and examined seriously on their confessions and denials, this having to be done, in order to regulate all this definitively. . . .

Deliberation of the Court of Mons, June 22, 1652

The trials of Antoinette Lescouffre and Suzanne Gaudry having been described to the undersigned, advocates of the Court of Mons, and [the Court] having been told orally that the peasants taking them to prison had persuaded them to confess in order to avoid imprisonment, and that they would be let go, by virtue of which it could appear that the confessions were not so spontaneous:

They are of the opinion that the office, in its duty, would do well, following the two preceding resolutions, to have the places of the marks that they have taught us about probed, and if it is found that these are ordinary marks of the devil, one can proceed to their examination; then next to the first confessions, and if they deny [these], one can proceed to the torture, given that they issue from bewitched relatives, that at all times they have been suspect, that they fled to avoid the crime [that is to say, prosecution for the crime of witchcraft], and that by their confessions they have confirmed [their guilt], notwithstanding that they have wanted to revoke [their confessions] and vacillate. . . .

Third Interrogation, June 27, in the presence of the afore-mentioned.

This prisoner being led into the chamber, she was examined to know if things were not as she had said and confessed at the beginning of her imprisonment.

—Answers no, and that what she has said was done so by force.

Asked if she did not say to Jean Gradé that she would tell his uncle, the

mayor, that he had better be careful . . . and that he was a Frank.
—Said that that is not true.

Pressed to say the truth, that otherwise she would be subjected to torture, having pointed out to her that her aunt was burned for this same subject.
—Answers that she is not a witch.

Interrogated as to how long she has been in subjection to the devil, and pressed that she was to renounce the devil and the one who misled her.
—Says that she is not a witch, that she has nothing to do with the devil, thus that she did not want to renounce the devil, saying that he has not misled her, and upon inquisition of having confessed to being present at the carol, she insisted that although she had said that, it is not true, and that she is not a witch.

Charged with having confessed to having made a horse die by means of a powder that the devil had given her.
—Answers that she said it, but because she found herself during the inquisition pressed to say that she must have done some evil deed; and after several admonitions to tell the truth:

She was placed in the hands of the officer of the *haultes oeuvres* [the officer in charge of torture], throwing herself on her knees, struggling to cry,

Figure 63. The Shackled Sorcerer.

Although this woodcut from Olaus Magnus' *Historia de gentibus septentrionalibus* presents an immense sorcerer, the shackling process was used as both investigative torture and punishment for guilty witches.

uttering several exclamations, without being able, nevertheless, to shed a tear. Saying at every moment that she is not a witch.

The Torture

On this same day, being at the place of torture.

This prisoner, before being strapped down, was admonished to maintain herself in her first confessions and to renounce her lover.

—Said that she denies everything she has said, and that she has no lover.

Feeling herself being strapped down, says that she is not a witch, while struggling to cry.

Asked why she fled outside the village of Rieux.

—Says that she cannot say it, that God and the Virgin Mary forbid her to; that she is not a witch. And upon being asked why she confessed to being one, said that she was forced to say it.

Told that she was not forced, that on the contrary she declared herself to be a witch without any threat.

—Says that she confessed it and that she is not a witch, and being a little stretched [on the rack] screams ceaselessly that she is not a witch, invoking the name of Jesus and of Our Lady of Grace, not wanting to say any other thing.

Asked if she did not confess that she had been a witch for twenty-six years.

—Says that she said it, that she retracts it, crying Jésus-Maria, that she is not a witch.

Asked if she did not make Philippe Corné's horse die, as she confessed.

—Answers no, crying Jésus-Maria, that she is not a witch.

The mark having been probed by the officer, in the presence of Doctor Bouchain, it was adjudged by the aforesaid doctor and officer truly to be the mark of the devil.

Being more tightly stretched upon the torture-rack, urged to maintain her confessions.

—Said that it was true that she is a witch and that she would maintain what she had said.

Asked how long she has been in subjugation to the devil.

—Answers that it was twenty years ago that the devil appeared to her, being in her lodgings in the form of a man dressed in a little cow-hide and black breeches.

Interrogated as to what her lover was called.

—Says that she said Petit-Grignon, then, being taken down [from the rack] says upon interrogation that she is not a witch and that she can say nothing.

Asked if her lover has had carnal copulation with her, and how many times. —To that she did not answer anything; then, making believe that she was ill, not another word could be drawn from her.

As soon as she began to confess, she asked who was alongside of her, touching her, yet none of those present could see anyone there. And it was noticed that as soon as that was said, she no longer wanted to confess anything.

Which is why she was returned to prison.

Verdict

July 9, 1652

In the light of the interrogations, answers and investigations made into the charge against Suzanne Gaudry, coupled with her confessions, from which it would appear that she has always been ill-reputed for being stained with the crime of witchcraft, and seeing that she took flight and sought refuge in this city of Valenciennes, out of fear of being apprehended by the law for this matter; seeing how her close family were also stained with the same crime, and the perpetrators executed; seeing by her own confessions that she is said to have made a pact with the devil, received the mark from him, which in the report of *sieur* Michel de Roux was judged by the medical doctor of Ronchain and the officer of *haultes oeuvres* of Cambrai, after having proved it, to be not a natural mark but a mark of the devil, to which they have sworn with an oath; and that following this, she had renounced God, Lent, and baptism and had let herself be known carnally by him, in which she received satisfaction. Also, seeing that she is said to have been a part of nocturnal carols and dances. Which are crimes of divine lèse-majesty:

For expiation of which the advice of the under-signed is that the office of Rieux can legitimately condemn the aforesaid Suzanne Gaudry to death, tying her to a gallows, and strangling her to death, then burning her body and burying it there in the environs of the woods.

At Valenciennes, the 9th of July, 1652. To each [member of the Court] 4 *livres*, 16 *sous*. . . . And for the trip of the aforementioned Roux, including an escort of one soldier, 30 *livres*.

33

COTTON MATHER
Witchcraft in North America
1689

In 1689, the Reverend Cotton Mather (1663–1728) preached a sermon in Boston entitled "A Discourse on Witchcraft," which was then printed and circulated in Massachusetts as a part of a larger collection, Mather's *Memorable Providences Relating to Witchcraft and Possessions* (Boston, 1689). Three years later, the witch-scare erupted in Salem.

From Burr, *The Witchcraft Persecutions*, pp. 2–5.

Such an Hellish thing there is as *Witchcraft* in the World. There are Two things which will be desired for the advantage of this Assertion. It should *first* be show'd

WHAT *Witchcraft* is;

My Hearers will not expect from me an accurate *Definition* of the *vile Thing;* since the Grace of God has given me the Happiness to speak without *Experience* of it. But from Accounts both by *Reading* and *Hearing* I have learn'd to describe it so.

WITCHCRAFT is the Doing of *Strange* (and for the most part *Ill*) Things by the help of *evil Spirits, Covenanting* with (and usually *Representing* of) the woful children of men.

This is the *Diabolical Art* that *Witches* are notorious for.

First. *Witches* are the Doers of *Strange* Things. They cannot indeed perform any proper *Miracles*; those are things to be done only by the *Favourites* and *Embassadours* of the *Lord*. But *Wonders* are often produced by them, though chiefly such Wonders as the Apostle calls in *2 Thes.* 2, 9. *Lying wonders.* There are *wonderful Storms* in the *great* World, and *wonderful Wounds* in the *little* World, often effected by these *evil Causes*. They do things which transcend the ordinary *Course* of Nature, and which puzzle the ordinary *Sense* of Mankind. Some *strange* things are done by them in a way of *Real Production*. They do really *Torment*, they do really *Afflict* those that their Spite shall extend unto. Other *Strange* Things are done by them in a way of *Crafty Illusion*. They do craftily make of the *Air*, the *Figures* and *Colours* of things that never can be truly created by them. All men might *see*, but, I believe, no man could *feel*, some of the Things which the *Magicians* of *Egypt* exhibited of old.

Secondly. They are not only *strange* Things, but *Ill* Things, that *Witches* are the Doers of. In this regard also they are not the Authors of *Miracles*: those are things *commonly* done for the *Good* of Man, *alwaies* done for the *Praise* of *God*. But of these *Hell-hounds* it may in a special manner be said, as in *Psal.* 52, 3. *Thou lovest evil more than good.* For the most part they labour to robb *Man* of his *Ease* or his *Wealth*; they labour to wrong *God* of His *Glory*. There is Mention of Creatures that they call *White Witches*, which do only *Good-Turns* for their Neighbours. I suspect that there are none of that sort; but rather think, *There is none that doeth good, no, not one.* If they *do good*, it is only that they *may do hurt*.

Thirdly. It is by virtue of *evil Spirits* that *Witches* do what they do. We read in *Ephes.* 2, 2. about the *Prince of the power of the air*. There is confined unto the *Atmosphere* of our *Air* a vast *Power*, or *Army* of *Evil Spirits*, under the Government of a Prince who employs them in a continual Opposition to the Designs of GOD: The Name of that *Leviathan*, who is the *Grand-Seigniour of Hell*, we find in the Scripture to be *Belzebub*. Under the Command of that mighty Tyrant, there are vast *Legions & Myriads* of Devils, whose *Businesses & Accomplishments* are not all the same. Every one has his *Post*, and his *Work*; and they are all glad of an opportunity to be *mischievous* in the World. These are they by whom *Witches* do exert their Devillish and malignant Rage upon their *Neighbours*: And especially Two Acts concur hereunto. The *First* is, Their *Covenanting* with the Witches. There is a most hellish *League* made between them, with various *Rites* and *Ceremonies*. The *Witches* promise to serve the *Devils*, and the

Devils promise to *help* the witches; *How?* It is not convenient to be related. The *Second* is, their *Representing* of the Witches. And hereby indeed these are drawn into *Snares* and *Cords* of Death. The Devils, when they go upon the *Errands* of the *Witches,* do bear their *Names*; and hence do *Harmes* too come to be carried from the *Devils* to the *Witches.* We need not suppose such a wild thing as the *Transforming* of those Wretches into *Bruits* or *Birds,* as we too often do.

It should next be proved *THAT* Witchcraft *is.*

The *Being* of such a thing is denied by many that place *a great part* of their *small wit* in derideing the Stories that are told of it. Their chief Argument is, That they never *saw* any Witches, therefore there are *none.* Just as if you or I should say, We never met with any *Robbers* on the Road, therefore there never was any *Padding* there.

Indeed the *Devils* are loath to have true Notions of *Witches* entertained with us. I have beheld them to put out the eyes of an enchaunted Child, when a Book that proves, *There is Witchcraft,* was laid before her. But there are especially Two Demonstrations that evince the Being of that Infernal mysterious thing.

First. We have the Testimony of *Scripture* for it. We find *Witchcrafts* often mentioned, sometimes by way of *Assertion,* sometimes by way of *Allusion,* in the Oracles of God. Besides that, We have there the History of diverse *Witches* in these infallible and inspired Writings. Particularly, the Instance of the *Witch* at *Endor,* in 1 *Sam.* 28. 7. is so plain and full that *Witchcraft* it self is not a more amazing thing, than any *Dispute* about the Being of it, after this. The Advocates of *Witches* must use more *Tricks* to make Nonsense of the *Bible,* than ever the *Witch* of *Endor* used in her Magical Incantations, if they would evade the Force of that famous History. They that will believe no *Witches,* do imagine that *Jugglers* only are meant by them whom the Sacred Writ calleth so. But what do they think of that law in *Exod.* 22. 18. *Thou shalt not suffer a Witch to live?* Methinks 'tis a little too hard to punish every silly *Juggler* with so great Severity.

Secondly. We have the *Testimony* of *Experience* for it. What will those *Incredulous,* who must be the only *Ingenious* men, say to This? Many *Witches* have like those in *Act.* 19. 18. *Confessed and shewed their deeds.* We see those things done, that is impossible any *Disease* or any *Deceit* should procure. We see some hideous *Wretches* in hideous *Horrours* confessing, *That they did the Mischiefs.* This *Confession* is often made by them that are owners of as much Reason as the people that laugh at all *Conceit* of

Witchcraft: the exactest Scrutiny of skilful Physicians cannot find any Distraction in their minds. This *Confession* is often made by them that are apart One from another, and yet they *agree* in all the Circumstances of it. This *Confession* is often made by them that at the same time will produce the *Engines* and *Ensignes* of their *Hellish Trade,* and give the standers-by an *Ocular Conviction* of *what* they do, and *how.* There can be no Judgment left of any *Humane Affairs,* if such *Confessions* must be Ridiculed: all the *Murders,* yea, and all the *Bargains* in the World must be meer *Imaginations* if such *Confessions* are of no Account.

Figure 64. The Hanging of the Chelmsford Witches.
This woodcut illustrated the reports of the Chelmsford Witches. Hanging was the punishment under English and American common law for crimes of witchcraft, while Scotland and the Continent burned convicted witches.

34

RICHARD BOVET
Demonology and Dilettantism
1684

Richard Bovet (b. 1641) was an undistinguished man of letters and country squire, who matriculated at Oxford (1657–58). He was a great admirer of Joseph Glanvil and Henry More (*No. 36*), and appears to have followed with close attention the Somerset witchcraft trials of the 1660's, which More and Glanvil used to great advantage. Having a wide acquaintance with country beliefs, he thus combined in his own mind strains of philosophical, judicial, and popular attitudes towards witchcraft. In 1684, he published his only known work, *Pandæmonium, or, The Dewil's Cloyster* which reflected these diverse tendencies. Although the work sold very poorly, and despite the obscurity of its author, it is a valuable compendium of common seventeenth-century beliefs.

Richard Bovet, *Pandaemonium,* tr. Montague Summers (Aldington, Kent, 1951), pp. 47–58, 98–99, 133–36.

*P*ropositions *of Assertions concerning Witches and Witchcraft. The Character of a Witch. Same Considerations of the Original of their power.* The last Chapter having designed that Idol Worship (as the Devil is therein proposed Objectively to be Adored) Is not only a great Countenancer, but Tends vastly to the promotion of Diabolical Confederacies. Before we proceed to a particular and Historical Account of Ancient and Modern Witches, it may be necessary a little farther to explain what we mean by a Witch; and how far the power of such a one may be understood. And this being a nice and difficult determination; The Candid Reader shall find very little new Asserted Notions either in Relation to their persons or practices; but we shall chuse to lay down what the most Unprejudiced, Learned, and Sober Writers of things relating to Matters of this Nature have upon their best search and Enquiry determined.

And first it is agreed that it is very difficult to prove such, or such a one to be a *Witch,* and it ought to be done with the greatest *Caution and Tenderness Imaginable:* The loss being greater on the part of *a false Testimony,* than on that of a *Supposed Criminal*; Infernal *Contracts* are not supposed to be made in the presence of Witnesses; being as hath been said, against the Law of *God* and *Man*; So that the Devil out of a seeming *regard* to the safety and *Immunity* of his *Prostitute* may omit the Ceremony of *Testes*; the black pupil acting with greater security when she apprehends none knows of, or is *privy* to the *Confederation.*

Yet is there no doubt but the Devil is as secure of his prey as if the whole world has subscribed a *Teste* to the Indenture; for by the consent of the party, he hath *Seisin* of her as his *Property*; which he will be sure never to part with, unless *Ejected by a stronger than He.* Those Hellish *Compacts* therefore, are Managed like the filthy *Intrigues* betwixt a *Fornicator* and his *Strumpet,* where it may be no *Eye sees them* that may Expose them to the penalties of Humane Laws; and it is difficult to prove matter of fact between them; but at last a Spurious off-spring, or a more Nauseous Rotteness unveils them to the world, and they linger out to a more Infamous Death, than if the Law had Chastised them; The Rotteness of their bones giving them more severe pains and Twinges than the Rod of Justice could have done: Not unlike this do some of these Infernal Prostitutes Escape the hand of the publick Justice until at last their loath'd and miserable Lives are seized as forfeitures to the Devil; and they are found (like *Faustus*) with broken Necks, or with some other wrack upon their Nauseous Bodies, that Evidently discovers their souls to have been *Extorted* from them, and that they have been *forcibly* Ejected *upon forfeiture* of *their Lease.*

Some too, may have been unjustly accused for Witches; either by an Ignorance of Causes *meerly Natural,* or misapplying Causes that in themselves are supernatural: So that the very same operations which to Intelligent, and Enquiring Philosophers, are meerly the product of Natural *Sympathies,* or *Antipathies* of *Heat,* or *Cold,* or the like, to the unskilful shall appear, as done by Art *Magical*, or *Diabolical*. So the *Freezing* a cup of snow-water to a Stool by the *fireside*, looks to some weak persons, with an Aspect very *strange* and *unaccountable*, whilst to those that consider and know the *restringent* Quality of the *Salt*, the others Admiration becomes almost Ridiculous.

It is acknowledged by all Naturalists that the power of Imagination hath had, and may have strange Effects, especially upon tender and Irrational Bodies, such as Children, Chickens, Lambs &c. according to that of *Virgil*,
Nescio quis Teneros Oculus mihi fascinat Agnos.

And very strange performances may be effected by an Exalted and Fixed Imagination, the Intention of which vastly contributes towards the Effecting things seemingly Impossible. The formation of the Child in the Mothers Womb (which if good Authority may be Credited) hath been Imputed to the force of an Imagination strongly possessed with such, or such a belief. And to this purpose, it is very remarkable what is by a learned pen related of a *Lady, who being used to wear patches, and that during the time she was with child, a Gentleman told her that her child would have such a patch in its forehead; and accordingly at the birth of the Child, such a spot was discerned in the place described,* and still remained in that same part of the Ladies Face, as a Testimony of the Impression a powerful Imagination may have on tender Bodies. Infinite more are the Experiments that might be mentioned of this kind, but if I should Enumerate never so many, it would nevertheless appear that the Feats, and performances of Infernal Confederacies vastly surpass whatsoever can be thought attainable in this kind; and this will be so Evident, by matters of Fact related in the following Collection that it would be needless to speak any thing more to it in this place.

Besides, if it be supposed that some have been suspected for Witches, barely for having deformed Bodies, Ill Aspects, or Melancholy Constitutions doth it any ways appear from hence, that there is really no such thing as a Witch? Or may it not with as much reason be alledged, that because some for having Arms found about them, have been wrongfully accused for being Robbers; that therefore there is no such thing as a High-way man. Such allegations as these, do not at all disprove the Existence of such Haggs.

Tho I must confess that there is no reason that any person (by reason of those *deformities* which may be only the Effects of *old Age*, or the product of some *disease*) should be presently Indicted and *trust up for a Witch*; nor can I Imagin that ever such a thing hath been in a Civilized Nation, without the concomitant circumstances of some other proofs: That would be a hard case indeed! But I think it will not be difficult to prove that there have been *some whose Insides have been blackened with as foul and damnable Confederacies as others*; who have notwithstanding appeared with Faces very *Charming*, and *Angelical*. For we have no account of any very Nauseous deformity that sate on the forehead of *Jesabel, Joan of Arc*, or *Joan Queen of Naples*. And perhaps the Attempts of these Hellish Agents may pass with less Suspicion, when under the plausible disguise of a *handsom Face*: For from Objects *Nasty* and *deformed*, men Naturally turn away, with a kind of *Innate Aversion* and *Contempt*; whilst under the *Charming Attraction* of a fair face, the *Magical Enchantment Insensibly* Steals upon *men. Nor is the Devil at any time more dangerous, than when he appears as an Angel of Light.*

Spotswood in his History of the Church of *Scotland*, book the 6th. page 383. Reports that there was one *Agnes Sampson* amongst the Witches and Sorcerers of that Kingdom, who was commonly called the *Wise Wife of Keith*, who was very remarkable; being (as he says) a Woman not of the sordid and base sort of Witches, in outward appearance, but of a Matron like, and grave Mein, settled, and seemingly Judicious in her answers; who upon her Examination declared, That she had a Familiar Spirit, which upon her Invocation usually appeared to her in a Visible form, & resolved her of doubtful Matters, especially concerning Matters relating to the Life or Death of persons lying sick, and that he had taught her, when she called him, to use the word *Holla Master*. Upon which he usually appeared to her. See *Wanly's Wonders of the little World*. lib. 5. chap. 20. *So that Deformity alone is no more an Argument of a Witch, than Beauty may be said to be an Evidence of a Whore.*

Sometimes, it is Objected, that some have come in and given Evidence against themselves; and being brought before Magistrates, have (it may be thought) causlesly accused themselves, by Confessing themselves to be Witches, and relating divers things by them done (as they have supposed) by the help of the Devil. And all this may be the Effect of a Deep Melancholy, or some Terrour that they may have been under: or perhaps an Argument that themselves have at the same time been under the Power of Witchcraft; or at least in some kind of Delirium of Phancy. So some Lunaticks have fancied themselves to be Kings, or Queens, and it hath been beyond the Power of the most Rational Arguments, and Demonstrations

Figure 65. The Inquisition at Work.

No tribunal, spiritual or lay, excited as much fear and fantasy as did that of the Holy Office, popularly called the Inquisition. This institution was responsible for rooting out and condemning first heretics, and later, witches. The representation here is a stylized eighteenth-century engraving.

to convince them of the contrary: But the self-accusations of such is as little to be credited, as the Self-Compurgation, and Applauses of others; without some more substantial Testimony.

It is Observable that Witches are commonly of the Female Sex, and some there are that confine that Term wholly to them: And ever since the prevalence of the First Temptation upon the first Woman; it is no wonder if the subtil Adversary still offer his Baits to such palats as are most desirous to taste Fruits forbidden; and more negligent in Enquiring into the Nature of what they Swallow. It was an Observation of *Fulgentius, Nescio quid habet Muliebre Nomen semper cum Sacris.* And it has been a long time observed of them, that if they incline to Virtue and Piety, few go beyond them; but if they take up with *Superstitious* and evil courses, none surpass them in Heights of Wickedness and mischief.

Tho these wretched Artists are commonly distinguished into those of the *Black,* and *White* orders; they are certainly the same, and cannot be said to differ in deeds of darkness, which admit of no difference of Colour, They are certainly both alike guilty in Compounding with the Devil. The black of those which are looked upon to do the most Mischief, because they commonly Torment mens bodies, or Injure them in their Estates; and the White, are reckoned to be such as restore people to health, and to goods lost: So that accordingly they have acquired the Names of *Good* and *Evil* Women. *But what Fellowship hath Light with Darkness, or what Communion hath Christ with Belial.* Both these deal in the same forbidden Arts, and Equally bring Clients to their Hellish Master. They may be said to be like the Glasiers boys about the Town, who Employ themselves to break the Neighbours windows, that their Masters may have the profit of mending them again.

Some Ancient Arts and Mysteries are said to be lost, but we have reason to believe that the Father of Mischief will not let fall any of those Trades by which he brings Souls to perdition, as long as he can have Scholars, and Servants to carry on his purposes.

So that we need not doubt the Continuance of that Ancient Devil-Craft, and Infernal Combination, as long as a Sordid Ignorance, Revengeful Malice, or Blind Superstition remain in the World. The Ignorant resort to it as to a School of Instruction, where they proceed and graduate themselves in the Cursed Mathematicks, and Mysteries of the Lower World. The Malicious apply themselves for Revenge, to wreak their spleens upon those they have Animosity against; and they are all the *better part of Mankind:* For if once they become in League with the Devil, they must be supposed to have espoused his Interest so far, as to *stretch out their Malice answerable to his Enmity, which is against all Mankind* in general, but particularly against those of the greatest *Integrity:* as is evident in the case of our *First Parents, Job,* our *Blessed Saviour and his Holy Apostles.* And in the Revelation of St. *John,* the Angel tells the Church of *Smyrna, that the Devil should cast some of them into prison that they might be Tryed.* And Luke 22. chap. 31. vers. He tells *Peter* that *Satan had desired to winnow him,* as they do wheat, but our Lord had prayed for him, *&c.* And this must be Imputed to that Enmity which was put between the seed of the Woman, and that of the Serpent; So that ever since the Apostate Angel hath by himself, and his wicked Agents, continually been Attempting to wreak his Revenge upon them.

The *Superstitious* are with as much ease, as any, drawn into the Fatal snare, for *they often become Witches, by endeavouring to defend themselves against Witchcraft.* These doubting that some Witch might have power to hurt them, arm themselves with the Devil's *Shield* against the Devil's *Sword:* Putting on the Armour of *Charms,* and *Spells* piecemeal by degrees; until at length they come to be Devil-fenc'd cap-a-pie: and so at first they are drawn in a *League Defensive;* until at last it comes to be declared *Offensive* too. That Art is quickly learnt; which wants nothing but *Credulity* and practice to attain it; and where the Devil once finds an *Invitation,* he ever after *Haunts.*

Of these Proficients in the *Black* Mysteries, there are some who at first begin with Feats rather diverting, than Hurtful; for they are sometimes entertained by Ludicrous and gamesom Spirits, who (to appearance) do things seemingly pleasant: but this *pastime* costs them dear in the End; for they play so long on the brink of Hell, until at length they tumble in, and sport with the devouring *Lyon,* until they are seized by his griping *Paw;* from whence They never after have power to Extricate themselves.

Others there are that are prevail'd with by none of these considerations; but take up the use of *Magical Forms,* and *Simples* by *Tradition:* Those that were their Predecessors deriving down to them the use of some *Mystical words,* or *Ceremonies* upon the recital of which, they acquire the knowledge of many strange, and remote secrets; and are Assisted in the performance of *things* much above the reach of a power meerly Humane. We have no reason to think it Improbable that the Apostate Spirit may have Obliged himself, upon the bare *naming,* or *repeating* such or such set forms of words (by himself, perhaps Appointed) to *attend* upon those that make use of them. And upon this account it is that *Balaam* and the Wisemen of *Nebuchadnezar* (mentioned in the book of *Daniel*) are acquitted by Learned men, from having a particular Covenant with the Devil, or acting by the Rules of the *greater Sorcery*.

And here I cannot omit relating a passage which was told me when I was a Shool-boy in the house of a Learned and Religious Divine in the Country, That there formerly Lived in the same house a Parson, who likewise taught the *Latin* tongue, and having several Lads under his care; they (one day when he was at Dinner at a Gentlemans house about a mile from the place) happened to go into his Study, and (whether out of Curiosity, or by accident, is uncertain) were reading in a book of his relating to that forbidden Art; the Lads continued reading, 'till divers Spirits came into the Room to them (as I remember) I was told in the Shape of boys, which seemed with a nimble motion to caper and play about them: Their Master, who was then at such a distance from them, and at dinner, had some Notice of what was doing at home, and immediately rose from table, and repaired to them, where he found them very perplexed at their new company, but knew not how to be rid of them but upon the coming in of their Master, they were soon discharged.

Not unlike to this may be the case of some, who having by them books of *Conjuration*, may perhaps ignorantly, and undesignedly peruse them, without any previous Compact; until at length their Inquisitive Inclinations are so wrought upon, as to make use of the more *Interdicted* means for their Information. Nor is it Improbable; but that some Students in *Astrology*, may (in their first Addresses to that Science) aim no farther than the satisfaction of their Curiosity, in the Knowledge of *Hidden* and *remote* Questions; and Future Events; Whilst those Mischievous Spirits (who like Beasts of prey) watching all Occasions to entrap and get them into their Envious reach: may work upon their overcurious and inquisitive Genius's to search after the more prohibited means of satisfying their sinful Curiosity. So that *Judicial Astrology* may well be lookt upon, as a fair Introduction to the Diabolical Art. And it seems not Improbable, but it might at first be set on foot as a *Lure* to draw the *Over-curious* into those snares that lye beyond it.

And whosoever but seriously Considers the Nature of those Questions, which the *pretenders to that Art* undertake to resolve, will find reason to think that they step somwhat beyond those bounds which are set to their *Enquiries*.

And it is too much to be doubted, that those who take upon them to *Predict* and Calculate of such Occult Contingencies, and Futurities; are not always free from Inticements and solicitations to the more dangerous Correspondencies.

Tho all this while it is not denied but that there may be an Observation of Sydereal and Planetical Motions, which falls not under the black Character of those Interdicted Arts; but if kept within the modest directions of Natural Speculation, may not only be Lawful, but of Good use, to Excite in us an Admiration and Adoration of *him that stretched out the Heavens like a Courtain, and bindeth up the sweet Influences of the Pleiades, Causing the Stars in their Courses to fight against such as Oppugn his Righteous purposes.* As we read in the Sacred pages.

Nor would we be thought to include all manner of Intimation of Future Events under the Notion of unlawful Divination; since it is very apparent, that as the practitioners of the Forbidden Study do by the Indication of the Devil and his wicked Angels, arrive to a Dear-bought Knowledge of things to come: So oftentimes it pleaseth God (by the blessed Guardians of his Saints, and) by the Ministry of Holy Spirits, to Impart to such as truly fear him, and call upon his Name, some certain Intimations of his Divine pleasure in relation to Mundane affairs, and the Changes that may happen either to his Church in general, or to particular Countries, Families, or Persons. Many Instances of this kind might be produced, of which, for proof some few shall be mentioned. Such was the Dream of *Nebuchadnezar,* Interpreted by the Prophet *Daniel,* and mentioned in the 4. *chap.* of that Prophesie and such was that Voice which was heard in the Temple before the destruction of *Jerusalem,* be well thought to be: When by a *Migremus Hinc,* an Alarm was given to the Jews to remove before the Storm of that dreadful War came upon them, which Occasioned the destruction of their City and Temple.

The late Reverend and Learned Bishop *Usher,* as is written in his Life, predicted the Massacre in *Ireland,* many Years before the bloody Execution of it. And King *James,* strangely discovered the horrid Powder Treason, by that letter to the Lord *Mont-Eagle;* which can hardly be imputed to any thing less than the Courteous Intimation, or Impulse of some good Genius. Nor is it at all unlikely that we are beholden to those Watchful Admonishers of us, for the seasonable Hints of approaching Calamities, which often shew themselves to us Either in Aerial, or other Prodigies. For these by the most

Considerate men of all Ages have been acknowledged to be the Prodroms of great Calamities, or Catastrophies.

So our Blessed Saviour tells us that there shall be *Signs* in the Heavens, and *Signs* in the Earth, before that great and terrible day of the Lord. And who knows, but these Indexes may be through the Care of those good and tender Guardians; who out of tenderness of our Welfare may give us those Cautions, and Admonitions to provide our selves against a day of Tryal. The dreadful desolations that happened in *Germany*, and *England*, in the Late unnatural Warrs (which whether or no they were presaged by them, yet certainly had many Tremendous Apparitions in the Air, and on the Earth &c. before those Calamities broke forth amongst them;) I say these are dismal Testimonies of the consequences of such Presages.

But these Kind of Predictions, as they are the effects of the *Benevolence* of Heaven, to us sinful Mortals, so they generally startle and awaken a secure and sinful World to meet God in the way of his Judgments: or if they have not that good effect on the sensual and Disobedient; they are at least Messengers of Joy, and Harbingers of Grace to those who apply themselves to Study the Voice of God in his Providences.

Whilst we are foretold in the Holy Scripture that *Wicked men and seducers shall wax worse & worse, deceiving, and being deceived.* For the Spirit of Delusion to which they adhere, shall betray them into gross mistakes, and palpable deviations; such are Generally Impenetrable by the Warning of Heaven, they are Judicially Blinded, and Infatuated, that they should not come to the knowledge of the Truth. Thus the Prophet *Ezekiel* tells us of a Spirit of Lying, which entered into the False Prophets, and they cryed *Peace, Peace*; when a sudden desolation, and destruction from the Lord was coming upon them. And this will be the dreadful case of those miserable Wretches who have given themselves up to the Conduct of the *Father of Lyes*; Who either *out of a belief that they have no souls*, have given themselves over to work Wickedness; Or else despising the Glories of a Blessed Eternity, have Listed themselves under the Banner of Satan, to Fight against the Power of the Omnipotent. And *that Atheism, Idolatry, Sensuality*, and *Debauchery*, have a Natural Tendence to promote this impious and Diabolical Confederacy, hath been hinted in the forgoing Pages. Which being so Regulary, Learnedly, and Largely Treated of by the Excellent pens of Dr. H. M. and Mr. J. G. before mentioned, in the second part of *Saducismus Triumphatus*; I shall presume to Wade no further in the

Argumentative, and Philosóphical part; but proceed now, to give an Account of the most Atested Relations of Ancient Witches; and thence descend to some very remarkable, and Credible Modern Relations, most of which have happened in these Few years, and will be attested by persons of Unquestionable Worth and Reputation now alive amongst us.

Giving an Account of divers most Remarkable Witchcrafts. Also a further Account of Dæmons, and Spectres, never before Published. By what hath been said in the foregoing pages, it is evident, that the Prince of Darkness hath a very large Dominion among the Sons of Men; That he hath his Temples, Altars, and Sacrifices: and though under new and different names, still draws off poor biggotted wretches to pay unto his Impious Shrines that Honour, Homage, and Adoration, which is only due to the *most High.* There are besides these, another sort of the Infernal Disciples, who give themselves up immediately to the Conduct, and disposal of the Apostate Angel, by entring into League, and Covenant with him, and giving themselves up to those Black, and Interdicted Mysteries, which justly are punished with death, both by the Divine, and Human Law. These have their Familiars of the dark Region, that assist them in the Execution of their Hellish purposes; by this means they attain to performances vastly trancending the capacity of Human Agents, as much as can be supposed that Spiritual, and Angelical Beings exceed in *Subtilty,* Agility, and Power, whatsoever can be pretended to by meer Mortals. It would swell this Volume to too large a bulk, should I speak of the divers ways and manners, by which they enter themselves Scholars to the School of Darkness; besides, divers learned and famous Authors have taken great pains herein. I shall therefore no longer detain the Reader from an account of divers very Remarkable Relations, never yet Printed; the Truth of which will be averred from Persons of unquestionable Reputation now alive; the things themselves having been done within the compass of these very few years: And if some sober, and ingenious Persons would undertake but to commend to the publick the Occurrences of this nature in every County; it would doubtless be a work very acceptable to all good men; and of great use for the conviction of others.

A Relation of a Gentleman that was cruelly Murthered by Witches, who made his Image of Wax, and stuck pins therein, April 78. *whereby he was miserably tormented, and died the Summer following.* In the West of *Scotland,* an Honourable Gentleman, Sir ———— *Maxwell* of *Pollock,* was taken with a grievous distemper, which by the vehemency of the Pain, hindred him from taking any rest, attended with continual sweating, through the vehemency of the Agony. His Pain resembled that which is caused by Punction, as if he had had so many Pins stuck in his side, but more vehement than a Pain excited by that can be conceived to be. Several Physicians were imployed to search into the Cause thereof, but none could find it out; nor could procure him ease by any Remedies: so that he lay in a comfortless Condition, expecting nothing, but to be racked with insupportable Tortures, till that long'd for Remedy, Death, should come. While he lay in this miserable Torment, it happened that a Woman (then pretending to be dumb) entred his House; and pointing to the Chamber where he was lying, made signs to those that were at that time in his House, to follow her out of doors; they at first took no notice of her, but she persisting therein, they went out with her, to see if they could understand her meaning. She led them into a House adjacent (a Tenant of this distressed Gentleman's,) and having entered the House, she gave signs to them to open a Chest there; whereupon they desired the Woman of the House to open the Chest, that they might satisfy their Curiosity in so far humouring her. The Woman conscious of her own Guilt, refused; whereupon they beginning to suspect there was more than ordinary in it, that made her so averse from it, broke it open, which when they had done, they found therein an Image of Wax, which they took out, and found a great many Pins stuck in the same side of it, as the Gentlemans Pain held him in his. They took out the Pins, and afterwards returning to the House, they asked the Gentleman how he found himself; who answered that he was altogether eased of his pain, and in a very good condition. Then they took the Pins, and stuck in the other side of the Image, when immediately the Gentleman cryed out of a pain that had seized him on his other side, as vehement as the former was. They took them out again, and he was eased as formerly. The Witch was had before a Justice, but I never heard that she was further troubled, whether for that that was not sufficient proof in Law to take away her life, or for some other reason I know not. The pretended dumb Woman was afterwards seized, and imprisoned at *Glasgow,* where she pretended to recover the use of her Tongue, and spoke, whereas before she seemed to be dumb. Several strange things were reported of her there; which being variously reported, I would not trouble the Reader with a Relation thereof; mentioning nothing herein but what I know to be of undoubted truth, and what was acknowledged by all. After she had been kept there for two or three weeks, she was transported to *Edinburgh,* and put in the *Cannon-gate* Prison, where she remained above half a year. She was several times had before the Council, and examined. A great many Persons out of Curiosity visited her, some of whom had better kept away; for if they were guilty of Love Intrigues, she used sufficiently to expose them, sparing neither Quality nor Sex. When any questioned how she came by that Knowledge, and charged her with having correspondence with the Devil, she made answer in the words of our Saviour; *If Satan cast out Satan, how can his Kingdom stand?* Denying that she had any Compact with the Devil, but affirming that it was a gift she had from her Birth. She was set at liberty, after having been a considerable time in Prison. But the Gentleman after her seizure, was taken with the same distemper, and died thereof.

35

HENRY MORE and
JOSEPH GLANVIL
Witchcraft and Philosophical Spiritualism

Henry More and Joseph Glanvil (1636–80), two philosophers of immense erudition and culture, were both associated with the movement in seventeenth-century English thought known as Cambridge Platonism. Both thinkers accepted a fundamental spiritual reality in the natural as well as the supernatural world, and saw a great danger to religious and Christian belief in the inroads of an anti-spiritualist mechanism and materialism that they identified with the thought of Descartes, Hobbes, and Spinoza. It is in this context that their writings on witchcraft must be understood.

If one could prove the existence of evil spirits, one would thereby demonstrate the reality of spiritual causes and agents in the natural world, and witchcraft offered for More and Glanvil such a proof. Predisposed to seeing spirits, evil and good, all about them in the world, More and Glanvil readily compiled case-histories of witchcraft, utilizing these "well-attested" tales as empirical evidence for the reality of spirit in the lives of men. Glanvil himself witnessed and publicized the activities of the "Demon of Tedworth," and he and More became a virtual clearing-house for similar relations by other men. Adding such empirical data to the scriptural sources of witchcraft-belief, they felt that they had completed a compelling case for witchcraft from both a traditional and a progressive, more scientific point of view.

Joseph Glanvil, *Sadducismus Triumphatus, Or full and plain Evidence concerning Witches and Apparitions . . . The Third Edition with Additions, The Advan-*

tages whereof, above the former, the Reader may understand out of Dr. H. More's account prefixed thereunto. In two parts. London, 1700. Part I, pp. 1–10; Part II, pp. 1–8, 101–105.

D_r. Henry More, his Letter with the Postscript to Mr. Joseph Glanvil, minding him of the great Expedience and Usefulness of his new intended Edition of the *Dæmon of Tedworth*. . . .

Sir,

When I was at London, I called on your Bookseller, to know in what forwardness this new intended impression of the Story of the *Daemon of Tedworth* was, which will undeceive the World touching that fame spread abroad, as if Mr. *Mompesson* and yourself had acknowledged the business to have been a meer Trick or Imposture. But the Story with your ingenious Considerations about Witchcraft, being so often printed already, he said, it behooved him to take care how he ventured on a new Impression, unless he had some new Matter of that Kind to add, which might make this new Edition the more certainly saleable; and therefore he expected the issue of that noised Story of the Spectre at *Exeter*, seen so oft for the discovering of a Murder committed some thirty Years ago. But the event of this business, as to juridical process, not answering expectation, he was discouraged from making use of it, many things being reported to him from thence in favour to the party most concerned. But I told him a Story of one Mrs. *Britton*, her appearing to her Maid after her Death, very well attested, though not of such a Tragical kind as that of *Exeter*, which he thought considerable. But of Discoveries of Murder I never met with any Story more plain and unexceptionable than that in Mr. *John Webster*, his display of supposed Witchcraft: The Book indeed itself, I confess, is but a weak and impertinent piece, but that Story weighty and convincing, and such as himself (though otherwise an affected Caviller against almost all Stories of Witchcraft, Apparitions) is constrained to assent to, as you shall see from his own Confession. I shall for your better ease, or because you haply may not have the Book, transcribe it out of the Writer himself, though it be something, about the Year of Lord 1632 (as near as I can remember, having lost my Notes and the Copy of the Letters to Sergeant *Hutton*, but am sure that I do most perfectly remember the Substance of the Story). Near unto *Chester*, in the Street, there lived one *Walker*, a Yeoman of good Estate, and a Widower, who had a young Woman to his Kinswoman that kept his house, who was by the Neighbours suspected to be with Child, and was towards the dark of the Evening one Night sent away with one *Mark Sharp*, who was a Collier, or one that digged Coals underground, and one that had been born in *Blakeburn* Hundred in *Lancashire;* and so she was not heard of a long time, and no noise or little was made about it. In the Winter time after, one James *Graham*, or *Grime* (for so in that Country they call them) being a Miller, and living about two Miles from the place where *Walker* lived, was one Night alone very late in the Mill grinding Corn, and about twelve or one o'Clock at Night, he came down the Stairs from having been putting Corn in the Hopper, the Mill doors being shut, there stood a Woman upon the midst of the Floor with her Hair about her Head hanging down and all Bloody, with five large Wounds on her Head. He being much affrighted and amazed, began to bless himself, and at last asked her who she was, and what she wanted? To which she said, "I am the Spirit of such a Woman, who lived with *Walker*, and being got with Child by him, he promised to send me to a private place, where I should be well looked to till I was brought in Bed and well again, and then I should come again and keep his House. And accordingly," said the Apparition, "I was one Night late sent away with one *Mark Sharp,* who upon a Moor," naming a place that the Miller knew, "slew me with a Pick," such as Men dig Coals withal, "and gave me these five Wounds, and after threw my body into a Coal-pit hard by, and hid the Pick under a Bank; and his Shoes and Stockings being bloody, he endeavoured to wash 'em, but seeing the Blood would not forth, he hid them there." And the Apparition further told the Miller that he must be the Man to reveal it, or else that she must still appear and haunt him. The Miller returned home very sad and heavy, but spoke not one Word of what he had seen, but eschewed as much as he could to stay in the Mill within Night without Company, thinking thereby to escape the seeing again of that frightful Apparition. But notwithstanding, one Night when it began to be dark, the Apparition met him again, and seemed very fierce and cruel, and threatened him, that if he did not reveal the Murder she would continually pursue and haunt him; yet for all this, he still concealed it until *St. Thomas Eve* before *Christmas*, when being soon after Sunset walking in his Garden, she appeared again, and then so threatened him, and affrighted him, that he faithfully promised to reveal it next Morning. In the Morning he went to a Magistrate and made the whole Matter known with all the Circumstances; and diligent search being made, the Body was found in a Coal-pit with five Wounds in the Head, and the Pick and Shoes and Stockings yet bloody, in every Circumstance as the Apparition had related unto the Miller; whereupon *Walker* and *Mark Sharp* were both Apprehended, but would confess nothing. At the Assizes following, I think it was at *Durham*, they were Arraigned, found Guilty, Condemned and Executed; but I could never hear they confessed the Fact. There were some that reported the Apparition did appear to the Judge, or the Foreman of the Jury, who was alive in *Chester* in the Street about ten Years ago, as I have been credibly informed, but of that I know no certainty: There are many Persons yet alive that can remember this strange Murder and the discovery of it; for it was, and sometimes yet is, as much discoursed of in the North Country as any thing that almost hath ever been heard of, and the relation Printed, tho' now not to be gotten. I relate this with the greater confidence (though I may fail in some of the Circumstances) because I saw and read the Letter that was sent to Sergeant *Hutton,* who then lived at *Goldsbrugh* in *Yorkshire,* from the Judge before whom *Walker* and *Mark Sharp* were tried, and by whom they were Condemned, and had a Copy of it until about the Year 1658, when I had it and many other Books and Papers taken from me; and this I confess to be one of the most convincing Stories, being of undoubted verity, that ever I read, heard or knew of, and carrieth with it the most evident force to make the incredulous Spirit to be satisfied that there are really sometimes such things as Apparitions. . . . This Story is so considerable that I make mention of it in my *Scholia* on my Immortality of the Soul, in my *Volumen Philosophicum,* Tom. 2. . . .

This Story of *Anne Walker* I think you will do well to put amongst your Additions in the new Impression of your *Dæmon of Tedworth,* it being so excellently well attested and so unexceptionable in every respect; and to hasten as fast as you can to that Impression, to undeceive the half-witted World, who so much exult and triumph in the extinguishing the belief of that Narration, as if the crying down the Truth of that of the *Dæmon of Tedworth,* were indeed the very slaying of the Devil, and that they may now with more gaiety and security than ever sing in a loud Note, that mad drunken Catch—"Hay ho! the Devil is Dead, etc."—which wild Song, though it may seem a piece of Levity to mention; yet believe me, the Application thereof bears a sober and weighty intimation along with it, *viz.* that these sort of People are very horribly afraid there should be any Spirit, least there should be a Devil and an account after this Life; and therefore they are impatient of any thing that implies it, that they may with a more full swing, and with all security from an after reckoning, indulge

Figure 66. The Burning of a Witch.
From a contemporary illustration of the burning of Urbain Grandier, convicted of bewitching the nuns at Loudun.

297

their own Lusts and Humours in this; and I know by long experience that nothing rouses them so out of that dull Lethargy of Atheism and Sadducism, as Narrations of this kind, for they being of a thick and gross Spirit, the most subtle and solid deductions of Reason does little execution upon them; but this sort of sensible Experiments cuts them and stings them very sore, and so startles them that by a less considerable Story by far than this of the Drummer of *Tedworth*, or of *Anne Walker*, a Doctor of Physic cried out presently, "If this be true, I have been in a wrong Box all this time, and must begin my account anew. . . ."

Indeed, if there were any Modesty left in Mankind, the Histories of the Bible might abundantly assure Men of the Existence of Angels and Spirits; but these Wits, as they are taken to be, are so jealous forsooth, and so sagacious, that whatever is offered to them by way of established Religion, is suspected for a piece of Politick Circumvention. . . .

Besides, though what is once true never becomes false, so that it may be truly said it was not once true; yet these shrewd Wits suspect the truth of things for their Antiquity, and for that very reason think them the less credible: Which is wisely done as of the old Woman the Story goes of, who being at Church in the Week before Easter, and hearing the Tragical Description of all the Circumstances of our Saviour's Crucifixion, was in such great sorrow at the reciting thereof, and so solicitous about the business, that she came to the Priest after Service with Tears in her Eyes, dropping him a Courtsie, and asked him how long ago this sad accident happened; to whom he answering, about fifteen or sixteen hundred Years ago, she presently began to be comforted and said, "Then in the Grace of God it may be true." At this pitch of Wit in Children and old Wives is the Reason of our professed Wit-would-be's of this present Age, who will catch at any slight occasion or pretence of mis-believeing those things that they cannot endure should be true.

And forasmuch as such course-grained Philosophers as those *Hobbians* and *Spinozians*, and the rest of the Rabble, slight Religion and the Scriptures, because there is such express mention of Spirits and Angels in them, things that their dull Souls are so inclinable to conceit to be imposable; I look upon it as a special piece of Providence, that there are ever and anon such fresh Examples of Apparitions and Witchcraft as may rub up and awaken their benumbed and lethargic Minds into a suspicion at least, if not assurance that there are other intelligent Beings besides those that are clad in heavy Earth or Clay; in this I say, methinks the divine Providence does plainly outwit the Powers of the dark Kingdom, permitting wicked Men and Women, and Vagrant Spirits of that Kingdom to make Leagues or Covenants one with another, the Confession of Witches against their own Lives being so palpable an Evidence, besides the miraculous Feats they play, that there are bad Spirits, which will necessarily open a door to the belief that there are good ones, and lastly that there is a God.

Wherefore let the small Philosophick Sir-Foplings of this present Age deride them as much as they will, those that lay out their pains in committing to writing certain well attested Stories of Witches and Apparitions, do real service to true Religion and sound Philosophy, and the most effectual and accommodate to the confounding of Infidelity and Atheism, even in the Judgement of the Atheists themselves, who are as much afraid of the truth of those Stories as an Ape is of a Whip, and therefore force themselves with might and main to disbelieve them, by reason of the dreadful consequence of them as to themselves. The Wicked fear where no fear is, but God is in the Generation of the Righteous; and he that fears God and has his Faith in Jesus Christ, need not fear how many Devils there be, nor be afraid of himself or of his Immortality; and therefore it is nothing but a foul dark Conscience within, or a very gross and dull constitution of Blood that makes Men so averse from these truths.

But however, be they as averse as they will, being this is the most accommodate Medicine for this Disease, their diligence and care of mankind is much to be commended that make it their business to apply it, and are resolved, though the peevishness and perverseness of the Patients makes them pull off their Plaster, as they have this excellent one of the Story of the *Dæmon of Tedworth* by decrying it as an Imposture, so acknowledged by both yourself and *Mr. Mompesson,* are resolved I say with Meekness and Charity to bind it on again, with the addition of new filletting. I mean other Stories sufficiently fresh and very well attested and certain. This worthy design therefore of yours, I must confess I cannot but highly commend and approve, and therefore wish you all good success therein; and so commit you to God, I take leave and rest,

Your affectionate Friend to serve you,
H.[ENRY] M.[ORE]

An Introduction to the Proof of the Existence of Apparitions, Spirits, and Witches: To the great usefulness and seasonableness of the present Argument, touching Witches and Apparitions in subserviency to Religion.

The Question, whether there are *Witches* or not, is not matter of vain Speculation, or of indifferent Moment; but an Inquiry of very great and weighty Importance. For, on the resolution of it, depends the Authority and just Execution of some of our *Laws;* and which is more, our *Religion* in its main Doctrines is nearly concerned. There is no one, that is not very much a stranger to the World but knows how *Atheism* and *Infidelity* have advanced in our days, and how openly they now dare to show themselves in Asserting and Disputing their vile Cause. Particularly the *distinction* of the *Soul* from the *Body,* the being of *Spirits,* and a *Future Life* are Assertions extremely despised and opposed by the Men of this sort, and if we lose those Articles, all Religion comes to nothing. They are clearly and fully Asserted in the Sacred Oracles, but those Wits have laid aside these Divine Writings. They are proved by the best Philosophy and highest Reason; but the Unbelievers, divers of them are too shallow to be capable of such proofs, and the more subtle are ready to Scepticize away those grounds.

But there is one Head of Arguments that troubles them much, and that is, the Topic of *Witches* and *Apparitions*. If such there are, it is a sensible proof of Spirits and another Life, an Argument of more direct force than any Speculations, or Abstract reasonings, and such an one as meets with all the sorts of *Infidels*. On which account they labour with all their might to persuade themselves and others, that *Witches* and *Apparitions* are but Melancholic *Dreams*, or crafty *Impostures*; and here it is generally, that they begin with the young men, whose understanding they design to Debauch.

They expose and deride all Relations of *Spirits* and *Witchcraft*, and furnish them with some little Arguments, or rather Colours against their *Existence*. And youth is very ready to entertain such Opinions as will help them to fancy [that] they are wiser than the generality of Men. And when they have once swallowed this Opinion, and are *sure* there are no *Witches*, nor *Apparitions*, they are prepared for the denial of *Spirits*, a *Life to come*, and all the other Principles of *Religion*. So that I think it will be a considerable and very seasonable service to it, fully to debate and settle this matter, which I shall endeavour in the following sheets, and I hope so, as not to impose upon myself or others, by empty Rhetorications, fabulous Relations, or Sophistical Reasonings, but treat on the Question with that freedom and plainness, that becomes one that is neither fond, fanciful nor credulous.

II: The true stating of the Question by defining what a Witch and Witchcraft is.

The Question is whether there are *Witches* or not. Mr. *Webster* accuseth the Writers on the Subject of defect, in not laying down a perfect Description of a *Witch* or *Witchcraft*, or explaining what they mean. What his perfect Description is, I do not know; but I think I have described a *Witch* or *Witchcraft* in my *Considerations*, sufficiently to be understood, and the Conception which I, and, I think, most Men have is, That *a Witch is one, who can do or seems to do strange things, beyond the Power of Art and ordinary Nature, by virtue of a Confederacy with Evil Spirits. Strange Things*, not *Miracles;* these are the extraordinary Effects of *Divine* Power, known and distinguished by their circumstances, as I shall show in due place. The *strange things* are *really* performed, and are not all *Impostures* and *Delusions*. The Witch *occasions*, but is not the *Principal* Efficient; she seems to do it, but the *Spirit* performs the wonder, sometimes immediately, as in *Transportations* and *Possessions*, sometimes by applying other Natural Causes, as in raising *Storms*, and inflicting *Diseases*, sometimes using the *Witch* as an *Instrument*, and either by the Eyes or Touch conveying Malign Influences: And these things are done by virtue of a *Covenant*, or *Compact* betwixt the *Witch* and an *Evil Spirit*. A *Spirit*, viz. an *Intelligent Creature* of the Invisible World, whether one of the Evil Angels called *Devils*, or an Inferiour *Daemon* or *Spirit*, or a wicked *Soul* departed; but one that is able and ready for mischief, and whether altogether Incorporeal or not, appertains not to this Question.

> *III: That neither the Notation of the Name*
> *that signifies indifferently, nor the false*
> *Additions of others to the Notion of a*
> Witch *can any way dissettle the Author's*
> *definition.*

This I take to be a plain *Description* of what we mean by a *Witch* and *Witchcraft:* What Mr. *Webster* and other Advocates for *Witches*, talk concerning the words whereby these are expressed, that they are improper and Metaphorical, signifying this, and signifying that, is altogether idle and impertinent. The word *Witch* signifies originally a Wise Man, or rather a Wise Woman. The same doth *Saga* in the Latin, and plainly so doth *Wizard* in English signify a Wise Man, and they are vulgarly called cunning Men or Women. An Art, Knowledge, Cunning they have that is extraordinary; but it is far from true Wisdom, and the word is degenerated into an ill sense, as *Magia* is.

So then they are called, and we need look no further, it is enough, that by the *Word*, we mean the *Thing* and *Person* I have described, which is

Figure 67. The Stylization of Witchcraft Motifs in the Seventeenth Century.
This title-page from Henry Grossius' *Magica de Spectris* illustrates the scenes of witchcraft and diabolism that were conventional by this time.

302

the common meaning; and Mr. *Webster* and the rest prevaricate when they make it signify an ordinary *Cheat*, a *Cozener*, a *Poisoner*, *Seducer*, and I know not what. Words signify as they are used, and in common use, *Witch* and *Witchcraft*, do indeed imply these, but they imply more, *viz.* Deluding, Cheating and Hurting by the Power of an *Evil Spirit* in *Covenant* with a wicked Man or Woman: This is our Notion of a *Witch*.

Mr. *Webster* I know will not have it to be a perfect Description. He adds to the Notion of the *Witch* he opposeth, *carnal Copulation* with the *Devil*, and the real Transformation into an *Hare, Cat, Dog, Wolf*; the same doth Mr. *Wagstaff*. Which is, as if a Man should define an Angel to be a Creature in the shape of a Boy with Wings, and then prove there is no such Being. Of all Men I would not have Mr. *Webster* to make my Definitions for me; we ourselves are to have the leave to tell what it is that we affirm and defend. And I have described the *Witch* and *Witchcraft*, that sober Men believe and assert. Thus briefly for Defining.

IV: *What things the Author concedes in this Controversy about* Witches *and* Witchcraft.

I shall let the Patrons of *Witches* know what I allow and grant to them;

First, I grant, That there are some Witty and Ingenious Men of the opposite Belief to me in the Question. Yea, it is accounted a piece of Wit to laugh at the belief of *Witches* as silly Credulity. And some men value themselves upon, and pride them in their supposed Sagacity of seeing the Cheat that imposeth on so great a part of Believing Mankind. And the Stories of *Witches* and *Apparitions* afford a great deal of Subject for Wit, which it is pity that a witty Man should lose.

Secondly, I own that some of those who deny *Witches* have no design against, nor a disinclination to Religion, but believe Spirits, and a Life to come, as other sober Christians do, and so are neither *Atheists, Sadducees* and *Hobbists*.

Thirdly, I allow that the great Body of Mankind is very credulous, and in this matter so, that they do believe vain impossible things in relation to it. That *carnal Copulation* with the *Devil*, and the *real Transmutation* of Men and Women into other Creatures are such. That people are apt to impute the *extraordinaries* of Art, of Nature to *Witchcraft*, and that their *Credulity* is often abused by subtle and designed *Knaves* through these. That there are Ten thousand silly lying Stories of *Witchcraft* and *Apparitions* among the vulgar. That infinite such have been occasioned by Cheats and *Popish*

Superstitions, and many invented and contrived by the Knavery of Popish Priests.[1]

Fourthly, I grant that Melancholy and Imagination have very great force, and can beget strange persuasions. And that many Stories of *Witchcraft* and *Apparitions* have been but Melancholy fancies.

Fifthly, I know and yield, that there are many strange natural Diseases that have odd Symptoms, and produce wonderful and astonishing effects beyond the usual course of Nature, and that such are sometimes falsely ascribed to *Witchcraft*.

Sixthly, I own, the *Popish* Inquisitors, and other Witch-finders have done much wrong, that they have destroyed innocent persons for *Witches*, and that watching and Torture have extorted extraordinary Confessions from some that were not guilty.

Seventhly and Lastly, I grant the Transactions of *Spirits with Witches*, which we affirm to be true and certain, are many of them very strange and uncouth, and that we can scarce give any account of the Reasons of them, or well reconcile many of those passages to the commonly received Notion of *Spirits*, and the State of the next World.

If these Concessions will do mine Adversaries in this Question any good, they have them freely. And by them I have already spoiled all Mr. *Webster's* and Mr. *Wagstaff's* and the other Witch-Advocates' Books, which prove little else than what I have here granted. And having been so free in Concessions, I may expect that something should be granted me from the other party.

ADVERTISEMENT: Those that are mentioned in the second Concession, though they are not *Atheists*, *Sadducees* nor *Hobbists;* yet if they deny *Witches*, it is plainly they are *Antiscripturists*, the Scripture so plainly attesting the contrary.

---

1. This concession, made in Part II of the *Sadducismus Triumphatus*, dramatically departs from the confident tone of Part I, the "Philosophical Considerations." There, discussing his opponents' charge that proponents of witchcraft-belief betray their credulity by accepting tales of transmutations and sexual relations between witch and devil, Glanvil wrote: "To this aggregate Objection I return, in the general, The more absurd and unaccountable these Actions seem, the greater confirmations are they to me of the Truth of those Relations, and the Reality of what the Objectors would destroy. For these Circumstances being exceeding unlikely, judging by the measures of common belief, 'tis the greater probability they are not Fictitious: For the contrivers of Fictions use to form them as near as they can conformably to the most unsuspected realities, endeavouring to make them look as like Truth as is possible in the main supposals. . . ." *Sadducismus Triumphatus*, ed. of 1700, I, p. 6. [Editor's note]

V: The Postulata *which the Author demands of his Adversaries as his just right.*

The demands that I make are: That whether *Witches* are or are not, is a question of Fact. For it is in effect, whether any Men or Women have been, or are in Covenant with *Evil Spirits*, and whether they by the *Spirits'* help, or the *Spirits* on their account perform such or such things.

Secondly, That matter of Fact can only be proved by immediate Sense, or the Testimony of others *Divine* or *Humane*. To endeavour to demonstrate Fact by abstract reasoning and speculation, is, as if a Man should prove that *Julius Caesar* founded the Empire of *Rome* by *Algebra* or *Metaphysics*. So that what Mr. *Webster* saith, That the true and proper mediums to prove the actions of *Witches* by, are *Scripture* and sound *Reason* and not the improper way of *Testimony* . . . is very Nonsense.

Thirdly, That the History of the *Scripture* is not all *Allegory*, but generally hath a plain literal and obvious meaning.

Fourthly, That some *Humane Testimonies* are credible and certain, *viz.* That they be so circumstantiated as to leave no reason of doubt. For our senses sometimes report truth, and all Mankind are Liars, Cheats and Knaves, at least they are not all Liars, when they have no Interest to be so.

Fifthly, That which is sufficiently and undeniably proved, ought not to be denied, because we know not how it can be, that is, because there are difficulties in the conceiving of it. Otherwise *Sense* and *Knowledge* is gone as well as *Faith*. For the *Modus* of most things is unknown, and the most obvious in Nature have inexplicable difficulties in the Speculation of them, as I have shown in my *Scepsis Scientifica*.

Sixthly and lastly, we are much in the dark, as to the *Nature* and *Kinds* of *Spirits*, and the *particular* condition of the other World. The Angels', Devils', and Souls' happiness and misery we know, but what kinds are under these generals, and what actions, circumstances and ways of Life under those States we little understand. These are my *Postulata* or demands, which I suppose will be thought reasonable, and such as need no more proof.

The Collection of Relations. Relation VIII: The Narrative of Mr. Pool, *a Servant and Officer in the Court to Judge* Archer *in his Circuit, concerning the Trial of Julian* Cox *for Witchcraft; who being himself then present, an Officer in the Court, noted as follows, viz.*

Julian Cox, aged about 70 Years, was *Indicted* at *Taunton* in *Somersetshire*, about Summer Assizes, 1663, before Judge Archer, then Judge of Assize there, for Witchcraft, which she practiced upon a young Maid, whereby her Body languished, and was impaired of Health, by reason of strange Fits upon account of the said Witchcraft.

The Evidence against her was divided into two Branches: First, to prove her a Witch in general: Secondly, to prove her Guilty of the Witchcraft contained in the Indictment.

For the proof of the first Particular: The first Witness was a Huntsman, who Swore that he went out with a Pack of Hounds to Hunt a Hare, and not far from *Julian Cox* her House, he at last started a Hare. The Dogs hunted her very close, and the third Ring hunted her in view, till at last the Huntsman perceiving the Hare almost spent, and making toward a great Bush, he ran on the other side of the Bush to take her up, and preserve her from the Dogs; but as soon as he laid Hands on her, it proved to be *Julian Cox*, who had her head groveling on the ground, and her Globes (as he expressed it) upward: He knowing her, was so affrighted that his Hair on his Head stood on end; and yet spake to her, and asked her what brought her there; but she was so far out of Breath, that she could not make him any Answer: His Dogs also came up with full Cry to recover the Game, and smelled at her, and so left off Hunting any farther. And the Huntsman with his Dogs went home presently, sadly affrighted.

Secondly, Another Witness Swore, That as he passed by *Cox* her Door, she was taking a Pipe of Tobacco upon the Threshold of her Door, and invited him to come in and take a Pipe, which he did, and as he was Smoking, *Julian* said to him, Neighbour, look what a pretty thing there is: He looked down and there was a monstrous great Toad betwixt his Legs, staring him in the Face: He endeavoured to kill it by spurning it, but could not hit it: Whereupon *Julian* bade him forbear, and it would do him no hurt; but he threw down his Pipe and went home (which was about two Miles off of *Julian Cox* her House) and told his Family what had happened, and that he believed it was one of *Julian Cox* her Devils.

After, he was taking a Pipe of Tobacco at home, and the same Toad appeared betwixt his Legs: He took the Toad out to kill it, and to his thinking, cut it in several pieces, but returning to his Pipe, the Toad still appeared: He endeavoured to burn it, but could not: At length he took a Switch and beat it; the Toad ran several times about the Room to avoid him, he still pursuing it with Correction: At length the Toad cried, and vanished, and he was never after troubled with it.

Thirdly, Another Swore, That *Julian* passed by his Yard while his Beasts were in Milking, and stooping down, scored upon the ground for some small time; during which time, his Cattle ran Mad, and some ran their Heads against the Trees, and most of them died speedily: Whereupon concluding they were Bewitched, he was after advised to this Experiment, to find out the Witch, *viz.* to cut off the Ears of the Bewitched Beasts and burn them, and that the Witch should be in misery, and could not rest till they were plucked out; which he tried, and while they were burning, *Julian Cox* came into the House, raging and scolding, that they had abused her without cause, but she went presently to the Fire, and took out the Ears that were burning, and then she was quiet.

Fourthly, Another Witness Swore, That she had seen *Julian Cox* fly into her own Chamber-window in her full proportion, and that she very well knew her, and was sure that it was she.

Fifthly, Another Evidence, was the Confession of *Julian Cox* herself, upon her Examination before a Justice of Peace, which was to this purpose: That she had been often tempted by the Devil to be a Witch, but never consented. That one Evening she walked out about a Mile from her own House, and there came riding towards her 3 Persons upon 3 Broom-staves, born up about a Yard and a half from the ground; 2 of them she formerly knew, which was a Witch and a Wizard that were Hanged for Witchcraft several Years before. The third Person she knew not; he came in the Shape of a black Man, and tempted her to give him her Soul, or to that effect, and to express it by pricking her Finger, and giving her Name in her Blood in token of it, and told her, that she had Revenge against several Persons that had wronged her, but could not bring her purpose to pass without his help, and that upon the Terms aforesaid he would assist her to be revenged against them; but she said, she did not consent to it. This was the sum of the general Evidence to prove her a Witch.

But now for the second Particular, to prove her guilty of the Witchcraft upon the Maid, whereof she was Indicted, this Evidence was offered.

It was proved that *Julian Cox* came for an Alms to the House where this Maid was a Servant, and that the Maid told her, she should have none, and gave her a cross Answer that displeased *Julian;* whereupon *Julian* was angry, and told the Maid she should repent it before a Night, and so she did; for before Night she was taken with a Convulsion Fit, and that after that left her, she saw *Julian Cox* following her, and cried out to People in the House to save her from *Julian*.

But none saw *Julian* but the Maid, and all did impute it to her Imagination only, And in the Night she cried out of *Julian Cox,* and the black Man, that they came upon her Bed and tempted her to Drink something they offered her, but she cried out, She defied the Devil's Drenches. This also they imputed to her Imagination, and bade her be quiet, because they in the same Chamber, with her, did not see or hear any thing, and they thought it had been her Conceit only.

The Maid the next Night expecting the same Conflict she had the Night before, brought up with her a Knife, and laid it at her Bed's head. About the same time of the Night as before, *Julian* and the black Man came again upon the Maid's Bed, and tempted her to Drink that which they brought, but she refused, crying in the audience of the rest of the Family, that she defied the Devil's Drenches, and took the Knife and stabbed *Julian*, and as she said, she wounded her in the Leg, and was importunate with the Witness to ride to *Julian Cox's* House presently to see if it were not so. The Witness went and took the Knife with him. *Julian Cox* would not let him in, but they forced the Door open, and found a fresh Wound in *Julian's* Leg, as the Maid had said, which did suit with the Knife, and *Julian* had been just Dressing it when the Witness came. There was Blood also found upon the Maid's Bed.

The Next Morning the Maid continued her Out-cries, that *Julian Cox* appeared to her in the House-wall, and offered her great Pins which she was forced to swallow: And all the Day the Maid was observed to convey her Hand to the House-wall, and from the Wall to her Mouth, and she seemed by the motion of her Mouth, as if she did Eat something; but none saw anything but the Maid, and therefore thought still it might be her Fancy, and did not much mind it. But towards Night, the Maid began to be very ill, and complained, that the Pins that *Julian* forced her to Eat out of the Wall, did torment her in all parts of her Body that she could not endure it, and made lamentable Out-cries for pain: Whereupon several Persons being present, the Maid was undressed, and in several parts of the Maid's Body several great swellings appeared, and out of the heads of the swellings, several great Pins' points appeared; which the Witness took out, and upon the Trial there were about 30 great Pins produced in Court, (which I myself handled) all which were Sworn by several Witnesses, that they were taken out of the Maid's Body, in manner as is aforesaid.

Judge *Archer*, who Tried the Prisoner, told the Jury, That he had heard that a Witch could not repeat that Petition in the Lord's-Prayer, *viz.* (*And lead us not into Temptation*) and having this occasion, he would try the Experiment, and told the Jury, that whether she could or not, they were not in the least measure to guide their Verdict according to it, because it was not Legal Evidence, but that they must be guided in their Verdict by the former Evidences given in upon Oath only.

The Prisoner was called for up to the next Bar to the Court, and demanded if she could say the Lord's Prayer? She said she could, and went over the Prayer readily, till she came to that Petition; then she said, "And lead us into Temptation," or "And lead us not into no Temptation," though she was directed to say it after one that repeated it to her directly; but she could not repeat it otherwise than is expressed already, though tried to do it near half a score times in open Court. After all which the Jury found her Guilty, and Judgement having been given within 3 or 4 days, she was Executed without any Confession of the Fact.

Scepticism, Doubt, and Disbelief in the Sixteenth and Seventeenth Centuries

By the end of the seventeenth century, such defenders of demonological and witchcraft-belief as Glanvil and More were engaged in a desperate struggle to halt the spread of scepticism and disbelief among the educated classes in Europe. The last decades of that century, however, witnessed the triumph of those who sought to end the active persecution of alleged witches and to alter the intellectual and theological systems whereby such persecution was deemed necessary and purposeful. Although occasional witch-scares and executions continued in the more remote areas of Europe, by the early eighteenth century witchcraft had ceased to be an intellectual and legal concern of educated men, except in so far as legal reformers sought to remove the laws dealing with the subject from the books. By the end of the century, witchcraft had become a topic of historical rather than contemporary interest.

The decline of active witchcraft-fear and belief can be studied with interest by a multitude of disciplines and from a multitude of explanatory perspectives, but it is, among other things, an intellectual event, and one reflected in the history of thought and philosophy. Europe's witches depended for their putative existence on specific systems of thought and modes of interpreting the natural and supernatural worlds; when men questioned or lost confidence in those systems or modes, or when new structures of inquiry and belief intervened in men's minds, the credibility or assumed usefulness of the witch-hunt could no longer be justified. This is what had occurred by the eighteenth century.

Scepticism, Doubt, and Disbelief

The intellectual components of this decline are many and complex, but can be grouped under several broad headings: the growth of anti-scholastic thought and the identification of the scholastic basis of contemporary witchcraft-belief; a growing aversion to the "credulity" and "superstition" of the common people, and the desire of educated men to distinguish themselves from these; the growth of philosophical systems and attitudes that provided natural accounts of phenomena that had formerly demanded supernaturalist and demonological explanations. To these should be added an emerging critical spirit among thinking men, whereby the antiquity and pervasiveness of beliefs and practices no longer added a presumption in their favor, but rather constituted a cause for suspicion and doubt.

Examples of selective and systematic scepticism were manifest already in the sixteenth century. Reginald Scot believed in the reality of witchcraft, but saw as illusory many of the fears and beliefs associated with it, seeking to discredit, among other things, the concept of a witches' sabbath (No. 36). The criteria by which men disabused themselves of any particular aspect of witchcraft-belief, however, were made available to investigators of other areas of the system as well. Montaigne, whose systematic scepticism was widely influential, demonstrated how easily men might deceive themselves when dealing with the unusual, and asked, in the face of the doubts he had raised, if men dare consider themselves certain enough to kill a fellow man in the name of such tenuous beliefs (No. 37). The recantations of men involved in witch-hunts, recantations and self-scrutinies arising from particular doubts concerning the signs and evidences of witchcraft, added to this growing legal and intellectual caution (Nos. 39, 41, 42).

In opposition to scholastic modes of thought, the seventeenth century witnessed the rise of philosophies in which there was no place for spiritual or supernatural causes of the events of the natural world. Arising from Descartes' categorical separation of the realms of matter and spirit, from experimental and mathematical science, and from contrary strains of deductive rationalism and empirical naturalism, mechanistic modes of explanation increasingly replaced accounts of spirit acting upon matter as satisfactory accounts of events in men's minds. Hobbes' thoroughgoing materialism left no room for spirits, evil or good, and he engaged in an often ironic metaphorical re-interpretation of his culture's beliefs in such beings (No. 40). Spinoza's pantheistic monism and naturalist mechanism invalidated such beliefs as well, and he attributed all demonology to philosophical naiveté and to historically-conditioned sectarian corruptions of our understanding of God and of the harmonious universe which manifests Him (No. 38).

Mechanists, materialists and pantheists all sought to change the intellectual paradigm upon which witchcraft belief depended. Few men, however, embraced the new systems of thought consistently and rigorously. Rather, most educated men lived within two worlds by the late seventeenth century, accepting much of traditional belief but adding to it a new awareness of the appeal of natural and mechanistic explanations where such were possible. The great sceptic and fideist Pierre Bayle never denied the theoretical bases of demonology and witchcraft; rather, he questioned the application of those beliefs in the particular, appealing to the critical intellect to avoid the superstitions of the vulgar and the uneducated, and he demonstrated how the same phenomena attributed to witchcraft could be accounted for by the natural operations of the imagination and the emotions of mankind (*No.* 43). Men increasingly felt that witchcraft was born of fear of and confusion about the created universe. Balthazar Bekker, a theologian and one of the most influential opponents of witchcraft-belief, attacked the entire demonological system as a lack of confident faith in the goodness and wisdom of the God he saw as Creator of the universe, and he offered naturalistic explanations of the role of the imagination and the credulity of men in the formation and sustenance of witchcraft and demonology (*No.* 44). From this combination of decreasing anxiety about the structure of the world men inhabit and increasing assurance of men's ability to understand that world in earthly terms, witchcraft, as a Western belief, was ultimately to founder.

36

REGINALD SCOT
Credulity and Witchcraft
1584

The last decades of the sixteenth century in England witnessed an upsurge in witchcraft trials, above all at the Assizes in Essex. Confessions and testimony revealed a deep-seated fear of the awesome powers of the witch to perform unnatural actions and a pervasive credulity among both the learned and the unlearned. In the face of this, a few voices raised themselves in sceptical opposition to popular notions of the witch and her powers and to the general sense that the testimony of the trials was manifestly true. Among these sceptical voices was Reginald Scot, whose *Discoverie of Witchcraft* (1584) called upon thinking men, especially churchmen, to reconsider their views of the witch and to reassess the nature of the judicial evidence.

Reginald Scot, *The Discoverie of Witchcraft* (1584), ed. Hugh Ross Williamson (Carbondale, Ill., 1962), Bk. I, ch. II, V, VI, IX: Bk. II, ch. I, IX, XVIII, XIX, XX; Bk. XVI, ch. I–III.

*T*he inconvenience growing by mens credulitie herein, with a reproofe of some churchmen, which are inclined to the common conceived opinion of witches omnipotencie, and a familiar example thereof. But the world is now so bewitched and over-run with this fond error, that even where a man shuld seeke comfort and counsell, there shall hee be sent (in case of necessitie) from God to the divell; and from the Physician, to the coosening witch, who will not sticke to take upon hir, by wordes to heale the lame (which was proper onelie to Christ: and to them whom he assisted with his divine power) yea, with hir familiar & charmes she will take upon hir to cure the blind: though in the tenth of S. *Johns* Gospell it be written, that the divell cannot open the eies of the blind. And they attaine such credit as I have heard (to my greefe) some of the ministerie affirme, that they have had in their parish at one instant, xvii. or xviii. witches: meaning such as could worke miracles supernaturallie. Whereby they manifested as well their infidelitie and ignorance, in conceiving Gods word; as their negligence and error in instructing their flocks. For they themselves might understand, and also teach their parishoners, that God onelie worketh great woonders; and that it is he which sendeth such punishments to the wicked, and such trials to the elect: according to the saieng of the Prophet *Haggai*, I smote you with blasting and mildeaw, and with haile, in all the labours of your hands; and yet you turned not unto me, saith the Lord. And therefore saith the same Prophet in another place; You have sowen much, and bring in little. And both in *Joel* and *Leviticus*, the like phrases and proofes are used and made. But more shalbe said of this hereafter.

S. *Paule* fore-sawe the blindnesse and obstinacie, both of these blind shepheards, and also of their scabbed sheepe, when he said; They will not suffer wholsome doctrine, but having their eares itching, shall get them a heape of teachers after their own lusts; and shall turne their eares from the truth, and shall be given to fables. And in the latter time some shall depart from the faith, and shall give heed to spirits of errors, and doctrines of divels, which speake lies (as witches and conjurers doo) but cast thou awaie such prophane and old wives fables. In which sense Basil saith: Who so giveth heed to inchanters, hearkeneth to a fabulous and frivolous thing. But I will rehearse an example whereof I my selfe am not onelie *Oculatus testis*, but have examined the cause, and am to justifie the truth of my report: not bicause I would disgrace the ministers that are godlie, but to confirme my former assertion, that this absurd error is growne into the place, which should be able to expell all such ridiculous follie and impietie.

At the assises holden at *Rochester*, Anno 1581, one *Margaret Simons*, the wife of *John Simons*, of *Brenchlie* in *Kent*, was araigned for witchcraft, at the instigation and complaint of divers fond and malicious persons; and speciallie by the meanes of one *John Ferrall* vicar of that parish: with whom I talked about that matter, and found him both fondlie assotted in the cause, and enviouslie bent towards hir: and (which is worse) as unable to make a good account of his faith, as shee whom he accused. That which he, for his part, laid to the poore womans charge, was this.

His sonne (being an ungratious boie, and prentise to one *Robert Scotchford* clothier, dwelling in that parish of *Brenchlie*) passed on a daie by hir house; at whome by chance hir little dog barked. Which thing the boie taking in evill part, drewe his knife, & pursued him therewith even to hir doore: whom she rebuked with some such words as the boie disdained, & yet neverthelesse would not be persuaded to depart in a long time. At the last he returned to his maisters house, and within five or sixe daies fell sicke. Then was called to mind the fraie betwixt the dog and the boie: insomuch as the vicar (who thought himselfe so privileged, as he little mistrusted that God would visit his children with sicknes) did so calculate; as he found, partlie through his owne judgement, and partlie (as he himselfe told me) by the relation of other witches, that his said sonne was by hir bewitched. Yea, he also told me, that this his sonne (being as it were past all cure) received perfect health at the hands of another witch.

He proceeded yet further against hir, affirming, that alwaies in his parish church, when he desired to read most plainelie, his voice so failed him, as he could scant be heard at all. Which hee could impute, he said, to nothing else, but to hir inchantment. When I advertised the poore woman hereof, as being desirous to heare what she could saie for hir selfe; she told me, that in verie deed his voice did much faile him, speciallie when he strained himselfe to speake lowdest. How beit, she said that at all times his voice was hoarse and lowe: which thing I perceived to be true. But sir, said she, you shall understand, that this our vicar is diseased with such a kind of hoarsenesse, as divers of our neighbors in this parish, not long since, doubted that he had the French pox; & in that respect utterly refused to communicate with him: untill such time as (being therunto injoined by M. D. *Lewen* the Ordinarie) he had brought frō *London* a certificat, under the hands of two physicians, that his hoarsenes proceeded from a disease in the lungs. Which certificat he published in the church, in the presence of the whole congregation: and by this meanes hee was cured, or rather excused of the shame of his disease. And this I knowe to be true by the relation of divers honest men of that parish. And truelie, if one of the Jurie had not beene wiser than the other, she had beene condemned thereupon, and upon other as ridiculous matters as this. For the name of a witch is so odious, and hir power so feared among the common people, that if the honestest bodie living chance to be arraigned thereupon, she shall hardlie escape condemnation.

A confutation of the common conceived opinion
of witches and witchcraft, and how detestable
a sinne it is to repaire to them for counsell
or helpe in time of affliction.

But whatsoever is reported or conceived of such manner of witchcrafts, I dare avow to be false and fabulous (coosinage, dotage, and poisoning excepted:) neither is there any mention made of these kind of witches in the Bible. If Christ had knowne them, he would not have pretermitted to invaie against their presumption, in taking upon them his office: as, to heale and cure diseases; and to worke such miraculous and supernaturall things, as whereby he himselfe was speciallie knowne, beleeved, and published to be God; his actions and cures consisting (in order and effect) according to the power of our witchmoongers imputed to witches. Howbeit, if there be any in these daies afflicted in such strange sort, as Christs cures and patients are described in the new testament to have beene: we flie from trusting in God to trusting in witches, who doo not onelie in their coosening art take on them the office of Christ in this behalfe; but use his verie phrase of speech to such idolators, as com to seeke divine assistance at their hands, saieng; Go thy waies, thy sonne or thy daughter, &c. shall doo well, and be whole.

It will not suffice to dissuade a witchmonger from his credulitie, that he seeth the sequele and event to fall out manie times contrarie to their assertion; but in such case (to his greater condemnation) he seeketh further to witches of greater fame. If all faile, he will rather thinke he came an houre too late; than that he went a mile too far. Trulie I for my part cannot perceive what is to go a whoring after strange gods, if this be not. He that looketh upon his neighbors wife, and lusteth after hir, hath committed adulterie. And truelie, he that in hart and by argument mainteineth the sacrifice of the masse to be propitiatorie for the quicke and the dead, is an idolater; as also he that alloweth and commendeth creeping to the crosse, and such like idolatrous actions, although he bend not his corporall knees.

In like manner I say, he that attributeth to a witch, such divine power, as dulie and onelie apperteineth unto GOD (which all witchmongers doo) is in hart a blasphemer, an idolater, and full of grosse impietie, although he neither go nor send to hir for assistance.

> *A further confutation of witches miraculous and*
> *omnipotent power, by invincible reasons*
> *and authorities, with dissuasions from such*
> *fond credulitie.*

If witches could doo anie such miraculous things, as these and other which are imputed to them, they might doo them againe and againe, at anie time or place, or at anie mans desire: for the divell is as strong at one time as at another, as busie by daie as by night, and readie enough to doo all mischeefe, and careth not whom he abuseth. And in so much as it is confessed, by the most part of witchmoongers themselves, that he knoweth not the cogitation of mans heart, he should (me thinks) sometimes appeere unto honest and credible persons, in such grosse and corporall forme, as it is said he dooth unto witches: which you shall never heare to be justified by one sufficient witnesse. For the divell indeed entreth into the mind, and that waie seeketh mans confusion.

The art alwaies presupposeth the power; so as, if they saie they can doo this or that, they must shew how and by what meanes they doo it; as neither the wiches, nor the witchmoongers are able to doo. For to everie action is required the facultie and abilitie of the agent or dooer; the aptnes of the patient or subject; and a convenient and possible application. Now the witches are mortall, and their power dependeth upon the analogie and consonancie of their minds and bodies; but with their minds they can but will and understand; and with their bodies they can doo no more, but as the bounds and ends of terrene sense will suffer: and therefore their power extendeth not to doo such miracles, as surmounteth their owne sense, and the understanding of others which are wiser than they; so as here wanteth the vertue and power of the efficient. And in reason, there can be no more vertue in the thing caused, than in the cause, or that which proceedeth of or from the benefit of the cause. And we see, that ignorant and impotent women, or witches, are the causes of incantations and charmes; wherein we shall perceive there is none effect, if we will credit our owne experience and sense unabused, the rules of philosophie, or the word of God. For alas! What an unapt instrument is a toothles, old, impotent, and unweldie woman to flie in the aier? Truelie, the divell little needs such instruments to bring his purposes to passe.

It is strange, that we should suppose, that such persons can worke such feates: and it is more strange, that we will imagine that to be possible to be doone by a witch, which to nature and sense is impossible; speciallie when our neighbours life dependeth upon our credulitie therein; and when we may see the defect of abilitie, which alwaies is an impediment both to the act, and also to the presumption thereof. And bicause there is nothing possible in lawe, that in nature is impossible; therefore the judge dooth not attend or regard what the accused man saith; or yet would doo: but what is prooved to have beene committed, and naturallie falleth in mans power and will to doo. For the lawe saith, that To will a thing unpossible, is a signe of a mad man, or of a foole, upon whom no sentence or judgement taketh hold. Furthermore, what Jurie will condemne, or what Judge will give sentence or judgement against one for killing a man at *Berwicke;* when they themselves, and manie other sawe that man at *London,* that verie daie, wherein the murther was committed; yea though the partie confesse himself guiltie therein, and twentie witnesses depose the same? But in this case also I saie the judge is not to weigh their testimonie, which is weakened by lawe; and the judges authoritie is to supplie the imperfection of the case, and to mainteine the right and equitie of the same.

Seeing therefore that some other things might naturallie be the occasion and cause of such calamities as witches are supposed to bring; let not us that professe the Gospell and knowledge of Christ, be bewitched to beleeve that they doo such things, as are in nature impossible, and in sense and reason incredible. If they saie it is doone through the divels helpe, who can work miracles; whie doo not theeves bring their busines to passe miraculouslie, with whom the divell is as conversant as with the other? Such mischeefes as are imputed to witches, happen where no witches are; yea and continue when witches are hanged and burnt: whie then should we attribute such effect to that cause, which being taken awaie, happeneth neverthelesse?

> *A conclusion of the first booke,*
> *wherein is fore-shewed the tyrannicall crueltie*
> *of witchmongers and inquisitors, with a request*
> *to the reader to peruse the same.*

And bicause it may appeare unto the world what trecherous and faithlesse dealing, what extreame and intollerable tyrannie, what grosse and fond absurdities, what unnaturall & uncivil discourtisie, what cancred and spitefull malice, what outragious and barbarous crueltie, what lewd and false packing, what cunning and craftie intercepting, what bald and peevish interpretations, what abhominable and divelish inventions, and what flat and plaine knaverie is practised against these old women; I will set downe the whole order of the inquisition, to the everlasting, inexcusable, and apparent shame of all witchmoongers. Neither will I insert anie private or doubtful dealings of theirs; or such as they can either denie to be usuall, or justlie cavill at; but such as are published and renewed in all ages, since the commensement of poperie established by lawes, practised by inquisitors, privileged by princes, commended by doctors, confirmed by popes, councels, decrees, and canons; and finallie be left of all witch moongers; to wit, by such as attribute to old women, and such like creatures, the power of the Creator. I praie you therefore, though it be tedious & intollerable (as you would be heard in your miserable calamities) so heare with compassion, their accusations, examinations, matters given in evidence, confessions, presumptions, interrogatories, conjurations, cautions, crimes, tortures and condemnations, devised and practised usuallie against them.

> *What testimonies and witnesses are allowed to*
> *give evidence against reputed witches, by the*
> *report & allowance of the inquisitors themselves,*
> *and such as are speciall writers heerein.*

Excommunicat persons, partakers of the falt, infants, wicked servants, and runnawaies are to be admitted to beare witnesse against their dames in this mater of witchcraft: bicause (saith *Bodin* the champion of witchmoongers) none that be honest are able to detect them. Heretikes also and witches shall be received to accuse, but not to excuse a witch. And finallie, the testimonie of all infamous persons in this case is good and allowed. Yea, one lewd person (saith *Bodin*) may be received to accuse and condemne a thousand suspected witches. And although by lawe, a capitall enimie may be challenged; yet *James Sprenger*, and *Henrie Institor*, (from whom *Bodin*, and all the writers that ever I have read, doo receive their light, authorities and arguments) saie (upon this point of lawe) that The poore frendlesse old woman must proove, that hir capitall enimie would have killed hir, and that hee hath both assalted & wounded hir; otherwise she pleadeth all in vaine. If the judge aske hir, whether she have anie capitall enimies; and she rehearse other, and forget hir accuser; or else answer that he was hir capital enimie, but now she hopeth he is not so: such a one is nevertheles admitted for a witnes. And though by lawe, single witnesses are not admittable; yet if one depose she hath bewitched hir cow; another, hir sow; and the third, hir butter: these saith (saith *M. Mal.* and *Bodin*) are no single witnesses; bicause they agree that she is a witch.

*The fifteene crimes laid to the charge of witches,
by witchmongers, speciallie by Bodin,
in Dæmonomania.*

They denie God, and all religion.

Answere. Then let them die therefore, or at the least be used like infidels, or apostataes.

They cursse, blaspheme, and provoke God with all despite.

Answere. Then let them have the law expressed in *Levit.* 24. and *Deut.* 13 & 17.

They give their faith to the divell, and they worship and offer sacrifice unto him.

Ans. Let such also be judged by the same lawe.

They doo solemnelie vow and promise all their progenie unto the divell.

Ans. This promise proceedeth from an unsound mind, and is not to be regarded; bicause they cannot performe it, neither will it be prooved true. Howbeit, if it be done by anie that is sound of mind, let the cursse of *Jeremie,* 32.36. light upon them, to wit, the sword, famine and pestilence.

They sacrifice their owne children to the divell before baptisme, holding them up in the aire unto him, and then thrust a needle into their braines.

Ans. If this be true, I maintaine them not herein: but there is a lawe to judge them by. Howbeit, it is so contrarie to sense and nature, that it were follie to beleeve it; either upon *Bodins* bare word, or else upon his presumptions; speciallie when so small commoditie and so great danger and inconvenience insueth to the witches thereby.

They burne their children when they have sacrificed them.

Ans. Then let them have such punishment, as they that offered their children unto *Moloch: Levit.* 20. But these be meere devises of witchmoongers and inquisitors, that with extreame tortures have wroong such confessions from them; or else with false reports have beelied them; or by flatterie & faire words and promises have woon it at their hands, at the length.

They sweare to the divell to bring as manie into that societie as they can.

Ans. This is false, and so prooved elsewhere.

They sweare by the name of the divell.

Ans. I never heard anie such oth, neither have we warrant to kill them that so doo sweare; though indeed it be verie lewd and impious.

They use incestuous adulterie with spirits.

Ans. This is a stale ridiculous lie, as is prooved apparentlie hereafter.

They boile infants (after they have murthered them unbaptised) untill their flesh be made potable.

Ans. This is untrue, incredible, and impossible.

They eate the flesh and drinke the bloud of men and children openlie.

Ans. Then are they kin to the *Anthropophagi* and *Canibals.* But I beleeve never an honest man in *England* nor in *France,* will affirme that he hath seene any of these persons, that are said to be witches, do so; if they shuld, I beleeve it would poison them.

They kill men with poison.

Ans. Let them be hanged for their labour.

They kill mens cattell.

Ans. Then let an action of trespasse be brought against them for so dooing.

They bewitch mens corne, and bring hunger and barrennes into the countrie; they ride and flie in the aire, bring stormes, make tempests, &c.

Ans. Then will I worship them as gods; for those be not the works of man nor yet of witch: as I have elsewhere prooved at large.

They use venerie with a divell called *Iucubus,* even when they lie in bed with their husbands, and have children by them, which become the best witches.

Ans. This is the last lie, verie ridiculous, and confuted by me elsewhere.

> *That the confession of witches is insufficient*
> *in civill and common lawe to take awaie life.*
> *What the sounder divines, and decrees*
> *of councels determine in this case.*

Alas! what creature being sound in state of mind, would (without compulsion) make such maner of confessions as they do; or would, for a trifle, or nothing, make a perfect bargaine with the divell for hir soule, to be yeelded up unto his tortures and everlasting flames, and that within a verie short time; speciallie being through age most commonlie unlike to live one whole yeare? The terror of hell fire must needs be to them diverslie manifested, and much more terrible; bicause of their weaknesse, nature, and kind, than to any other: as it would appeere, if a witch were but asked, Whether

Figure 68. The Witch of Endor and Seventeenth-Century Philosophical Spiritualism.

This frontispiece from the German translation of Glanvil's *Saducismus Triumphatus* reflects the renewal of biblical motifs among the philosophical spiritualist defenders of witchcraft beliefs in the later seventeenth century. The scene is the famous one of Saul evoking the spirit of Samuel through the Witch of Endor.

she would be contented to be hanged one yeare hence, upon condition hir displesure might be wreked upon hir enimie presentlie. As for theeves, & such other, they thinke not to go to hell fire; but are either persuaded there is no hell, or that their crime deserveth it not, or else that they have time enough to repent: so as, no doubt, if they were perfectlie resolved heereof, they would never make such adventures. Neither doo I thinke, that for any summe of monie, they would make so direct a bargaine to go to hell fire. Now then I conclude, that confession in this behalf is insufficient to take awaie the life of any body; or to atteine such credit, as to be beleeved without further proofe. For as *Augustine* and *Isidore*, with the rest of the sounder divines saie, that these prestigious things, which are wrought by witches are fantasticall: so doo the sounder decrees of councels and canons agree, that in that case, there is no place for criminall action. And the lawe saith, that The confession of such persons as are illuded, must needs be erronious, and therefore is not to be admitted: for, *Confessio debet tenere verum & possibile.* But these things are opposite both to lawe and nature, and therfore it followeth not; Bicause these witches confesse so, *Ergo* it is so. For the confession differeth from the act, or from the possibilitie of the act. And whatsoever is contrarie to nature faileth in his principles, and therefore is naturallie impossible.

The law also saith, *In criminalibus regulariter non statur soli confessioni rei*, In criminall cases or touching life, we must not absolutelie stand to the confession of the accused partie: but in these matters proofes must be brought more cleare than the light it selfe. And in this crime no bodie must be condemned upon presumptions. And where it is objected and urged, that Since God onelie knoweth the thoughts, therefore there is none other waie of proofe but by confession: It is answered thus in the lawe, to wit: Their confession in this case conteineth an outward act, and the same impossible both in lawe and nature, and also unlikelie to be true; and therefore *Quod verisimile non est, attendi non debet.* So as, though their confessions may be worthie of punishment, as whereby they shew a will to commit such mischeefe, yet not worthie of credit, as that they have such a power. For, *Si factum absit, soláque opinione laborent, é stultorum genere sunt;* If they confesse a fact performed but in opinion, they are to be reputed among the number of fooles. Neither may any man be by lawe condemned for criminall causes, upon presumptions, nor yet by single witnesses: neither at the accusation of a capitall enimie, who indeed is not to be admitted to give evidence in this case; though it please *M. Mal.* and *Bodin* to affirme the contrarie. But beyond all equitie, these inquisitors have shifts and devises enow, to plague and kill these poore soules: for (they say) their fault is greatest of all others; bicause of their carnall copulation with the divell, and therefore they are to be punished as heretikes, foure maner of waies: to wit; with excommunication, deprivation, losse of goods, and also with death.

And indeede they find lawe, and provide meanes thereby to mainteine this their bloudie humor. For it is written in their popish canons, that As for these kind of heretikes, how much soever they repent and returne to the faith, they may not be reteined alive, or kept in perpetuall prison; but be put to extreame death. Yea, *M. Mal.* writeth, that A witches sinne is the sinne against the Holie-ghost; to wit, irremissible: yea further, that it is greater than the sinne of the angels that fell. In which respect I wonder, that *Moses* delivered not three tables to the children of Israell; or at the leastwise, that he exhibited not commandements for it. It is not credible that the greatest should be included in the lesse, &c.

But when these witchmongers are convinced in the objection concerning their confessions; so as thereby their tyrannicall arguments cannot prevaile, to imbrue the magistrates hands in so much bloud as their appetite requireth: they fall to accusing them of other crimes, that the world might thinke they had some colour to mainteine their malicious furie against them.

Of foure capitall crimes objected against witches, all fullie answered and confuted as frivolous.

First therefore they laie to their charge idolatrie. But alas without all reason: for such are properlie knowne to us to be idolaters, as doo externall worship to idols or strange gods. The furthest point that idolatrie can be stretched unto, is, that they, which are culpable therein, are such as hope for and seeke salvation at the hands of idols, or of anie other than God; or fixe their whole mind and love upon anie creature, so as the power of God be neglected and contemned thereby. But witches neither seeke nor beleeve to have salvation at the hands of divels, but by them they are onlie deceived; the instruments of their phantasie being corrupted, and so infatuated, that they suppose, confesse, and saie they can doo that, which is as farre beyond their power and nature to doo, as to kill a man at *Yorke* before noone, when they have beene seene at *London* in that morning, &c. But if these latter idolaters, whose idolatrie is spirituall, and committed onelie in mind, should be punished by death; then should everie covetous man, or other, that setteth his affection anie waie too much upon an earthlie creature, be executed, and yet perchance the witch might escape scotfree.

Secondlie, apostasie is laid to their charge, whereby it is inferred, that they are worthie to die. But apostasie is, where anie of sound judgement forsake the gospell, learned and well knowne unto them; and doo not onelie imbrace impietie and infidelitie; but oppugne and resist the truth erstwhile by them professed. But alas these poore women go not about to defend anie impietie, but after good admonition repent.

Thirdlie, they would have them executed for seducing the people. But God knoweth they have small store of Rhetorike or art to seduce; except to tell a tale of Robin good-fellow be to deceive and seduce. Neither may their age or sex admit that opinion or accusation to be just: for they themselves are poore seduced soules. I for my part (as else-where I have said) have prooved this point to be false in most apparent sort.

Fourthlie, as touching the accusation, which all the writers use herein against them for their carnall copulation with *Incubus*: the follie of mens credulitie is as much to be woondered at and derided, as the others vaine and impossible confessions. For the divell is a spirit, and hath neither flesh nor bones, which were to be used in the performance of this action. And since he also lacketh all instruments, substance, and seed ingendred of bloud; it were follie to staie overlong in the confutation of that, which is not in the nature of things. And yet must I saie somewhat heerein, bicause the opinion hereof is so stronglie and universallie received, and the fables hereupon so innumerable; wherby *M. Mal. Bodin, Hemingius, Hyperius, Danaeus, Erastus*, and others that take upon them to write heerein, are so abused, or rather seeke to abuse others; as I woonder at their fond credulitie in this behalfe. For they affirme undoubtedlie, that the divell plaieth *Succubus* to the man, and carrieth from him the seed of generation, which he delivereth as *Incubus* to the woman, who manie times that waie is gotten with child; which will verie naturallie (they saie) become a witch, and such a one they affirme *Merline* was.

> *A request to such readers as loath to heare*
> *or read filthie and bawdie matters (which of*
> *necessitie are heere to be inserted) to passe over*
> *eight chapters.*

But in so much as I am driven (for the more manifest bewraieng and displaieng of this most filthie and horrible error) to staine my paper with writing thereon certeine of their beastlie and bawdie assertions and examples, whereby they confirme this their doctrine (being my selfe both ashamed, and loth once to thinke upon such filthinesse, although it be to the condemnation thereof) I must intreat you that are the readers hereof, whose chaste eares cannot well endure to heare of such abhominable lecheries, as are gathered out of the bookes of those witchmongers (although doctors of divinitie, and otherwise of great authoritie and estimation) to turne over a few leaves, wherein (I saie) I have like a groome thrust their bawdie stuffe (even that which I my selfe loath) as into a stinking corner: howbeit, none otherwise, I hope, but that the other parts of my writing shall remaine sweet, and this also covered as close as may be.

> *A conclusion, in maner of an epilog, repeating*
> *manie of the former absurdities of witchmongers,*
> *conceipts, confutations thereof, and of the*
> *authoritie of James Sprenger and Henrie Institor*
> *inquisitors and compilers of M. Mal.*

Hitherto you have had delivered unto you, that which I have conceived and gathered of this matter. In the substance and principall parts wherof I can see no difference among the writers heereupon; of what countrie, condition, estate, or religion so ever they be; but I find almost all of them to agree in unconstancie, fables, and impossibilities; scratching out of *M. Mal.* the substance of all their arguments: so as their authors being disapproved, they must coine new stuffe, or go to their grandams maids to learne more old wives tales, whereof this art of witchcraft is contrived. But you must know that *James Sprenger*, and *Henrie Institor*, whom I have had occasion to alledge manie times, were copartners in the composition of that profound & learned booke called *Malleus Maleficarum*, & were the greatest doctors of that art: out of whom I have gathered matter and absurditie enough, to confound the opinions conceived of witchcraft; although they were allowed inquisitors and assigned by the pope, with the authoritie and commendation of all the doctors of the universitie of *Collen*, &c: to call before them, to imprison, to condemne, and to execute witches; and finallie to seaze and confiscate their goods.

These two doctors, to mainteine their credit, and to cover their injuries, have published those same monsterous lies, which have abused all Christendome, being spread abroad with such authoritie, as it will be hard to suppresse the credit of their writings, be they never so ridiculous and false. Which although they mainteine and stirre up with their owne praises; yet men are so bewitched, as to give credit unto them. For proofe whereof I remember they write in one place of their said booke, that by reason of their severe proceedings against witches, they suffered intollerable assaults, speciallie in the night, many times finding needdels sticking in their biggens, which were thither conveied by witches charmes: and through their innocencie and holiness (they saie) they were never miraculouslie preserved from hurt. Howbeit they affirme that they will not tell all that might make to the manifestation of their holines: for then should their owne praise stinke in their owne mouthes. And yet God knoweth their whole booke conteineth nothing but stinking lies and poperie. Which groundworke and foundation how weake and wavering it is, how unlike to continue, and how slenderlie laid, a child may soone discerne and perceive.

> *By what meanes the common people*
> *have beene made beleeve in the miraculous*
> *works of witches, a definition of witchcraft,*
> *and a description thereof.*

The common people have beene so assotted and bewitched, with whatsoever poets have feigned of witchcraft, either in earnest, in jest, or else in derision; and with whatsoever lowd liers and couseners for their pleasures heerein have invented, and with whatsoever tales they have heard from old doting women, or from their mothers maids, and with whatsoever the grandfoole their ghostlie father, or anie other morrow masse preest had informed them; and finallie with whatsoever they have swallowed up through tract of time, or through their owne timerous nature or ignorant conceipt, concerning these matters of hagges and witches: as they have so settled their opinion and credit thereupon, that they thinke it heresie to doubt in anie part of the matter; speciallie bicause they find this word witchcraft expressed in the scriptures; which is as to defend praieng to saincts, bicause *Sanctus, Sanctus, Sanctus* is written in *Te Deum*.

And now to come to the definition of witchcraft, which hitherto I did deferre and put off purposelie: that you might perceive the true nature thereof, by the circumstances, and therefore the rather to allow of the same, seeing the varietie of other writers. Witchcraft is in truth a cousening art, wherin the name of God is abused, prophaned and blasphemed, and his power attributed to a vile creature. In estimation of the vulgar people, it is a supernaturall worke, contrived betweene a corporall old woman, and a spirituall divell. The maner thereof is so secret, mysticall, and strange, that to this daie there hath never beene any credible witnes thereof. It is incomprehensible to the wise, learned or faithfull; a probable matter to children, fooles, melancholike persons and papists. The trade is thought to be impious. The effect and end thereof to be sometimes evill, as when thereby man or beast, grasse, trees, or corne, &c; is hurt: sometimes good, as whereby sicke folkes are healed, theeves bewraied, and true men come to their goods, &c. The matter and instruments, wherewith it is accomplished, are words, charmes, signes, images, characters, &c; the which words although any other creature doo pronounce, in maner and forme as they doo, leaving out no circumstance requisite or usuall for that action: yet none is said to have the grace or gift to performe the matter, except she be a witch, and so taken either by hir owne consent, or by others imputation.

> *Reasons to proove that words and characters*
> *are but bables, & that witches cannot doo*
> *such things as the multitude supposeth they can,*
> *their greatest woonders prooved trifles,*
> *of a yoong gentleman cousened.*

That words, characters, images, and such other trinkets, which are thought so necessarie instruments for witchcraft (as without the which no such thing can be accomplished) are but bables, devised by couseners, to abuse the people withall; I trust I have sufficientlie prooved. And the same maie be further and more plainelie perceived by these short and compendious reasons following.

First, in that *Turkes* and infidels, in their witchcraft, use both other words, and other characters than our witches doo and also such as are most contrarie. In so much as, if ours be bad, in reason theirs should be good. If their witches can doo anie thing, ours can doo nothing. For as our witches are said to renounce Christ, and despise his sacraments: so doo the other forsake *Mahomet,* and his lawes, which is one large step to christianitie.

It is also to be thought, that all witches are couseners; when mother *Bungie,* a principall witch, so reputed, tried, and condemned of all men, and continuing in that exercise and estimation manie yeares (having cousened & abused the whole realme, in so much as there came to hir, witchmongers from all the furthest parts of the land, she being in diverse bookes set out with authoritie, registred and chronicled by the name of the great witch of *Rochester*, and reputed among all men for the cheefe ringleader of all other witches) by good proofe is found to be a meere cousener; confessing in hir death bed freelie, without compulsion or inforcement, that hir cunning consisted onlie in deluding and deceiving the people: saying that she had (towards the maintenance of hir credit in that cousening trade) some sight in physicke and surgerie, and the assistance of a freend of hirs, called *Heron*, a professor thereof. And this I know, partlie of mine owne knowledge, and partlie by the testimonie of hir husband, and others of credit, to whome (I saie) in hir death bed, and at sundrie other times she protested these things; and also that she never had indeed anie materiall spirit or divell (as the voice went) nor yet knew how to worke anie supernaturall matter, as she in hir life time made men beleeve she had and could doo.

The like may be said of one *T.* of *Canturburie*, whose name I will not litterallie discover, who wonderfullie abused manie in these parts, making them thinke he could tell where anie thing lost became: with diverse other such practises, whereby his fame was farre beyond the others. And yet on his death bed he confessed, that he knew nothing more than anie other, but by slight and devises, without the assistance of anie divell or spirit, saving the spirit of cousenage: and this did he (I saie) protest before manie of great honestie, credit, & wisedome, who can witnesse the same, and also gave him good commendations for his godlie and honest end.

Againe, who will mainteine, that common witchcrafts are not cousenages, when the great and famous witchcrafts, which had stolne credit not onlie from all the common people, but from men of great wisdome and authoritie, are discovered to be beggerlie slights of cousening varlots? Which otherwise might and would have remained a perpetuall objection against me. Were there not three images of late yeeres found in a doonghill, to the terror & astonishment of manie thousands? In so much as great matters were thought to have beene pretended to be doone by witchcraft. But if the Lord preserve those persons (whose destruction was doubted to have beene intended thereby) from all other the lewd practises and attempts of their enimies; I feare not, but they shall easilie withstand these and such like devises, although they should indeed be practised against them. But no doubt, if such bables could have brought those matters of mischeefe to passe, by the hands of traitors, witches, or papists; we should long since have beene deprived of the most excellent jewell and comfort that we enjoy in this world. Howbeit, I confesse, that the feare, conceipt, and doubt of such mischeefous pretenses may breed inconvenience to them that stand in awe of the same. And I wish, that even for such practises, though they never can or doo take effect, the practisers be punished with all extremitie: bicause therein is manifested a traiterous heart to the Queene, and a presumption against God.

But to returne to the discoverie of the aforesaid knaverie and witchcraft. So it was that one old cousener, wanting monie, devised or rather practised (for it is a stale devise) to supplie his want, by promising a yoong Gentleman, whose humor he thought would that waie be well served, that for the summe of fourtie pounds, he would not faile by his cunning in that art of witchcraft, to procure unto him the love of anie three women whome he would name, and of whome he should make choise at his pleasure. The yoong Gentleman being abused with his cunning devises, and too hastilie yeelding to that motion, satisfied this cunning mans demand of monie. Which, bicause he had it not presentlie to disbursse, provided it for him at the hands of a freend of his. Finallie, this cunning man made the three puppets of wax, &c: leaving nothing undone that appertained to the cousenage, untill he had buried them, as you have heard. But I omit to tell what a doo was made herof, and also what reports and lies were bruted; as what white dogs and blacke dogs there were seene in the night season passing through the watch, mawgre all their force and preparation against them, &c. But the yoong Gentleman, who for a litle space remained in hope mixed with joy and love, now through tract of time hath those his felicities powdered with doubt and despaire. For in steed of atchieving his love he would gladlie have obteined his monie. But bicause he could by no meanes get either the one or the other (his monie being in huckster's handling, and his sute in no better forwardnes) he revealed the whole matter, hoping by that meanes to recover his monie; which he neither can yet get againe, nor hath paied it where he borrowed. But till triall was had of his simplicitie or rather follie herein, he received some trouble himselfe hereabouts, though now dismissed.

37

MICHEL de MONTAIGNE
Ignorance and Witchcraft

In a sixteenth-century France torn apart by religious war and passionate, dogmatic hatreds, the tolerant and worldly Michel de Montaigne (1533–95), fideistically rational and sceptically devout, called for an admission of ignorance by men and a moderation in their actions towards each other that challenged the right of the fanaticism of the hunt after witches and, indeed, after heretics in general. As his motto, Montaigne took the phrase "Que sais-je?," "What do I know?" The answer was to be a humbling one for an honest man. Given how little one knew, and how uncertain the foundations of *human* judgment, how could a man kill another in the name of human knowledge and judgment? In his essay, "Of Cripples," the implications of such a sceptical attitude for witchcraft persecutions are made clear.

Michel de Montaigne, *The Complete Essays of Montaigne,* tr. Donald M. Frame (Stanford, Cal., 1965), pp. 784–92.

I was just musing, as I often do, on how free and vague an instrument human reason is. I see ordinarily that men, when facts are put before them, are more ready to amuse themselves by inquiring into their reasons than by inquiring into their truth. They leave aside the cases and amuse themselves treating the causes. Comical prattlers!

The knowledge of causes belongs only to Him who has the guidance of things, not to us who have only the enduring of them, and who have the perfectly full use of them according to our nature, without penetrating to their origin and essence. Nor is wine pleasanter to the man who knows its primary properties. On the contrary, both the body and the soul disturb and alter the right they have to the enjoyment of the world by mixing into it the pretension to learning. Determining and knowing, like giving, appertains to rule and mastery; to inferiority, subjection, and apprenticeship appertains enjoyment and acceptance. Let us return to this habit of ours.

They pass over the facts, but they assiduously examine their consequences. They ordinarily begin thus: "How does this happen?" What they should say is: "But does it happen?" Our reason is capable of filling out a hundred other words and finding their principles and contexture. It needs neither matter nor basis; let it run on; it builds as well on emptiness as on fullness, and with inanity as with matter: Suited to give solidity to smoke. (Persius.)

I find that in almost every case we ought to say: "That is not so at all." And I would often use that reply, but I dare not, for they cry out that it is an evasion produced by feeblemindedness and ignorance. And I am ordinarily obliged to play the fool for company's sake and discuss frivolous subjects and stories which I entirely disbelieve. Besides, it is truly a little rude and quarrelsome flatly to deny a statement of fact. And few people fail, especially in things of which it is hard to persuade others, to affirm that they have seen the thing or to cite witnesses whose authority stops us from contradicting. Following this custom, we know the foundations and causes of a thousand things that never were; and the world skirmishes amid a thousand questions of which both the pro and the con are false. *The false is so close to the true that the wise man should not trust himself in so dangerous a spot* [Cicero].

Truth and falsehood are alike in face, similar in bearing, taste, and movement; we look upon them with the same eye. I find not only that we are lax in defending ourselves against deception, but that we seek and hasten to run ourselves through on it. We love to embroil ourselves in vanity, as something in conformity with our being.

I have seen the birth of many miracles in my time. Even when they are smothered at birth, we do not fail to foresee the course they would have taken if they had lived out their full age. For it is only a matter of finding the end of the string, and we can unwind as much as we want. And there is more distance between nothing and the smallest thing in the world than there is between this and the biggest.

Now the first persons who are convinced of a strange initial fact, as they spread their story, feel from the opposition they meet where the difficulty of persuasion lies, and go and calk that place with some false patch. Besides, *by the innate desire in men to foster rumors diligently* [Livy], we naturally scruple to return what has been lent us without some interest and addition from our own stock. The private error first creates the public error, and afterward in turn the public error creates the private error. Thus this whole structure goes on building itself up and shaping itself from hand to hand; so that the remotest witness is better instructed about it than the nearest, and the last informed more convinced of it than the first. It is a natural progression. For whoever believes anything esteems that it is a work of charity to persuade another of it, and in order to do so does not fear to add out of his own invention as much as he sees to be necessary in his story to take care of the resistance and the defect he thinks there is in the other person's comprehension. . . .

There is nothing on which men are commonly more intent than on making a way for their opinions. Where the ordinary means fail us, we add command, force, fire, and the sword. It it unfortunate to be in such a pass that the best touchstone of truth is the multitude of believers, in a crowd in which the fools so far surpass the wise in number. *As if anything were so common as lack of sense!* [Cicero.] *A fine evidence of sanity is the multitude of the insane!* [Saint Augustine.] It is a difficult thing to set one's judgment against accepted opinions. The first conviction, taken from the subject itself, seizes the simple; from them it spreads to the able, under the authority of the number and antiquity of the testimonies. For my part, in a matter on which I would not believe one, I would not believe a hundred ones. And I do not judge opinions by their years. . . .

Many abuses are engendered in the world, or, to put it more boldly, all the abuses in the world are engendered, by our being taught to be afraid of professing our ignorance and our being bound to accept everything that we cannot refute. We talk about everything didactically and dogmatically. The style in Rome was that even what a witness deposed to having seen with his own eyes, and what a judge decided with his most certain knowledge, was drawn up in this form of speech: "It seems to me." It makes me hate probable things when they are planted on me as infallible. I like these words, which soften and moderate the rashness of our propositions: "perhaps," "to some extent," "some," "they say," "I think," and the like. And if I had had to train children, I would have filled their mouths so much with this way of answering, inquiring, not decisive—"What does that mean? I do not understand it. That might be. Is it true?"—that they would be more likely to have kept the manner of learners at sixty than to represent learned doctors at ten, as they do. Anyone who wants to be cured of ignorance must confess it. Iris is the daughter of Thaumas. Wonder is the foundation of all philosophy, inquiry its progress, ignorance its end. I'll go further: There is a certain strong and generous ignorance that concedes nothing to knowledge in honor and courage, an ignorance that requires no less knowledge to conceive it than does knowledge.

In my youth, I read about the trial of a strange case, which Corras, a counselor of Toulouse, had printed, about two men who impersonated one another. I remember (and I remember nothing else) that he seemed to me, in describing the imposture of the man he judged guilty, to make it so marvelous and so far surpassing our knowledge and his own, who was judge, that I found much rashness in the sentence that had condemned the man to be hanged. Let us accept some form of sentence which says "The court understands nothing of the matter," more freely and ingenuously than did the Areopagites, who, finding themselves hard pressed by a case that they could not unravel, ordered the parties to come back in a hundred years.

The witches of my neighborhood are in mortal danger every time some new author comes along and attests to the reality of their visions. To apply the examples that the Holy Writ offers us of such things, very certain and irrefragable examples, and bring them to bear on our modern events, requires greater ingenuity than ours, since we see neither their causes nor their means. It belongs perhaps only to that most powerful testimony to say to us: "This is a miracle, and that, and not this other." God must be believed in these things, that is truly most reasonable; but not, by the some token, one of us, who is astonished at his own narrative (and he is necessarily astonished unless he is out of his senses), whether he tells it about someone else or against himself.

I am sluggish and tend to hold to the solid and the probable, avoiding the ancient reproaches: *Men put greater faith in those things that they do not understand* [author unknown]. *By a twist of the human mind, obscure things are more readily believed* [Tacitus]. I see indeed that people get angry, and I am forbidden to doubt on pain of execrable insults. A new way of persuading! Thank God, my belief is not controlled by anyone's fists. Let them bully those who accuse them of holding a false opinion;

I accuse them only of holding a difficult and rash one, and condemn the opposite affirmation, just as they do, if not so imperiously. *Let them appear as probable, not be affirmed positively* [Cicero].

He who imposes his argument by bravado and command shows that it is weak in reason. In a verbal and scholastic altercation these people may have as good an apparent case as their contradictors; but in the effective consequences they draw from them, the latter have much advantage.

To kill men, we should have sharp and luminous evidence; and our life is too real and essential to vouch for these supernatural and fantastic accidents. As for druggings and poisonings, I put them out of my reckoning; those are homicides, and of the worst sort. However, even in such matters they say that we must not always be satisfied with confessions, for such persons have sometimes been known to accuse themselves of having killed people who were found to be alive and healthy.

In those other extravagant accusations, I should be inclined to say that it is quite enough that a man, whatever recommendation he may have, should be believed about what is human; about what is beyond his conception and of supernatural effect, he should be believed only when some supernatural approbation has sanctioned him. This privilege that it has pleased God to give to some of our testimonies must not be cheapened and communicated lightly.

My ears are battered by a thousand stories like this: "Three people saw him on such-and-such a day in the east; three saw him the next day in the west, at such-and-such a time, in such-and-such a place, dressed thus." Truly, I would not believe my own self about this. How much more natural and likely it seems to me that two men are lying than that one man should pass with the winds in twelve hours from the east to the west! How much more natural that our understanding should be carried away from its base by the volatility of our untracked mind than that one of us, in flesh and bone, should be wafted up a chimney on a broomstick by a strange spirit!

Let us not look for outside and unknown illusions, we who are perpetually agitated by our own home-grown illusions. It seems to me that we may be pardoned for disbelieving a marvel, at least as long as we can turn aside and avoid the supernatural explanation by nonmarvelous means. And I follow Saint Augustine's opinion, that it is better to lean toward doubt than toward assurance in things difficult to prove and dangerous to believe.

A few years ago I passed through the territory of a sovereign prince, who, as a favor to me and to beat down my incredulity, did me the kindness of letting me see, in his own presence and in a private place, ten or twelve prisoners of this nature, and among others one old woman, indeed a real witch in ugliness and deformity, long very famous in that profession. I saw both proofs and free confessions, and some barely perceptible mark or other on this wretched old woman, and I talked and asked questions all I wanted, bringing to the matter the soundest attention I could; and I am not the man to let my judgment be throttled much by preconceptions. In the end, and in all conscience, I would have prescribed them rather hellebore than hemlock. *It seemed to be a matter rather of madness than of crime* [Livy]. Justice has its own corrections proper for such maladies.

As for the objections and arguments that worthy men have brought up against me, both on this subject and often on others, I have not felt any that are binding and that do not admit of a solution more likely than their conclusions. It is true indeed that the proofs and reasons that are founded on experience and fact I do not attempt to disentangle; moreover they have no end to take hold of; I often cut them, as Alexander did his knot. After all, it is putting a very high price on one's conjectures to have a man roasted alive because of them.

38

BENEDICT de SPINOZA
Reason, Man, and the Devil

Benedict de Spinoza (1632–77) was an excommunicated Dutch Jew who articulated a rationalistic yet mystical pantheism in which the whole of reality was conceived of as a manifestation of the Divine, of the Perfect and Infinite Being of which all things that are were merely modes. In such a scheme there was no room for real evil, for Satan, for suspensions of natural (for Spinoza, divine) laws, that is to say, no room for the conceptions upon which witch-craft-belief depends. If man would clarify his theological concepts, Spinoza insisted, the existence of subsidiary agents of evil would appear contradictory to the reality that must flow from the nature of the Divine.

Benedict de Spinoza, The Political Works, ed. A. G. Wernham (Oxford, 1958), pp. 269–71.

Most men, however, believe that the unenlightened violate the order of nature rather than conform to it; they conceive men in nature as a state within a state. They maintain, in fact, that the human mind is not produced by natural causes at all, but is the direct creation of God, and is so completely independent of every other thing that it has an absolute power to determine itself and use reason correctly. But experience teaches us only too well that it is no more in our power to have a sound mind than to have a sound body. Moreover, since everything does all it *can* do to preserve its own being, we cannot have the slightest doubt that, if it *were* as much in our power to live by the precept of reason as it is to be led by blind desire, all men *would* be guided by reason, and *would* order their lives wisely; which is very far from being the case. For everyone is captivated by his own pleasure. Nor do theologians dispose of this difficulty by their dogma that the cause of this weakness is the vice or sin which arose in human nature through the fall of our first ancestor. For if even the first man had as much power to stand as to fall, if his mind was sound and his nature uncorrupted, how, with his knowledge and foresight, could he possibly have fallen? Their answer is that he was deceived by the Devil. Then who was it that deceived the Devil himself? Who, I ask, made the very foremost of all intelligent creatures so insane that he wished to be greater than God? For surely, if the Devil had a sound mind, he must have been doing all he could to preserve himself and his own being? Again, if the first man himself was sound in mind and master of his own will, how could he possibly have allowed himself to be seduced and tricked? If he had the power to use reason correctly, he could not have been deceived; for he must have done everything in his power to preserve his own being and his own sound mind. Now the hypothesis is that he did have the power to use reason correctly: therefore he must have preserved his sound mind, and could not have been deceived. This, however, is shown to be false by the story told about him; and so we must admit that the first man did not have it in his power to use reason correctly, but was subject to passions like ourselves.

39

ALONSO SALAZAR de FRIAS
The Grand Inquisitor of Spain
on Witchcraft and Delusion
1610

As more critical and cautious thought spread throughout learned Europe, and as educated men began to dissociate themselves from the beliefs and attitudes of the uneducated, scepticism about witchcraft-persecutions and trial procedures increasingly made its presence felt among the officers of civil and ecclesiastical institutions. No more striking example of this could be found than the person of the Grand Inquisitor of Spain explaining the need to cease the dangerously self-fulfilling witch-hunts.

"Antonio [sic] Salazar de Frias to the Supreme Court of Spain," in Charles Williams, *Witchcraft* (London, 1941), pp. 252–53.

Considering the above with all the Christian attention in my power, I have not found even indications from which to infer that a single act of witchcraft has really occurred, whether as to going to aquelarres, being present at them, inflicting injuries, or other of the asserted facts. This enlightenment has greatly strengthened my former suspicions that the evidence of accomplices, without external proof from other parties, is insufficient to justify even arrest. Moreover, my experience leads to the conviction that, of those availing themselves of the Edict of Grace, three-quarters and more have accused themselves and their accomplices falsely. I further believe that they would freely come to the Inquisition to revoke their confessions, if they thought that they would be received kindly without punishment, for I fear that my efforts to induce this have not been properly made known, and I further fear that, in my absence, the commissioners whom, by your command, I have ordered to do the same, do not act with due fidelity, but, with increasing zeal are discovering every hour more witches and aquelarres, in the same way as before.

I also feel certain that, under present conditions, there is no need of fresh edicts or the prolongation of those existing, but rather that, in the diseased state of the public mind, every agitation of the matter is harmful and increases the evil. I deduce the importance of silence and reserve from the experience that there were neither witches nor bewitched until they were talked and written about. This impressed me recently at Olague, near Pampeluna, where those who confessed stated that the matter started there after Fray Domingo de Sardo came there to preach about these things. So, when I went to Valderro, near Roncesvalles, to reconcile some who had confessed, when about to return the alcades begged me to go to the Valle de Ahescoa, two leagues distant, not that any witchcraft had been discovered there, but only that it might be honored equally with the other. I only sent there the Edict of Grace and, eight days after its publication, I learned that already there were boys confessing.

40

THOMAS HOBBES
Demonology as Unsound Philosophy
1651

Thomas Hobbes (1588–1679) was a materialist and mechanist for whom the concepts of witchcraft—indeed, concepts involving spiritual agents of any kind—were philosophically inconceivable and insignificant. In Book IV of *Leviathan,* Hobbes interprets the meaning of scriptural passages concerning witchcraft as metaphorical, a device that men unwilling to admit the interaction of matter and spirit but unwilling to abandon scripture will utilize, less ironically than Hobbes, to reconcile their various intellectual and religious commitments.

Thomas Hobbes, *Leviathan* (1651), Bk. IV, ch. 45–46.

*O*f *Daemonology, and other Reliques of the Religion of the Gentiles.* The impression made on the organs of Sight, by lucide Bodies, either in one direct line, or in many lines, reflected from Opaque, or refracted in the passage through Diaphanous Bodies, produceth in living Creatures, in whom God hath placed such Organs, an Imagination of the Object, from whence the Impression proceedeth; which Imagination is called *Sight*; and seemeth not to bee a meer Imagination, but the Body it selfe without us; in the same manner, as when a man violently presseth his eye, there appears to him a light without, and before him, which no man perceiveth but him-selfe; because there is indeed no such thing without him, but onely a motion in the interiour organs, pressing by resistance outward, that makes him think so. And the motion made by this pressure, continuing after the object which caused it is removed, is that we call *Imagination*, and *Memory*, and (in sleep, and sometimes in great distemper of the organs by Sicknesse, or Violence) a *Dream*: of which things I have already spoken briefly, in the second and third Chapters.

This nature of Sight having never been discovered by the ancient pretenders to Naturall Knowledge; much lesse by those that consider not things so remote (as that Knowledge is) from their present use; it was hard for men to conceive of those Images in the Fancy, and in the Sense, otherwise, than of things really without us: Which some (because they vanish away, they know not whither, nor how,) will have to be absolutely Incorporeall, that is to say Immateriall, or Formes without Matter; Colour and Figure, without any coloured or figured Body; and that they can put on Aiery bodies (as a garment) to make them Visible when they will to our bodily Eyes; and others say, are Bodies, and living Creatures, but made of Air, or other more subtile and aethereall Matter, which is, then, when they will be seen, condensed. But Both of them agree on one generall appellation of them, *Daemons*. As if the Dead of whom they Dreamed, were not Inhabitants of their own Brain, but of the Air, or of Heaven, or Hell; not Phantasmes, but Ghosts; with just as much reason, as if one should say, he saw his own Ghost in a Looking-Glasse, or the Ghosts of the Stars in a River; or call the ordinary apparition of the Sun, of the quantity of about a foot, the *Daemon*, or Ghost of that great Sun that enlighteneth the whole visible world: And by that means have feared them, as things of an unknown, that is, of an unlimited power to doe them good, or harme; and consequently, given occasion to the Governours of the Heathen Common-wealths to regulate this their fear, by establishing that *Daemonology* (in which the Poets, as Principall Priests of the Heathen Religion, were specially employed, or reverenced) to the Publique Peace, and to the Obedience of Subjects necessary thereunto; and to make some of them Good *Daemons*, and others Evill; the one as a Spurre to the Observance, the other, as Reines to withhold them from Violation of the Laws.

What kind of things they were, to whom they attributed the name of *Daemons*, appeareth partly in the Genealogie of their Gods, written by *Hesiod*, one of the most ancient Poets of the Graecians; and partly in other Histories; of which I have observed some few before, in the 12. Chapter of this discourse.

Figure 69.
The frontispiece of Glanvil's *Saducismus Triumphatus* showing six scenes from well-known seventeenth-century witch cases.

344

The Graecians, by their Colonies and Conquests, communicated their Language and Writings into Asia, Egypt, and Italy; and therein, by necessary consequence their *Daemonology*, or (as St. *Paul* calles it) *their Doctrines of Devils*: And by that meanes, the contagion was derived also to the Jewes, both of *Judaea*, and *Alexandria*, and other parts, whereinto they were dispersed. But the name of *Daemon* they did not (as the Graecians) attribute to Spirits both Good, and Evill; but to the Evill onely: And to the Good *Daemons* they gave the name of the Spirit of God; and esteemed those into whose bodies they entred to be Prophets. In summe, all singularity if Good, they attributed to the Spirit of God; and if Evil, to some *Daemon*, but a *kakodaimon*, an Evill *Daemon*, that is, a *Devill*. And therefore, they called *Daemoniaques*, that is, *possessed by the Devill*, such as we call Madmen or Lunatiques; or such as had the Falling Sicknesse; or that spoke any thing, which they for want of understanding, thought absurd: As also of an Unclean person in a notorious degree, they used to say he had an Unclean Spirit; of a Dumbe man, that he had a Dumbe Devill; and of *John Baptist* (*Math.* 11. 18.) for the singularity of his fasting, that he had a Devill; and of our Saviour, because he said, hee that keepeth his sayings should not see Death in *aeternum, Now we know thou hast a Devill; Abraham is dead, and the Prophets are dead*: and again, because he said (*John* 7. 20.) *They went about to kill him*, the people answered, *Thou hast a Devill, who goeth about to kill thee?* Whereby it is manifest, that the Jewes had the same opinions concerning Phantasmes, namely, that they were not Phantasmes, that is, Idols of the braine, but things reall, and independent on the Fancy.

Which doctrine if it be not true, why (may some say) did not our Saviour contradict it, and teach the contrary? nay why does he use on diverse occasions, such forms of speech as seem to confirm it? To this I answer, that first, where Christ saith, *A spirit hath not flesh and bone*, though hee shew that there be Spirits, yet hee denies not that they are Bodies: And where St. *Paul* saies, *We shall rise spirituall Bodies*, he acknowledgeth the nature of Spirits, but that they are Bodily Spirits; which is not difficult to understand. For Air and many other things are Bodies, though not Flesh and Bone, or any other grosse body, to bee discerned by the eye. But when our Saviour speaketh to the Devill, and commandeth him to go out of a man, if by the Devill, be meant a Disease, as Phrenesy, or Lunacy, or a corporeal Spirit, is not the speech improper? can Diseases heare? or can there be a corporeall Spirit in a Body of Flesh and Bone, full already of vitall and animall Spirits? Are there not therefore Spirits, that neither have

Bodies, nor are meer Imaginations? To the first I answer, that the addressing of our Saviours command to the Madnesse, or Lunacy he cureth, is no more improper, then was his rebuking of the Fever, or of the Wind, and Sea; for neither do these hear: Or than was the command of God, to the Light, to the Firmament, to the Sunne, and Starres, when he commanded them to bee: for they could not heare before they had a beeing. But those speeches are not improper, because they signifie the power of Gods Word: no more therefore is it improper, to command Madnesse, or Lunacy (under the appellation of Devils, by which they were then commonly understood,) to depart out of a mans body. To the second, concerning their being Incorporeall, I have not yet observed any place of Scripture, from whence it can be gathered, that any man was ever possessed with any other Corporeall Spirit, but that of his owne, by which his body is naturally moved.

Our Saviour, immediately after the Holy Ghost descended upon him in the form of a Dove, is said by St. *Matthew* (Chapt. 4. 1.) to have been *led up by the Spirit into the Wildernesse*; and the same is recited (*Luke* 4. 1.) in these words, *Jesus being full of the Holy Ghost, was led in the Spirit into the Wildernesse*: Whereby it is evident, that by *Spirit* there, is meant the Holy Ghost. This cannot be interpreted for a Possession: For Christ, and the Holy Ghost, are but one and the same substance; which is no possession of one substance, or body, by another. And whereas in the verses following, he is said *to have been taken up by the Devill into the Holy City, and set upon a pinnacle of the Temple*, shall we conclude thence that hee was possessed of the Devill, or carried thither by violence? And again, *carryed thence by the Devill into an exceeding high mountain, who shewed him them thence all the Kingdomes of the world*: Wherein, wee are not to beleeve he was either possessed, or forced by the Devill; nor that any Mountaine is high enough, (according to the literall sense,) to shew him one whole Hemisphere. What then can be the meaning of this place, other than that he went of himself into the Wildernesse; and that this carrying of him up and down, from the Wildernesse to the City, and from thence into a Mountaine, was a Vision? Conformable whereunto, is also the phrase of St. Luke, that hee was led into the Wildernesse, not *by*, but *in* the Spirit: whereas concerning His being Taken up into the Mountaine, and unto the Pinnacle of the Temple, hee speaketh as St. Matthew doth. Which suiteth with the nature of a Vision.

Again, where St. Luke sayes of Judas Iscariot, that *Satan entred into him, and thereupon that he went and communed with the Chief Priests, and Captaines, how he might betray Christ unto them*: it may be answered, that by the Entering of *Satan* (that is the *Enemy*) into him, is meant, the hostile and traiterous intention of selling his Lord and Master. For as by the Holy Ghost, is frequently in Scripture understood, the Graces and good Inclinations given by the Holy Ghost; so by the Entring of Satan, may bee understood the wicked Cogitations, and Designs of the Adversaries of Christ, and his Disciples. For as it is hard to say, that the Devill was entred into Judas, before he had any such hostile designe; so it is impertinent to say, he was first Christs Enemy in his heart, and that the Devill entred into him afterwards. Therefore the Entring of Satan, and his Wicked Purpose, was one and the same thing.

But if there be no Immateriall Spirit, nor any Possession of mens bodies by any Spirit Corporeall, it may again be asked, why our Saviour and his Apostles did not teach the People so; and in such cleer words, as they might no more doubt thereof. But such questions as these, are more curious, than necessary for a Christian mans Salvation. Men may as well aske, why Christ that could have given to all men Faith, Piety, and all manner of morall Vertues, gave it to some onely, and not to all: and why he left the search of naturall Causes, and Sciences, to the naturall Reason and Industry of men, and did not reveal it to all, or any man supernaturally; and many other such questions: Of which nevertheless there may be alleged probable and pious reasons. For as God, when he brought the Israelites into the Land of Promise, did not secure them therein, by subduing all the Nations round about them; but left many of them, as thornes in their sides, to awaken from time to time their Piety and Industry: so our Saviour, in conducting us toward his heavenly Kingdome, did not destroy all the difficulties of Naturall Questions; but left them to exercise our Industry, and Reason; the Scope of his preaching, being onely to shew us this plain and direct way to Salvation, namely, the beleef of this Article, *that he was the Christ, the Son of the living God, sent into the world to sacrifice himselfe for our Sins, and at his comming again, gloriously to reign over his Elect, and to save them from their Enemies eternally*: To which, the opinion of Possession by Spirits, or Phantasmes, are no impediment in the way; though it be to some an occasion of going out of the way, and to follow their own Inventions. If wee require of the Scripture an account of all questions, which may be raised to trouble us in the performance of Gods commands; we may as well complaine of Moses for not having set downe the time of the creation of such Spirits, as well as of the Creation of the Earth, and Sea, and of Men, and Beasts. To conclude, I find in Scripture that there be Angels, and Spirits, good and evill; but not that they are Incorporeall, as are the Apparitions men see in the Dark, or in a Dream, or Vision; which the Latines call *Spectra*, and took for *Daemons*. And I find that there are Spirits Corporeall, (though subtile and Invisible;) but not that any mans body was possessed, or inhabited by them; And that the Bodies of the Saints shall be such, namely, Spirituall Bodies, as St. Paul calls them.

Neverthelesse, the contrary Doctrine, namely, that there be Incorporeall Spirits, hath hitherto so prevailed in the Church, that the use of Exorcisme, (that is to say, of ejection of Devills by Conjuration) is thereupon built; and (though rarely and faintly practised) is not yet totally given over. That there were many Daemoniaques in the Primitive Church, and few Mad-men, and other such singular diseases; whereas in these times we hear of, and see many Mad-men, and few Daemoniaques, proceeds not from the change of Nature; but of Names. But how it comes to passe, that whereas heretofore the Apostles, and after them for a time, the Pastors of the Church, did cure those singular Diseases, which now they are not seen to doe; as likewise, why it is not in the power of every true Beleever now, to doe all that the Faithfull did then, that is to say, as we read (*Mark* 16. 17.) *In Christs name to cast out Devills, to speak with new Tongues, to take up Serpents, to drink deadly Poison without harm taking, and to cure the Sick by the laying on of their hands,* and all this without other words, but *in the Name of Jesus,* is another question. And it is probable, that those extraordinary gifts were given to the Church, for no longer a time, than men trusted wholly to Christ, and looked for their felicity onely in his Kingdome to come; and consequently, that when they sought Authority, and Riches, and trusted to their own Subtility for a Kingdome of this world, these supernaturall gifts of God were again taken from them. . . .

An *Image* (in the most strict signification of the word) is the Resemblance of some thing visible: In which sense the Phantasticall Formes, Apparitions, or Seemings of visible Bodies to the Sight, are onely *Images*; such as are the Shew of a man, or other thing in the Water, by Reflexion, or Refraction; or of the Sun, or Stars by Direct Vision in the Air; which are nothing reall in the things seen, nor in the place where they seem to bee; nor are their magnitudes and figures the same with that of the object; but changeable, by the variation of the organs of Sight, or by glasses; and are present oftentimes in our Imagination, and in our Dreams, when the object is absent; or changed into other colours, and shapes, as things that depend onely upon the Fancy. And these are the Images which are originally and most properly called *Ideas*, and *Idols*, and derived from the language of the Graecians, with whom the word *Eido* signifieth to *See*. They are also called *Phantasmes*, which is in the same language, *Apparitions*. And from these Images it is that one of the faculties of mans Nature, is called the *Imagination*. And from hence it is manifest, that there neither is, nor can bee any Image made of a thing Invisible.

It is also evident, that there can be no Image of a thing Infinite: for all the Images, and Phantasmes that are made by the Impression of things visible, are figured: but Figure is a quantity every way determined: And therefore there can bee no Image of God; nor of the Soule of Man; nor of Spirits; but onely of Bodies Visible, that is, Bodies that have light in themselves, or are by such enlightened.

Of Darknesse from Vain Philosophy, and Fabulous Traditions

By *Philosophy*, is understood *the Knowledge acquired by Reasoning, from the Manner of the Generation of any thing, to the Properties; or from the Properties, to some possible Way of Generation of the same; to the end to bee able to produce, as far as matter, and humane force permit, such Effects, as humane life requireth.* So the Geometrician, from the Construction of Figures, findeth out many Properties thereof; and from the Properties, new Ways of their Construction, by Reasoning; to the end to be able to measure Land, and Water; and for infinite other uses. So the Astronomer, from the Rising, Setting, and Moving of the Sun, and Starres, in divers parts of the Heavens, findeth out the Causes of Day, and Night, and of the different Seasons of the Year; whereby he keepeth an account of Time: And the like of other Sciences.

By which Definition it is evident, that we are not to account as any part thereof, that originall knowledge called Experience, in which consisteth Prudence: Because it is not attained by Reasoning, but found as well in Brute Beasts, as in Man; and is but a Memory of successions of events in times past, wherein the omission of every little circumstance altering the effect, frustrateth the expectation of the most Prudent: whereas nothing is produced by Reasoning aright, but generall, eternall, and immutable Truth.

Nor are we therefore to give that name to any false Conclusions: For he that Reasoneth aright in words he understandeth, can never conclude an Error:

Nor to that which any man knows by supernaturall Revelation; because it is not acquired by Reasoning:

Nor that which is gotten by Reasoning from the Authority of Books; because it is not by Reasoning from the Cause to the Effect, nor from the Effect to the Cause; and is not Knowledge, but Faith.

41

FRIEDRICH SPEE
A Jesuit Criticizes the Persecutions
1631

Friedrich Spee was a Jesuit and poet assigned the painful task of being confessor of witches condemned to death during the persecutions at Würzburg
in the late 1620's. Appalled by the method of the trials, Spee published an
anonymous attack upon the persecution in 1631, the *Cautio Criminalis,* which
became celebrated later in the century, when the philosopher Leibniz
revealed the identity of its author.

From Burr, *The Witch Persecutions,* pp. 30–35.

*W*hat, *now, is the outline and method of the trials against
witches to-day in general use?—a thing worthy Germany's consideration.*
I answer: . . .

1. Incredible among us Germans and especially (I blush to say it) among
Catholics are the popular superstition, envy, calumnies, back-bitings, insinu-
ations, and the like, which, being neither punished by the magistrates nor
refuted by the pulpit, first stir up suspicion of witchcraft. All the divine
judgments which God has threatened in Holy Writ are now ascribed to
witches. No longer do God or nature do aught, but witches everything.

2. Hence it comes that all at once everybody is clamoring that the magistrates proceed against the witches—those witches whom only their own
clamor has made seem so many.

3. Princes, therefore, bid their judges and counselors to begin proceedings against the witches.

4. These at first do not know where to begin, since they have no testimony or proofs, and since their conscience clearly tells them that they ought not to proceed in this rashly.

5. Meanwhile they are a second time and a third admonished to proceed. The multitude clamors that there is something suspicious in this delay; and the same suspicion is, by one busybody or another, instilled into the ear of the princes.

6. To offend these, however, and not to defer at once to their wishes, is in Germany a serious matter: most men, and even clergymen, approve with zeal whatever is but pleasing to the princes, not heeding by whom these (however good by nature) are often instigated.

7. At last, therefore, the judges yield to their wishes, and in some way contrive at length a starting-point for the trials.

8. Or, if they still hold out and dread to touch the ticklish matter, there is sent to them a commissioner [*Inquisitor*] specially deputed for this. And, even if he brings to his task something of inexperience or of haste, as is wont to happen in things human, this takes on in this field another color and name, and is counted only zeal for justice. This zeal for justice is no whit diminished by the prospect of gain, especially in the case of a commissioner of slender means and avaricious, with a large family, when there is granted him as salary so many dollars per head for each witch burned, besides the fees and assessments which he is allowed to extort at will from the peasants.

9. If now some utterance of a demoniac or some malign and idle rumor then current (for proof of the scandal is never asked) points especially to some poor and helpless Gaia, she is the first to suffer.

10. And yet, lest it appear that she is indicted on the basis of rumor alone, without other proofs, as the phrase goes, lo a certain presumption is at once obtained against her by posing the following dilemma: Either Gaia has led a bad and improper life, or she has led a good proper one. If a bad one, then, say they, the proof is cogent against her; for from malice to malice the presumption is strong. If, however, she has led a good one, this also is none the less a proof; for thus, they say, are witches wont to cloak themselves and try to seem especially proper.

11. Therefore it is ordered that Gaia be haled away to prison. And lo now a new proof is gained against her by this other dilemma: Either she

Figures 70–72. The
Craft and its Critics.

THE

Difcovery of Witchcraft:

PROVING,

That the Compacts and Contracts of WITCHES
with *Devils* and all *Infernal Spirits* or *Familiars*, are but
Erroneous Novelties and Imaginary Conceptions.

Alfo difcovering, How far their Power extendeth in Killing, Tormenting,
Confuming, or Curing the bodies of Men, Women, Children, or Animals,
by Charms, Philtres, Periapts, Pentacles, Curfes, and Conjurations.

WHEREIN LIKEWISE

The Unchriftian Practices and Inhumane Dealings of
Searchers and *Witch-tryers* upon *Aged, Melancholly,* and *Superftitious*
people, in extorting Confeffions by Terrors and Tortures,
and in devifing falfe Marks and Symptoms, are notably Detected.

And the Knavery of *Juglers, Conjurers, Charmers, Soothfayers, Figure-Caflers,
Dreamers, Alchymifts* and *Philterers*; with many other things
that have long lain hidden, fully Opened and Deciphered.

ALL WHICH

Are very neceffary to be known for the undeceiving of *Judges, Juftices,*
and *Jurors,* before they pafs Sentence upon Poor, Miferable and Ignorant People;
who are frequently Arraigned, Condemned, and Executed for *Witches and Wizzards.*

IN SIXTEEN BOOKS.

By REGINALD SCOT *Efquire.*

Whereunto is added
An excellent Difcourfe of the *Nature* and *Subftance*
OF

DEVILS and SPIRITS,

IN TWO BOOKS:

The *Firft* by the aforefaid *Author:* The *Second* now
added in this *Third Edition,* as Succedaneous to the *former,*
and conducing to the compleating of the *Whole Work:*
With *Nine Chapters* at the beginning of the *Fifteenth Book*
of the *DISCOVERY.*

LONDON:

Printed for *Andrew Clark,* and are to be fold at Mris. *Cotes's* near
the *Golden-Ball* in *Alderfgateftreet,* 1 6 6 5.

Figure 70. Title
Page of Reginald
Scot's *Discovery of
Witchcraft.*

The elaborate title
indicates the levels
of Scot's attack upon
both current witch
beliefs and the judi-
cial institutions used
to prosecute them.

then shows fear or she does not show it. If she does show it (hearing forsooth of the grievous tortures wont to be used in this matter), this is of itself a proof; for conscience, they say, accuses her. If she does not show it (trusting forsooth in her innocence), this too is a proof; for it is most characteristic of witches, they say, to pretend themselves peculiarly innocent and wear a bold front.

12. Lest, however, further proofs against her should be lacking, the Commissioner has his own creatures, often depraved and notorious, who question into all her past life. This, of course, cannot be done without coming upon some saying or doing of hers which evil-minded men can easily twist or distort into ground for suspicion of witchcraft.

13. If, too, there are any who have borne her ill will, these, having now a fine opportunity to do her harm, bring against her such charges as it may please them to devise; and on every side there is a clamor that the evidence is heavy against her.

14. And so, as soon as possible, she is hurried to the torture, if indeed she be not subjected to it on the very day of her arrest, as often happens.

15. For in these trials there is granted to nobody an advocate or any means of fair defense, for the cry is that the crime is an excepted one,[1] and whoever ventures to defend the prisoner is brought into suspicion of the crime—as are all those who dare to utter a protest in these cases and to urge the judges to caution; for they are forthwith dubbed patrons of the witches. Thus all mouths are closed and all pens blunted, lest they speak or write.

16. In general, however, that it may not seem that no opportunity of defense has been given to Gaia, she is brought out and the proofs are first read before her and examined—if examine it can be called.

17. But, even though she then denies these and satisfactorily makes answer to each, this is neither paid attention to nor even noted down: all the proofs retain their force and value, however perfect her answer to them. She is only ordered back into prison, there to bethink herself more carefully whether she will persist in her obstinacy—for, since she has denied her guilt, she is obstinate.

18. When she has bethought herself, she is next day brought out again,

---

1. *Crimina excepta* were those in which, by reason of their enormity, all restraints upon procedure were suspended. Such were treason, and, by analogy, treason against heaven—heresy, that is, and especially witchcraft. In dealing with the latter an added ground for severity was found in the belief that the Devil might aid supernaturally his allies. [Burr's note]

and there is read to her the sentence of torture—just as if she had before answered nothing to the charges, and refuted nothing.

19.   Before she is tortured, however, she is led aside by the executioner, and, lest she may by magical means have fortified herself against pain, she is searched, her whole body being shaved, . . . ; although up to this time nothing of the sort was ever found. . . .

21.   Then, when Gaia has thus been searched and shaved, she is tortured that she may confess the truth, that is to say, that she may simply declare herself guilty; for whatever else she may say will not be the truth and cannot be.

22.   She is, however, tortured with the torture of the first degree, i. e., the less severe. This is to be understood thus: that, although in itself it is exceeding severe, yet, compared with others to follow, it is lighter. Wherefore, if she confesses, they say and noise it abroad that she has confessed without torture.

23.   Now, what prince or other dignitary who hears this can doubt that she is most certainly guilty who thus voluntarily without torture confesses her guilt?

24.   Without any scruples, therefore, after this confession she is executed. Yet she would have been executed, nevertheless, even though she had not confessed; for, when once a beginning has been made with the torture, the die is already cast—she cannot escape, she must die.

25.   So, whether she confesses or does not confess, the result is the same. If she confesses, the thing is clear, for, as I have said and as is self-evident, she is executed: all recantation is in vain, as I have shown above. If she does not confess, the torture is repeated—twice, thrice, four times: anything one pleases is permissible, for in an excepted crime there is no limit of duration or severity or repetition of the tortures. As to this, think the judges, no sin is possible which can be brought up before the tribunal of conscience.

26.   If now Gaia, no matter how many times tortured, has not yet broken silence—if she contorts her features under the pain, if she loses consciousness, or the like, then they cry that she is laughing or has bewitched herself into taciturnity, and hence deserves to be burned alive, as lately has been done to some who though several times tortured would not confess.

27.   And then they say—even clergymen and confessors—that she died obstinate and impenitent, that she would not be converted or desert her paramour, but kept rather her faith with him.

28.   If, however, it chances that under so many tortures one dies, they say that her neck has been broken by the Devil. . . .

29.   Wherefore justly, forsooth, the corpse is dragged out by the executioner and buried under the gallows.

30.   But if, on the other hand, Gaia does not die and some exceptionally scrupulous judge hesitates to torture her further without fresh proofs or to burn her without a confession, she is kept in prison and more harshly fettered, and there lies for perhaps an entire year to rot until she is subdued.

31.   For it is never possible to clear herself by withstanding and thus to wash away the aspersion of crime, as is the intention of the laws. It would be a disgrace to her examiners if when once arrested she should thus go free. Guilty must she be, by fair means or foul, whom they have once but thrown into bonds.

32.   Meanwhile, both then and earlier, they send to her ignorant and headstrong priests, more importunate than the executioners themselves. It is the business of these to harass in every wise the wretched creature to such a degree that, whether truly or not, she will at last confess herself guilty; unless she does so, they declare, she simply cannot be saved, nor share in the sacraments.

33.   The greatest care is taken lest there be admitted to her priests more thoughtful and learned, who have aught of insight or kindliness; as also that nobody visits her prison who might give her counsel or inform the ruling princes. For there is nothing so much dreaded by any of them as that in some way the innocence of any of the accused should be brought to light. . . .

34.   In the meantime, while Gaia, as I have said, is still held in prison, and is tormented by those whom it least behooves, there are not wanting to her industrious judges clever devices by which they not only find new proofs against Gaia, but by which moreover they so convict her to her face (an 't please the gods!) that by the advice of some university faculty[2] she is then at last pronounced to deserve burning alive. . . .

35.   Some, however, to leave no stone unturned, order Gaia to be exorcised and transferred to a new place, and then to be tortured again, in the hope that by this exorcism and change of place the bewitchment of taciturnity may perhaps be broken. But, if not even this succeeds, then at last

2. It was sometimes the juristic, sometimes the theologic, faculty of a university which was called on for such advice, the crime of witchcraft being subject to both secular and ecclesiastical jurisdiction. [Burr's note]

they commit her alive to the flames. Now, in Heaven's name, I would like to know, since both she who confesses and she who does not perish alike, what way of escape is there for any, however innocent? O unhappy Gaia, why has thou rashly hoped? why hast thou not, at first entering prison, declared thyself guilty? why, O foolish woman and mad, wilt thou die so many times when thou mightst die but once? Follow my counsel, and before all pain declare thyself guilty and die. Thou wilt not escape; for this were a disgrace to the zeal of Germany.

36. If, now, any under stress of pain has once falsely declared herself guilty, her wretched plight beggars description. For not only is there in general no door for her escape, but she is also compelled to accuse others, of whom she knows no ill, and whose names are not seldom suggested to her by her examiners or by the executioner, or of whom she has heard as suspected or accused or already once arrested and released. These in their turn are forced to accuse others, and these still others, and so it goes on: who can help seeing that it must go on without end?

37. Wherefore the judges themselves are obliged at last either to break off the trials and so condemn their own work or else to burn their own folk, aye themselves and everybody: for on all soon or late false accusations fall, and, if only followed by the torture, all are proved guilty.

38. And so at last those are brought into question who at the outset most loudly clamored for the constant feeding of the flames; for they rashly failed to foresee that their turn, too, must inevitably come—and by a just verdict of Heaven, since with their pestilent tongues they created us so many witches and sent so many innocent to the flames.

39. But now gradually many of the wiser and more learned begin to take notice of it, and, as if aroused from deep sleep, to open their eyes and slowly and cautiously to bestir themselves. . . .

46. From all which there follows this corollary, worthy to be noted in red ink: that, if only the trials be steadily pushed on with, there is nobody in our day, of whatsoever sex, fortune, rank, or dignity, who is safe, if he have but an enemy and slanderer to bring him into suspicion of witchcraft. . . .

42

1693
The Recantation of the Salem Jurors

In 1692 a witchcraft-scare and persecution occurred in the Puritan colony of Salem, Massachusetts, in the course of which a score of convicted witches were put to death. This was one of the last major witch-scares in the western world. The effect of the events in Salem, however, far from rekindling the active hunt after sorcerers, was further to intensify men's rapidly growing scepticism concerning such persecutions; for in its aftermath, those who had convicted their fellow-citizens formally recanted their sentences and admitted the error of their actions. This recantation does not in any way question the theology of witchcraft-belief; rather, it was as if the jurors had put to themselves Montaigne's challenge and had failed to find the necessary inner conviction: Did we know enough to put these men and women to death on the basis of our conjectures? Salem represented as much the crisis of confidence in the validity of witchcraft persecution as it did any continuity of practices.

From *The Witchcraft Delusion in New England: Its Rise, Progress, and Termination,* with preface, introduction, and notes by Samuel G. Drake (Roxbury, Mass., 1866), pp. 134–35.

W e, whose names are under written, being in the year 1692 called to serve as jurors in court at Salem on trial of many, who were by some suspected guilty of doing acts of witchcraft upon the bodies of sundry persons:

We confess that we ourselves were not capable to understand, nor able to withstand, the mysterious delusions of the powers of darkness, and prince of the air; but were, for want of knowledge in ourselves, and better information from others, prevailed with to take up with such evidence against the accused, as, on further consideration and better information, we justly fear was insufficient for the touching the lives of any (Deut. xvii. 6) whereby we fear we have been instrumental, with others, though ignorantly and unwittingly, to bring upon ourselves and this people of the Lord the guilt of innocent blood; which sin the Lord saith, in scripture, he would not pardon (2 Kings xxiv. 4), that is, we suppose, in regard of his temporal judgements. We do therefore hereby signify to all in general (and to the surviving sufferers in special) our deep sense of, and sorrow for, our errors, in acting on such evidence to the condemning of any person; and do hereby declare, that we justly fear that we were sadly deluded and mistaken; for which we are much disquieted and distressed in our minds; and do therefore humbly beg forgiveness, first of God for Christ's sake, for this our error; and pray that God would not impute the guilt of it to ourselves, nor others; and we also pray that we may be considered candidly, and aright, by the living sufferers, as being then under the power of a strong and general delusion, utterly unacquainted with, and not experienced in, matters of that nature.

We do heartily ask forgiveness of you all, whom we have justly offended; and do declare, according to our present minds, we would none of us do such things again on such grounds for the whole world; praying you to accept of this in way of satisfaction for our offence, and that you would bless the inheritance of the Lord, that he may be entreated for the land.

Foreman, Thomas Fisk,	Th. Pearly, sen.
William Fisk,	John Peabody,
John Bachelor,	Thomas Perkins,
Thomas Fisk, jun.	Samuel Sayer,
John Dane,	Andrew Eliot,
Joseph Evelith,	Henry Herrick, sen.

43

PIERRE BAYLE
Superstition and the Imagination
1703

Pierre Bayle (1647–1706) spent his intellectual life in a solemn dialectic of reason and faith. He abhorred, above all, the arrogance of self-confident dogmatism, and sought to demonstrate to his contemporaries the rational, empirical and historical difficulties at the center of the positions and theses they espoused with such assurance of their own reasonableness, indicating, in his own mind, the necessity of a tolerant faith respecting the rights of conscience. In his writings on witchcraft, Bayle combined three vital strains of seventeenth-century thought: a scepticism of popular and traditional opinion; a Cartesian mechanism which sought simpler, wholly natural explanations of phenomena thought to be beyond the powers of nature; and a desire for tolerance and peace that rejected the use of torture and stake for the victims of religious enthusiasm. Bayle never theoretically attacked the theological basis of witchcraft belief; that would have been an unacceptable dogmatism for him. Rather, he challenged the right of men to assign confidently certain phenomena to the category of witchcraft and to maintain explanations that contemporary wisdom ought to know enough to reject. He was, in this sense, less an innovator than an upholder of the tradition of Weyer and Montaigne.

Pierre Bayle, *Résponse aux Questions d'un Provincial,* 4 Parties (1703), in *Oeuvres Diverses de M. Pierre Bayle,* 4 vols. (La Haye, 1727), Vol. III, Pt. 2, pp. 559–62. Tr. A. C. K.

Pierre Bayle

You know that in several provinces of France, in Savoy, in the Canton of Bern, and in several other parts of Europe, all one hears of is witchcraft, and that no town or hamlet is so small that it has no one reputed to be a witch. Tales of apparitions and evil spells are endless in number; the heads of little children are filled with them, and that makes them completely credulous and timorous with regard to such things. You hear of nothing else among the common people but that an illness has been given to such and such persons by a witch, and that it has been cured either by the same witch, or by one of his confreres. And the truth is that they go running to those types as soon as they decide that an illness comes from a spell. It is moreover true that several ill persons are cured by such means, but it is no less true that these cures, and these illnesses, are an effect of the dominion that the imagination exercises over the other faculties of the body and the soul. This dominion is sometimes so despotic that nothing can prevail against it. An imagination that is alarmed by the fear of a witch's spell can overthrow the animal constitution, and produce those extravagant symptoms that exasperate the most expert medical doctors. This same imagination, forearmed with confidence that the spell has been lifted, and that the witch has sworn to it, by virtue of several words that she babbled over some herbs, arrests the course of the disease. It was maintained by the anxieties of the mind and by the panic-stricken terrors of the soul; it ceases from the time that the person believes himself delivered from the charm. Tranquility of the heart and inward joy return, and allow the faculties to regain their interrupted functions.

I understand, thus, that it is very possible for a woman to persuade herself that someone has put the Devil into her body. All that is necessary for this is that she be asked if the witch whom she suspects made any grimaces near her, at the time that she believes she was put under a spell, and muttered several words which are preliminary to the evocation of the Demon that someone wants to make enter her. It is enough to tell her that he is a man who has put many other people under the possession of the Devil. She thereupon will believe herself a veritable possessed person, and will act in the way that she knows possessed people act; she will scream, she will jump up and down, and so on and on. . . .

A similar persuasion can easily enter the mind of those devout nuns who read many treatises filled with stories of temptations and apparitions. They

Figure 71. Balthasar Bekker.
The author of *Le Monde enchanteé* and one of the most articulate critics of witchcraft beliefs in the seventeenth century.

attribute to the malice of Satan the wicked thoughts that come to them, and if they observe an obstinate strength in their temptations, they imagine that he persecutes them close at hand, that he haunts them, and finally that he lays hold of bodies. Angela de Fulgino, a great name among the Mystics, seems to me to be in good faith when she relates that the Devils, not content with inspiring her with evil desires, beat her terribly. The description that she gives of the pains that they made her suffer in her body and in her soul would inspire compassion in the most hardened of hearts. They excited such a flame of impurity in her body that she could not repress its force except by material fire; but her confessor forbade her this remedy. They chased all of the virtues from her soul, which caused her an unbelievable agony, and so furious an anger that she came very close to tearing herself apart, and sometimes it drove her to the point of beating herself horridly. "I suffered incessantly, from these demons, torments and passions of the spirit which were incomparably sharper and more numerous than those of the body. . . . When, in my soul, all virtues had been overthrown and had fled, and my soul could not oppose this, there was such a grief in my soul that anything could make it lament because of its desperate grief and anger. Indeed, I weep incessantly sometimes, and sometimes such great anger rises up in me that I am wholly torn to pieces. Sometimes I am not able to control myself, so that I strike myself horribly, and from this striking, my head sometimes swells up, as do my other members. . . . I perceive that I am given up to many demons who bring back to life those vices which I abhor and which were dead [in me], and they bring in [me] other vices which I never had." No more than with Job's body, there was no part of her body that the Devils had not struck. "There are numberless torments of the body inflicted by many demons many times. Indeed, I believe that the afflictions and passions which I have described now may be corporeal. For there is in me now no member which has not suffered horribly. Never am I without anguish, never do I rest without languor. I am broken and fragile, and filled with pain, so that it is possible only to lie prone. There is no member in me that has not been beaten, twisted and punished by the demons, and I am always ill and always swollen and full of pain in all my body. Only with immense pain may I move myself, and only with complete exhaustion may I rest. Nor indeed am I able to take enough food to keep myself alive."[1] I would not dare to suspect her of any

1. *The Life of Angela de Fulgino*, ch. 19. [Bayle's note]

falsehood; I believe that she is speaking sincerely. But see what the imagination is capable of, once unhinged by too contemplative a life.

I have gone on a bit too much with the story of this woman, and I have quoted sections of it at too great a length, because I remembered that you did not put too much stock in what I wrote to you about the bitterness that accompanies the devout life. You have persisted in telling me that mystics seem to you to be the happiest men in the world. It was thus necessary to convince you by means of a great example that they do not always enjoy "those illapsus and those ineffable sweetnesses" that you have read in their writings.

It is not necessary for me to give you proofs of the force of the imagination: you will find enough of them in the books that have been published on this matter,[2] and you are not unaware of what everyone says, that there is nothing more important to an ill person than having a full confidence in the skill of his doctor, and in the virtues of the medications. The fear of death inspires so much grief and so many worries in ill persons, even if they say nothing about it, that these increase their illness much more than remedies diminish it, and very often become great obstacles for the remedies to overcome. Remove this cause, give a full confidence to the ill person, and he will have a tranquil mind, and that will be his cure. It is thus that monks famous for their holiness and the gift of miracles and that sacred relics have been able to cure many men. It is thus that imposters have broken the fever of several persons into a sweat, persons to whom they had promised this operation by means of sympathetic properties. The internal agitation with which a person prepares himself for this effect in a warm bed is the true sudorific of those people. If credulous folks with an easily impressed imagination alone fell into the hands of these imposters, the latter almost never would be disparaged.

I beseech you not to accuse of fraud those who protest that phantoms have appeared to them, for the tales that they have read or heard told about these sorts of apparitions were able to leave so deep a mark upon their brain that the animal spirits cannot fall upon these marks without vigorously stimulating the idea of a specter. If a lively attention to those latter objects, accompanied by fear, unsettles the imagination, be assured that the action of the animal spirits upon this mark will be stronger than the action of

2. Bayle, in a footnote, refers his reader to Malebranche's *De la recherche de la vérité*, Book II, "and above all to the last chapter, where he speaks of witches and werewolves." [Editor's note]

light upon the optic nerves. The imagination thus will be stronger than sight, and will paint its objects as if they were present, in such a way that although a person may be awake he will believe that one sees a thing which is not present to the eyes, but only to the internal senses. Consider a bit what happens in our dreams. The most reasonable heads become extravagant while sleeping, and create chimeras more bizarre than those of the madmen whom one shuts up in the asylums. These objects of dreams appear as if they were present to the external senses: one believes that one sees Fauns and Satyrs, that one hears a tree or a river talking, etc. From whence does that come? From the fact that the action of the senses is interrupted, and the imagination rules. The same thing will happen in much the same way to those who are not asleep, if by the effect of some fear, or of some great internal emotion, the acts of the imagination have more force than those of sight, hearing, etc.

I could not restrain myself from making you recall something which is undoubtedly very common in your Province, and which visibly demonstrates what the imagination can accomplish. Several men are unable to consummate their marriage, and believe that this impotence is the effect of a spell. From then on, the newlyweds regard each other with an evil eye, and their discord at times descends into the most horrible enmity: the sight of one makes the other shiver. What I tell you here are not old-wives'-tales, but certain and incontestable facts which only too often come into the sight and ken of all the neighbors in the provinces, where much faith is put in the traditions of witchcraft. The common opinion is that the witches visit this evil service upon newlyweds by pronouncing certain words during the nuptial benediction; but it is also said that the witches must tie several knots in a ribbon, or in a rope, from which comes the vulgar expression, "knotting the braid." They add that if the fiancees sleep together before the wedding, the spell is no longer to be feared. That is why there are some good mothers who consent to anticipating the wedding night in order to foil the witch. But I can tell you that there are examples of folks married for a long time who come to hate each other, and to believe that a witch has given them this mutual aversion. There are also examples of an aversion incited among brothers, or among cousins, or among domestics of different sexes; I speak of that aversion whose features make people judge that witchcraft is involved in it. Thus one must not take as a general maxim what several authors say, that one cannot "knot the braid" with regard to concubines. I don't have to tell you that people are certain that if the witch undoes the knots of the rope he undoes the spell, and that if the rope falls into the hands of anyone who can untie it, all the wizardry disappears, and that there always are hailstorms if one restores it to its original state. Neither do I have to tell you that a witch is often begged to raise the spell, and offered some gift in payment. I must suppose that all these things are known to you.

But in order to show you that there is only imagination involved in these things, it would suffice to report to you a little adventure that I can guarantee is completely true. I knew a peasant who, having married a widow, and being unable to consummate his marriage, persuaded himself that the braid had been knotted, and had great trouble bearing this patiently. Several weeks passed without any change except that he became daily more dissatisfied, and his wife more displeased. They nevertheless went together to their work: now one day as they were working on their vines, it began to rain, and they took refuge in one of those huts of vine-shoots that are put up in the middle of vineyards to be used as refuges in case of rain. They were scarcely in there when it thundered and hailed. The good man then remembered the tradition that it hails every time the braid is unknotted for someone, and imagining that it was his being unknotted, he felt all his virility returning to life, and consummated his marriage on the spot. Wouldn't you say that he had the same auspices as Dido and Aeneas? He related the thing so naively when the occasion presented itself, that there was no room for doubt of his ingenuousness. I am not so certain of another adventure told to me, which is about a man who found himself in the same situation as this peasant, and felt himself cured as soon as he was told that a small boy, who was looking for nests, had found a rope with several knots in a haystack, and that he had had the patience to untie all these knots, one after the other, and that while he worked a bit of hail fell. That was undoubtedly a pious fraud. This tale was told only to make the person believe that he was no longer under the spell.

M. Venette, Medical Doctor of La Rochelle, has published a fact which gives us here a more convincing proof. "About thirty-five years ago," he relates, "Pierre Burtel . . . working for my father in one of his country houses, told him something so unfavourable about me one day, that I was obliged the next day to say to Burtel, the cooper, that, to avenge myself, I would knot his braid when he married, which he was going to do in a little while with a servant from our neighborhood. This man truly believed what I said to him, and although I spoke only in jest, nevertheless these fake threats made so strong an impression on his mind, already preoccupied with spells, that after being married, he spent almost a month without being able to sleep with his wife. He felt desires to embrace her tenderly many times, but, when he had to execute what he was resolved upon, he found himself impotent; his imagination being thus overburdened with ideas of witchcraft. On the other side of this, the wife, who was well built, felt as much coldness towards him as he had towards her; and because this man did not caress her, hatred quickly took ahold of her heart, and she manifested for him the same repugnances that he had for her. It was thus a good game to hear them tell everyone that they were bewitched, and that I had knotted the braid for them. At this point I repented of having mocked so simple a man in such a way, and I did everything that one could do on this occasion to persuade them that this was not the case: but the more I protested to the husband that what I had said were only trifles to avenge myself on him, the more he abhorred me and believed that I was the author of all of his troubles. The curé of Notre-Dame, who had married them, even used all his wit and all his prudence to settle this affair. Finally, he succeeded better than I had in bringing this to an end, and by his efforts broke the spell after twenty-one days."[3]

He uses this example to prove what he just had established, that the impotence that is alleged to be caused by witchcraft comes only from a susceptible imagination.

Let us cite as well Pierre Pigray, who strongly refutes those who suppose that the braid is knotted by "a certain ceremony that is performed by saying several sacred words." It is most notorious, he says, "that the least passion of the mind prevents and turns us away from this [sexual] pleasure: it is most certain that it can be knotted without any ceremony, that is to say, that the member of a cold, fearful, melancholy and apprehensive man can be rendered weak and puny, simply by telling him that it has been knotted for him; the fear and apprehension that he will have (the force of which suffices not only to trouble us in this act, but to make us fall into great and extreme illnesses) alone will render him for a time impotent and inept; but in the case of a sanguine, healthy, strapping man, without apprehension or any passion of the mind, it is impossible for all of the enchanters to benumb him, if he is alongside of a subject whom he loves, or to prevent him from doing well and executing his natural function. I saw an honor-

3. Venette, *Tableau de l'amour* (ed. of 1696), pp. 595 ff. [Bayle's note]

able personage, fallen into this difficulty, for whom it never had been thought to knot the braid; but from the fear of that alone, he fell into this impotence for some time. And the remedy used to cure this evil demonstrates well enough the abuse, namely (it is said), to make the woman pee into a ring, as if that had the power to cure the husband. It is true that it does not matter whatever the remedy be, provided that it removes and cures the passion of the mind."[4]

There is hardly a superstition of greater antiquity than that which attributes to certain words the quality of bestowing or curing illnesses. Those who have understood that words cannot be the physical cause of such effects resort to upholding the position that they operate by an "explicit" or "implicit" pact with the Demon. But to refute them, it suffices to say that if those who used these words made use of others according to their fantasy, they would produce the same effects. I have read somewhat that Hemmingius, a most famous Theologian, quoted two barbarous verses in one of his sermons, and added, to amuse himself, that they could chase away fever. One of his listeners made the attempt on his valet, and cured him, and soon after, word of the remedy spread, and it happened that several feverish people found themselves well by virtue of it. Learning of that, Hemmingius felt obliged to say that he had spoken in that way in fun, and that it was only a witticism. From that moment on, the remedy was a failure; people no longer put any faith in it.[5] In the second volume of the *Aventures d'Assouci,* you will see how cures that pass for supernatural can be effected without any magic.

---

4. Pigray, *Chirurgie mise en Théorie et Pratique*, Book VII, Chapter 7, pp. 434-435. [Bayle's note]

5. Jean Christien Frommann, *De Fascinatione* (Nuremberg, 1675), Book II, Chapter 9, p. 432; see also Francisco Moncaejo Fridevalliano Atrebatio, *Disquisitio de magia devinatrice et operatrice* (Leipzig, 1683), p. 167. [Bayle's note]

44

BALTHASAR BEKKER
Rational Theology and Witchcraft
1691

Balthasar Bekker (fl. 1691) was a Dutch pastor and Cartesian rationalist who wrote what was in many ways the seventeenth century's most fundamental and influential critique of demonology and witchcraft-belief, *The Enchanted World,* which first appeared in Dutch in 1691 and was soon translated into French, German and English. Armed with an optimistic rational theology that challenged the powerful role given to the Devil in witchcraft-belief, an abhorrence of inherited "superstition" that refused to elevate tradition and folklore to the status of sound belief, and a mechanistic sense of human "disorders" of the imagination, Bekker undertook to analyze and to negate the components of Christian witchcraft-belief. Putting his critical reason to work in the areas of scriptural interpretation, formal theology, natural history and natural philosophy, and offering alternative explanations of generally accepted witchcraft incidents, Bekker was one of a handful of seventeenth-century thinkers preparing the conceptual and intellectual path for a complete renunciation of the demonological beliefs that had stood the tragic test of time for centuries.

Balthasar Bekker, *Le Monde Enchanté,* 4 vols. (Amsterdam, 1691), Vol. III, ch. 3, art. 4–6; Vol. IV, ch. 33, art. 1–9. Tr. A. C. K.

O*n alleged pacts between man and Satan.* Leaving aside what concerns Scripture on this question, to make use of it in its proper place,

Figure 72. The Satirical Frontispiece of Christian Thomasius' Attack on Witchcraft. The text reads: "My reader! Do you still deny the reality of the Magic Mountain? This page shows you it clearly. You see the witches' choir stand out upon it plain. Ah, how I fool myself, it exists only on paper."

Reason teaches me enough to know that men's wills can never be under compulsion; so that it is of no value to say that they do with its assent that to which they are coerced. Of two necessary evils, there is one to be chosen; and if that is done voluntarily, it is not in order to take one of them upon oneself, but in order to avoid the other, when one cannot escape both of them. One does not wish for either of these two evils, but rather for one less than the other. Thus, the Devil must not imagine that he possesses the will of those men whom he has obliged to sign the contract that exists between him and them. It is true that they are not exempt from sin by virtue of this; on the contrary, they grieviously trespass against God: first, by signing this contract, in which the will chooses as the lesser of two evils that which is in reality the greater; secondly, by being the occasion of all the evil that the Devil himself does, but by their means, granted for the sake of argument that it occurs in such a way. But no one can say, however, that he agrees of his own will to the Pact to which he is forced by the Devil himself.

Now if God, after the perfidious rebellion of this evil Spirit, still gives him permission to do harm, particularly to men, against their will, how would that harmonize with the Justice of God, since this evil Enemy would be able to harm man only by making use of the most infamous and cruel means imaginable? For who would dare to say that the Devil is allowed to commit the greatest of crimes to prevent him from committing lesser ones? And who can deny that it is a much greater evil to bind oneself to the Devil, by a contract signed with one's own hand and with a vow, and to give oneself to him in body and soul by an express denial of God, than to sin simply by seduction and by weakness? And isn't it the same way, that to do evil unto man against his will, and to afflict him only on earth with temporal pains, as the Devil surely would do without the aid of this pact, if he could, is an infinitely lesser evil than to force him to obligate himself to do evil, and to sacrifice himself body and soul to this evil Spirit, in order to be damned eternally? You can see a little, thus, the good reason that these men [defending the concept of the voluntary pact] have invented, in order to make us believe that the Devil, without the aid of this Pact that they attribute to him, cannot effect any evil.

But leaving that aside, a man, they say, would not be able to avoid being tormented by the Devil, if this evil Spirit were not limited by being unable to harm anyone without the aid of such a Pact. For having as his goal nothing else but the doing of harm, what man is there who could escape from him, if he could effect it at his pleasure? There would be no one, thus, (following their line of reasoning), who would be assured of his body, or his life, or of the salvation of his soul, what with this Spirit being on the watch over all things. I must admit, however, that I should expect these arguments only from persons who believed in no other Spirits except the Devils, who did not know even of a God, or a Saviour, and who imagined that the world was filled entirely with evil Spirits. For me, since I believe that there are Spirits, I also believe that there are as many good ones for the preservation of men as there are evil ones for their ruin. And if it is granted that, on the other hand, the good Spirits, that is to say the holy Angels, or even the tutelary Spirits, following the ancient opinion of the Pagans, have as much inclination to secure the good for men as the others have a penchant for doing evil unto them, it follows necessarily that no one would be in dire peril of suffering or committing evil, because the good Angels not being limited in their power, their care for the preservation of men always would have its effect; and, moreover, that they would be as favorable to men as the Devils are opposed to them. Thus the affair would remain between the two, and the Devil would have no advantage.

> *That it is evident, from everything that has been said up to this point, that there is nothing whatsoever, neither of illusions, nor of apparitions of Spirits, nor of Divinations, nor of Magic, in the manner of which men speak of these:*

If I had been obliged to bring together all the examples [of witchcraft, apparitions, spells, etc.], not all of those which are extant, but only those which I have had in my hands, I should never have finished, so many are there in such great quantity everywhere. But having chosen those which are the best known or the most famous, as well as those which have recently occurred close to us, and about which, as a consequence, one can best inquire, it seems to me that this should be sufficient to convince any person who is disinterested and who loves the truth. To wit, that no one has had any experience whatsoever of that Magic, whatever name one can give to it, which occurs through the contrivance or the operations of the Devil, or by virtue of a Pact contracted with him; nor any whatsoever of the least act of evil Spirits upon man or upon any thing of which man knows. Among all those I have cited, there is not a single example in which the chief circumstances are not incomplete, lacking something that would be necessary if one desired to draw conclusions from them; there is not one whose certainty is not doubtful, and which doesn't lack solid evidence; there is not one in which one doesn't have good cause to suspect that there is deception. Several of these have occurred, but simply by virtue of the imagination, and several to which far more scope was given than was theirs, by virtue of prejudice alone. And beyond that, all that is natural that is found in these is simply something unusual, of whose cause, for the most part, we are ignorant. There is, thus, no other Magic than that which is in the imagination of men; there are no Phantoms, no Divination, nor any obsession which is from the Devil.

In saying this, I limit my explanation to the exclusion of the Devil, without seeking to deny, by virtue of this, any kind of Magic, if one wants to give that name to it. For seeing how everything of which we have spoken has not been fabricated, nor forged only in the imagination, but rather, for the most part, has occurred in fact, we must say that experience teaches us that there truly is a Magic, and that more of the world is bewitched than is thought: namely, those who have been deceived by the cunning of others, or those to whom others have secretly done harm, or both. The people of Macon, of Tedworth, of Sainte Anneberg, of Campen and of Beckington, certainly have been bewitched, that is to say, they have been pitifully deceived. In the two latter places, it was the warlocks and the witches themselves whom people thought bewitched. In the other places, the observations that should have been made were not made, because it was thought (or even it was said), that this was the Devil [before them]. The Priests and Nuns of Loudun had performed the Magic themselves, for which Grandier was burned at the stake, although he was innocent. And elsewhere, the Judges in a matter of Magic were themselves the Magicians. The Devils who made themselves seen and heard were in the brains of men; if not, they were made of flesh and bones. This Zachary, this Devil who hid himself in a ring, was a great Magician, since he duped so many people for so long a time. And if we turn to fact, this Catherine of Harlingen, of whom we spoke in Chapter Thirty-One [revealing her to be a fraud], was a Sorceress . . . in that same sense. . . .

But those who preserve the ordinary meaning [of magic, or witchcraft] make use of this expedient: they do not deny that many things attributed to the Devil occur following the proper but secret course of nature, or occur from the trickery of men, but deny that it follows from this that they are all of the same order. For let us suppose, they say (so that they are taken for men who make suppositions), that of a hundred adventures believed to be Sorcery, there are ninety-nine which are not, yet one must not infer from this that the hundredth could not so be. But I don't want to appear less stingy than they, and I will also say, if we suppose that out of a hundred tales that are called sorcery, it be proven that one of them is not, one must demonstrate why the other ninety-nine would be sorcery: for could there possibly be one of these that could be resolved with less difficulty [by a supposition of witchcraft] than this one out of a hundred was by natural means? And if I am now only one case away from the end of the hundred, it would take a great deal of difficulty to stop me from reaching my goal. Unless those persons show me one of the hundred which is so entirely above the ordinary forces of Nature, that there could be no other thing involved except these Spirits. . . .

There is no argument so absurd as that of attributing an unusual effect to an occult or unknown cause, but above all, to these sorts of [spiritual] intellects, as people want to do, in order to draw as a consequence that they have the power and the capacity to do such things. Why not rather investigate deeply into knowledge of Nature, in order to be able to unite things corporeal to things corporeal? For if I encounter something which has not yet been proven, but which nevertheless is of the same nature as something else, what reason do I have to look for another cause than that which I already have found at work in the other? Suppose that I see a new style of slippers that is beautiful, and such as I never have seen the likes of in the shop of any shoemaker, nor on anyone's feet: must I infer from this that it was neither a shoemaker nor his servant who made them, but rather a baker or a tinker? Nevertheless, it would not be so strange a thing that a baker or a tinker should have made a pair of slippers, since they have hands and feet just like other people, as it would be to say that a Spirit had done a corporeal thing, or, which is the same thing, that a body does spiritual things. It is simply that I have not yet been in all the shops; or perhaps that a former style is being revived that would not seem so strange to the old folks as it does to me. Moreover, I have not investigated the secrets of nature in such a way that I could know what she is yet capable of doing again, and I have not thumbed through books in such a way that there could not be in them certain things formerly known to be natural things, but that pass today for witchcraft.

I have been speaking here only of things that truly happen; what a greater vanity would it not be if I wanted to seek beyond nature the cause of things that do not happen? For if a thing said to have happened never occurred, it has no cause. Now we have seen in all the examples cited above, that the majority of things occur only by virtue of deception, or lack of knowledge, or inadvertence, or that by virtue of the imagination, they have been seen as other things than what they were. What wisdom can there be in all this to bother one's head over the question of what the Devil does or does not do, what he can and cannot do? Imaginary Theology goes even further, when details are missing from some affair that does not have its likeness in the ancient histories, as is the case with the wife of Abbekerk. Such a thing immediately gets attributed to the Devil, and the books of the Theologians and Philosophers are rummaged through [to find supporting evidence]. If it isn't found there, something is invented, so that the affair can still be attributed to the Devil, and the inference is made that he could well have done it. And when it is seen how much difficulty there is in reconciling these things with the laws of Divine Providence, to the extent that they are known to us, something must be said of this matter: either one has recourse to some Author who believed things to be as we want them, or else several passages of Scripture are twisted in order to favor such a view—but always while making the reservation that it was done by the permission of God or by his secret judgments.

How else would it be possible that such questions as our Voetius asked could have been posed?—*Voetius, part. I, pag. 944–971.*

I will cite several of these here to serve as samples of the others.

"If the Devil can appear in the form of a true believer, or of a saint, either dead or alive?"—*pag. 944.*

"If the Devil cannot appear in the form of a Lamb or a Dove or even a Man, without some recognizable defect or deformity?"—*pag. 946.*

"If the Devil can act directly upon the rational memory?"—*pag. 965.*

"If the Devil's actions extend to the mental faculties not only of men awake, but also of sleepers?"—*pag. 965–6.*

"If there are no evil thoughts without a proximate and current inspiration from the Devil?"—*pag. 966.*

"If the Devil can act upon a thing which is distant from him, and by means of what quality which issues from him?" And several other questions of the same sort, which depend on this or follow from it—*pag. 967.*

"If the Devil can make the Elements flow more rapidly than they do, make them burn more quickly than they do, and make them softer or harder?"—*pag. 968.*

"If the Devil can produce, essentially, the Elements, or destroy them; for example, if he can change air into water, and vice-versa?"—*pag. 968.*

"If the Devil truly can eat, or if he only does so in appearance, like the charlatans?"— *pag. 970.*

There are many other such questions, but I limit myself to these. He asks "how the Devil can enter a solid place, when he has a body?"—*pag. 971.* I did not believe it worth the trouble to reveal his answers to the other questions, because it would take too long, but here I must do it. "Is it," he says, "because these bodies [that the Devil assumes] are ofttimes so subtle, that they penetrate as easily as light does, by means of the pores? Or because he forms these bodies, on the spot, from the light, or from some other substance that might be in the room? Or finally, because he opens and shuts the windows without being perceived, because these bodies are too heavy or dense? Or because he removes stones or beams from the wall or from the grating, and afterwards returns them to place?" What do you make of such an answer, Reader, which consists of three or four questions? Does it not increase the obscurity of the difficulty, rather than resolve it? But to speak of things as they are, he doesn't pose enough questions. For I would ask him how the body is seen when it appears, since it is more subtle than the air, which cannot be seen because of its subtlety? Secondly, who manifested more power or wisdom: either God, when He formed the body of Adam with visible and palpable substance, or His accursed creature, if it is true that he has always formed visible bodies from all kinds of substances that he finds. Finally, consider this infernal architect, who, in the winking of an eye, can break, remove, disassemble, replace and reconstruct, at his pleasure, the doors, windows, roof-tiles, lattices and stones of a house.

That is how lost one becomes, when one goes beyond the limits of Nature, and when one wants to go beyond revelation. For where does Reason teach us anything of all that? Or where indeed is the Scripture which imputes such acts to the Devil? What does it serve man, thus, to believe what is said of all this? The prejudice which is thrown at him again and again makes it so easy for man to believe all of this, and superstition reinforces this ease. That occurs because one hears it unceasingly shouted, by the so very ordinary practice of preaching and writing, in which it is asserted without end that the Devil involves himself in all sorts of things; and because of ignorance and lack of experience concerning the secrets of nature; and because of the desire men have to appear more savant in occult things than in things which are known. But above all, man is forced, as soon as he meets something which arrests his judgment, to throw it back upon the Devil. He can do this in all safety, and without being fearful of passing for idiotic, stupid, wicked or impious. But if he should happen to put into doubt, and even more, if he should deny that the Devil can be the author of the thing, he is called an Atheist, because he falls back upon a God, and he limits himself to only One, Who created, Who governs and Who maintains all things. What other reason could one find to convince Atheists, than to produce these examples of visions, phantoms, Magic and obsession? As if there had to be no God, if it were not true that the Devil acted upon men in all sorts of encounters? If you answer yes, why could He not do by means of his Angels the things which cannot be done naturally, or rather, by the force of Nature, of which man still does not know the thousandth part?

Index of Illustrations

Index of Illustrations